ART S

Published by Melbourne Books
Level 9, 100 Collins Street,
Melbourne, VIC 3000
Australia
www.melbournebooks.com.au
info@melbournebooks.com.au

Title: Artful Lives: The Cohen Sisters
Author: Penny Olsen
ISBN: 9781922779182

NATIONAL LIBRARY OF AUSTRALIA

A catalogue record for this book is available from the National Library of Australia

Front cover image: 'Portrait of Yvonne'. A gift to Von from her lover, Noel. Painting by Noel Wood, 1945. Credit: Cairns Gallery Art Collection, 1999.11, Cairns. Gift of Yvonne Cohen and Valerie Albiston under the Australian Government's Cultural Gifts Program

Back cover image: 'The Velvet Hat'. Val dressed for the city. Painting by Pat Goldman, 1945. Credit: Private collection

ARTFUL LIVES

From Melbourne to the Islands:
The Artful Lives of the Cohen Sisters

Penny Olsen

M
MELBOURNE BOOKS

For my family: past, present and future.

CONTENTS

INTRODUCTION

> *Romance is in all of us. We long to fashion romantic careers for ourselves.*
>
> —Valerie Frankel-Cohen (1936)

> *Romance: a quality or feeling of mystery, excitement, and remoteness from everyday life.*
>
> —Oxford Dictionaries

Left to my own devices, I took in the tiny landing-come-study above the living room. In 1997—after a lifetime's fascination with my cousins, Valerie and Yvonne Cohen—I had announced that I would like to write their biography. The sisters, 'Val and Von', as we referred to them in one breath, were the first cousins of my adored maternal grandmother and, for as long as I could remember, family stories of their unconventional lifestyle had fed my imagination.

I came to know them best later in their lives, when their wings had been clipped by life, but their vigour and mischievous sense of fun still came to the fore. But now, Von was in a nursing home following a devastating series of strokes, and Val lived alone in the house they had shared for a decade. Indeed, they had spent most of their lives together, as close as twins (fraternal twins perhaps), with entirely different looks and personalities. Both, each in their own way, were beauties and painters. Val, however, sometimes described herself as more journalist than artist.

For much of their adult lives, after touring the world during the Great Depression, the sisters had spent winters on Timana, their tiny palm-clad island in Far North Queensland, often unclad themselves. The remainder of the year they lived in a small co-operative at Templestowe, attending galleries and the theatre, enjoying the vibrant Melbourne art scene. To me, especially when I was younger, it all seemed impossibly romantic.

Upstairs, in Val's small writing space, I surveyed the scene. As if in waiting, three tables lined the wall, alike only in the narrow space each claimed. On the empty-drawered central table, an elderly, pale-blue Adler sat heavily on an aging lime-green mat. Stacked beside the machine were the 1978–1987 edition of *Writers' & Photographers' Marketing Guide,* a few newsletters from the Victorian arm of the Fellowship of Australian Writers, and a 1990 *Bulletin of the Australian Women's Art Register*. Above the typewriter, sadly cracking in a yellowing linen mount, hung a wondrously serene oil painting of a horse-drawn hay-wagon at a crossroads, its lower right monogrammed 'M.E.C.'—their father, Morris Edwin Cohen.

To the right, the lowest paint-splattered member of the table trio was strewn with spare ribbons, carbon paper and a fat 1952 *Chambers Twentieth Century Dictionary*, the latter bought at Collins Book Depot in Bourke Street and covered in carelessly hand-stitched olive-green silk, frayed from frequent use, with a good many pages repaired with tape aged to shades of amber. To the left, two cardboard cartons crowded the closed, fold-out top of the tallest and most handsome table—'Writing' scrawled in black marking pen along the side of one and the other branded 'Victorian Apples'. Both overflowed with manuscripts, published works, part-finished stories and scraps of ideas in blue biro. A solo sentence on one shred read: 'the moon rose glistening silver on the banana leaves'. Most were articles drawn from a very full life, their typed pages—characterised by a handful of capital letters hovering above their page-mates—held together by rusting paperclips and heavily corrected by hand.

In one beguiling article, destined for a magazine or newspaper, Val describes her first trip north, after a failed love affair, to the Far North Queensland islands:

> Escaping a Melbourne winter and hankering to travel through Europe again, I made the 84-hour trip, the last leg on a train lumbering north from Townsville, in search of sun and a palm tree. Tully was like a frontier town out of the American Wild West—two pubs, a handful of shops and a sugar mill. After a wait, a cup of tea and a watery corned beef sandwich, I was offered a lift with the stores for the island. Scratching madly at the sandflies, I helped load the boat, and from the river it lurched across over the bar into the rough sea, this city girl all the while assuring the boatman that I was alright as I clung, faint and white-handed, to the side. It was dusk as we made the island and the relief of a calm bay with a little landing at the foot of an avenue of coconut palms. Two bronzed figures emerged from the shadows to meet me. A short time later Hugo, Noel and I shared drinks and talk of books and painting on the verandah of a bungalow set in a lush garden. All thoughts of Italy were swept aside and a few months later I returned with my sister.

Sitting there in Val's writing space, I pondered the daunting task ahead. The cushions of her canvas director's chair matched the sunny mustard, gold and lemon striped curtains edging a meter-wide, fully windowed wall. In the soft Melbourne sunshine, the rambling garden led my eye to the Yarra River, gently winding below, and beyond to the sharp, stylish shapes of central Melbourne. It was a peaceful place. The only other occupants of the room were an elegantly narrow, black and tan woven basket to home discarded writings, and, opposite the window, two small glowing pastels of turn-of-the-century Melbourne, again by Morris.

Downstairs, the modest lounge rooms—one for each sister—were decorated with their own paintings among others by the likes of Ian Fairweather, Ada Plante and Roger Kemp, and pottery by the Boyds. In their studios, buried deep among the artistry of a lifetime—oil on board paintings of hens feeding around a palm-framed house, a lush island rising from the sea, and portraits of lovers—lay stacked and waiting to be rediscovered. There was so much to tantalise and not a little to unravel and explain. But how would I begin? The islands of Far North Queensland seemed a world away.

My family had been entertained by stories of the freedoms of island life, of free-thinking, left-leaning colleagues, and of the well-chosen artwork about the house. Inconsistencies left us baffled and not a little curious. Atop the tall dining room cabinet stood a row of over a dozen carved wooden figures from the islands to Australia's north. Arranged from largest to smallest, their explicit appendages faced the wall. If we commented, we were told that 'the cleaner turns them around'. Late into the night, Val listened to the right-wing shock-jocks on commercial radio and, by day, defended them to the last. Even her well-matched sunny drapery didn't tally with her appearance: Salvation Army op-shop dressed, shod and hand-bagged. Von, less politically conservative and better dressed, tended to be Val's passive accomplice. Occasionally, when Val went too far, an 'Oh, sis' or 'That's enough' signalled revolt and hinted at a stronger character than was usually evident.

Pre-arranged outings for meals often began with Val's perverse, 'I just had a big bowl of porridge for breakfast' and ended with her forceful protest at the price if the sisters had offered to pay. Von, on the other hand, quietly enjoyed good food—a decent meal. This was something not encouraged at home, where discounted, end-of-life supermarket goods were the staple and months-old crackers with fish paste were routinely offered to visitors. We anticipated and enjoyed these little quirks. At Christmas, each sister would send a small, creatively hand-made card, with a well-coined message inside; a delightful change from the usual store-bought card's 'best wishes for the festive season'. For many years, Val liked to include a single one-dollar scratchie, each one bought from a different outlet, which supposedly increased our chances of winning. Sadly, none of us ever did.

As amused as we were by the sisters' antics, occasionally their behaviour dismayed. Regularly, we heard stories of kindnesses—fish given to them at the local Saturday farmers' market, baskets of seasonal vegetables left on their doorstep, paintings acquired gratis, and services provided at cut rates. As we came to know them better, we realised that this benevolence didn't just happen. The vegetable basket was left by a widower: 'He's keen on me … sometimes I don't even bother opening the door to him,' Val would scoff. Not infrequently, Val would agree to a fee for mattress disposal, repairs to the car, or whatever, then simply pay what she decided it was worth—always significantly less than the going rate, of course—and refuse to budge. A feisty little elderly woman versus a burly tradesman? It was no contest.

A trip to the butcher with Val was revelatory. She wanted a lamb chop for dinner, 'just one'. The first was too big; she couldn't possibly eat that much, she announced, all the while rifling through her purse. The second chop apparently also cost too much, eliciting a, 'How about that little one there' from Val, still seemingly counting her coins. Before she could reject that little wisp of flesh, the bemused butcher quickly wrapped it and gave it to her, waiving away payment. The 'we're just poor, helpless, penniless, little old ladies' routine worked time after time. She was shameless. Even the dentist who cared for her teeth settled for a cut-price or one of her leftover paintings. Yet, as the family knew, and many friends suspected, the sisters were never without significant means.

With the biography in mind, we began interviews in 1997. Von's memory was failing and too often Val's stories seemed just that: stories, repeated and polished so that they had lost freshness and even, I suspected, veracity. Always inclined to be mischievous, Val would play games, promising to leave the answer to my question in an envelope to be opened when they were both 'gone', all the while winking at Von. Von, for her part, would smile serenely, possibly feeling that it was easier not to challenge her domineering sibling. Frustrated and worried that it may have become unwelcome, or was never really welcome, I decided to abandon the project.

More than a decade passed and so too those two fascinating sisters. It was 2013 and my Melbourne-based brother and sister-in-law, Peter Woollard and Artemis Georgiades, who looked after Val in her final years, had recently retired. A request arrived from the Perc Tucker Gallery in Townsville for permission to use the sisters' work in a forthcoming exhibition 'To the Islands' (the title of one of Val's paintings). Peter, as one of Val's executors, agreed. We decided that the time was right to venture north to fulfill our promise to take their ashes to Timana, their very own island. The exhibition would be a bonus; a chance to see their work hung beside paintings by Noel Wood, Roy Dalgarno and Fred Williams, and tapestries by Deanna Conti and Bruce Arthur. The show opened in mid-October in Townsville before moving to Cairns in January.

We hoped that November, the early wet season, would be kind. The three of us met at Cairns Airport and hired a car for the two-hour drive south through cane-country, past lush mountainsides, to Mission Beach. We settled into the house we had rented on a bluff over the beach, congratulating ourselves for choosing a spot with a magnificent view of tiny Timana, centre-stage, flanked on the left by the dominant, double-humped Dunk Island and behind-left by lower-lying Bedarra. Within two hours the tranquil island scene was obliterated by torrential rain, pelting in from the north, whipped by a gale that bowed the palms almost to the ground. Telephoning

Fozzy and Nancy's water taxi service, as arranged, we were told that the forecast was for more of the same, with a possible lull in a couple of days. They advised us not to get our hopes up, as the tides and the weather had to coordinate; which was unlikely within the time we had. That first night, while the house trembled around us, we joked that the sisters weren't happy to be back.

As the fury outside gradually subsided, it was replaced by the unfamiliar *tuk tuk tuk* of the resident geckos, which hunted insects across improbable surfaces as we drifted off to sleep. Miraculously, we woke to sunshine, a restored view and a totally revised forecast. We spent the day exploring southwards, spending time at Tully with its little railway station, and Townsville, where, excitedly, we viewed the evocative exhibition.

The day after, on a high tide and in dazzling sunshine, Fozzy dropped us at Timana, scarcely ten minutes by launch from the coast. To say that little blip in the ocean took our breath away, that it was a magical, picture-postcard tropical island, hardly does it justice. What I feared would be a dreadfully sad occasion was immediately lightened by our surroundings: the green hillside, pale sand and gin-clear, gently lapping water. Fish jumped in the shallows and pigeons cooed in the trees. Truly, everything sparkled.

After a brief discussion about where to perform the deed—both on land and sea, we decided—and my brother's mighty struggle to open the sisters' well-sealed canisters with a Stanley knife, we waded into the wide shallows. I scattered half of Von's ashes and we watched as they settled prettily into a silvery crescent beneath the water. Peter followed suit with Val's ashes—black lumps which floated heavily on the gentle swell, refusing to sink. After a brief moment of horror, we looked at each other and collapsed into gales of laughter. Artemis, on shore, was perplexed—this was hardly a dignified send-off—but we who saw could only enjoy the visual metaphor for the sisters: one deliciously wicked, the other a more gentle, wistful soul.

The urge to tell their story returned with force. Val had left me a couple of boxes full of drafts of her writings, letters, photographs, catalogues and an unfinished autobiography, labelled 'articles & magazines for Penny' and initialled 'V.A.' Among the papers were two and a half sheets of paper, a list of the major remembered events in her life—some of them dated—interspersed with instructions such as 'remember burglars & mother's jewellery. My lies' and 'read article on Deanna Conti our first and last tenant on Timana'. I took these as permission to tell their story.

1

THE ESPLANADE

Elwood

(1911 – 1930)

The childhood of Valerie and Yvonne Cohen began in a big house on the wave-washed esplanade at Elwood, and ended abruptly with a tragedy. How these formative years helped to shape my cousins' lives, I can only surmise. Certainly, there were reverberations from these earliest days and one upshot, in Val's words, was that 'there was a lot of living'.

The sisters were born at 'Sevilla', the house their father built in about 1910 and named after one of his favourite European destinations. Val arrived in the winter of 1911 and Von three years later. Their parents, Morris and Viva, had married in August 1910, at the ages of forty-five and thirty-one, respectively, and there were no further children. Val's memoirs suggest that the two girls were more than enough.

Their home was one of the first on the esplanade, in the budding Melbourne suburb of Elwood. According to Val, Sevilla was '… cold and uncomfortable by today's standards … inside sacrificed to a magnificent staircase, outside sea winds thrashed the verandahs

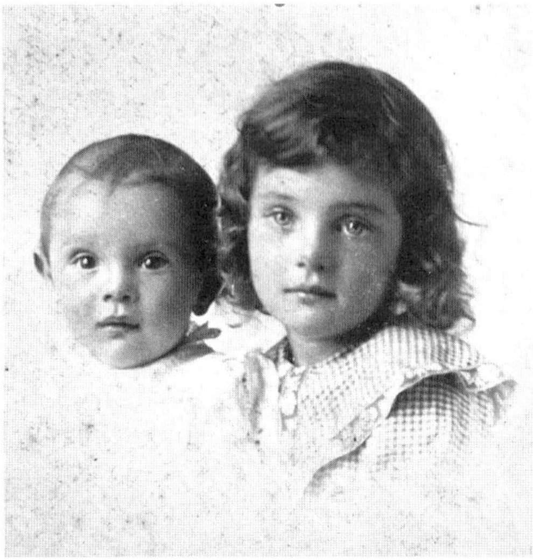

Studio photograph of the sisters; Val aged three years and Von aged eight months. March 1915

and assaulted the struggling garden.' The windows would have been misted by the sea, especially in winter, but when the house came on the market after two decades of family life, number 45 Ormond Esplanade was made to sound much more welcoming. Billed as 'a most attractive two-storied, balconied brick residence', it was, the advertisement continued, right on the sea front *and* with glorious views of the city, in perfect condition, spacious, tasteful and well-designed; with four main bedrooms, two maid's rooms and two indoor bathrooms, with 'hot and cold water to all points'. In the yard were various outbuildings, 'choice flower gardens, lawns, rock-gardens, and crazy paths, fernery, decorative fishpond, and wall fountain' and a 'small but well cultivated vegetable garden'.

Their mother, Viva, managed the household:

> Mother with her quiet organisation saw each morning that the baker delivered hot loaves of white bread, the milkman filled the jugs with cream-topped milk, the butcher and grocer delivered orders, the vegetables arrived in a hooded

> wagon. Every year, a little sewing woman came to stay and make us new dresses.

The live-in help included a housemaid and the cook, Mrs Mack. Mrs Ma, as the girls called her, came to the house temporarily and stayed sixteen years, until retirement. Observed through Val's young eyes, she was a sad, somewhat scandalous case:

> Middle aged and dumpy, she would bustle about the big kitchen with its one fire stove. As a young girl she had run away from the Channel Isles, escaping by sailing ship to Australia. The man who bedded her on that foul three-month voyage left her pregnant. The daughter she would eventually produce would also one day discard her, ashamed of her peasant mother. In all those years with us, Mrs. Ma never received mail or visitors. On her days off she would sit in her tiny room overlooking the backyard … But, she would gladly roast the sacks of coffee beans Father imported from Brazil, jug the hares he shot, and gut the fish he caught.

Every few years Viva placed an advertisement in *The Argus* for a nursery housemaid or day-time lady companion for the two children: 'easy position, comfortable seaside home … take Brighton electric tram to Bendigo Avenue'. The last such ad was published in December 1920, when the sisters were six and nine, and specified 'middle-aged'.

The girls played in the washhouse and, encouraged by their mother, left notes for the fairies:

> As children Mother kindled our imagination. We believed her when she said there were fairies at the bottom of the garden. There, among the flowers, we left messages for them, which disappeared like our baby teeth, plucked from a bedside glass of water for three pence a price. Father was proud of his two young daughters, although I never recall him reading us stories or cuddling us.

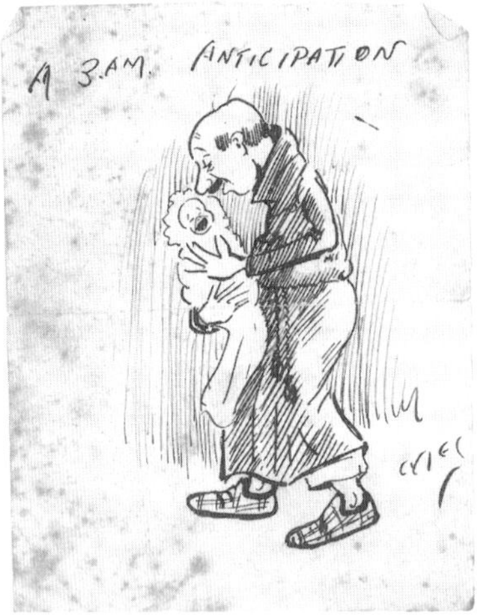
A 3.AM. ANTICIPATION

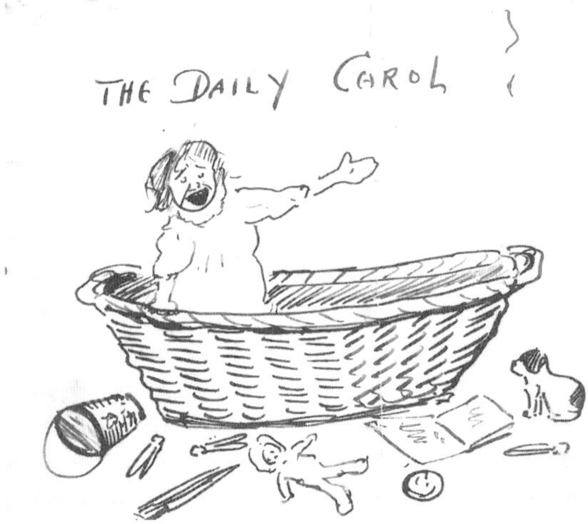
THE DAILY CAROL

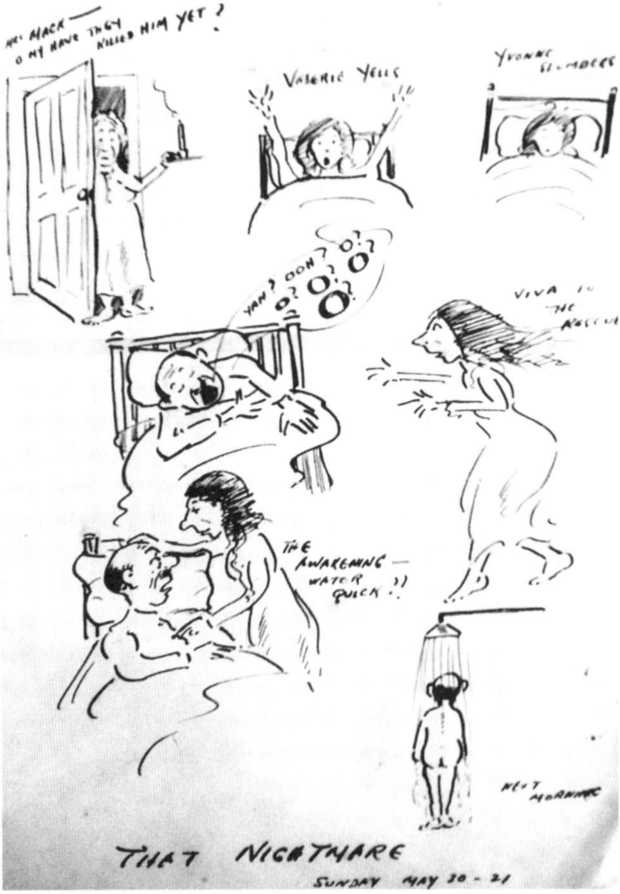
MRS MACK—
O MY HAVE THEY KILLED HIM YET ?
VALERIE YELLS
YVONNE SLUMBERS
YAH ? OOH ? O ? O ? O ? O ?
VIVA TO THE RESCU
THE AWAKENING— WATER QUICK !!
NEXT MORNING
THAT NIGHTMARE
SUNDAY MAY 20 - 21

'Father', Morris, was a director of the family company, S. Cohen & Sons, a successful hardware business with little to tempt the sisters:

> In his wholesale warehouse, he would leave us to make a choice of anything we fancied. How could two little girls find something of interest among those floors of hardware but a few coloured rings for the legs of fowls.

Val liked to visit Father's 'smoke room', with its sweeping views across the bay, and look through his box of stereoscopic slides, taken during trips abroad in the earliest years of the twentieth century. However, to get there she had to climb the grand staircase and, on the first landing, pass a cupboard with a crackled glass window. She sped across that landing, never daring to look at the cupboard. After two burglaries, and the theft of her mother's jewellery, she feared that a face might appear behind the pane.

Von was a frail youngster. Interviewed in 1988, she remembered, 'I was a weak sort of child, I was always sick, [there was] always something ill around me.' At one stage a person came to the house to give her strengthening exercises. Val, on the other hand, and by her own account, was lively and frequently in trouble for her tantrums and lies. Faced with punishment, she would take refuge under the stairs with Von, roped in as her accomplice, or flee to the branches of the peach tree in the front yard. From her safe-tree, she could see the beach on the far side of the narrow reserve, where the local bag-lady sometimes rested, her bicycle piled high with curious possessions. This 'unkempt old lady', dubbed 'Anxious Florrie', and an elderly Chinese man, who came padding down the back lane yoked with two bamboo baskets, formed indelible memories from that time. For her misbehaviours, Val was told that she would be given away to this scarily unfamiliar Asian man. When the impact of that threat lessened, he was replaced by the mythical 'Miss Butterworth's, in the You Yangs'. From the top veranda, their mother would point to the mountains across the bay, saying, 'Miss Butterworth's is just the right place for a naughty little girl who kicks, spits and pulls her sister's hair.'

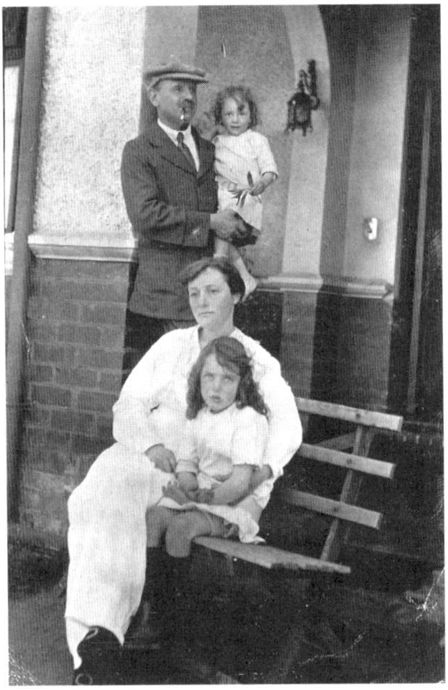

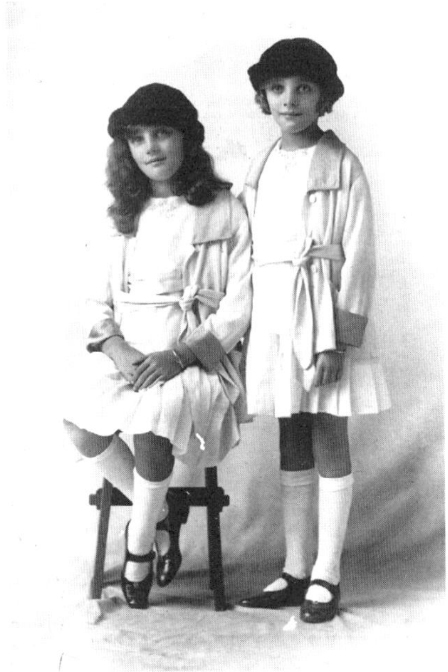

left: Morris, holding two-year-old Val, and Viva with Val, age five, in front of Sevilla, the family home. November 1916

right: Val and Von, aged eleven and eight. 1922

Many evenings, the girls' parents played duets on the upright piano that stood in the spacious hall, singing tunes from Gilbert and Sullivan, or listened to operatic records on the horned gramophone. Unappreciative of the music, the sisters squabbled as they squatted on the floor, tossing Jacks; the actual knucklebones of sheep.

The foreshore was a quiet place until the late 1920s when, a few blocks south of Sevilla, St Kilda Council responded to public demand by erecting a sea-bathing pavilion, which provided change rooms, a place to leave belongings, and showers. But even in the mid-1910s, on public holidays large numbers of picnickers would arrive from the inner suburbs in horse-drawn carriages. They parked in the shade of the huge pine trees flanking the earth road, just around the corner from Sevilla. On hot days, the young sisters liked to carry water to the horses.

Sometimes the girls accompanied their father to the Point Ormond jetty, where he fished. His catches, taken home for Mrs Mack to prepare, left the sisters with a lifelong love of fish, especially garfish cooked simply in a frying pan. Their father also took them for regular early morning swims, having taught them breaststroke as they lay giggling, face down on their beds. Their mother rarely joined them: 'She had a firm dislike of cold water. The few times I remember her attempting it was under a scorching summer sun and even then she didn't get completely wet,' Val recalled. One dip, Val got more of an education than intended, and in writing of the incident, she revealed something of her adult personality:

> … the leg of Father's limp cotton costume slipped sideways, of which he was completely unaware. In disbelief my young eyes gazed at some lumps hanging out. To me nudity was unknown so I had no way of becoming acquainted with the male testicles. Once I'd run away when a man exposed himself, alarmed by that unfamiliar sight, but with Father I just stared. Years later, when I reached menstruation, Mother felt it was her duty to explain the little she knew about sex. Embarrassed, she made a timid attempt. 'Don't bother,' I brazenly boasted, 'At school we talk all about that!'

The First World War apparently largely passed the young sisters by; the exception being seven-year-old Val's vivid memory of the Armistice celebrations of November 1918. With her mother, she took the dummy along the tree-lined cable tramway of St Kilda Road, past the stately homes. They sat on the bench seats reserved for women and children, alongside ladies in boned collars and long skirts, with their gloved hands demurely clasped. Her mother—who paid little attention to contemporary fashion and 'still wore stiff laced corsets that enhanced her slender figure'—quietly explained only that they were going to Bourke Street to see the march: 'Our boys from Gallipoli need a big welcome home.' The boys surely got one. Thousands of Melbournians

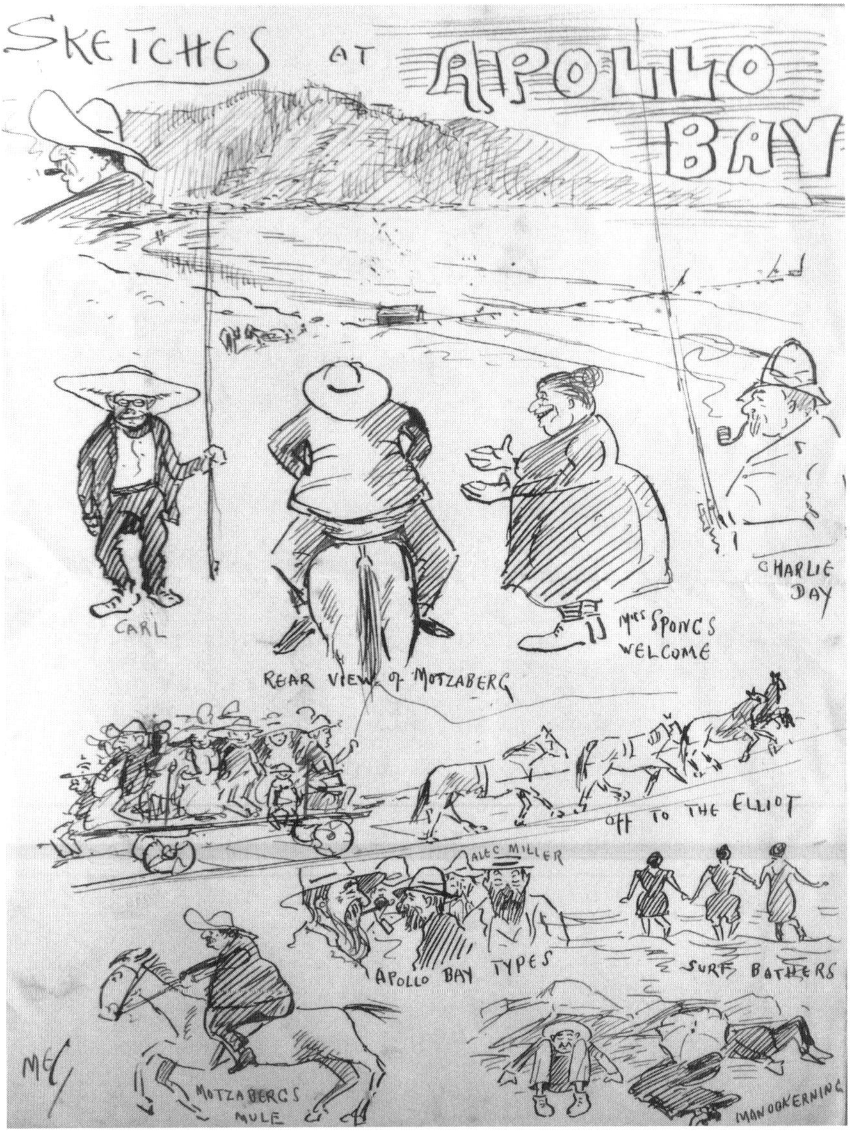
SKETCHES AT APOLLO BAY
CARL
REAR VIEW OF MOTZABERG
MRS SPONGS WELCOME
CHARLIE DAY
OFF TO THE ELLIOT
ALEC MILLER
APOLLO BAY TYPES
SURF BATHERS
MOTZABERGS MULE
MANOOKERNING
MEC

lined the streets to honour the returning heroes and welcome back friends and family members—the first of the Anzacs to come home. Val squeezed between the people to where she could, '… just catch a glimpse of flags waving, crowds cheering—soldiers passed, some with feathers in their hats, some with medals.'

The next month, December 1918, Spanish influenza arrived in Melbourne. The devastating epidemic had been on the move since mid-year and, when it finally burned out at the end of 1919, had taken more lives worldwide than the Great War. By January there were sufficient cases for Victoria to be quarantined, and strict procedures were enacted to limit the virus's spread—theatres and schools were required to close. The already sickly Yvonne must have been a real concern to the family.

Not far from home, in Ormond Road, Val attended Miss Perry's primary school; apparently a private concern. There, Val claimed, she was seldom out of trouble. She fought with the other girls and was caught ringing the school bell early, gleefully watching the other children running along the street in fear that they would be late for class.

In 1920, post-war and post-epidemic, both girls were enrolled at Firbank Church of England Girls' Grammar School (now Firbank Grammar) in Brighton. Brighton, next door to Elwood, was another up-and-coming fashionable, well-to-do, outer suburb, with the homes of professionals and prosperous businessmen set among market gardens, nurseries and dairy farms. The school, with its highly respected headmistress, catered for some 300 bright local girls from Christian families. Reportedly, physical education and domestic science were in demand, whereas Latin, maths and science—recent additions to the curriculum—were seldom taken up. Girls were frequently reminded of the value of charitable works, good citizenship and service to Empire. Several clubs were on offer, including music, drama, camera and literary groups.

Sport was compulsory—two days a week. Tennis was the favourite and the high standard of the game at Firbank ensured that the school

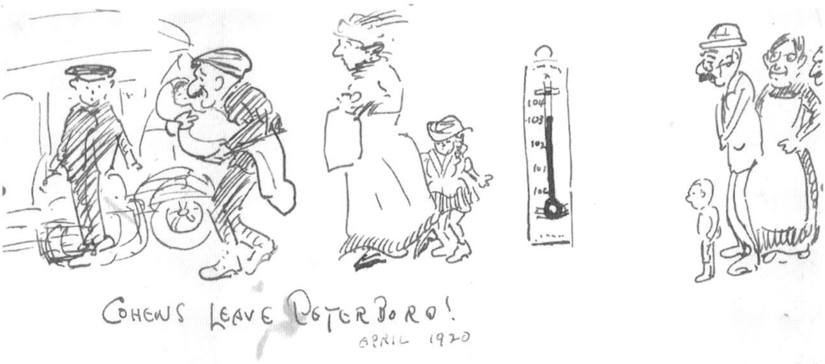

performed well at interschool events. Swimming carnivals were held at the Brighton Baths, set at the end of an old pier that shook when bikes or children ran along it. The boys' baths, on the pier side, and the smaller, girls' baths, opposite, were divided by iron railings below water and a paling fence above. A shrill whistle indicated that the no consorting rule had been breached. Neck-to-knee costumes were regulation wear. Firbank took over the boys' baths for their annual aquatic carnival, held on the first high tide Saturday in March. The shivering girls took part in novelty events such as the balloon race and duck-diving, and few tackled the 100-metre. Despite regular swims with their father, there is no evidence that the sisters excelled at competitive swimming.

In the autumn of 1920, possibly for Easter, the Cohen family travelled west by rail to Timboon then by coach to Peterborough; a picturesque town (and good fishing spot) set on a steep bluff overlooking the Southern Ocean. The holiday ended with Val in the maternity hospital at Warrnambool, spotty and feverish with measles; the highly contagious disease that, at its worst, can cause seizures and death, especially in young children. She was unable to stay—'maternity and measles don't mix', the matron told her father—and the family took the train home to Elwood. With one very sick child and another sickening, Morris booked an entire carriage for the family. He distracted his suffering daughters with stories of holidays spent, before marriage, at Apollo Bay, a little farther east. For years, Morris had spent Christmas at Apollo Bay with his brothers, the girls' uncles. The only way they could get there was by a small supply boat caught near the docks on the Yarra River and they had many a wild trip around the coast. Morris fleshed out his anecdotes with amusing descriptions of the locals and, a clever caricaturist, also lampooned them in pencil.

Back at Firbank, to her consternation Val discovered that there were two other girls named Valerie in her class. This must have been significant: seventy-seven years later, when she was eighty-six, Val remembered that one of the other Valeries received the highest marks for a set essay on horses, while she came second: 'Perhaps this was the beginning of my interest in writing,' she suggested. It was also an early sign of her strongly competitive streak. At the end-of-year speech nights of 1920 and 1921, as recorded in *The Argus*, Val received an 'honour' prize along with a couple of other girls, including a 'V. Rigg', surely her rival—one of the other Valeries.

The sisters took the tram to school but the long walk home proved too demanding for Von. So, in 1922 or 1923, their mother found them places at a school closer to home, where they stayed for a 'wasted year', according to Val:

> It was a remarkably progressive school for its time. The Headmistress was French, a language she promised we would soon speak fluently. This never happened. Half the time the class would wander to the beach at the end of the street. Nobody seemed to notice.

This may have been Elsternwick State School, on Murphy Street, about a kilometre from the sea and less than two from the Cohen family home. In 1923, as Val recalled, Von contracted a severe case of scarlet fever (suffering temporary hearing loss) and both girls missed a lot of school.

The next year, the sisters started at St Michael's Girls Grammar, an

Anglican school in St Kilda, about four kilometres from home. At the December speech night, it was announced that with 235 pupils, and more wishing to enrol, the school would be expanded and 'lighted and ventilated in the most modern way'. That March, a school holiday was declared and the family joined thousands of spectators gathered on Point Ormond Hill and the St Kilda foreshore to watch the warships of the British Fleet entering Port Phillip Bay. The broadsheets reported that twenty-two aircrafts flew overhead and a choir of 700 children from St Kilda's two State primary schools sang 'Rule Britannia'.

The new building at St Michael's had wide corridors, indoor toilets, and spacious classrooms with large blackboards. The all-season uniform was a navy serge tunic that was required to be no more than ten inches from the ground, worn with a white, long-sleeved blouse, red and navy striped school tie, thick black stockings and black, rubber-soled shoes. In the mid-1920s, many of the girls had their long hair cut to a fashionable bob, with or without a 'shingle' (fringe).

As at Firbank, the students were encouraged to do sport, and they attended concerts, recitals and dances, as was expected from a good school education. Academic excellence was an increasing priority and senior teachers at the school were required to have university degrees. Even so, few girls, around half the class, sat for the Leaving Certificate exams and many left after Intermediate.

With the Cohen girls finally settled at school, and with Von in better health, Morris decided to take Viva on an overseas trip—her first. Leaving their daughters with his sister-in-law, they sailed for London in January 1925, on the *RHS Orama*. Mid-year, an article in Sydney's *Sunday Times* charted the couple's progress. They had just passed through Paris on their way to Norway, Denmark and Sweden: 'Mr. Cohen is the well-known Melbourne artist, and he has been commissioned during his trip round the world to do sketches for several Australian papers.'

Left in the care of Susie, their widowed aunt, and cousins nineteen-year-old Mathew and eighteen-year-old Jeanette, Valerie and Yvonne

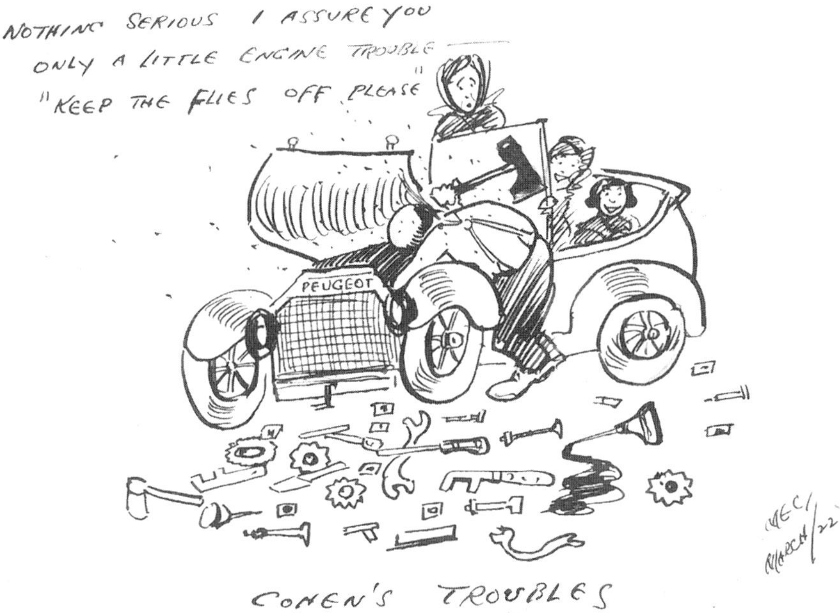
NOTHING SERIOUS I ASSURE YOU
ONLY A LITTLE ENGINE TROUBLE
"KEEP THE FLIES OFF PLEASE"
PEUGEOT
MEC
MARCH/22
COHEN'S TROUBLES

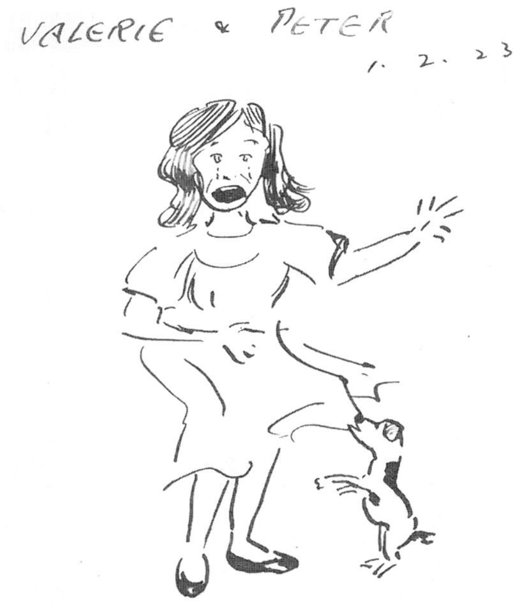
VALERIE & PETER
1. 2. 23

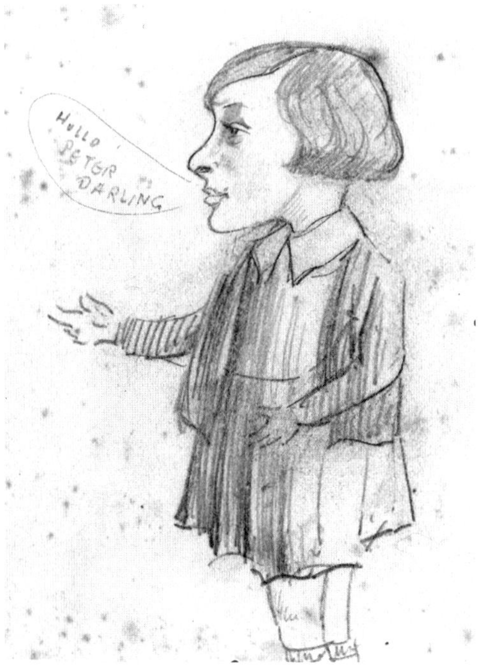

fretted. As Val remembered years later, ‘How we hated those older cousins. They bossed us mercilessly. During those nine months they made our lives miserable and we couldn’t wait to get home. Oh joy when that day arrived.’

While counting the days until their parents’ return, Von turned eleven and Val fourteen. On arrival home in late October, her father announced that it was time for Val to learn how to drive. ‘You can practice on our next holiday,’ he promised. The family set off for Sydney in their Peugeot, perhaps intending a visit to Viva’s widowed father, the girls’ grandfather. Val recalled, ‘Carefully, I drove across the mountains … the earth road had once been a bullock track, twisting and turning through the forest. There was little choice of overnight accommodation in those days. Not Mother’s idea of comfort.’

In 1926, Von must have had some respite from her health problems. As a tall, slender eleven-year-old, she ran strongly at the St Michael's autumn sports day, coming first in the seventy-five yards under-12s and second in the fifty yards under-16s. *The Michaelian*, the school magazine, recorded that she was also Captain of Form IVb. She enjoyed mapping and drawing, but little else, and struggled scholastically given her broken record of formal schooling. Still, mid-year, her creative little essay, titled 'An argument', was deemed interesting enough to be published in the magazine as an example of work from the junior school.

Val was also strong at sports. Each year at St Michael's, she was a member of the running team and a goalie in the basketball team. Despite her claims to being a poor student, she was Form Captain in second term of 1926 and won honour prizes for her schoolwork in 1926 and 1927.

In May 1926, the papers reported, hundreds of schoolgirls turned out at Toorak Oval, flags festooned the railings, and the girls were resplendent in their school colours. Val, a short but speedy fourteen-year-old, finished second in the under-16s seventy-five-yard dash, and Von ran third in the under-14s 100-yards. Still, St Michael's lost the Challenge Cup to the sisters' old school, Firbank.

The following year, the intra-school sports day was held in April in the grounds of Grimwade House. As usual, the mothers' committee provided afternoon tea and the fathers' committee officiated. *The Michaelian* reported that, 'Yvonne Cohen only won from Elaine Schneider by a half-point in the under 14 events. Yvonne came second to Olive in the Championship.' It was to be Von's last year at school; she fell ill again and her parents withdrew her for the last time. She had just turned thirteen.

School records show that Val stayed on till the end of 1928, when she was seventeen, though she later claimed, '... at recess one morning when I was barely sixteen I gathered up my books and hat and returned home.' Later still, she had herself dropping out at thirteen: 'I'm never going back. Miss Nichols hates me, she tried to stop me playing in the school's matches because I'm so hopeless at maths and spelling,' she wailed. With her sister too sickly to attend school, eventually her parents relented, but they insisted that the girls continue to be educated. So:

> Somehow, an Oxford graduate, Sister Ernestine, was found and together with my sister and four friends we made up a class—taught to think, to question, not just to accept. She was a remarkable teacher. Between sessions on science, art and literature, we sent to the Emily McPherson College for cooking, millinery and dressmaking classes.

The Emily McPherson Domestic College (now part of the Royal Melbourne Institute of Technology; RMIT) had been open only a couple of years. A tram ride from the esplanade at Elwood, it was located on the corner of Russell and Victoria Streets in central Melbourne. Housed in a new, state-of-the-art building, the college was open to women fifteen years or older. It aimed, the brochures claimed, 'To train girls for professional and commercial employment', such as matrons of schools and other institutions; laboratory workers with commercial firms; demonstrators of commercial food and other products; teachers of domestic science; and hospital dietitians.

While Sister Ernestine proved a great success, the girls' domestication did not. Records in the RMIT archive show that the only subject the sisters completed was the second term of Cookery Grade 1, in which they performed poorly in theory (Val 33 per cent and Von 39 per cent), better in practice (67 per cent and 62 per cent). As for dressmaking, Val remembered, 'one term, one skirt, one pleat a week'.

Most likely, the sisters were more interested in socialising than studying. In October 1929, they and three other young women hosted a dance at Fawkner Park Kiosk, on Toorak Road, with one hundred guests. The sisters, closer than ever, were budding socialites, and garnered their earliest appearance in *Table Talk*, Victoria's longstanding weekly social magazine. 'Miss Valerie Cohen' was reported to have worn a dress of 'ankle length white taffeta, embroidered in red and green cherries', while 'Miss Yvonne Cohen' chose 'pink taffeta with bands of tulle'.

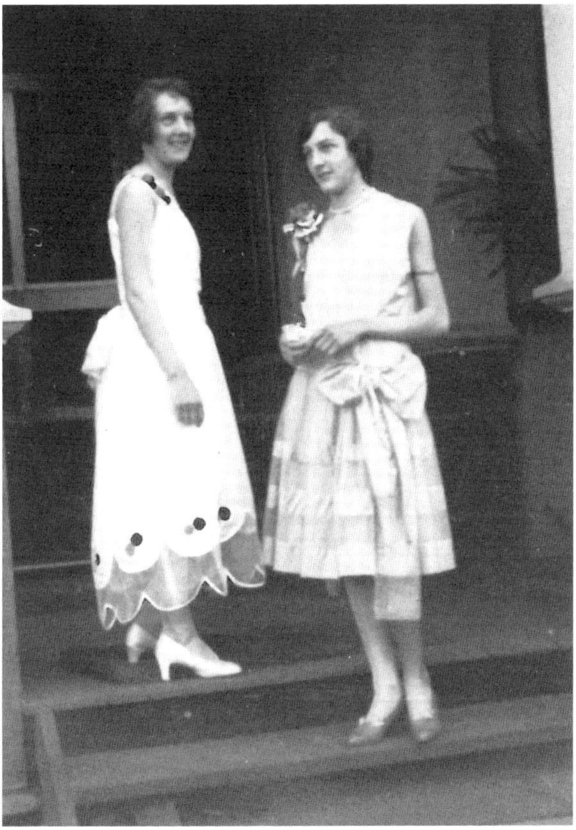

Val (left) aged eighteen and Von fifteen. Inscribed on the back, 'Val and Von off to their first ball.' October 1929

The following year, 1930, the sisters enrolled at the National Gallery Art School. They completed their second term with the drawing master, William (Billy) Beckwith McInnes; one of the requirements before progressing to the painting school. Evening classes were held five nights a week in a long tin shed annexed to the gallery, located on Swanston Street in the city. Sometime-student George Johnston described it as a harshly lit, confusing space, scattered with staring eyeballs and casts of dismembered body parts of various proportions set against '... the startling contrast of the girl students in their floral smocks moving with indifference beneath the uncoloured fig-leaves of naked gods.'

Later in life both sisters claimed that they did not take up art until after their father's death. Interviewed in 1988, Von, told Mary Newsome:

> We'd go with him when we were children at weekends because he'd go off sketching and we'd go to the coast or we'd go to the country, and Val and I … we wouldn't sketch, we'd go for walks and pick wildflowers while he sketched scenery, but then when we were about 16, 17, we got interested in learning to paint so we went to the National Gallery … But while Dad was alive we just didn't, he was a bit disappointed that we wouldn't attempt it.

But, in 1930, when the sisters began art classes at the Gallery, Morris was still very much alive.

The sisters' teacher, McInnes, was a society portraitist and seven-time winner of the Archibald Prize. In Victoria, the debate over Modernism was only just beginning, but the conservative McInnes was said to have had no intellectual interest in art—rather, he viewed it as a craft to be learned. According to the *Australian Dictionary of Biography*, he was 'regarded with some affection even by the most radical of his students'.

Interviewed late in life, both sisters, then devoted followers of George Bell, took the stance typical of those who had broken away from what they regarded as the staid gallery school. Von claimed, '… it was so boring because we were only allowed to use, not crayons, that black stuff—charcoal, and we could only do fractions of the face. We could do a nose one day, or an ear the next day.'

Val agreed that they spent 'the whole time doing eyes and noses' from plaster casts and statues. She added that they saw McInnes only once, and learned most from fellow students, including the Roger Kemp, a handsome twenty-two-year-old, who also began classes at the gallery in 1930. Roy Dalgarno and Neil Douglas, who were to figure later in their lives, were completing their final year. Despite the school's traditional teachings, many fellow students went on to achieve fame as Modernists.

The young sisters—Val, aged eighteen at the start of the year, and Von, at fifteen surely the baby of the class—probably enjoyed the freedom, the mixed sex classes (having attended girls' schools) and the attention from older students, and had little thought of Modernism. Indeed, it was likely that they were a little overwhelmed. Still, looking back, Val maintained that they were unhappy with the teaching, felt like they would never be allowed into the painting studio and left to study design at Melbourne Technical School under Murray Griffin. In fact, it was several years before they signed on with Griffin. Their lives were about to be turned upside down.

2

'FATHER': MORRIS E. COHEN

Ballarat and Melbourne

(1865–1906)

Valerie and Yvonne spent the last half of 1930 attending drawing classes at the National Gallery Art School. They were still living in the family home by the sea at Elwood. Their father, Morris, not long retired, was also spending more time on his artwork, mainly landscapes drawn with pastels.

In June, their father attended the screening of a documentary on New Guinea—filmed and 'vividly' portrayed by 'Australia's most travelled cameraman', William J. Jackson. The event appealed to Morris's love of travel and exotic peoples. He determined to see the Australian protectorate for himself, booking a passage on the steamer *Marsina*, departing from Sydney for the ports of Rabaul and Bougainville, via Brisbane and Samarai, and returning via the Solomon, Norfolk and Lord Howe Islands. Early in August, he left frosty Melbourne on the Sydney express and a week later arrived in the sweltering tropics to begin his island hop.

Morris was inspired to write an article on his impressions—titled 'Cruising around tropical islands'—published in *The Australian*

Traveller and illustrated with his sketches of New Guineans and caricatures of fellow passengers. At his first stop, Samarai, a twenty-three-hectare island on the north-eastern tip of New Guinea, then a significant regional trading port, a delighted Morris found himself:

> ... surrounded by copper-coloured lithe savages, with frizzy mops of hair dyed from saffron yellow to salmon pink, adorned with scarlet hibiscus flowers, ears hanging with fantastic shells, bones ... I am enchanted by the intensity of the green foliage, the graceful swaying coconut palms, the hedges of crimson and dappled gold ... I set up my painting gear and am surrounded ... They watch and criticise every stroke; yell with delight as I feature a familiar object. There comes a picturesque type with a huge basket perched on his head. Authoritative voices shout at him not to move. He stands statue-like and the excitement intensifies as he emerges on the picture.

Lacking the usual currency of twisted black sticks of tobacco, Morris traded sketches for tropical fruits and goods. His account continues with great enthusiasm for the colours, the lush fragrant vegetation, and the happy, relaxed people, fishing and trading the abundant produce.

The days went by, 'a joy to an artist'. Steaming through the Buka Passage, Morris was enchanted: '... forest-clad mountains, flocks of white cockatoos scream ... palm-embroidered islands, so peaceful, so colourful in their intensity of haunting green harmonies,' he wrote. He could almost be describing the island group, and lifestyle, that not many years later so captivated his daughters.

Early the next year, Morris decided to take the family for a four- or five-week holiday in Tasmania, to tour the island in search of scenic landscapes and fish. On Friday 27 March 1931, with Viva and the two girls, he drove their car onto the steamer *Nairana* to cross Bass Strait for Launceston. Sunday, they motored to Scamander, a quiet town on the northeast coast known for its fine fishing, pretty surf beaches and mild climate. There, they checked into the Scamander Hotel, widely promoted as 'one of the most favoured holiday resorts in Tasmania'; a particular attraction being the abundance of bream in the wide Scamander River. The modern hotel boasted tennis courts and a social hall and offered free boats and bait to patrons.

Morris had long enjoyed sketching, fishing and hunting—legacies from his early years growing up in the burgeoning gold-mining town of Ballarat. In October 1854, his father, Simon (Simeon) Cohen, in the midst of a cholera epidemic, had sailed from Liverpool on *Champion of the Seas*. It was the speedy clipper's maiden voyage, taking just seventy-three days. The ship arrived in Port Phillip Bay on Christmas Eve with 780 passengers—the Cohen family listed among the second-class and intermediate travellers. A passenger was recovering from smallpox, so the ship was placed in quarantine for a few days while the sails were fumigated and the passengers' clothes boiled. Simon had spent the past decade in England, where he met and, in Sheffield in 1853, married, Jeanette Greenthal (also known as Grunthal or Greendale). His birthplace, however, was Bomst, in Posen, a province of the contested territory of Prussia, now the Poznan region of Poland.

Simon and Jeanette arrived in Ballarat in early 1855—the year the city was declared a municipality—and Simon set up an ironmongery (hardware) business. Ballarat was very much a mining town, prosperous and expanding, with a high demand for goods and mining equipment, but still reeling in the wake of the bloody battle of the Eureka Stockade for greater rights for miners.

The next year, being of 'good character and respectability', Simon was naturalised—along with about thirty other Ballarat storekeepers, mostly born in Poland and surrounds—becoming a British subject. Between 1852 and 1873, he and Jeanette had at least nine children, six boys and three girls, seven of whom survived to adulthood. According to *The Ballarat Star*, Morris Edwin, the second youngest son, was born at the family home in Albert Street, Ballarat East, on 26 May 1865—not 1866, as is often cited.

Simon expanded his business, invested in mining and other ventures and involved himself in civic affairs and local philanthropic causes. His initial store, 'S. Cohen, wholesale and retail ironmonger', was located centrally, in Main Road, opposite the Star Hotel. It catered largely to miners, offering mostly imported products such as shovels, sluice forks, extra heavy picks and axes, grinding stones, blasting powder and fuses, quicksilver and ropes. As the business grew, travelling salesmen were employed to service towns popping up in more remote locations across the Australian colonies and the extension of the railway from Geelong in 1862 opened further markets and access to ports. With the continued growth of Ballarat, the waning of the gold rush in the 1870s and its replacement by agriculture and manufacturing, the store switched to tools for the garden city, more general hardware, more furnishings, and gear for sportsmen.

As Simon's sons reached their majority they joined the company, which became 'S. Cohen & Sons' of Sturt Street. In 1888, the company moved headquarters to Melbourne and eventually built a large warehouse there. With offices in Ballarat and London, by 1917 its operations catered to much of settled Australia.

Morris studied art at the School of Design at the Mechanics Institute, founded by James Oldham in 1870. That first year, Oldham—a talented amateur painter and etcher—taught watercolour and pastel to seventy-seven students, twelve of them ladies and the rest 'youths', aged nine to twenty. The school was such a success that in 1877 Oldham hired Thomas Price to teach the more advanced pupils such as Morris's close friend David Davies, the star pupil.

Morris's entries in his homemade diary for the Christmas holidays of 1881, when he was sixteen, give an insight into his interests. His brief daily notes, from 14 December to 4 January 1882, show that he spent time with his brothers Henry, Fred and 'Doll' or 'Dolly' (Adolph), and friends, exploring in the buggy, riding the pony, sailing, hunting and birding, rowing and fishing. In the evenings they played cards (snaps), or met downtown or at the lake and botanic gardens. On December 20, Morris went to hear the 'Nightingale Serenaders' at the Mechanics Institute and, on the evenings of 27–29 December, entertainment was provided by a visiting company, who sang and performed pantomime, ventriloquism and mind-reading. But Morris's main summer activity is obvious: he was attending a holiday art course at the School of Mines.

In 1884, his teacher Price was the driving force behind staging a ground-breaking exhibition of 395 of the best paintings from Europe, Melbourne and Ballarat, funded by local businessman and art-lover James Oddie. People flocked to the free exhibition at the Town Hall, which ran for three weeks and was even open into the evening. A reviewer for *The Argus* was impressed, averring, 'Ballarat has distinguished itself by being the first city in the colony to hold an exhibition composed of works of art exclusively.' A room at the top of the stairs was dedicated to paintings by students, Morris included. The *Catalogue of the Ballarat Fine Art Exhibition* lists his contributions, both oils, as: number 317, 'Gip', sale price £2 10s; and number 331, 'Puzzled', £5. His titles stood out among the more descriptive names, such as 'misty mornings' and 'evening glows'. This was the first public airing of his artwork.

The historic Ballarat art exhibition had been such a success that it helped fuel the idea to build an art gallery in the city. A committee was formed to make: 'A plea for art culture ... the expression of man's instinctive love of the beautiful.' Morris was on the committee when they decided to buy the old post office site. The result of their labours was the impressive Ballarat Fine Art Public Gallery and Museum, which opened in June 1890.

By then the Cohen family had moved to Melbourne, where Morris became involved with Victorian Artists Society (VAS), popularly referred to as 'The Vics'. The Vics held monthly 'smoke nights' as well as exhibitions and boasted a membership of around 400. The selection committee, made up of professional artists, accepted Morris's oil, 'Twilight on The Yarra', for the VAS's May 1889 exhibition at the National Gallery, where it hung alongside the likes of well-established artists Arthur Streeton, Frederick McCubbin, John Lambert, Jessie Traill, JA Turner and Ada Plante.

The next year—1890—was difficult for the family. S. Cohen & Sons had just moved their Melbourne headquarters from Post Office Place to Lonsdale Street and Victoria was suffering a deep economic depression following years of reckless speculation and too little business and enterprise. In February, Simon, Morris's father, died aged sixty-five, at his home in St Kilda. Simon's concern for his children (as stated in his will) was 'maintaining, educating and bringing them up in a manner suitable to their station in life'. Perhaps unusually for the time, he left his sons and daughters an equal share in his estate: income from the business and stocks and shares in the colony, or from the profits of their sale. Barely three months later, the family was rocked by the death of Henry, just thirty-three. This left Joseph (about thirty-one years old), Fred (twenty-six), Morris (twenty-five) and Adolph (twenty-three) in charge of the family business.

With the loss of his father and eldest brother, the family business consumed more of Morris's time, and he painted less. Then, six years later, Joseph left S. Cohen & Sons to start his own business and Carrie, the eldest of the siblings, lost her husband, Maurice Sloman, leaving her with teenaged daughters to care for. Both events added greatly to Morris's responsibilities. Still, throughout his life, as often as he could, he spent weekends and holidays sketching, shooting and fishing and he remained an inveterate caricaturist, doodling on any scrap of paper to hand—envelopes, the backs of invitations, and theatre programs.

Late in 1891, Morris appears to have made a trip to the New Zealand's South Island for business, and to visit relatives and go fishing. He painted a Fiordland scene—possibly Mitre Peak, Milford Sound—in oil on a Windsor and Newton canvas, dated 1892. However, his entry in VAS winter exhibition that year was closer to home, No. 94 'A Sunny Day, Cranbourne'.

Five VAS exhibitions passed without contribution from Morris. Then, quite possibly he spent his 1889 to 1900 Christmas holidays painting, because three of his oils were accepted for the January 1900 show: 'The Sundowner'; 'View of The Domain, Sydney'; and 'Watson's

ARCH 4, 1905. THE AUSTRALASIAN TRAVELLER.

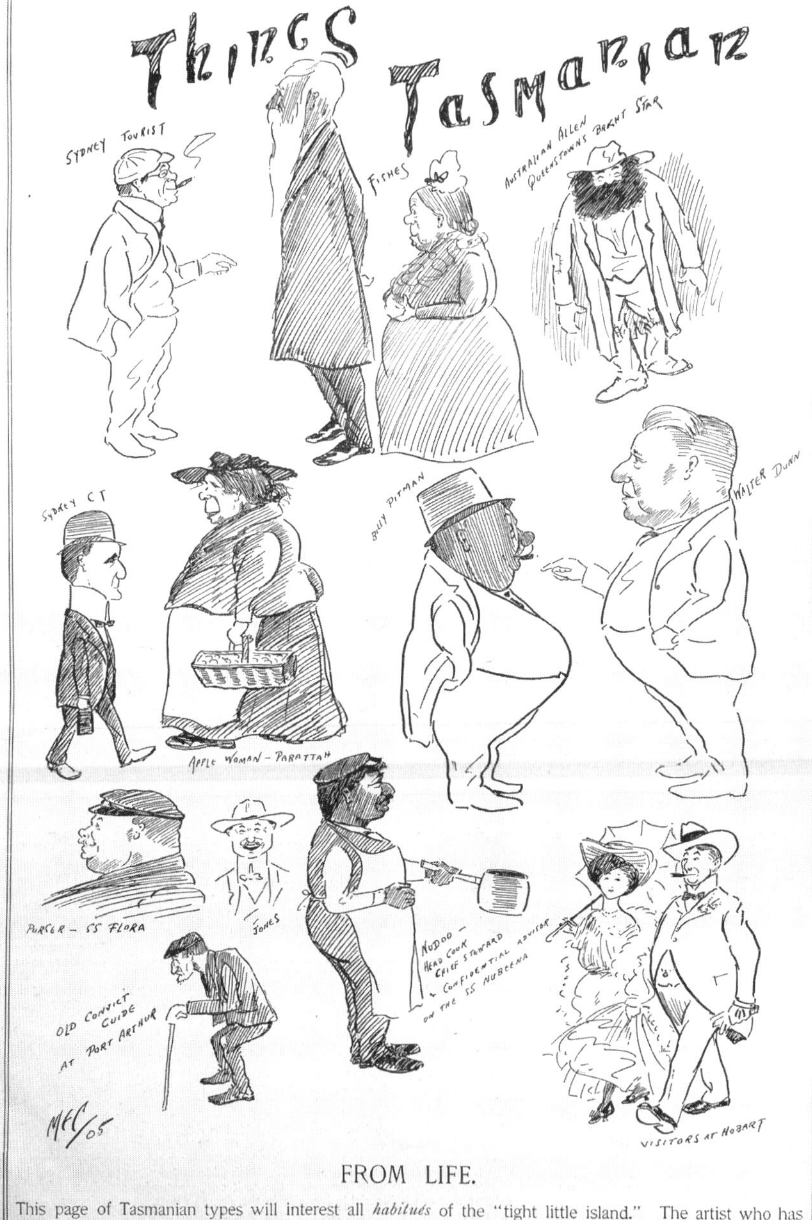

FROM LIFE.

This page of Tasmanian types will interest all *habitués* of the "tight little island." The artist who has caught them "on the wing" (!) is Mr. Morris E. Cohen, a well-known member of the C.T.A. of Victoria.

Bay'. The first painting, priced at thirty-five guineas, was among two of Morris's which travelled to Sydney as part of the Commonwealth Show of January 1901, which also included work by Tom Roberts and Blamire Young and a much-lauded painting by Morris's buddy, John Longstaff. A reviewer from *The Evening News* made special mention of 'a graceful painting by M. Cohen', titled 'View of River'—a steal at ten guineas.

In 1892, Morris joined the influential Commercial Travellers' Association (CTA), which was to become a significant aspect of his life. From its dusty beginnings in 1880, when horse-drawn vehicles were the norm for commercial travellers—and trains or ships on some routes—the association aimed to improve conditions for members. Hotel and pubs around the colony became associates and offered special rates to members. By 1899, the Victorian branch of the CTA had built handsome premises in Flinders Street, with room for 200 diners, thirty-one bedrooms, a meeting room, library and billiards room. On opening day, the building attracted 2000 visitors. Lord Brassey, the Governor of the Colony of Victoria, and his wife attended the inaugural dinner, as well as the Bishop of Melbourne and various ministers, union leaders, and businessmen.

Thereafter, Victorian CTA members could meet, dine and be entertained at what was effectively a gentleman's club and alternative to the snobby Melbourne Club. The organisation also held hugely successful Easter carnivals, picnics, and other family events, with hotly contested races and competitions. In 1905, the first edition of the CTA's journal, *The Australasian Traveller*, appeared, promising advertisers a circulation of 4000 monthly. It was enlivened by Morris's caricatures of Tasmanian 'habitués' he had encountered on his many visits to the island. The newspaper contained articles for women and children as well as items of interest to commercial travellers, and often featured illustrated travel stories, which must have had strong appeal for Morris, who contributed articles on his own travels.

In July 1905, the business was going well. Morris left Fred and Adolph in charge while he took time off to see the world. From

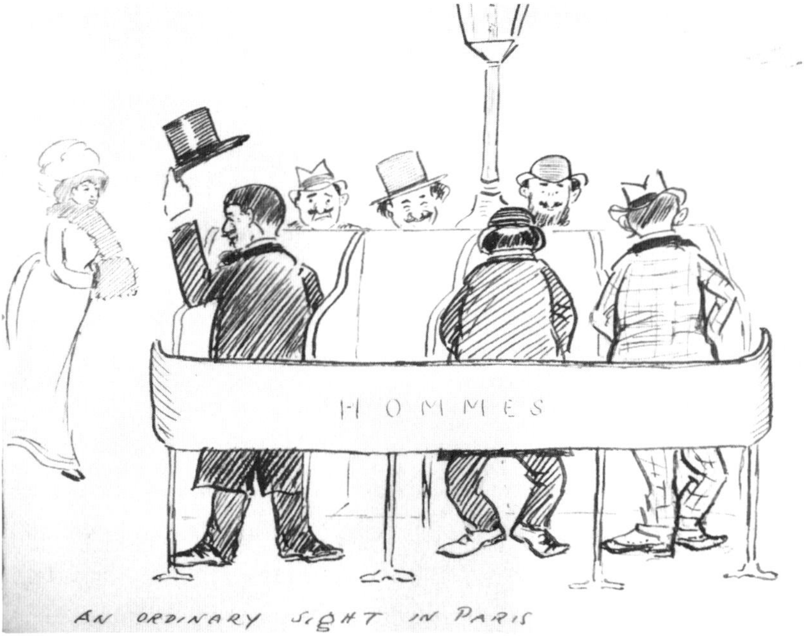
HOMMES
AN ORDINARY SIGHT IN PARIS

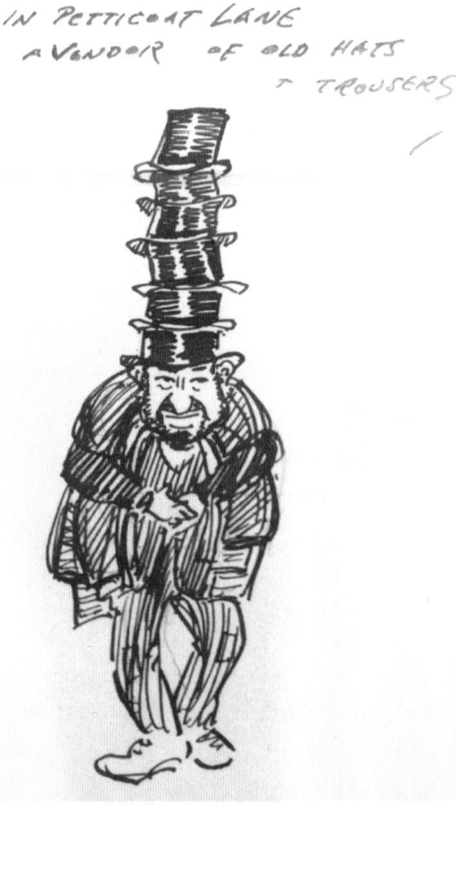
IN PETTICOAT LANE
A VENDOR OF OLD HATS
+ TROUSERS

Sydney, he took a first-class cabin on the steamer *Manuka*. A cartoon mailed home from the United States lampoons the extent of tipping expected in the unfamiliar country. From North America (Canada, then USA), he sailed for England and the Continent. While he was in Europe, in February 1906, his mother Jeanette, the family matriarch, died aged seventy-two years, at 'Quamby', Crimea Street, St Kilda; the house she shared with Morris and Fred, and their sister, the widowed Carrie (Caroline), and her children.

There was little Morris could do but journey on, through France, Switzerland, Holland and Spain, painting whenever he could. Along the way, as well as sketches, he sent home several articles, which were published in *The Australasian Traveller.* James Davies, the energetic editor, wrote the introduction to Morris's 'spirited notes' and 'pungent pen and ink drawings'. Several were caricatures of 'types'—English, Spanish, French, Dutch—still others covered Egypt and Israel. He also documented his travels in pastel, capturing some beautiful landscapes.

From Spain, Morris wrote disapprovingly of Barcelona bullfights and glowingly of Granada's glorious Alhambra:

> … perched on a craggy hill overlooked by the Sierra Nevada, surrounded by exquisite gardens and lime trees, where nightingales warble in the moonlight, and the gurgle of marble fountains, with the tinkling of mule bells far, far down below in the olive and orange groves, are the only sounds that break the stillness.

Then it was on to Egypt and the Holy Land; the latter a popular destination for turn-of-the-century travellers and the subject of many lectures and slide shows in Australia at the time, one of which may have peaked Morris's interest and influenced his choice of destination. He began his article in exotic Egypt:

> Cairo, its capital, is one of the most interesting cities of the world, with its clashing of Eastern and Western peoples, its refinement and barbarism, its enlightenment and

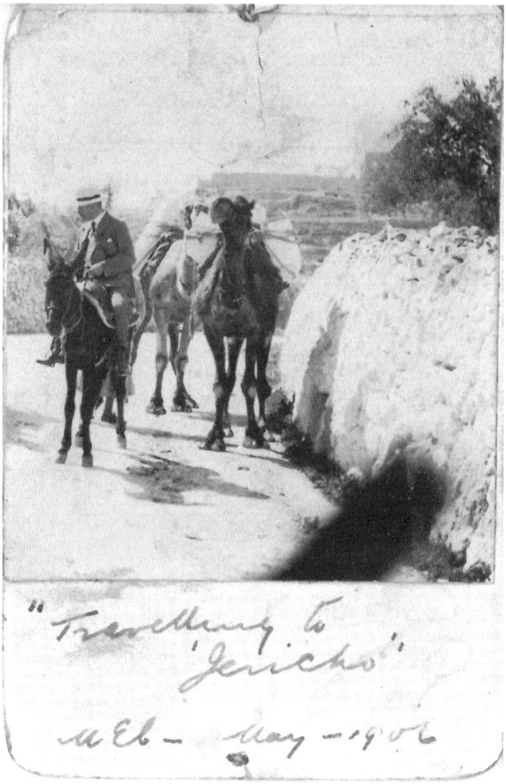

Invitation to Morris's solo exhibition 'Around the World Colour Sketches'. 1906

paganism, all jostling in the labyrinth of its streets ... Here camel caravans dodge motor cars ... European princes and swarthy Bedouins, Americans and Arabs, elegant French and English ladies, and dirty, dishevelled dervishes—all mix in a sort of jumbly *mélage*. In its native quarter and bazaars, the conglomeration is even more pronounced ... inky-black Nubians, copper-coloured Bedouins, cunning Arabs, veiled women, shouting, yelling vendors of all wares—from live monkeys to stuffed crocodiles ... 'Emshe Emshe' (go away) I shout to an Arab girl who bothers me to purchase a bowl of milk while I am busy painting the intense colouring of an

> Arab village … my boy endeavours to effect a sale for the lady by assuring me it's 'Verra good milka, master; she gets it from a married donkey', but no business results.

After a camelback tour of the desert and a visit to the pyramids, Morris took a steamer to Jaffa, the Gate of the Holy Land. He was shocked by the filth, smell and noise: 'Here is a seething mass of mixed humanity, fighting like jackals for possession of my baggage.' The train ride to Jerusalem was a welcome escape from the chaos. It steamed through the fertile valley of Sharon, past groves of oranges and olives, and wide swathes of wheat and oats. The 'peasants', Morris noted, wore clothes out of the Bible and plodded behind camel, bull and donkey-drawn ploughs. After four hours of rocky, barren goat-grazed passes, he was delighted to '… pull up at the Holy City, just as the sinking sun guilds its ancient domes and minarets with ruddy gold.' Again, he was struck by the diversity—people in 'comic-opera costumes' from every corner of the earth. Finding a quiet café, he settled down to 'sip a doll's house cup of thick, fragrant Turkish coffee' and watch the passing parade.

From Jerusalem, Morris rode with a guide to Bethlehem, where he tried to photograph and sketch the people, but was rebuffed because of the Mohammedan belief that taking an image weakens the subject. He travelled on, by mule and camel, to the Mount of Olives, Bethany, Jehosophat and Jericho, and other Biblical towns 'bristling with interest and scintillating with colour'.

After a nine-month odyssey, Morris returned home to Elwood and, in June 1906, had his own 'Exhibition of Around the World Colour Sketches' at Bernard's Picture Gallery in Collins Street. Invitations were printed on a small card—on the verso was stuck an evocative sepia photograph of Morris on the road to Jericho.

3

MORRIS AND MARRIAGE

Melbourne

(1907–1931)

Throughout his life, Morris maintained a strong interest in the doings of the art world. Even when he had little time for his own art, he attended exhibitions and kept up his friendships with David Davies, John Longstaff and Robert Taylor Ghee, who all became artists in the public eye.

Morris, Davies and Taylor Ghee; the latter four years Morris's junior; were born in Ballarat. Longstaff, four years Morris's senior, was born at Clunes, thirty kilometres away. The artistically talented colleagues enjoyed various degrees of recognition as artists. Longstaff, later Sir John, became a famous portraitist and five-time winner of the Archibald Prize. The introspective Davies—nicknamed 'Moonlight Davies' for his skills in depicting twilight scenes—left Australia in 1896 to teach and paint in France and England and is represented in major Australian galleries. Taylor Ghee, like Morris, remained an amateur. He worked as an optician, frequently exhibited, and was collected by the National Gallery of Victoria. As for Morris, after his death, it was left to his daughters to shepherd his paintings into major national and regional galleries.

Another Ballarat boy, Arthur Phillips, became a 'leading expert on company and mining law', and acted as solicitor for the Cohen's company as well as for the family. Phillips was seven years younger than Morris, but they were more than business colleagues. After Morris moved to Melbourne, on holidays he and Longstaff often stayed at Phillips's property, 'Yarra Grange', a white two-storey, brick and stone house on nearly 1000 hectares of river frontage, between Melbourne and Healesville. Together, they sketched, hunted and fished. Visitors included Nellie Melba, the celebrated soprano, supporter of artists and collector of art and antiques, who lived at nearby Coomb Cottage. Apollo Bay was another favourite holiday destination, where for decades the Cohen family and friends enjoyed ocean fishing. Morris loved its unspoiled shoreline and isolation; access then was from the open ocean and the difficulty of safe landing was a concern.

Early 1909, Morris again indulged his love of overseas travel to picturesque places. At the beginning of March, he was in New Zealand to paint amongst the rugged peaks of the South Island. He stayed at a rest house at the far end of Lake Te Anau, where the biting insects foiled his every attempt to set up his easel: '... swarms of murderous sand flies infest the whole region, and for a painter, seeking to depict the beautiful, never was such a plague,' he reported to readers of *The Australasian Traveller*. After a few days, he gave up and set off with a rucksack to cross the mountains towards Milford Sound via McKinnon Pass.

> The trail is through a fine beech and pine forest, dense and verdant; intense green and russet mosses carpet the earth, and every tree trunk is correspondingly clothed, while festoons of hanging mosses trail from tree to tree like drapings of delicate green lacery.

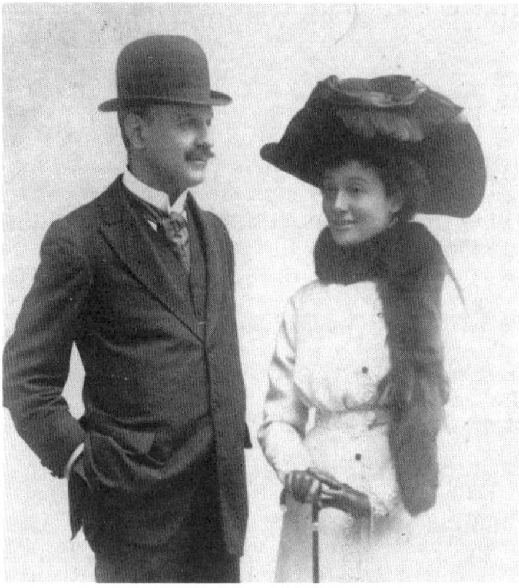

Morris and Viva's engagement photo, inscribed on the back by Von, 'When Mother and Daddie were engaged.' July 1910

After five days of such 'wandering' with his companions, he reached the spectacular Sutherland Falls, at the time believed to be the tallest waterfall in the world. On the zig-zag return descent to the little ferry, he passed two ladies struggling up with their heavy skirts hitched: 'With a sudden scream the skirts were instantly rung down,' he later wrote, and he sketched them trapped good-naturedly in the awkward moment.

Morris returned to Melbourne briefly, before taking the train to Sydney to cross the Pacific in the RMS *Marama* and spend most of the year in North America, visiting the Rocky Mountains and other scenic areas. The vessel departed in April from Circular Quay, packed with passengers on the popular route—first stop Vancouver. Among the passengers, many of whom he caricatured, along with the captain and crew, was a circus troupe which included Bebe, a clown; Marco, the lion tamer; and the circus manager, 'a most excitable German.'

It may have been Morris's final fling, for he married the next year—the last of his siblings to do so. On 5 July 1910, he announced his engagement to Viva May Frankel of Sydney. Wasting no time, in August they were wed in Randwick, at her father's home. Rabbi Cohen of Sydney's Great Synagogue, where Viva's father was the

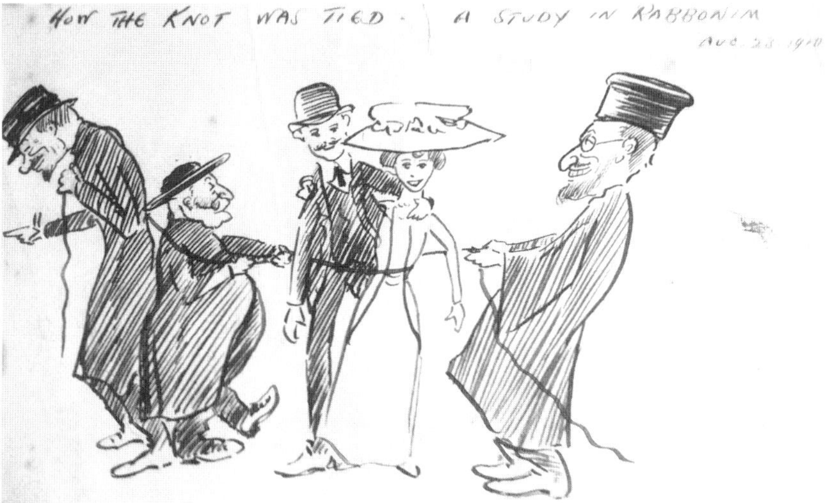

secretary, tied the knot. Morris created a charming caricature of the happy event and, many years later, their daughter Valerie described the couple's formal engagement photo: 'Her rare beauty was hidden under large hats as she stood beside this well-proportioned man with his trim moustache, bald head and dark eyes shining with a great sense of humour.'

Like Morris, Viva came from a family of nine children. Born in May 1879, she was the youngest of the four daughters of Annie (neé Cohen) and Simeon Frankel, who had married in Melbourne in 1863. The lively thirty-one-year-old had for some years been the honorary secretary of the Jewish Girls' League and had gained some notice as an actress in amateur musical theatre. She appeared regularly with various clubs, singing and reciting at get-togethers, hospitals and charitable functions. Around 1908, when she performed with the popular Sydney Comedy Club (SCC), Viva was singled out as among 'the pick of Sydney's amateurs'. Another show, *The Tame Cat*—a light comedy—a reviewer wrote, '... attracted a large and fashionable audience ... woman parts were played by Misses Viva Frankel and Elsie Prince, both very clever girls and attractive beyond dispute.'

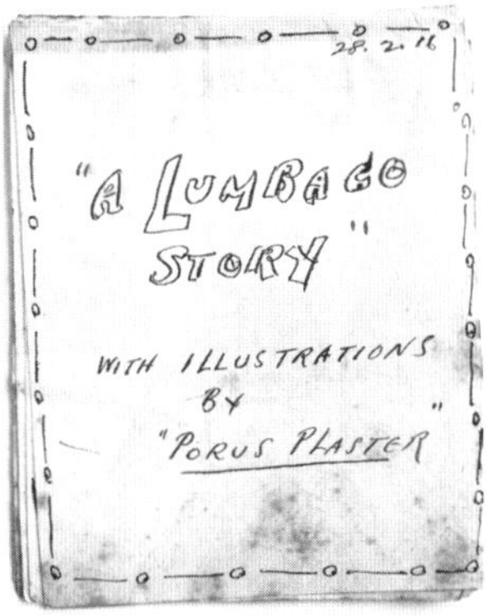
28. 2. 16
"A LUMBAGO STORY"
WITH ILLUSTRATIONS BY "PORUS PLASTER"

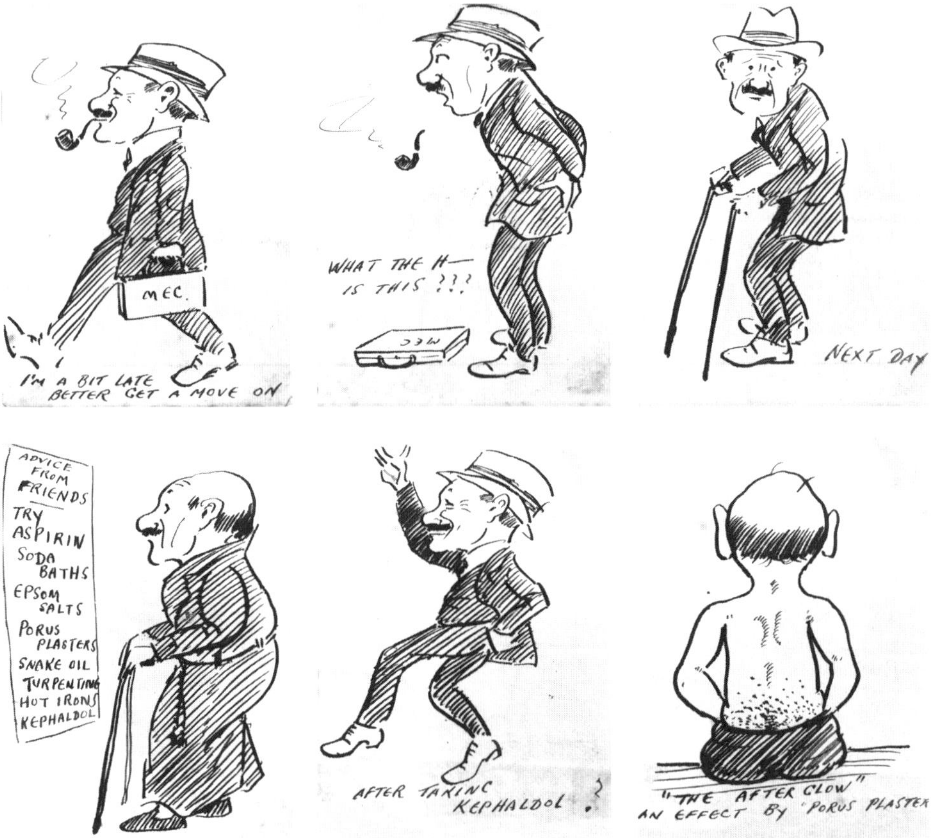
MEC
I'M A BIT LATE BETTER GET A MOVE ON
WHAT THE H— IS THIS ???
MEC
NEXT DAY
ADVICE FROM FRIENDS
TRY
ASPIRIN
SODA BATHS
EPSOM SALTS
PORUS PLASTERS
SNAKE OIL
TURPENTINE
HOT IRONS
KEPHALDOL
AFTER TAKING KEPHALDOL ?
"THE AFTER GLOW" AN EFFECT BY "PORUS PLASTER

A few days before Morris and Viva's wedding, the Jewish Girls' Guild held a farewell for Viva, their 'popular' secretary, and presented her with a gift. Viva took part in the program of recitals and music. Whether she knew it or not, it was her also farewell from the stage. As a married woman, she carried on her good works in support of institutions such as the Foundling Hospital and Infants Home and the Red Cross, and she and Morris often sang around the piano at home, but she never again performed in public.

Ten months after the wedding, Valerie was born on 10 July. In another three years, on 28 June, Yvonne arrived, completing the family. Valerie, in the 1990s, remembered her parents' relationship thus:

> In their strange way they showed respect and understanding for each other … [yet] I never remember seeing Father either kissing Mother or taking her in his arms. She was a graceful, sensitive woman who lived solely for the welfare of her husband. Her world revolved around his desires and comfort. She might lie on the edge of the marital bed lest she disturb the poor sleeper. Summer would see her running wildly up the street in search of the ice man, should the ice have melted in that wooden chest and the jelly be unset for dinner. There could be no failures when Father returned home. Often he would come home with what he called a 'sick headache', now known as a migraine. He'd lie in a darkened room while my Mother my sister and I crept about fearful of disturbing him.

Later events suggest that Morris's headaches may have been symptomatic of a heart problem. He also suffered from lumbago. Still, he took great pleasure in life, especially the holidays. His humour is evident in his many joyful caricatures of himself, friends and family and anyone else of interest. He sketched on anything to hand. Not infrequently, he would embarrass his daughters by doodling on the pristine tablecloth. Cartoons of outings to tearooms such as the Mia Mia and the Wattle in Collins Street show him 'assisting'

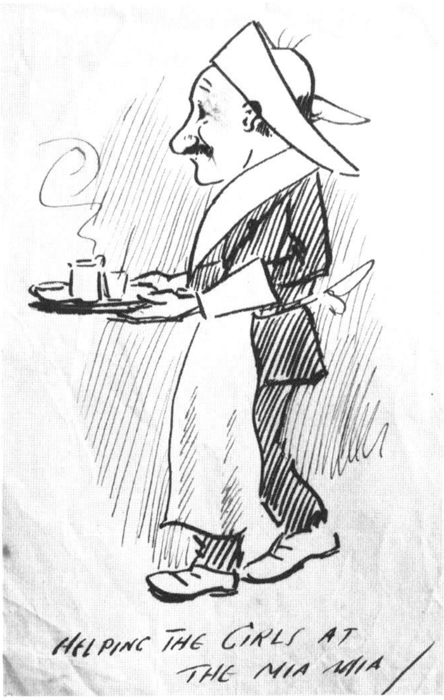

the waitresses. Others feature restaurant chefs, speakers at public lectures, orchestra conductors, or participants in shipboard activities. It seems that his pen and wry eye were never still. He was Jewish but unafraid of lampooning his Hebrew colleagues in Melbourne and the radical, ring-locked sects that he struck overseas. He traded cartoons with Reverend Jacob Danglow, Minister of the St Kilda Hebrew Congregation, who, in a letter of May 1922, thanked Morris for the 'welcome provoker of mirth'. Although the family had strong Jewish roots, apparently, their daughters received a secular upbringing.

Morris's recreational interests (hunting, fishing, painting) form a strong theme among his sketches, but music and other entertainments were clearly happy aspects of his life with Viva. With Viva's background in amateur theatre, they keenly attended productions and musical performances at venues such as the Lido and the Lyric. Fritz Hart, distinguished composer, conductor and director of the Albert Street Conservatorium, and champion of (Dame) Nellie Melba, and others, was a firm friend and visited their home. Later, Fritz lent his support to composer and pianist Margaret Sutherland, who was to figure in Val's life. Morris's artistic friends, Longstaff and Taylor Ghee—the latter viewed by the sisters as a 'tall, forbidding figure'—often came to Sevilla.

Morris himself was no shrinking violet. In a 1912 letter to the editor of *The Argus*, he wrote an articulate defence of his lifelong friend David Davies, then living in France:

> When criticising the two fine seascapes of David Davies, at the Artists' Society exhibition, you state that he has fallen under the influence of Julius Olhsen. I beg to state the position should, indeed, be reversed ... it is generally admitted by artists of the Newlyn School that Davies taught and inspired Ohlsen considerably. [However,] recent work by both painters show a wide difference in technique and character ... Davies portrays the quiet unobtrusive sweetness of nature, while Ohlsen treats the broad, brilliant, and dashing effects of light and shade. Both men's works have their exquisite charm. Ohlsen's pictures are eagerly bought by the public, while Davies's are keenly sought after by artists.

Despite these loyal artistic friendships, and newspaper reports that Morris was 'widely known' and 'esteemed by all who knew him', Valerie considered him 'a bit of a loner'. Regardless, Christmas and Easter Holidays were spent with family and friends in country Victoria, and Hobart, anywhere with fishing or hunting or sketching opportunities. Peterborough, Lorne, Lakes Entrance, Rokeby, Maryville, Yarra Grange, Mount Macedon, Kalimna, Westernport, Mount Dandenong and French Island, and his old haunt, Apollo Bay, feature amongst Morris's cartoons and pastels. 'On those holidays,' Valerie recalled, 'Father tried to encourage my sister and me to draw but we preferred to walk and gather wildflowers. Only many years later did we become involved with art when it was too late to benefit from his knowledge.'

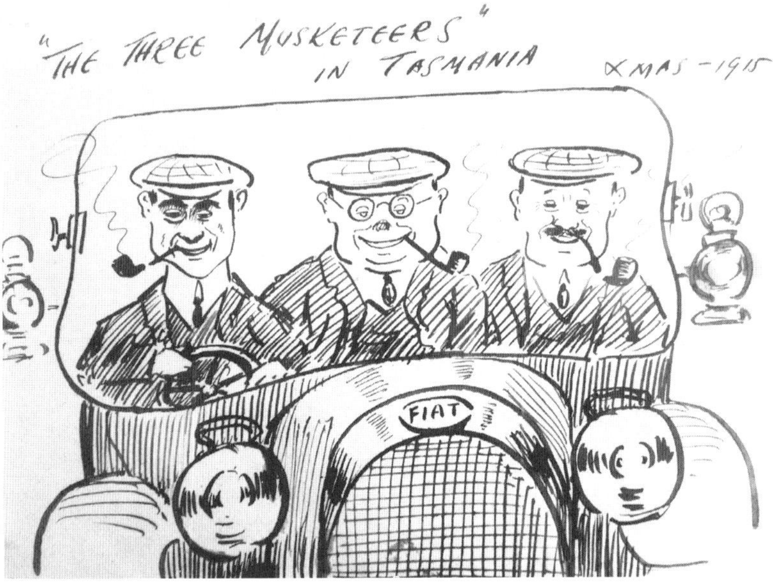

Von did, however, remember doing a small pastel with him when she was about twelve, and, unlike her sister, admitted to some influence: 'We were taking it in, that's how it all developed.'

Before his marriage, Morris had put his oil paints aside and taken up pastels, a technique taught to him many years before by Oldham. Perhaps the medium allowed him to finish a work quickly, without the drying time needed for oils, or perhaps he wished to distinguish himself from the many fine landscape artists who worked in oils. Then again, the paint fumes may have exacerbated his migraines. For whatever reason, pastels, imported from France, became his medium. Unusually, he rubbed them in, which gives his landscapes a watercolour-like appeal, moody and Impressionistic, anticipating the work of slightly later tonalists such as Clarice Beckett, in particular, and Max Meldrum. Looking at the pastels today, they are remarkable.

Towards end of 1912, S. Cohen & Sons had moved into a grand new warehouse in Queen Street. The business was extremely busy with retail and well as government contracts for hardware items. Around that time, Morris was also on the committee of the Elwood and South Kilda Progress Association, battling for matters such as better lighting, installation of a sewage system and limiting the size of allotments, but after two years he excused himself due to business pressures. In the 1920s, he joined the boards of several mining companies. Some weekends, Val recalled, to escape the stresses of work, '… he'd shut himself away in the spare room, refusing to be disturbed' while he painted. Unlike his caricatures, which showed a fondness for humanity, his paintings captured landscapes.

The Great War, the First World War, brought further stress for Morris; keeping him busy given his business interests. There must have been joy and relief when war ended. However, over the next three years the number of remaining Cohen sons rapidly diminished. In August 1919, Adolph, the youngest, died aged about fifty-two, leaving his widow and two children. Dolly was remembered in his obituary as a great sportsman: 'One of the best field shots in the State … president and a committee-man of the Melbourne Gun Club … active member of the Victorian Golf Club, and an ardent fisherman.' Then, a year later, Joe passed away, age sixty-two, who had been 'a frequent visitor to the Far East, and was widely known both commercially and in sporting circles'. Brother Fred followed, in July 1922, at the age of fifty-eight. He was also great angler and one of the founding members of the Commercial Travellers' Club. The family history of heart problems was taking its toll, leaving Morris, then a vulnerable fifty-seven-year-old, as the last of the five sons and sole governing director of S. Cohen & Sons.

Just two years on, in September 1924, another Cohen heart gave out. Daisy, Morris's fifty-year old sister, died in bizarre circumstances. As reported in *The Argus*, she was downstairs with her daughter aged nineteen years, son ten, and two domestic servants, when they heard loud noises upstairs. She went upstairs to investigate while the others rang the police. The room was deserted, but drawers and cupboards had been ransacked and their contents strewn about. As the others arrived in the room, Daisy collapsed and died shortly after.

Possibly believing that he should travel while he could, Morris left his daughters with their aunt, Adolph's widow, and took Viva on a grand tour of Europe; her first trip overseas. In early January 1925, the staff of S. Cohen & Sons farewelled the couple over dinner at the Commercial Travellers' Club and presented Morris with a camera and travel rug and Viva with a bag. After a train ride to Sydney, Morris and Viva sailed from Woolloomooloo, travelling as saloon passengers on *RMS Orama*. Mid-year, an article in Sydney's *Sunday Times* reported on the couple's progress:

> Mr. and Mrs. Cohen left Australia at the beginning of the year in the 'Orama'; got off the ship at a Mediterranean port, and have been travelling up through Italy and France ever since. They will not return to Melbourne till the end of the year. One cannot travel far in Europe these days without running across Australians, or, at least, traces of them.

The English, Scottish and Australian Bank issued Morris and Viva with a circular Letter of Credit for an aggregate amount of £2000. Their withdrawals charted their extensive journey. They spent two-thirds: drawing on the note in Colombo, on the *Orama*, Naples, Palerma, Taormina, Naples, Rome, Monte Carlo, Nice, Marseille, Paris, Rouen, London, Exeter, London, Windemere, London, Oslo, Copenhagen, Hamburg, Berlin, Salzberg, Vienna, Venice, Naples, and finally, on the 25th of October, on the *Oronsay*.

While in France, Morris had a happy reunion with David Davies and bought home one of Davies's recent oil paintings, 'Chateau at Dieppe'. As ever, he carried his sketchpad, chronicling their travels and the people they met. He also carried a letter from the editor of the CTA journal, recently renamed *The Australian Traveller*, introducing him as an authorised representative of the newsletter: '... we shall appreciate any courtesies or facilities for obtaining information on our behalf, or for sketching.' Morris contributed five articles from his travels. 'Wanderings in Sicily', 'Wanderings through Norway' and 'Doings in Germany' were all printed in 1925, the first while he was still abroad. 'European types' appeared the following January. A further note, 'In a Cornish fishing village'—a charming story of an encounter with a beer-soaked teller of tall tales—seems not to have been submitted.

Arriving in Sicily, Morris was struck by the poverty and decay of once fine buildings, yet the narrow lanes were full of life and colour. He and Viva stayed in a converted monastery in the centre of the island where, he wrote:

> Decrepit villages cling to precipitous craggy mountain-sides, with some ancient castle or monastery on the peak. Goats and black sheep browse in almost inaccessible places, while mules with panniers toil up the picturesque mountain paths, their jingling bells sounding sweetly in the still air … The most popular resort is Taormina … a veritable paradise for artists … The ancient Greek theatre and colosseum are here, with Mount Etna, snow-covered and smoking furiously, alongside. The Sicilian homes, some of great beauty, are cut into the hillside; gardens redolent with brilliant flowers, olive and orange groves with their intoxicating fragrance, are everywhere, while the almond trees in blossom are as a veil of translucent pink on the mountain sides. More than twenty artists of various nationalities are here, their easels set up.

In contrast to historic Sicily, Morris observed, Norway was a contented modern European country, shining clean, alcohol-free, with wholesome smorgasbords. But, like Sicily, it was Arcadia for a landscape artist:

> Norway in summer is a land of exquisite beauty. The map shows a long coast-line jagged and indented with fjords that extend some hundreds of miles inland … These deep-green narrow waterways, twisting and winding between mighty mountain-sides clothed in birch, fir, larch … up almost to the snowline, where the ice-capped tops are usually buried

> in the clouds … Far, far up, on impossible ledges, are seen handkerchief-sized farms, with tiny matchboxes glued on their sides—the houses and barns.

Germany, on the other hand, seemed far from contented. Germans were suffering from the deflation of the mark, following on from the immediate post-war flow of cash into the country to take advantage of high interest rates. From a corpulent, shaven-domed Berliner, drinking deeply from a gigantic mug of beer, Morris heard a common refrain, *Ja, Deutschland ist kaput.*

The ten-month journey inspired Morris to pen an entertaining poem, 'Doing Europe', presumably for friends and family on return. It begins with fishing in Norway's 'placid green waters' and ends with a whirlwind trip to Florence and its galleries and churches and then Naples, where the exhausted travellers were glad to board the *Oronsay* for Australia:

> Don't wake us for a week to our steward I said
> I swallowed a whisky then coiled up in bed
> Land Ho cried the lookout afar on the lee
> Its Australia I smell it as plain as can be
> We hop down the gangway our dear ones embrace
> Yes Europe's all right but Australia's *the* place.

If Morris and Viva were proud to call Australia home, the girls were overjoyed to have their parents back. But it was not long before another Cohen heart gave out: Carrie, the eldest, and Morris's only surviving sibling died in July 1926.

Exactly two years on, Russell Pty Ltd took over S. Cohen & Sons, retaining Morris as one of the directors. Morris was relieved, finally, to be able to take a back seat. He caricatured himself as a dog, breaking its chain and bounding joyfully towards the fishing spots of Portsea and Hastings, leaving behind a bowl of 'worry soup' outside a doghouse labelled 'S. Cohen & Sons'.

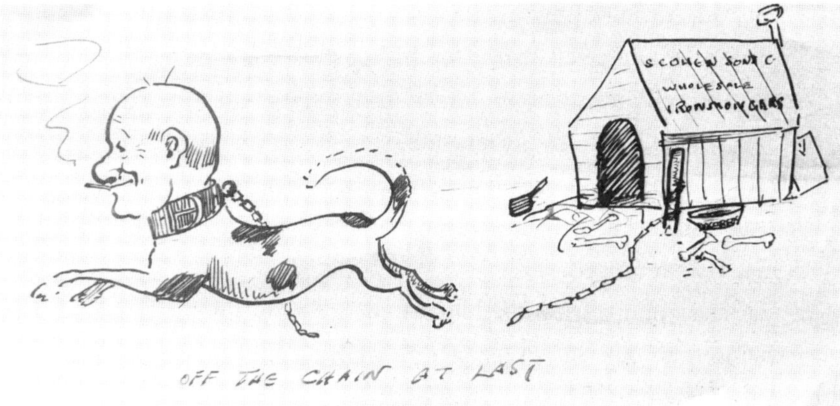
WHOLESALE
OFF THE CHAIN AT LAST

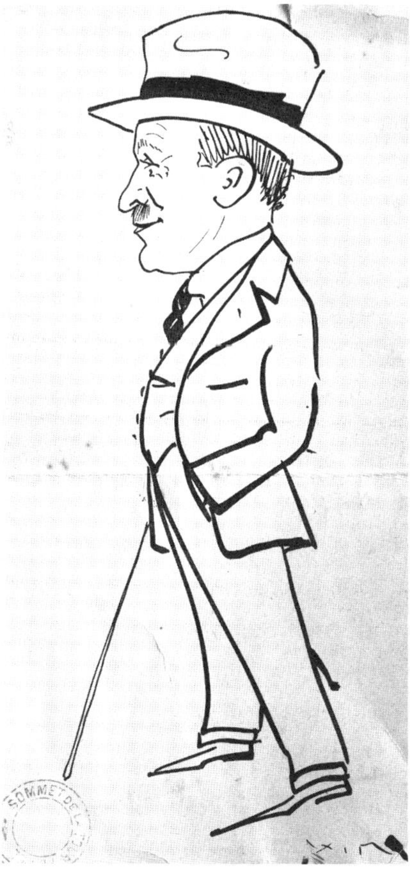

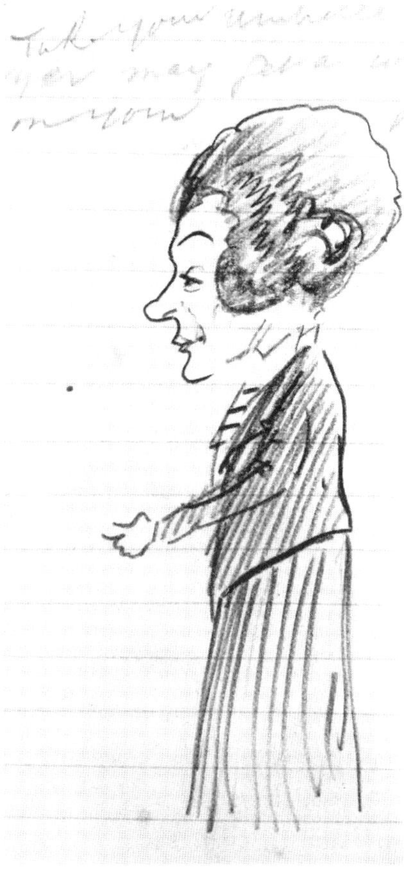

Fishing was not the only thing on Morris's mind: from 25 October to 10 November 1928, three of his pastels were hung in a mixed 'Exhibition of Paintings by Australian Artists' in the Fine Art Society's Rooms on Exhibition Street. He was in good company: Arthur Streeton, Hans Heysen, George Lambert, Margaret Preston, Thea Proctor, Roy de Mestre and Tom Roberts were among the twenty-seven artists represented.

Morris's paintings must have made a favourable impression. The following year he was given a one-man exhibition at the Society's rooms. Over sixty of his landscapes of Melbourne and surrounds, and places visited on his travels overseas, were on show from August 1st for two weeks. Nearly half sold on the opening day: 'a considerable success', according to *The Age*.

Whereas a few reviewers weren't sure that pastel, mainly used for figure and portrait painting, was the appropriate medium for landscape, the reviewer for *The Age* was more open-minded: '... at his best, in pictures such as Hay gathering near Healesville, Harvesting at Yarra Grange and Morning on Lake Geneva, he shows a competent grip of the landscapist's problem of light, space and colour.'

The Australasian Traveller also found much to admire in Morris's work:

> Pastel bas been used by a fair number of Australian artists, but usually for figure work. A few have experimented with the medium for landscape, but not to a large extent. Mr. Morris E. Cohen, however, has made pictures of the kind, and his capable work forms a display of an unusual nature at the gallery of the Fine Art Society ... With much variety in choice of subject, there is interesting treatment both of country which invites the use of brilliant colour and of landscape of quiet charm. Many of the pictures are from Europe, and the colour associated with mountain scenery has appealed to Mr. Cohen both there and in Australia and New Zealand. Other work introduces autumn tints, seaside and river scenes, farm

CATALOGUE

		Guineas	
1.	Morning on Lake Geneva, from Les Avants	20	
2.	Moonlight and Low Tide, Western Port Bay	12	
3.	Hay-gathering Near Healesville	8	8
4.	Building the Stacks	6	
5.	Farm Scene Near Tallarook	7	
6.	Evening Glow, "The Remarkables," N.Z.	10	
7.	Half-Moon Bay	6	6
8.	Blackwoods on the Mountain Top	7	
9.	Wattles on the Upper Yarra	4	4
10.	Mount Sir Donald, British Columbia	20	
11.	The Sunlit Flat	8	8
12.	The Evening Clood	4	4
13.	Morning—Rokeby Farm, Near Tallarook	8	
14.	Autumn Tints, Gisborne	10	10
15.	Lake Zum-am-zee, Tyrol	25	25
16.	Palermo, Sicily	12	
17.	Innsbruck, Tyrol	20	
18.	Careston Castle, Scotland	15	
19.	Evening at Marysville	5	5
20.	Sunset in the Tropics	5	
21.	View from Mt. Dandenong	7	
22.	Autumn in Tasmania	6	
23.	Springtime at Marysville	8	
24.	The Road to Ferntree Gully	5	5
25.	A Woodland Peep, Marysville	3	
26.	A Frosty Moonlight	5	
27.	Twofold Bay	7	7
28.	Near Trawool	5	
29.	Farm Scene Near Trawool	5	
	Forward		£ 82
	Forward	Guineas	82
30.	Port Arthur, Tasmania	8	
31.	The Gleam	3	
32.	Gipsy Point	3	3
33.	Hay Cocks Near Healesville	5	5
34.	The Silent River	7	
35.	Yarra Grange	8	
36.	Moonlight on the Indian Ocean	6	6
37.	On Cape Woolamai	Lent	
38.	A Grey Morning	Lent	
39.	Forest of St. Germaine, France	10	
40.	Autumn	7	7
41.	Twofold Bay	8	8
42.	Beaumaris Bay, Evening	7	7
43.	Autumn, Gardens, Fitzroy Street, St. Kilda	6	
44.	Back Beach, Sorrento	5	
45.	Near Templestowe	7	
46.	An Old Garden, Healesville	8	
47.	Autumn, Alexandra Drive	7	
48.	Sunshine and Shadows, Doncaster	7	7
49.	On the Goulburn	6	6
50.	Gordon River, Tasmania	10	10
51.	Gorse in Springtime	6	
52.	The Genoa River, Gipsy Point	7	
53.	Elwood Beach	6	
54.	The Old Station Near Kiami, N.S.W.	8	
55.	Ruins of Greek Theatre, Toamina, Sicily	7	7
56.	Harvesting at Yarra Grange	7	
57.	Autumn Morn	7	
58.	Wattle Grove, Lilydale Creek	7	
59.	Moonlight on Port Phillip Bay	8	
60.	Lake Wakatipu, N.Z.	10	10
61.	Evening Glow on Mt. Donna Buang	10	10
62.	Wattles on the Yarra	4	4
63	?		6
64	?		44
			182
			£191. 2. 0

The catalogue from Morris's exhibition of August 1929, in the Fine Art Society's Rooms on Exhibition Street, with handwritten notes of sales

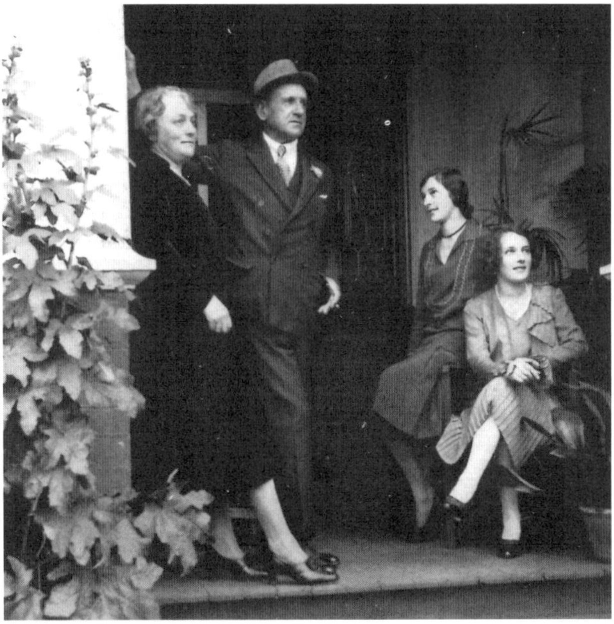

Possibly the last photo of the family together, at Sevilla. Val aged nineteen (right) and Von sixteen. November 1930

> subjects, decorative trees, and old-world buildings. There is much to observe in the exhibition.

Blamire Young, art critic for *The Herald*, and an artist himself, was also approving: 'His medium is pastel, which he manages with skill and reserve ... In his handling of evening skies, when the absence of shadow welds the whole landscape into a glowing mass of colour, Mr. Cohen is particularly successful.'

A young George Bell, for *The Sun News-Pictorial*, was even more complimentary:

> Mr. Cohen is an amateur ... a very talented one ... A happy choice of subject, a knack of pleasant composition, and a delicate sense of colour combine in producing good works of great charm ... a noticeable feature of these picture is the capability of the drawing.

Morris must have been much encouraged. Val always claimed that he was a 'natural artist', untrained, declaring to interviewer, artist James Gleeson, 'He was completely self-taught; he had no lessons at all, ever.' But that was clearly not the case. Nor did she seem to realise how involved he was in promoting the arts. Early in 1925, for instance, he was one of the three delegates representing country galleries to meet the State Treasurer to lobby for increased funding.

With the success of his solo show in 1929, Morris began preparing for another exhibition. In 1930, he travelled to the islands of New Guinea, sketching along the way. Then, in March 1931, he bundled Viva and their daughters into the car, packed his sketchpad and fishing gear and headed to Tasmania for a month's getaway touring the island.

On Sunday 29 March the family settled in at the Scamander Hotel and explored the resort's surroundings in the gentle sunshine. The following day, before breakfast, Morris and the girls took out one of the hotel's boats. An oar apiece, the sisters rowed down the river towards the sea, while their father steered in the stern. The three stopped at a lagoon and enjoyed a walk across a sandspit on the ocean beach. Returning to the dinghy, the girls attempted to row back up the river to the jetty but could make no headway against the tide running swiftly out the narrow river-mouth. Their father took over the oars. By then the boat was being swept through the channel and over the bar. The girls leapt into the metre-deep water and called to their father to follow. A few seconds later, they saw Morris jump over the bow and cling to it. A wave broke over the boat, and that was the last they saw of him.

4

DEPRESSION-TIME TRAVEL

Melbourne and overseas

(1931 – 1937)

That terrible last Monday of March 1931, the two sisters last saw their father clinging to the beleaguered dinghy. Within seconds, the outgoing tide swept it over the wave-washed bar at the mouth of the river. While their mother watched horrified from the hotel, the girls struggled ashore and raised the alarm. As Valerie wrote some sixty years later:

> The Tasmanian sketching trip had only just started for us all when the tragedy occurred … From the hotel window [Mother] had seen the boat overturn at the mouth of the river and seen my sister and me struggling up the long stretch of surf beach. Somehow we'd managed against the strong current to swim ashore.

Morris was quickly lost to sight. Onlookers watched powerlessly as the dinghy was rushed out to sea. There were no suitable rescue facilities at the resort and the police had to arrange for a motor-launch to be taken from the water at St Helens and ferried down by lorry. That afternoon, the weather worsened, hampering the search. Val remembered, 'All night my sister and I huddled beside Mother, distressed, waiting, hoping.'

The next day, police and numerous residents patrolled the beaches until after midnight, and the search widened and continued into the first day of April. The 'Scamander Tragedy', as it quickly became known, was widely reported, even in Queensland and New Zealand. It was all so public. Arthur Phillips, the family's friend and solicitor, suggested that Viva and her daughters stay for a while at his Healesville estate, 'Yarra Grange':

> This kindly bachelor suggested that we take advantage of his holiday property with its peace and quiet to recover. Father had stayed and painted there many times in the white two-storey house, shot over the river flats and visited the neighbouring properties of Dame Nellie Melba and Baron de Pury.

It would be some time before their ordeal would be over. Viva, Val and Von prepared a joint statement to the police. As well as describing the events, they had to testify as to Morris's state of mind. They made note of the fact that he was a strong swimmer and experienced with boats. Another of Morris's colleagues, Major Alexander Donaldson Spiers, offered a reward of £20 for the recovery of the body. While some newspaper reports described Morris as 'elderly', Spiers told the police that Morris looked younger than his sixty-five years. Spiers's description of his friend continued:

> Bald on top of head. Height about 5 foot 6 or 7, clean shaven, weight about 9 stone. Fawny tweed trousers, light fawn shirt, buttoned plus-four sports coat with strap cross the back. Brown boots size 7 white soft collar and blue tie. He had a walking stick, letter of credit and fairly large wad of notes.

Three weeks after the accident, a boat was found washed up on a beach about ten miles south of Scamander. Investigation showed that it was the missing rowboat, no. 6, its bow split and its bottom pocked with holes. Then, in early June—just before the inquest into Morris's death—on Shelly Beach, about two miles south, human remains were discovered: 'a human foot, with boot and sock, and some distance away a human bone'.

The inquest opened on 22 June but was adjourned until 3 July. Spiers was in Tasmania on other business and took the opportunity to view the grisly find. He gave testimony that the boot was the sort that Morris wore, with a rubber sole of the type he had specially attached to his fishing boots.

Dr Henry Shannon, GP, testified that Morris and Viva had sought his advice in January that year. They were worried because, after helping a fisherman pull up his boat, Morris had been troubled by breathlessness and a racing heart. The doctor found that Morris's heart was enlarged and his 'heart sounds' were poor. He warned Morris that, given the family history of cardiac arrest, 'exertion might aggravate his condition very seriously'. Shannon told the coroner that he believed that the events on 30 March were such that exertion and emotional disturbance would have been enough to cause heart failure and immediate death. After hearing all the evidence, the coroner returned the verdict: 'That the remains were those of Morris Edwin Cohen, who came by his death by drowning at Scamander, in Tasmania, on March 30, 1931; and that the cause of death was accidental.'

The application for probate was still to come. Phillips handled the arrangements but the details of the day had to be revisited and were repeated in the broadsheets for all read. Finally, at the end of July, Viva and the girls could get on with their lives. In his will, Morris '... left real estate of a gross value of £9,766, and personal property of a gross value of £3,725 to his wife and daughters, subject to numerous gifts to other relatives.' There were also stocks and shares in various mining and other companies, among them the highly successful Carlton &

United Breweries and its predecessors, headed by Montague Cohen. Family legend has it that, as Morris walked the streets, he tossed coins to down-and-outers, laughingly claiming that they would all come back via the pub.

In the meantime, Viva and the girls had gone back to Sevilla, their home by the sea at Elwood. Of course, it was difficult. Von had only just turned seventeen. In her mid-seventies, when interviewed about her father, she said, 'We were sad, Val and I ... It was an awful experience and something you never forget.' Similarly, Val recalled:

> Returning to the old house by the sea we were sad without Father. Mother was completely lost. All her life she had left everything of importance to Father ... Now in middle age she couldn't even drive. More and more she began to turn to me ... She tried hard over the next year to overcome the emptiness till finally she decided to sell the house and take my sister and I overseas.

Instead of selling, they let the house to Spiers, Morris's friend and business associate—both men were on the board of Aberfoyle Tin Company. And, when the *RMS Mongolia* sailed from Melbourne in early March 1932, the three Cohen women were onboard, headed for Adelaide, Bombay, London and ports between. It was the sisters' first trip abroad. The one-class P & O tourist cruiser, catering for Depression-era travellers, was a disappointment for their mother, but the girls enjoyed the many and varied entertainments—and the men. In 1990, Val recalled:

> In 1932 I stepped aboard ... in a black and white cotton dress and a straw hat pulled down to hide a face covered in a pimply rash. I was still suffering from the shock of Father's death but undaunted by my first trip out of Australia. Underlying my grief was an intense excitement. The conditions onboard were basic but not even the accommodation and poor food troubled me. Mother, always fastidious, would turn

> her sad face away from the plates of greasy mutton. For my sister and I, shipboard activities were just one continuous round of games, dancing and romance. My young military companion took me ashore at Colombo—my first glimpse of the colourful East. He spoke fluent Hindi. We wandered through the labyrinth of bazaars, out along the coast to Mt. Lavinia, and up the winding road to Kandi, sailing the same evening for Bombay. There my young Brigadier refused to say goodbye, overstaying his leave trying to persuade me that I'd really like life on the North West Frontier. Came Suez, he said his farewell while strings of camels and Arabs plodded past beside the canal. From Suez, we made a rushed trip to Cairo to see its pyramids and tombs, then sailed on through the blue Mediterranean. The three-week voyage ended one cold wet morning at Tilbury [London].

Val's young Brigadier was in fact an Australian Captain in the Ghurkas, whose next posting was to India; it was later that he became a Brigadier. 'Can you imagine me a Brig's wife?!', Val asked me in 1997.

The family stayed at the Grantleigh Court Hotel in Hyde Park, central London. The hotel was modern, with central heating; its ads promised that it was 'unsurpassed for comfort, cuisine, service, homeliness'. Their mother was happy. A young family acquaintance arrived to escort the sisters around London and that first day ended at a dinner dance at a venue on the Thames. Val continued her account:

> A few days later I had my twenty-first birthday. It was the year of the brilliant concert at the Albert Hall at which fourteen-year-old Yehudi Menuhin took the applause beside the aged composer Sir Edgar Elgar; the year the young dancer Margot Fonteyn captivated audience after audience; while at the Redfern Galleries the painter Ian Fairweather—an artist we were to meet years later in Far North Australia—was showing canvasses from China.

She appears to have muddled the facts though, perhaps conflating her first two trips to Europe. In 1932, she turned twenty-one in July; Yehudi Menuhin turned sixteen that same year and although he did make a recording in London just before Val's birthday, the concert with Elgar was held in Paris in 1933. Fonteyn was only thirteen and living in China in 1932; Fairweather too was in China and his first canvasses were not hung in the Redfern Galleries until 1935.

But, to let Val continue her account: 'In London we raced from one historic site to the next, imbibing and digesting history'. She had a new paramour, who took her to clubs, dinners, parties and dives. The latter, with their men and mistresses, transgender and homosexual patrons, white ties, top hats and beautiful cars, fed Val's thirst for experience, because she had decided that she wanted to be a writer. Her doomed escort was just a convenience—he pursued her to Australia, only to be left with her mother. 'He was nice but a bore,' Val sniffed.

Later in the year, the three women left exciting London—where paintings by Monet and Pissarro made a particular impression—to tour the rest of the country:

> Finally it was time to explore the British Isles. From the car-yard I drove the Essex bang into Trafalga Square … We criss-crossed England, Scotland and Wales, devouring the sights of castles, churches, cathedrals, finally coming to rest at a thatched cottage outside Guilford. It was when Stanley Parker, the gossip writer for Melbourne's 'Table Talk' and his brother Ken, a photographer, came to stay that we discovered our ghost. Locked doors opened, keys lay in the middle of the room, lumps of clay were found on the bed, while at night in the garden was heard the stamping of horses. From the villagers we learnt of the headless horseman who stamped outside all the haunted houses.

The Parkers were Melbourne-born. Stanley, some three years older than Val, was a caricaturist as well as a writer for the social weekly, *Table*

Talk. Most likely these events occurred on the sisters' third overseas tour, because Stanley lived in London from 1936, where he drew for the *Bystander* and *Tatler*. Indeed, an article in *The Argus* indicates that in April 1936, the Cohen sisters gave an afternoon farewell cocktail party at their flat in Roslyn Court, South Yarra, for the two brothers, and the Pyke sisters, Guelda and Mollie, who were all soon to leave for London on the *Orsova*. *Table Talk* reported that the flat was decorated creatively with green and red peppers—'a welcome change from the usual autumn foliage'. A twenty-four-year-old Lina Bryans, later to become a significant artist, was said to be among the best dressed of the guests, looking stunning in a tailored flannel suit. A buffet supper, followed by a game of roulette, rolled the party on until midnight.

Ship's records, newspaper reports and Valerie's own articles indicate that the three women; Viva, Val and Von; made three grand world tours: 1932–1933; 1934–1935; and 1936–1937, with shorter travels between. Valerie's unpublished account, 'Raking through the embers', ends their 1932 overseas trip with a visit to a relative in South Africa, but, like their fun with the Parker brothers, that too seems to have occurred during 1936–1937.

On that first journey abroad in 1932, Viva arranged for their aunt and her eldest sister, Mrs Amy Leicester (my great-grandmother), to join them from New Zealand. After some family time in London and surrounds, Amy embarked for home in February 1933 and Viva and daughters followed in April on the *Oronsay*.

The Cohens arrived back to an Australia in the depths of the Great Depression, the economy had collapsed and one-third of workers were unemployed. It seems to have had little impact the sisters' lives. A couple of months later, Val was on a ship again. After her friend, Leila Pirani, a writer nearly twenty years her senior, was involved in an accident in her sports car, they made a last-minute decision to take a three-week 'winter pleasure cruise' to Port Moresby via the Great Barrier Reef. On the *Otranto*, while the captain navigated the tricky waters of the reef, the passengers were said to be '... basking in the sunshine, dancing in the moonlight, or sleeping soundly in their cabins.'

On return to Melbourne, Viva bought an apartment at Roslyn Court, 434 St Kilda Road. Spiers, their tenant at Sevilla, needed to vacate for a business trip to England, and the house at Elwood was put on the market. The family home went to auction and sold on 22 October 1933, having, in the months before, been thoroughly renovated by one of Melbourne's leading architects.

As she had when Morris was alive, Viva continued her association with charities such as the Red Cross. At their mother's urging, Val and Von followed her lead. In August they were helping Queenie Sloman, their (once hated) cousin, with a flower stall that graced the foyer of a highly successful matinee at the Athenaeum Theatre in support of the Melbourne District Nursing Society's appeal.

As well as art, the sisters were then keen on fashion. At Caulfield in April 1934, Von—with her creative friends Guelda and Mollie Pyke—was spotted amongst the other punters wearing '… a mulberry red felt hat to match her suit of mulberry red and black finely striped tweed.' It was most likely their friend Parker at *Table Talk*, who reported that, a week later, the mother and daughters sailed again for England on the *Oronsay*, embarking on their second and most extensive world tour. Much later, Val explained:

> We [she and Von] both wanted to return to Europe, especially Italy. Acquiring a three-month rail pass we would explore art galleries, museums and the hill villages of Tuscany, like San Gimignano where life had changed little over the centuries. Each evening the bullock carts were brought inside the massive stone walls, the gates shut and in the medieval square the people would dance and sing. By morning the peasant women could be seen carrying washing on their hips down the hillside to the stream that flowed through the vale of Chianti. This ancient place abounded in history. Inspired, I wrote my first article. Melbourne *Age* accepted it. Like Father,

> who had written and illustrate articles on his travels, I had made a beginning. My next article was from one of Europe's special places, St Paul de Vence, in the Alpes Maritime. There, the proprietor of the little albergo showed us paintings artists had left in lieu of payment. 'They're just gathering dust', the old man said as we crowded into the little room above the vine-covered verandah, 'perhaps one day they'll be worth a few francs, I don't understand them'. Against the wall rested Picabias, Signacs, Derains and Lucien Jacques. At that time our appreciation of such art was minimal for we had never spoken to Father about art or his artist friends. Since his death I had grown used to Mother's highly nervous disposition. She wasn't happy travelling, but needed her daughters' companionship. My sister and I wanted to continue, so we all wandered over Sweden, Holland, Switzerland, from where I was to write further articles. Finally, we returned to London to explore more of the history, the dives of the deviant, and the exclusive nightclubs of the West End, all adding to copy before we left for the USA and Canada.

While in England, the three Cohens joined the eight or nine thousand people 'commanded' to attend the inaugural Royal Garden Party at Buckingham Palace, the first big outing for little Princess Elizabeth. After the lavish event, in late October 1934 they crossed the Atlantic to New York on the *Manhattan* to tour North America for a few months.

While the family was away, their cousin (my grandmother), with her husband and daughter, stayed in their St Kilda Road flat waiting for their own house in Landen Place, Toorak, to be built. My mother, aged eleven, was told not to look at the raunchier publications in their packed bookcase, but of course she did.

On disembarking back in Melbourne in January 1935, the Cohen trio was met by the Parkers. Stanley sketched the sisters and their souvenirs for *Table Talk*. The accompanying article outlined their European adventure and revealed a little of their time in the USA:

> Well, the Cohens, Valerie and Yvonne, are back again after their world tour! When I saw Yvonne coming down the gangway the other day she said, 'I feel just like a travelling circus!' and certainly what with leis, brilliant hued baskets from Pango, her easel, paints and palette, her tennis racket and various mascots, including an adorable native bear perching on her shoulder ('and given me ironically enough in California') she certainly looked it! They have had the most wonderful tour—London, and a different theatre every night—all over England and Scotland, Switzerland for the sport (where they distinguished themselves by climbing to the top of Mt. Blanc), Germany, a mad week in Paris, and of course Italy, for this was actually their goal, as they wanted to further their art studies. This was their favorite of all countries. 'It has everything,' says Valerie; 'perfect mountain country and the most beautiful lakes in the world, and then the cities and their statuary, their paintings and the music, their wine and their flowers! I really think that I must be a spiritual child of Italy. I feel it is my home.'
>
> After this they had a look at the New World and spent a few months in New York ... Their visit to Radio City was almost as interesting as their visit to Hollywood, where they watched Charles Laughton rehearsing in his new film, and 'met everyone—but Garbo.' They used to have their meals at the famous Brown Derby, where all the stars would party with their make-up still on.

That year two Laughton movies were released: *Mutiny on the Bounty,* starring Clarke Gable as Bligh with the then unknown Australian actor Errol Flynn as Fletcher Christian; and *Les Misérables,* based upon the famous Victor Hugo novel. The Hollywood restaurant that the sisters frequented was indeed enjoying its heyday and there was a good chance of seeing the likes of Bing Crosby, Gary Cooper, Cary Grant, Barbara Stanwyck, Mickey Rooney, and assorted wannabes.

After Hollywood, *Table Talk* revealed, came Honolulu, with its leis and hula dancing. There was no mention that the sisters were travelling with their mother, but it was reported that they were about to sail to New Zealand to 'climb a volcano', and, presumably, to see Viva's sister and their other relatives.

If they did indeed visit New Zealand, it was quick. The three Cohens were soon on a cruise to the islands to Australia's north. From Singapore, they returned to Melbourne in early August 1935, on the premium liner *Nieuw Holland*, marketed as one of the two great white yachts of the Dutch KPM line. Ports between included Batavia (Jakarta), Semarang, Surabaya, Bali, Brisbane and Sydney. Disembarking in a Singapore-bought paddy hat, Val caught the attention of a newspaper photographer. For Val, as for Von, Bali was *the* standout destination, inspiring an article and a lifelong love of such languid, luxuriant places. Val wrote:

> Crowded market scenes under shady banyan trees, long rolls of lazy blue surf through leaning palms, vivid little fish in the island corals, crazy high mountains, emerald lakes, girls with dazzling hibiscus flowers tucked in their long black sleek hair, where it falls into a huge knob on their glossy shoulders, water buffalo tilling the rice fields, nude gay children running, laughing and hugging their precious fighting cocks—all these scenes and many more flash through the kaleidoscope that is Bali, crowned by a mighty pagoda, strange festivals, the heavy scent of brilliant flowers and the beat of bamboo gamelans.

The Melbourne *Herald* accepted Val's essay on Bali, published in November. Ever after, she liked to make the point that she used the payment to buy her first typewriter, with the intention of becoming a writer. Her article makes the rather romantic case that the simple Balinese way of life—'children of nature'—free of the 'rushing and bustling' of the western world, brings contentment. Her late father had had a similar reaction to the tropics when he visited New Guinea just five years before.

Still restless and unsettled after their wide-ranging travels, Val and Von decided it was time to see more of their home State. They convinced their long-suffering mother to accompany them on a three-week caravanning trip over the Christmas and New Year period. Then, in the New Year, there were more parties. Mid-February, the sisters were on the organising committee for a 'very cherry' Leap Year party, held by members of the amateur group Melbourne Little Theatre at the Lawn Tennis Association Clubhouse in Kooyong. *Table Talk* reported that:

> Many amusing items were given by members in an informal programme arranged by Mr Dick Webb. Around the walls of the ballroom, notices giving the rules of behavior at a Leap Year party made an unusual decoration, and caused the guests much amusement, while bowls of belladonna lilies and colorful phlox and zinnias were set across the mantelpiece to complete the decorative scheme.

In the first six months of 1936, Val and Von again began art lessons, this time taking a class at Melbourne Technical College (now RMIT) with the new drawing master, Murray Griffin. Griffin was conservative, but his use of colour and design meant that he could be considered a Modernist. But, by May, the sisters had embarked on another extensive overseas tour, beginning with San Francisco. 'Melbourne Chatter', a gossipy social column in *The Bulletin* alludes to their extraordinarily privileged lives:

> Val and Yvonne Cohen must have been born under a lucky star, for they are leaving with their mother on Saturday in the Monterey for the U.S.A. and even further afield. Only a few months ago this family of three enjoyed a holiday to Java and Bali, and in four years they have been twice to Europe and once round the world. They are ideal travelling companions,

> for they are all interested in art. The girls are taking their painting kit and movie camera. Val says she won't come home until she has seen Russia, so that means visas for three to the U.S.S.R.
>
> One of the week's farewell parties to Mrs. Frankel Cohen and her daughters was a dinner at the Windsor, given by Mr, and Mrs. Alexander Spiers. There were posies for all the feminine guests; Mrs. Cohen's, of tiny buds and hyacinths, melted into her misty chiffon frock. A master craftsman of flowers created an original seascape for the centre of the table; a ship composed of green hydrangea petals sailed over a sea of autumn leaves, funnels being of pink rosebuds from which came puffs of white tulle smoke. Nautical dolls paced the decks as captain and crew.

Val's expressed determination to visit Russia may have been more her desire to be interesting than reality. I could find no evidence that she or the family visited Soviet-era Russia—then mainly a destination for a small number of progressive western intellectuals. Val surely would have written about such an unusual destination.

If Val's article on the medieval town of San Gimignano, in Italy, was indeed her first effort at travel writing, as she later remembered, it took some time to be published, and her Bali story actually appeared first. The Melbourne *Herald* ran her reports on European cities between January 1936 and March 1937: the first on Holland, then on San Gimignano, followed by the Swiss Alps and, finally, Sweden.

Val's focus was on human interest. Keeping up with the times, her articles are illustrated not with sketches, but with her own photographs. They would have appealed to the average Australian, then very isolated from the rest of the world. She writes of the quaint costumes, flaxen hair and stiff caps worn along the waterways of the Zyder Zee; Chianti and the romantic, crumbling villages of Italy; and smorgasbord and snaps in serious Sweden. She describes a funicular ride on the Jungfrau Railway, to the top of the Swiss Alps, past hayfields and hotels perched on steep peaks, ski-fields and glaciers, of cocktails and fairy-lights. The latter article offended one reader, who wrote to the editor, horrified at the banality and commercialism depicted in the face of such a glorious landscape: 'I have lived unforgettable months among the world's giants, where the ineffable glory of moonlight upon snow-field and rock is not, as yet, improved by fairy-like coloured lights,' he protested. Val kept the cutting—perhaps as a souvenir of the first 'review' of her writing, however sarcastic.

By July, the Cohens were in England, and a columnist for 'Melbourne Chatter' passed on to readers some of the contents of an earlier letter from Val, written:

> … on the train bound from Los Angeles to the Grand Canyon in Arizona. Even the air-conditioned car was uncomfortable, for the temperature outside was 120 deg. Val, describing fashions in and around Los Angeles, is critical about midsummer deshabille. Women wander round the streets in shorts. One vision who didn't seem to cause more than a momentary flicker of surprise wore a hat, a playsuit, sandals and stockings separated from the brief little pants by suspenders, and an expanse of bare leg.

After the sisters 'complained that fellow-guests in most London hotels were seldom under ninety', Viva bought a Morris Minor and rented 'Stoatley', a beautiful old house in Surrey, complete with resident ghost. They toured the countryside and drove to London for the sales, which, according to 'Melbourne Chatter', Viva 'disliked intensely as an accumulation of all kinds of rubbish since 1066'. They planned, the following year, to join the crowds gathering in London from all over the British Empire for the coronation of King George VI and his wife, Queen Elizabeth. About May, when the coronation festivities began, they moved to a hotel close to the city.

Before departing England, for £5, they sold their little car to Australian artist and stage designer John Rowell, who had been commissioned to make two paintings of the coronation ceremony and was in London with his family. From Southampton, on July 9th, the Cohens boarded *The Stirling Castle* for Cape Town, South Africa, travelling first class. Viva had been unwell for a while and decided that it was time to return home. But first, she would take her daughters to visit her second eldest brother, Harry, about eleven years her senior, who had left Sydney for South Africa when she was still a child. In a subsequent travel article, Valerie described their African experience:

> We would sail for South Africa via the Cape and visit him in Johannesburg. From Cape Town to Johannesburg the country was reminiscent of parts of Australia except for the indigenous population that surfaced from those deep Joberg mines. Our new-found uncle was round and jolly. He suggested that he drive us all to Kruger Park for a few days. On entering that great strip of South Africa teeming with wildlife uncle's automatic revolver was sealed. Even in those days South Africans never drove without a gun. The park was enormous; every fifty miles or so along the earth roads would be found a collection of roundavels [circular, often thatched, buildings with a conical roof]. Before sunset all travellers had to find accommodation. Natives patrolled the encircling fences; outside marauding animals fought and killed each other, their cries making the night hideous. 'These animals aren't tame' had blazed across a Joberg paper before we had left for the park and lions had forced some travelers, who had vacated the safety of their car, to crawl under it to safety. 'Don't lean out', uncle had said, chewing away on his biltong as our car slowed to separate a pride of lions so close we could have touched them. Everywhere the land moved with an assortment of game. The Kruger had been an experience. The variety of animals, the birds, the waterholes where these collections drank after the early morning kills, were experiences to dwell on as we bucketed across the ocean towards Australia.

By mid-September, the trio were back in Melbourne, arriving from Durban on the *Nestor*, initially staying at The Chevron on St Kilda Road, Melbourne's most modern hotel, before moving back into their South Yarra apartment. The newspapers picked up on their doings. 'Melbourne Chatter' reported only their views on the fashions they encountered during their extraordinary seventeen months on the other side of the world:

> They found fashion in New York color-crazy, with all the smart women wearing printed materials in a mixture of colors so bright as to be almost garish. Floral effects in blends of primary colors were almost loud enough to scream. In the travellers' opinion the New Yorkers missed the bus. It was the women in Stockholm who looked the loveliest—and the smartest. They favored black, which made a perfect foil for their fair hair and clear, natural complexions. The most decorative figures the girls saw in Paris were the widows making the very most of fashion's fancy for halo hats on the back of the head and flowing veils. Their widows' weeds are a joy to behold. Folds of soft georgette fall from crown to waistline. One can shop better in Melbourne than in Paris, where things are expensive and Australian money goes nowhere. These wideawake lasses noted that Austria was making itself felt in London. All over the West End there are little shops stocked with Austrian goods, and many fashions bear the ornamental stamp of that country.

On return from this final grand tour, Von was describing herself as an artist. Although she would have been well aware of the conversations on modern art that were shaking up the conservative Melbourne art scene, it seems that she had not yet embraced Modernism. In an interview for *The Argus*, she commented that she had been puzzled by an ultra-modern exhibition of Belgian art that they had attended in one of London's newest galleries. Reportedly, she said:

> When someone asked the attendant in charge if she could explain the pictures, she told them there was no need for explanation—one had only to gaze at the colours, which were so marvellous in themselves that there was no need for form or any of the conventional techniques.

An accompanying photo of Von descending the gangplank from the *Nestor* shows that the sickly, skinny, younger sister with 'straggling hair round her oval face', as Val had described her, had blossomed an elegant young woman of twenty-three. Two days later, the fashionable sisters were spotted at an art opening:

> Corded ribbon as a trimming for woollen suits must be a recent fashion from abroad for the Misses Yvonne and Valerie Cohen, who returned on Monday after a visit to Europe, [and] were noticed yesterday at the opening of the exhibition of paintings by Mrs. Gwen Barringer wearing suits illustrating this novel idea. Buttons made of tightly rolled ribbon fastened the front of the deep parma violet woollen suit worn by Miss Yvonne Cohen. Tiny bows of the ribbon adorned her wide brimmed summer-weight felt hat, and tied under the high turned-down collar of her jacket. Her sister was wearing a cape suit of dove grey flannel. The cape was laced round the edges with navy blue corded ribbon. Her smart little grey felt hat was trimmed with a matching navy band.

Earlier that year, George Russell, the large hardware company that had acquired S. Cohen & Sons, was liquidated—a victim of the severe economic recession. The Cohen sisters, however, had sailed through the Great Depression in style.

5

TO THE ISLANDS AND WAR

South Yarra and Dunk Island

(1938–1939)

After their final trip to England, Val and Von decided that it was time to settle down in Melbourne and become more serious about art. They went in search of a teacher, as Val explained:

> Our first request for tuition was to Louis McCubbin. This quiet portly man had a studio in Collins Street but was unable to impart his knowledge. 'Study these art books', was all he'd suggest. After a short unproductive period we joined the students at the Melbourne Technical College, working with Murray Griffin and on Saturday afternoons landscape painting with John Rowell at his Bayswater home. With little technique but a lot of desire, we began sketching out-of-doors with our artist friends Neil Douglas, Lina Bryans and Jock Frater. Like Father, I enjoyed landscape but attempted it in a very different style.

Closer to each other than ever after their travels, they re-enrolled at Melbourne Technical College on Latrobe Street, a short tram ride from their St Kilda Road apartment. In February 1938, they started Full Day Art with drawing master Griffin and other teachers such as painting master John Rowell and his brother William.

Rowell had trained under McCubbin, soaking up his Impressionistic approach to light and colour. He emphasised sound technique and taught the sisters the outdoor skills of painting sea and sky and of mixing colour on a palette. Yet, Val complained, 'He took us along dusty roads to paint gum trees—nothing *pretty*.' Rowell was 'an awfully nice man', Von said, but painting with him and his other students in the hills of Bayswater became tedious: 'Anyway we got bored stiff up there because it was just one place looking at a gum tree and he'd say "Now we'll all do that gum tree" and I thought, how boring.'

Looking for more colour and diversity, later, in 1938, Val found it. With first term over by the end of May, Val—fleeing either a difficult love affair, the Melbourne winter, or both—boldly determined to head north. A travel agent recommended Dunk Island—at the time promoted by the Queensland Tourist Bureau as Australia's premier getaway location in the Far North, then far off the usual tourist track. The little resort, nestled in the foothills surrounding beautiful Brammo Bay on the lee side of the island, had opened just two winters before. Arriving in July, after a lengthy train journey, Val made the 'rough as billyo' crossing from the jetty at the mouth of the Hull River, pretending to be unfazed, but clinging white-knuckled to the side of the boat. Safely ashore, she recalled, 'This island filled me with delight, immediately I fell in love with its tropical environment, its isolation.'

In her later writings, Val remembered that the resort 'never seemed to get off the ground', but newspaper reports and tourist brochures of the 1930s suggest otherwise. With the owner's social connections and access to the media, it quickly became fashionable, at least for a favoured few. Even though it was a work in progress, the little resort was well-equipped and the services were appropriately relaxed. There were half a dozen chalets, a small bar by the beach, a dining room on the hill, and a hall for 'entertainment'. The location had the added allure and historical interest of former resident Edmund J. Banfield, journalist and self-styled beachcomber, who had lived beside the bay with his wife Bertha for twenty-three years and died there in 1923. Banfield's hugely popular books—*My Tropic Isle* (1911), *The Confessions of a Beachcomber* (1918), *Last Leaves from Dunk Island* (1925)—at once romanticised life on the island and demonstrated a deep understanding of its cyclone-prone climate, fauna, flora and anthropology.

During Banfield's time, other writers and artists were attracted to the escape and romance of the Far North. Naturalists Charles Barrett and Alec Chisholm wrote about Dunk's fauna, and the newly wed, disabled Dorothy Cottrell eloped from her family's station in western Queensland to live there from February to July 1923. Her first novel, *The Singing Gold*, was an international success. The realities of the runaways' attempt to live more or less self-sufficiently on the island soon caught up with them but, on arrival, the tropical island seemed incredibly evocative. 'The divine setting for adventure, for youth, for Love; never to me quite real,' she wrote:

> There were wistful brown casuarinas against a smoke-blue horizon; ragged yellow-flowered beach hibiscus among the sedge; … slender stemmed jungle palms clinging to the cliff-face; … clear green shallows blotched with purple, and reefs smeared in henna and pink, and a sea of glass-like silver. A little chalk-white beach, that at its northern end was pressed and overlapped by the glistening jungle, brilliant, living, enamelled with sunlight. The water rolled and shished gently amongst the tiny shell and coral fragments at our feet … A big blue butterfly passed like a swift hard-blue flame … Scrub hens called in the jungle-brush … There was life and colour and light, and life, life, life ...

Like Val, Australia was waking to the attractions of its tropical islands. In the winter of 1931, Frederick McCubbin, the sisters' sometime-art teacher, was commissioned by the Australian National Travel Association to tour and paint the Whitsunday Islands, to Dunk Island's south. On show in Melbourne the following year, his seventy-two paintings brought the tropics to the south. They were, according to *The Argus*, 'A revelation to those who have never looked upon the tropical shores of North Queensland, where the skies are of a matchless blue, and the vegetation is barbaric and exotic in its colouring.'

More and more writers and artists were sharing the joys of the Australian tropics, yet to be discovered by the general public. In 1932, the Palmers, Vance and Nettie—then Australia's foremost literary figures—joined them. The Palmers escaped civilisation for over eight months to camp on Green Island, 130 kilometres north of Dunk. Anticipating loneliness and solitude, instead they were struck by another aspect of the tropics: the many memorable, relaxed encounters with all sorts of visitors, as Palmer observed.

> That year seems full of an extraordinary richness in human contacts—friendships formed in queer circumstances, remembered conversations around campfires or on heaving decks at midnight, memories of strange characters with outlines a little more emphatic than those of the ordinary beings of urban life.

A young Robert Campbell, later to be McCubbin's successor as Director of the National Gallery of South Australia, camped on the beach at Brammo Bay for six or so months with his wife; fishing, beachcombing and painting. In August 1934, thirty of Campbell's paintings of the tropics were hung in Brisbane. 'On viewing them one wonders that more Australian painters do not seek that area, so fertile in subjects for the brush and so prolific in inspiration,' wrote a reviewer for *The Courier-Mail*.

In the winter of 1933, Queensland journalist Freda Barrymore visited the brand-new Dunk Island resort as a guest of media mogul Sir Keith Murdoch and Lady Murdoch. Barrymore contributed an article to the quarterly magazine, *The Home*, which extolled 'The Romantic Isles' as places to 'seek peace far from the world'. At Dunk Island, she met the Campbells, and, she writes, after a 'refreshing swim in the clear, calm waters of Brammo Bay' …

> … we came out as if reborn, re-vitalised anyhow. Later we swam again, explored gullies and heights, listened to birds, went in search of oysters, collected a variety of exquisite shells, pieces of coral, walked and talked of the things that flood the mind when the heart is light and energy plentiful.

Earlier in the year, in another article entitled 'Let's buy a Queensland tropic isle', Barrymore had suggested that increasing numbers of winter visitors to North Queensland, seduced by the idea of an island of one's own, were seeking to buy or lease, and predicted that 'island life is about to be fashionable'.

During her visit to Dunk, and the Campbells, 'Nugget'—a beachcomber with a mass of curly, white hair—and a few regulars were the only residents on Dunk Island. However, as Barrymore foresaw, change was on the doorstep. It came not from Australia, but London.

In July 1935, Hugo Brassey—a dashing young Etonian; son of a wealthy, well-connected family, and grandnephew of Lord Brassey; pre-Federation Governor of the Colony of Victoria—married Christa von Bodenhausen; a beautiful, adventurous, German heiress. The newsworthy couple had met just three weeks earlier, when the baroness was presented at court. Hugo had not long emerged from a much-publicised and speculated upon on-off engagement to film star Lili Damita, by then Mrs Errol Flynn.

The Brassey family owned several large pastoral leases in Australia, which Hugo had visited pre-marriage, his activities as an eligible young bachelor often making the newspapers. For a wedding gift, Captain Brassey, Hugo's father, bought him a chunk of Dunk Island; then marked by just a scattering of beach shacks. The newlyweds were soon living there several months of the year in the old Banfield bungalow, between cruising the Pacific on their launch, the *Sunbeam*, and socialising on the mainland.

The island offered solitude, but the Brassey's enjoyed entertaining, and life just off the Queensland coast, not too far from civilisation, was good. Brassey had a pilot's licence and his wife was seeking to have hers recognised in Australia, so access to the island was easy. Stores could be purchased at Tully and delivered with the mail twice a week. An article in *The Courier-Mail* focussed on Christa:

> With her golden hair bleached by the sun to a fairer shade on the top, since she seldom wears a hat, her skin a rich, even tan, where it is left uncovered by her beach frocks with their sleeveless, backless tops and brief wrap-over skirts, Mrs. Hugo Brassey is a modern incarnation of the sun-worshipper … Now thoroughly accustomed to life on the island, Mrs. Brassey enjoys fishing and boating—she can handle a motor boat as well as any of the men on the island—supervising the laying out of lawns and gardens, swimming, and also supervising all the domestic arrangements. Each day the menus are brought to her by the French chef for her inspection, and she is often able to suggest new ideas, many of which have been gleaned from her experience of British and Continental entertaining.

The Brasseys built a new house and opened a small resort. In the winter of 1938, when Val holidayed there, for £4.10 per week at high season rates, the resort offered a handful of bungalows with baths and wide verandas, an enclosed seawater pool, floodlit at night, a bar and a dance hall. Meals were served uphill in the old Banfield bungalow, reached along a palm-lined avenue. Cows provided fresh milk, cream and butter, and fowls provided meat and eggs. Vegetables, coconuts, mangoes and other tropical fruits thrived in the rich soil. Tourists from the south arrived by train at Tully ('on the Sunlander'), about thirty kilometres inland by road, where they were collected by car or flown in to land on the sand of Mission Beach. The island itself was reached by boat from a jetty on the Hull River, or direct from the beach.

Val found the resort laidback, 'run with the utmost simplicity', but, she allowed, 'tinged with a certain amount of comfort'. On her return south, she wrote an article titled 'Where the telephone can't ring. The islands of the Barrier Reef', which was published in *The Age*. She had been captivated, bitten by the island bug:

> To own an island! How many of us have longed for that dream to come true, that we might creep away to a tiny corner all our own, untouched, unknown, except as a pinprick on a map? The South Sea Islands—silhouettes of palms, warm nights, romance. ... and yet here at our feet is the key to fairyland—the isles of the Great Barrier Reef. Little groups of islands and coral atolls scattered on the edge of the tropics, with a lure and enchantment all their own ... I idled away hours watching vivid tropical fish, looking at bunches of coloured coral. There were rocks clustered with oysters, there was surf, sunshine and abundant time ... [for] Dreaming, fishing, lazing in the sun, forgetting the jangle of the city. If you want all of this ... then the tropic isle of Coonanglebah is where it really comes true.

On Dunk, Val met the artist Noel Herbert Wood and picked up his preference for the Indigenous Australians' name for the island, interpreted by Banfield to be 'Coonanglebah', the 'island of peace and plenty'. In the mid-nineteenth century, the Indigenous population of the island was estimated to be 400, but they were long gone by Banfield's time.

The 'Family Islands', so named by James Cook when he passed seaward in 1770, are the traditional lands of the Djuru, from the coastal mainland, and Bandjin, the saltwater people. Cook named the largest of the 'family', the father, for George Montagu-Dunk, Earl

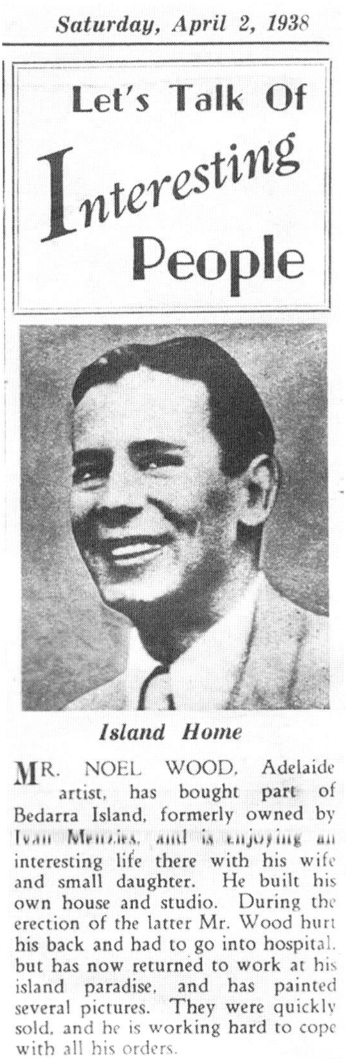

Saturday, April 2, 1938

Let's Talk Of Interesting People

Island Home

MR. NOEL WOOD, Adelaide artist, has bought part of Bedarra Island, formerly owned by Ivan Menzies, and is enjoying an interesting life there with his wife and small daughter. He built his own house and studio. During the erection of the latter Mr. Wood hurt his back and had to go into hospital, but has now returned to work at his island paradise, and has painted several pictures. They were quickly sold, and he is working hard to cope with all his orders.

An urbane looking Noel in an early article on his choice to live and paint on Bedarra with his wife and child; later articles make no mention of family. The *Australian Women's Weekly* 2 April 1938 p. 2

of Halifax and Sandwich. Later, the other islands and islets were also given European names: Richards or Allason (Bedarra or Biagurra), the mother and Thorpe (Timana or Timanoo), and ten other 'children'; most with white-gold sandspits on their north-western edge. Coonanglebah is the only of these three musical Indigenous names which failed to stick.

As Val wrote in 1938, Noel, living on Bedarra, walked with her along the beach and they swam in the gentle surf. He made her tea in a small cave in the rocks, which he used as a fireplace. Noel showed Val the spot where the breezes blew night and day and he planned to build a studio. 'I simply couldn't exist in a city. After this freedom it would kill me stone dead in a month,' he told her. When the studio was finished, she quotes him saying that he would '… be able to have a couple of fellow artists up. Competition gives stimulus and that's what I sometimes lack. One's apt to get stale working month after month alone.' Sitting on the veranda of his self-made bungalow, with its garden of fruits and vegetables, Val exclaimed for the nth time, 'What a Paradise you have here!' She was smitten:

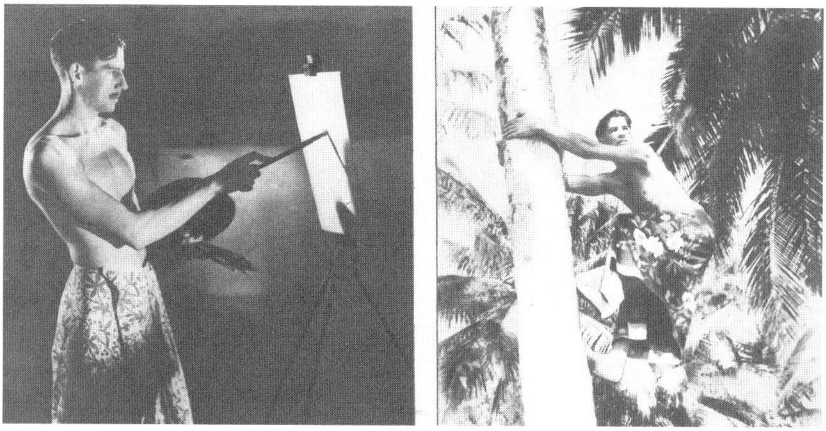

Two images of Noel that explain the attraction Val felt on first encounter in 1938. The accompanying article described him as an artist and modern day Robinson Crusoe, living on a lonely island, where, he said, 'Peace, a simple life, magnificent climate, no taxation, few worries, are the attractions.' The photographer captured him painting in one his trademark colourful sarongs and climbing a palm tree 'with the agility of an aborigine.' *Pix* 1 March 1939, p. 36

> We talked of art, music, books. Although he was literally cut off from the world, his knowledge was profound ... We talked until it was dusk. I was loath to leave, but I had seven miles [it's actually 4 miles, 7 km] to sail to Coonanglebah, where I was to stay. With great reluctance I climbed into the waiting boat, clutching an armful of wild orchids. On the beach stood a tall figure, his scarlet sarong dim in the evening light. 'Come again', he shouted, waving a bronzed arm, 'A little company is good for me'.

Hugo is not mentioned. In other of Valerie's accounts, however, he was very much present alongside Noel to greet her on this first arrival at Dunk Island:

> It was dusk as we made the island and the relief of a calm bay with a little landing at the foot of an avenue of coconut palms. Two bronzed figures emerged from the shadows to meet me.

> A short time later Hugo, Noel and I shared drinks and talk of books and painting on the verandah of a bungalow set in a lush garden. All thoughts of Italy were swept aside and a few months later I returned with my sister.

A third version, in Val's 'The Dunk Island story', begins similarly with a lengthy trip in a little motor rail from Townsville to Tully and a long wait for the boatman, and arrival at dusk. However, in this rendering, Val was met at Dunk Island by a 'dishevelled looking man' with a limp, 'a rope holding up ragged pants, and a vast expanse of hairy chest'. It was the manager, who took her to her cabin, directed her to head up the hill for dinner and disappeared into the dark. The managers at that time were the Polloks. Arthur Pollok was the brother of Lady Gowrie, the Governor-General's wife.

In yet other recounts, Von is present on that first trip north. As the sisters told Gavin Wilson, curator and author of an exhibition and catalogue *Escape Artists: Modernists of the Tropics*:

> We arrived in Tully and went to the pub and said 'how do we get to Dunk Island?' … We got to the channel in difficult conditions and onto the island. In the distance we could see these two creatures lurking behind palm trees—one was Noel Wood, the other Hugo.

Val's own article, 'Early neighbours on a Barrier Reef island', written in the 1990s, is yet another variation: the sisters are together when they meet Noel for the first time; not on Dunk Island, but Bedarra:

> It was a sparkling winter's afternoon in the late thirties, when Hugo Brassey, the owner of Dunk Island, whizzed us over in his new toy, a speed boat, the only one in the district, to his artist friend Noel Wood … as the boat nosed into the shallows of Doorila Bay, a willowy young man came casually from the palms, a sarong twisted around his waist … He led the way along a narrow track … to his hidden abode. Inside it was dim and cool, simple as any Tahitian dwelling with its walls of plaited palm … He offered coffee … we sat on

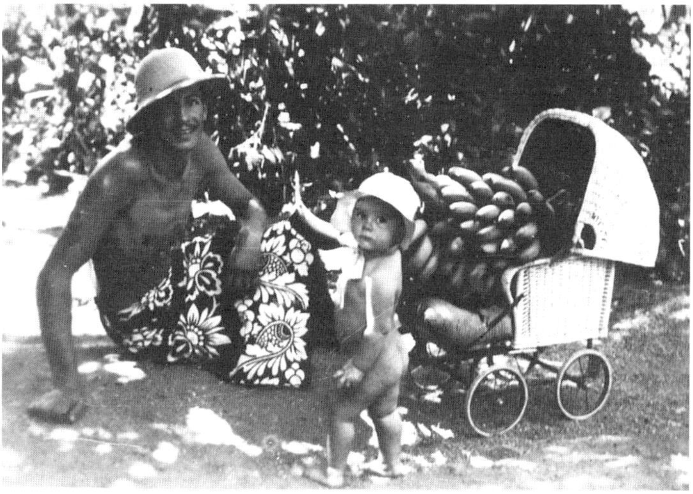

Noel and daughter Ann with a pram full of bananas. c.1939

> the swept earth floor … Hugo squatting like some handsome bronzed Buddha, slim, youthful.

What is clear and consistent is that Val was not only taken with the place, but dazzled by its cultivated, bronzed, sarong-clad men. That winter of 1938, Val turned twenty-seven; Hugo one year her senior and Noel one year her junior. Brassey was newly divorced and had put the Dunk Island resort on the market. However, in the absence of serious buyers, he continued to develop it. He had just bought a new launch to ferry tourists, and applied for a license to sell alcohol. He was also planning an airstrip.

Noel, who spent considerable time on Dunk Island and occasionally worked as a labourer for his friend Brassey, was married, and a new father. Strathalbyn-born, after studying art at the South Australian School of Art, he had worked in Melbourne as a photographic model for *Vogue* and tried his hand at fashion drawing. In August 1933, he married Eleanor Weld Skipper, a member of Adelaide society. Noel's father, the Reverend Thomas Wood, an unorthodox Church of England minister, conducted the ceremony. Eleanor was a fellow artist of some talent. She was related to the Skippers of Montsalvat, the Victorian artists' colony. For about two years, Noel and Skip—or Pisky, as he called her—lived in a small cottage on Kangaroo Island, 'Eumalla', owned by Noel's brother. Noel painted consistently: portraits, landscapes and still-life, mostly in oils. In September 1935, he was part of a group show, followed in November by a well-received solo exhibition, both held at the Society of Arts Gallery in Adelaide. By December that year, as Eleanor told the social columnist of *The Mail*, the young couple were considering '... taking one of the Barrier Reef islands, where Mr. Wood will carry on with his painting.' Apparently, inspired by a letter in *The Queenslander*, Noel was seeking to escape society and live simply and self-sufficiently.

With the proceeds from the recent exhibitions, the Woods bought a Model T Ford and set off for Far North Queensland with their fox terrier, Louse. They first sampled island life on Havannah, near Palm Island, but it soon proved too difficult, so they returned southwards to Townsville and eventually to Dunk Island. In mid-1936, Nugget, the resident beachcomber, ferried Noel across the water to Bedarra Island, less than seven kilometres from Dunk, giving him only half an hour to look around before the tide turned. It was time enough. The day before Christmas, with Eleanor providing the funds, Noel purchased fifteen acres of land at Doorila Bay on the north-eastern corner of Bedarra, then owned by an English syndicate headed by Jack Harris. Harris and the Woods, with Nugget as witness, signed a Memorandum of Agreement for a price of £3 an acre.

During their first weeks on the island, the couple lived in a tent and cleared the 'jungle', built a temporary home of palms and planted their first crops. Eleanor, pregnant and unwell, temporarily returned to Adelaide. She was idealistic and full of enthusiasm for the future. In November, she was interviewed by Elisabeth George from the women's pages of *The Advertiser,* who began her article, 'Perhaps every woman finds a secret echo in her heart to that most romantic of ambitions, "an island of one's own"', and continued with Eleanor's description of Bedarra:

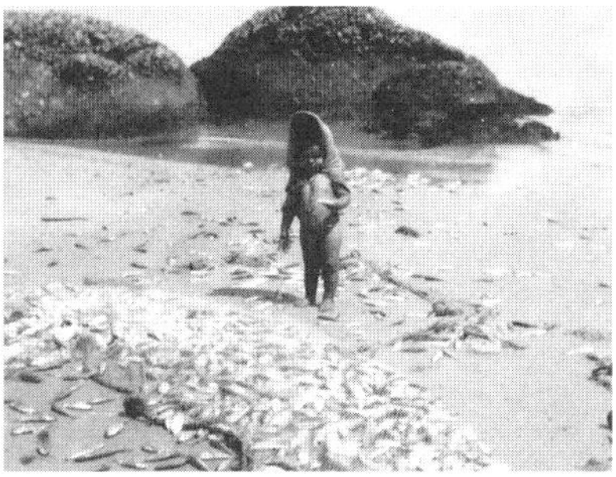

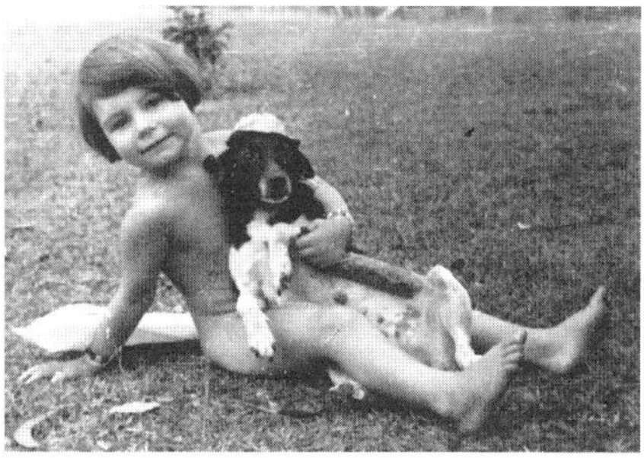

left: Gini, when she was left in Noel's care, amid a good haul of sardines, butterfish, and hammer-heads caught with a single throw of the net. 1938

right: Gini and Louse on the islands at Christmas. After the Woods' breakup, Ann and Gini were raised separately for a time. December 1939

> A little jewel of an island, with tall timber, spring water, and a population of most brilliant birds and butterflies. There are cocoanuts and pawpaws, orchids to make a collector's heart ache with longing, and rainbow colored fish reflected in crystal waters ... There are patches of good soil near springs that will be used for growing rice, coffee and other crops, and all vegetables will be home grown.

On 11 January 1937, Eleanor gave birth to their first daughter, who they named Virginia (Gini) Maray Wood. With Gini, Eleanor returned to the islands. In about September, Noel's mother Fanny, a member of the pioneering Herbert family of Yankalilla, South Australia, took the train from Adelaide to pay her first and only visit to their island home. That November, Eleanor contributed an article to *The Advertiser* upon summer's arrival on Bedarra. Noel, she wrote, had finished his first shack, and acquired a goat and kid, six laying hens and a rooster. She may well have written the piece in Adelaide, for it was about that time that, after a marital spat, Eleanor left Gini on the island with Noel for a couple of months. Noel fed Gini goat's milk and bananas and kept one eye out for her while, with a mattock, he cut a track up to a freshwater spring.

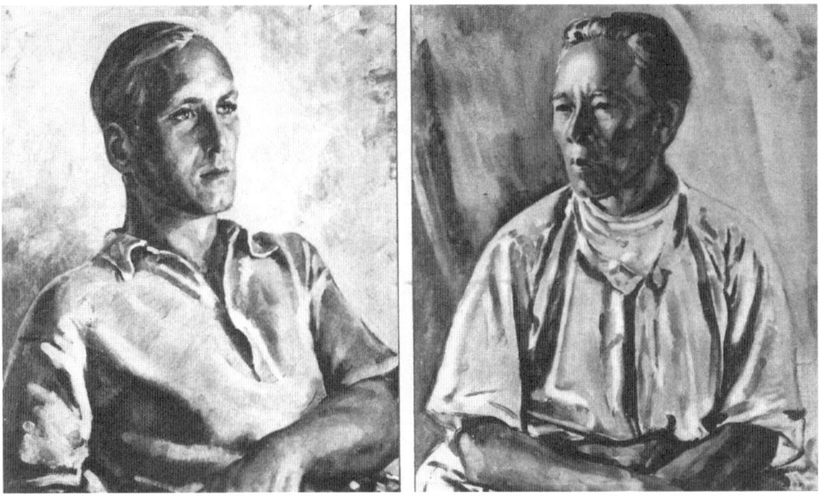

Noel's handsome portraits of Hugo Brassey, the owner of Dunk Island resort, and Charlie Nazan, his handyman, in 1938. *Pix* 1 March 1939, p. 37

By year's end, Eleanor was back on Bedarra. She was pregnant again and relieved to find Gini plump and healthy. In February 1938, according to *The Australian Women's Weekly*, she and Noel were holidaying on Dunk Island—taking a break from Bedarra—where Eleanor was writing about wildflowers and Noel was painting. In April, they were back at Doorila Bay, and the same magazine reported that Noel was 'enjoying an interesting life there with his wife and small daughter'. They had gained neighbours, the Colemans—former farmers who had purchased the remainder of Bedarra and were building on a spit across the island.

In June, Eleanor went home to Adelaide with Gini, where, on 25 September 1938 at Glenelg, their second and last child, Ann Oenone Wood, was born. In the meantime, one or both of the beautiful, artistically inclined Cohen sisters arrived on Dunk Island for a carefree winter holiday—newspaper records suggest that it was just the wilful Val, who seems to have holidayed for a month or so in June-July and returned later that winter with Von.

With a house of sorts built, land cleared and fruits and vegetables planted, Noel finally had more time to paint. By the following year, having destroyed his early attempts to capture the tropics, he had accumulated enough island paintings and portraits for an exhibition in Sydney. It had been three years since his last show, in Adelaide, and the exhibition would introduce him to new audiences.

In January, *The Courier-Mail* reported that Noel—described as the artist 'who lives alone on Bedarra Island'—flew to Sydney with Hugo. The Sydney show opened on the last day of February 1939, in the David Jones Gallery in Market Street. It was attended by Lady Gowrie, wealthy friends of Hugo's, and other members of society. Apparently, Noel stayed in a studio apartment in Elizabeth Bay, possibly Hugo's, where he painted a portrait of Mrs Joan Collins; a well-known socialite and friend of Hugo's. In March, a feature on Noel appeared in *Pix* magazine, which covered the exhibition and, like *The Courier-Mail*, described him as living a 'solitary existence'—no mention of a wife or family.

Noel's exhibition was on show for three weeks before moving to Melbourne's Riddell Galleries, to be opened by George Bell on the last day of May. Among his works were portraits of Hugo and his Aboriginal-Malay gardener and roustabout, Charlie, as well as the islands. The *Sydney Morning Herald* critic was enthusiastic:

> Mr. Wood rejoices in the lush colour of it all the hard blue shadows; the pale green and the dark green; the flat grey of a bay under a rainshower. There is no monotony in the series. Each picture has an air of novelty, as though it were seen with a keen, unspoiled eye, Mr. Wood must be set down as one of Australia's most forceful painters. And, considering that he has scarcely been heard of until now, that is a distinct surprise.

In Melbourne, Harold Herbert, well-known art critic for *The Argus*, predicted that 'Mr. Wood's studies will intrigue Melbourne's art-loving public', and Peggy MacIntyre for *Art in Australia* confidently announced, 'Noel Wood's paintings of tropical foliage burst on Sydney

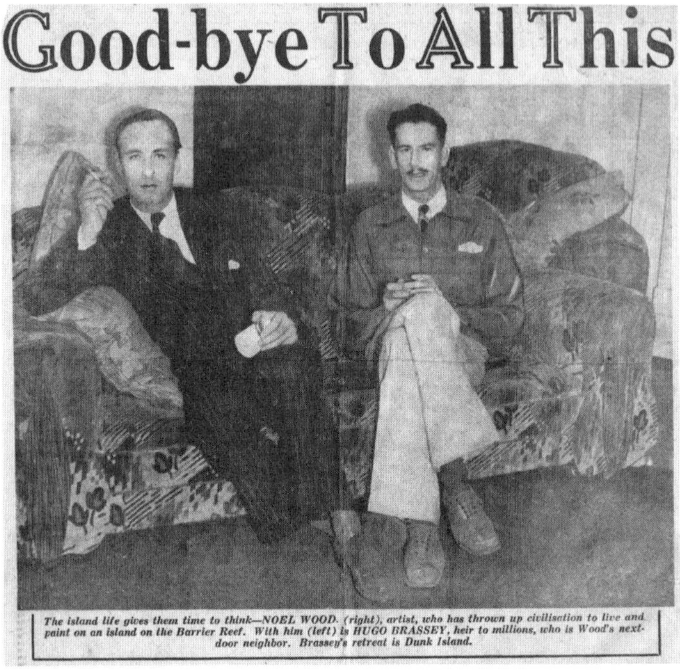
Good-bye To All This

The island life gives them time to think—NOEL WOOD. (right), artist, who has thrown up civilisation to live and paint on an island on the Barrier Reef. With him (left) is HUGO BRASSEY, heir to millions, who is Wood's next-door neighbor. Brassey's retreat is Dunk Island.

Hugo Brassey (left) and Noel on a visit to Sydney. Noel's comment on the article was that 'people think we look like a pair of homosexuals.' *Smith's Weekly* 22 July 1939, p. 17

with an unexpected freshness and charm … [and] earned for him a definite and prominent place in Australian art.'

While Noel's solo exhibition hung in Melbourne, in his home State a selection of 170 works from the Australian Academy of Art were on show in the Adelaide National Gallery. Amongst the paintings, etchings and sculpture that stood out, according to *The News*, were: 'Two extremely vital and powerfully painted pictures … garden scenes by Noel Wood, acclaimed in Melbourne by critics of advanced views as the finest landscapes in the show.'

In June, Noel—on an artistic high—was still in Melbourne, possibly staying with the sisters, and he wrote a favourable review of the inaugural exhibition of the Contemporary Art Society (CAS), at the National Gallery. Arch-conservative, Herbert, however, like other resisters of Modernism, considered that many works were derivative, if not 'grotesque', yet he found a handful of artists worthy of brief mention, including Von—'convincing in a sketch of banana trees'. Val did not contribute, but a portrait of Von, titled 'Yvonne', was exhibited by the sisters' friend, architect Patricia (Pat) Goldman.

The Cohen sisters had finished another term of art studies at the MTC in autumn, after which they spent time with Noel in preparation for his exhibition. Their doings provided copy for 'Melbourne Chatter'. Mid-April, the column noted them entertaining friends. As Noel and Alan and Wilfred McCulloch, all artists, were present, they played a game of 'mystery drawings' with a reward of chocolate frogs for the person who first guessed what the abstract drawings represented.

On 8 July, Noel returned triumphant to Dunk Island on one of the Airlines of Australia flights that were ferrying guests from Townsville and Cairns to land on Brassey's new airstrip. The airstrip made the island (which was receiving wide coverage in media) even more accessible. Noel, 'the celebrated landscape artist', and his exotic lifestyle, was also in the public eye. Interviewed in mid-May while painting a self-portrait tiled 'The Man with the Open Door' in a Collins Street studio, he was described as having lived alone on Bedarra for three years, growing his own food and painting in a colourful sarong. Eleanor and the children had been written out of his history.

Nonetheless, his very real wife Eleanor returned to the islands in about August, with baby Ann. On arrival, she was given a frosty welcome by Noel, who sat on the veranda with Hugo, watching her struggle from the jetty and along the beach with suitcase, pram and baby. Apparently, Hugo—a newly divorced man—had been encouraging Noel to shed his domestic responsibilities, enjoy himself and pursue his art. 'You don't need a wife and screaming brats,' he apparently told Noel in front of Eleanor.

That winter of 1939, both sisters again holidayed on the islands. They swam, trailed for fish and camped, exploring with Noel and Hugo in his new speedboat. The two men, Val said, 'widened our horizons', introducing them to '... writers Celine and Thomas Wolfe ... and the modern music of Australian composer Margaret Sutherland.' Noel was a wonderful raconteur, never lost for words—able to quote long passages from the many books he read. The handsome Hugo '... wandered about ... picturesque in sarongs, dog at heal, a tin of Capstans constantly in hand, slim, bronzed and as lithe as a panther ... the antithesis of the dark, willowy, sensitive Noel'.

Eleanor is absent in Val's accounts, though they must have met her that winter. Nor were the sisters naïve about playboy Hugo, whose reputation preceded him. As Charlie apparently told Val: 'I no care if he mix 'em blankets with ladies too much. He good to me.'

With all this mischief on the islands, the trouble that had been brewing internationally must have seemed far away. Nevertheless, change became inevitable: two days after the invasion of Poland on the first of September 1939, Great Britain declared war on Germany. In 1979, Val remembered of that time:

> It didn't seem real that balmy evening, amongst the palms Banfield had planted, to hear war declared from a battery wireless ... Hugo, before he hurried away, offered his bungalow and Charlie ... During the next nine months we learnt a lot from the serene old man.

In reality, the sisters were back in Melbourne by October of 1939, photographed for *The Argus* assisting at a fundraiser in aid of the French Red Cross, so they could not have spent as long as nine months learning from Charlie. Had Val also forgotten that in November that year, her article on Charlie—'Tropical vignettes: Glimpses of North Queensland'—was published in *The Age*? In it she described him unkindly, and in complete opposition to her later recollections, as a slow-witted 'old Black'; a hermit who 'few dared to go near' and who believed that he received messages from his long-dead boss 'Raymond', an error for Edmund Banfield. She further claimed that, despite her curiosity, Charlie was secretive about the medicinal plants he used; an important part of his Indigenous knowledge. She also circulated what seems be a quirky north Queensland yarn about Charlie's marriage to a Scottish woman: 'Romance! It had come into his life in an extraordinary way. It was a real Robinson Crusoe love affair, and has become one of the legends of the coast.' As Val presented it, the couple mainly conversed in signs and eventually the woman returned to Scotland with their ten-year-old son. However, 'Apparently she has not entirely forgotten her hermit husband, for each Christmas she sends him a tin of shortbread.'

More genuine was her description of the place that was to become their almost half-time home:

> Days of cloudless blue skies, nights so still that even the starry heavens are reflected in the sea … To fish at night in the still waters of North Queensland must be experienced to be believed. I have been under a crescent moon and a myriad of huge stars with water so clear and quiet that everything is reflected. Garfish have leapt in shoals round the boat. Scrub hens have called from dense Jungle; in the pandanus trees at the shore edge I have listened to the monotonous knock-knock of the carpenter bird [Long-tailed Nightjar], for the silver night holds only these sounds.

In October, the broadsheets report, Hugo was off-island, holidaying in Beaudesert with his good friends, Mr and Mrs John Collins, who frequently visited Dunk Island, before flying with them to Sydney for the Spring Race meetings. He was enjoying a brief hiatus until the end of the month, when he was made honorary Aide-de-Camp to the Governor-General, his uncle, whose previous aides had been recalled to England. That too was transitory: in early December, Hugo was appointed a sub-lieutenant in the anti-submarine section of the Royal Australian Navy and was on his way to Europe.

As for Noel, his quest for a simple life, free of responsibility, was further compromised. Hugo left him to oversee the running of the Dunk Island resort.

6

CRUISING THE ISLANDS

Timana and South Yarra

(1940–1941)

The beauty of the islands and relaxed lifestyle—'simplicity, tinged with a certain amount of comfort', as Val put it—greatly appealed to the sisters. According to Val, one calm day, Nugget rowed them across from Dunk to explore Timana. Another evening, while they were out fishing, Hugo had suggested that they buy the isle: 'a casual remark dropped as we trailed for kingfish around Fortyfoot one dawn, as the sun rose crimson from the horizon.' They set their hearts on acquiring Timana, the little island between the mother, Dunk, and father, Bedarra. Fortuitously, Nugget mentioned to Von that Cardwell Council was discussing what to do about Timana's current owners, who had no interest in the island or in paying the rates. Never ones to miss an opportunity, the sisters offered to pay the back rates and were successful in securing the island. Or, so they claimed, even believed.

Tiny Timana is everyone's image of an idyllic tropical isle—a luxuriantly vegetated peak rising from a clear cerulean sea, edged by a sweep of white sand protected by a fringing reef. Unlike, say, Paul Gauguin's Tahiti or Donald Friend's Bali, it is a continental island, the tip of a former mountain, now separated from the mainland only by the relatively narrow Hinchinbrook Channel.

Edmund Banfield thought that, in outline, Timana resembled a jockey's cap: 'the sandspit towards the setting sun forming the peak, a precipice covered with scrub and jungle, the back.' Mighty milkwood trees, shallow-rooted but anchored by giant buttresses, their canopy emerging from the tangle of the forest to tempt the gales. One, occupied for generations, contained the nest of an osprey, and, according to Banfield, was raided by only the finest of Aboriginal climbers—to take the chicks whose down was used for hair ornaments.

Most of the twenty-acre island is more or less inaccessible. As Val wrote, '… once off the sand spit, Timana's foreshore is all rock, and, at the end of the island, perpendicular faces are hung with ferns and orchids.' The only habitable area lies just inland of the spit. There, in the rich soil, the sisters would quickly grow fruits and vegetables and forage over the fringing reef at low tide for fish and oysters.

Val also enjoyed Timana's rich history, reflected in her published articles. She wrote of signs of Aboriginal use, middens and artefacts, and of the early visits by Europeans mapping and exploring the coasts. The Barrier Reef islands had been avoided by most early European navigators since Cook's *Endeavour* came to grief a bit further north. But in June 1918, the *Mermaid*, captained by Philip Parker King, charted the coast. Unlike many of its neighbours, Timana is accessible by boat at high tide, so the ship's botanist, Allan Cunningham, asked to be put ashore to collect plants. Nearly thirty years later, Owen Stanley, captain of the *Rattlesnake*, was sent by the British Admiralty to survey the inner passage of the Great Barrier Reef in the hopes of finding a quick, safe trade route to the East Indies. In May 1848, Thomas Huxley, the biologist on the voyage, was landed on Timana to shoot the plentiful cockatoos they had spotted from the ship. The dense 'jungle' foiled Huxley in his pursuit of parrots for the pot and, finding no water on Timana, the ship moved on to anchor off Dunk, where the Aboriginal peoples allowed the crew to access a stream and bartered shellfish for biscuits. Young and bored, Huxley recorded that he was miserable in the tropics—at that time of year, the rain was ceaseless, the ship stank, and he hated being 'steamed in this manner'.

Generally, the sisters avoided the northern wet season, preferring the drier, calmer winters. In the autumn of 1940, they flew north with their mother, arriving on 11 April at Townsville on a Stinson airliner, enroute to a holiday on Dunk Island, as the local papers recorded. Germany had just invaded France, but at that time there was little thought of invasion of Australia and the resort was still open. On the mainland though, floods were diverting trains and blocking roads. Twenty guests returning from the island after Easter spent a day wading through twelve miles of water, up to their chest at times, towing their luggage partway in a boat, to reach Tully from the Hull River. Reportedly, they arrived bedraggled but in good spirits and most attended a compensatory party organised by the Government Tourist Bureau.

It was Nugget who made possible the sisters' move to Timana. Just as he had helped Robert Campbell and his wife in 1931, he took the sisters under his wing. Described as a stocky little man with a shock of curly white hair, Nugget was well-read, with a trunkful of classics mouldering in the climate. Years before, he had deserted his respectable family and gone outback, working as a drover, in a circus, whatever and wherever, before finding his way to Banfield's Dunk Island. On the island, one of his tasks was to light the night-lights at the jetty to guide shipping. He also supplied black oysters from his lease on the islet Kumboola, accessible by foot at low tide, and acted as a ranger for the part of Dunk Island that is now a national park.

Initially, Val and Von 'drew a sketch in the damp sand for simple house', to be built among the trees edging the sandspit. Nugget set to work, preparing the site, planting fruits and vegetables—initially bananas and peanuts—and organising the building of their bungalow. It would be raised, like a Queenslander, to catch the breezes, with one large room upstairs, hung front and back with verandas, and with a couple of small rooms and open living space beneath.

While Nugget worked, the sisters and their mother shared Brassey's bungalow with Charlie, who was looking after it for his boss. Despite Val's harsh initial assessment, by all other accounts, Charlie was widely liked. He kept the gardens neat and the house swept, boiled water for the women's baths and lit the fire for them. He was very proud of his old gramophone and selection of records. Famously, the sounds of the darkly humorous song, 'With her head tucked underneath her arm', signalled to the resort his bedtime. Remembering him in 2009, more honestly than in some of her early published articles, Val described him as '... a marvellous old man. He used to take Von and I into the jungle to show us ... toothache cures and all the native cures ... all the plants and things.'

The sisters went fishing and painting with Noel, who had found a manager-lessee for the resort and was overseeing him on Brassey's behalf. Noel and Von both sketched a peacefully sleeping Gini, Noel's three-year-old daughter. In her unpublished memoir, Val wrote that, when they first met, Noel was 'separated from his wife and two young daughters', but that clearly was not the case. At that time, his daughter Ann was not yet born. What's more, the sisters must also have met Eleanor, who, at least until mid-1940, seems still to have been planning a life on the islands with Noel and their two daughters. That June, she was elected secretary to the newly formed Dunk Island branch of the Red Cross, with Val as treasurer and Von and Viva as committee members. The Cohens had been active in the organisation in Melbourne. On the King's Birthday holiday (16 June), the branch held a fundraising day on the island, with coconut shies, hoop-la and other attractions, which drew a reasonable crowd from Tully. Not long after, Eleanor left for good with the two children. Noel wrote very occasional letters to his daughters, with little sketches, but they seldom saw him and did not visit Bedarra again until they were adults.

That winter of 1940, Jean Devanny, writer and communist agitator, was on a getaway to Far North Queensland, one of her favourite destinations. Like many, Devanny found the reef and sea restorative and the people relatively free of the economic, class, gender and time strictures of the south. The Communist Party had just been outlawed and the authorities—concerned that Devanny would distribute communist literature and foment trouble amongst the cane-cutters—were tracking her. Dressed in men's shirts and trousers, Devanny and her travel companion Rose eventually wandered to Dunk Island. The resort, Devanny considered, was too commercial, 'vulgarised' and a bit run-down. Devanny sought out Noel, who clearly charmed the forty-six-year-old but, at least that day, didn't fit his saronged stereotype:

> We learned that Noel Wood, the painter whose exhibition in Sydney in 1939 had created exceptional interest, was on Dunk for the day … We ran him to earth later on and, sitting on the verandah of one of Brassey's infernally horrible 'Swiss chalet' huts, listened to him talk … Wood is a handsome man. His great velvety eyes fix on one straightly. His perfect teeth are gold-filled. He seemed out of focus in that spot, with his townified clothes and good grooming. Certainly there was nothing Gauguinish about him. His talk was frank and willing.

Devanny also met Nugget and they compared the merits of the writings of Ion Idreiss with those of Banfield; Nugget firmly believed the latter to be more honest. The resort's absent owner, Nugget told Devanny, was 'no nonsense … handsome but short-tempered'. Devanny also encountered Charlie and the sisters:

> Charley Nazan, son of an aboriginal mother and Malay father, conducted us through Brassey's home and orchid house. Two women students were domiciled in the former, and in one room were stacked their rather immature artistic efforts.

Val and Von may not have disagreed with her assessment. Heavily influenced by Noel, they were striving to shed what they called the 'look and put' approach to painting. As Noel explained to Devanny,

'Realism is taught by the punk rules of Australian and British art schools … it's the devil's own job to forget to copy nature—instead of painting objectively, if you get me.'

No sooner had Noel's wife and daughters departed than Noel's life again became complicated. Despite, or perhaps because, it was wartime, several long-staying visitors arrived on Bedarra, all fired up with the dream of an artists' colony in the sunny tropics. Writer Guy Morrison, his wife and two young children appeared. So too did painters John Busst and Roy Dalgarno.

Busst, who had been influenced by his time living at Montsalvat, was receiving a stipend from his wealthy father and planned to help finance the putative island colony, but he soon decided to go his own way. He leased the peninsula on the north-eastern corner of Bedarra and had a log cabin built. Inevitably, tensions arose.

Whether Noel really intended to start a colony is debatable. His daughters believe it was unlikely because he valued his solitude, or the idea of solitude, apart from the company of whoever was his latest woman. In an interview with *The New Yorker* some years later, Noel suggested that the Morrisons arrived 'unannounced'. Morrison saw it differently. He wrote that he had been among the many journalists who met Noel in Sydney during his successful exhibition. After a few drinks together, and Noel's evocative descriptions of his back-to-nature lifestyle, the young, idealistic Morrison was hooked. It seems that Noel suggested that Morrison come to the island, never intending him to stay, nor considering that he might have a family. But Morrison quit his job, packed up house and family, and with 150 books, a portable gramophone, twelve albums, and little else, arrived at Noel's bungalow.

The rain was unceasing, Noel had to improvise beds and it was a stretch to feed those six extra mouths. None of them had any money, his guests tired of the rationing and the monotonous diet. Occasionally, Busst came to the rescue. After a few weeks, Noel convinced Morrison to build a little palm house of his own and demonstrated how to plait the palm fronds. Eventually, the sun came out, but tensions continued in the crowded isolation, particularly disputes over boundaries. Noel had no concept of how much land he had bought—evidently it turned out to be smaller than he imagined.

On the other side of Bedarra, the Colemans had paying guests, among them Englishman Dick Greatrix and Frenchman Pierre (Pete) Huret, who were travelling the world looking for a tropical place to settle. Greatrix and Huret fell in love with Bedarra and made an offer to the aging Colemans, who, later in the 1940s, sold them their share of the island, allowing Busst to retain his lease.

After a year on the island, Morrison wrote, his family were 'exceedingly glad to return to the terrors of civilisation'. Some years later, after the war, he published a humorous, semi-fictional account of the adventure. Only the names were changed: 'Moan-ahra' was the possibly Kabbalistic name for Bedarra; 'Paul' was Noel; and 'Merton', Busst. Arguably, the tale could be read as clever satire: a commentary on communal life. In the manner of the times, it was unimaginatively and appallingly homophobic and racist. Morrison portrayed 'Frick' and 'Berry' (Huret and Greatrix), as 'the Americans', mincing and lisping and avoiding paying taxes. Charlie, from Dunk Island, was, '... old man, brown and bony ... When I walked towards him I found that he was quite hideous. His face had the prominent brows of the Australian aboriginal, but his small yellow eyes slanted upward like those of an oriental.'

As brutal and insensitive as it was, the book was a good yarn and well-received by the public, funding Morrison's move to England to further his career in literary journalism. As for the Cohen girls, who the Morrisons would have met, Morrison wrote that Paul (Noel) had a 'dame' on Brown (Dunk) Island, who Merton (Busst) was also visiting. Eventually, Paul discovered Merton 'entertaining' her on the beach at Bedarra, adding to the friction between the two men. Surely, this was one of the sisters.

'Larry', another of the minor characters in Morrison's book, was Roy Dalgarno, who the sisters knew from their brief time at the National Gallery School a decade earlier. Dalgarno had just begun to take painting seriously and, with the help of a sponsor, was in the north to paint workers around Cairns, Tully and the South Johnstone canefields. Dalgarno dabbled in communism, but proved too bohemian for the party, according to Devanny, who described his arrival at a meeting on the mainland: '... silence fell upon the group in the striking figure he made, with his heavily-bearded, bronzed and sensitive face, stippled with sweat, and his stocky body clothed in a fanciful plaid shirt and paint-smeared dungaree shorts.'

In September 1940, with Dalgarno, Noel left his crowded island and flew south to Brisbane to organise a joint exhibition. Together they contributed sixty-four paintings and ten chalk drawings, the latter by Dalgarno. In December, the president of the Royal Queensland Art Society and Dalgarno's mentor opened the show. The reviews were strong and the crowds 'thronged'; well over half of the artworks sold, a near record number for a Brisbane exhibition and remarkable for wartime. As usual, the artists' 'idyllic' lifestyles were the focus:

> The two painters [Noel and Roy] have made their headquarters on Bedarra, where they have built a studio of plaited palm leaves. There they have obviated the distraction of having to work for a living. The soil on Bedarra is so generous that preparing a meal is reduced to picking a papaw, and the chief imports from the mainland are tobacco and tea. Although the work of both painters reflects the intensity of sunlight on the coast, it reveals divergent angles of approach to the tropical scene. Noel Wood has been preoccupied primarily with the effects of light and shade and vivid contrasts of colour. Roy Dalgarno has tackled the human side of his new environment, seeking material in the canefields, the hotels, the native colonies, and the faces of native men and women.

The sisters and their mother missed the exhibition—towards the end of November, they had returned south. Before they left, Viva paid £279 and 5s to Mr Cox, which she recorded in her little notebook as first payment on 'Valerie and Yvonne's Timana House'. Thanks to Nugget, building supplies had been accumulating for some time. In the school holidays a carpenter and plumber, their wives and children, arrived for a working holiday, pitching their tents on Timana. Nugget supervised, making sure that the upper storey was cyclone-proofed, bolted securely to the heavy Cyprus pine posts, and the supports protected against the ravages of termites. Sheltering beneath, a bathroom, galley and spare room, and an open space for dining began to take shape. The sister helped by lugging bags filled with shell grit to surface the lower floor.

With all these happenings on Timana, the sisters might not have had a care in the world. Yet, the war was looming ever closer. In July, Val, Von and Viva raised £5 which, on behalf of Dunk Island, Val had sent to the Lord Mayor's Fund for the war effort in Melbourne. Noel somehow escaped service, perhaps by growing food for the troops. In September he donated paintings to be sold as part of an exhibition in Townsville to raise money for the war fund. Sometime during that year, he and the sisters must have received the concerning news that their friend Hugo had narrowly escaped death in an air and sea battle off Norway. His ship went down and, under machinegun fire, the crew evacuated and took shelter in a cave for forty-eight hours before being rescued by a little Norwegian fishing smack. Back in action later in the year, the newspapers reported, Hugo was wounded. The following year, 1941, Dalgarno joined the RAAF as a camouflage artist and was sent to Darwin.

In 1940, Von again contributed two works to the CAS's annual exhibition and sale, held at David Jones Gallery in Sydney. Val contributed for the first time, with a painting of the fruit and vegetable patch on Dunk Island, 'Garden at Coonanglebah'. The catalogue outlined five propositions, obviously intended to challenge the

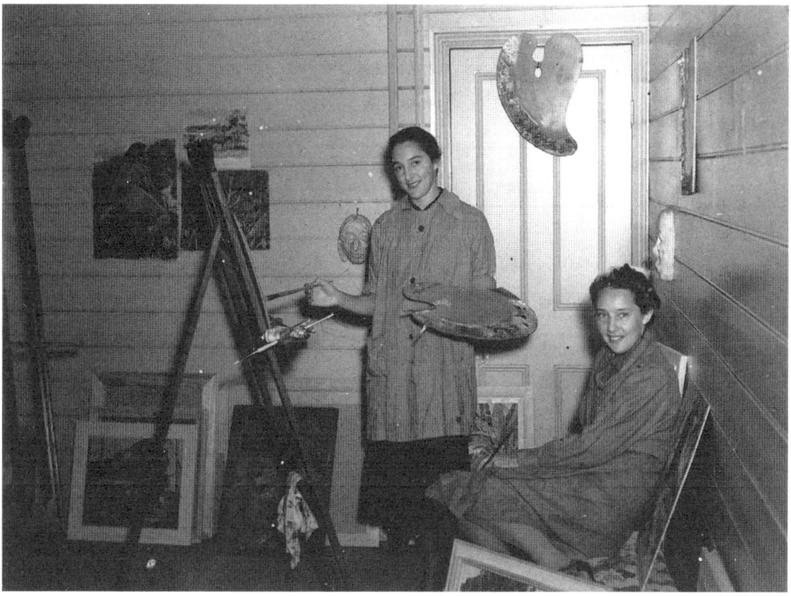

Val (seated) and Von (at the easel) in smocks in a studio, about the time that they first exhibited, in February 1941 at Riddell Galleries, in aid of the war funds, or possibly earlier. Herald Feature Services, Melbourne

conservatives: '… there can be no art without life; there can be no life without growth; there can be no growth without change; there can be no change without controversy; vital art-work is controversial and displeasing to the majority.' The ploy, if it was one, worked, record numbers of viewers attended and the show had to be extended twice, running for six weeks to accommodate the crowds.

Viva had always wanted her girls to do charitable work, but they were determined in their desire to be artists—with the war effort, they found a way to do both. They donated a few of their earliest tropical paintings to Red Cross events at Melbourne's Athenaeum theatre. At a March 1940 fundraiser, a little painting of Val's attracted the attention of a reviewer for *The Argus*, who considered that her 'Grey Morning Queensland' was among the 'most outstanding' of the 117 catalogued works, which included paintings by the sisters' friends, John Rowell, Anne Montgomery and Adrian Lawlor. Then, in 1941, after eight or nine months of painting on the islands, with the pick of their oils, the sisters had their own exhibition at Riddell Galleries in aid of the patriotic funds. Margaret Maclean organised the fortnight-long show, opened by celebrated soprano Gladys Moncrieff on 18 February. The reviews tended to be lacklustre, possibly made from a conservative viewpoint, mostly simply comparing the sisters' approaches. *The Bulletin* opined:

> Two Melbourne sisters, Yvonne and Valerie Cohen, have been painting Dunk the islet on the Queensland coast which Banfield made world-famous. With its bananas, mangoes and palm-trees bathed in brilliant sunshine it looks a delectable place, but obviously difficult to paint. Valerie Cohen's efforts appear to give more of the vividness of the color and the violence of the light than her sister's.

The Argus reviewer also felt the sisters had missed the mark but found their work more alike:

> There is a strong similarity in the work of the two sisters. Both are in love with strong, unmodulated colour, and neither has much feeling for subtlety and nuance. As a consequence the Dunk Island here depicted is as brazen a terrain as that of melodrama. The pictures undoubtedly convey something of the luxuriant growth, the burning sunshine, the tropical urgency of their subject matter, but it is difficult to believe that the island itself contains no more of beauty than the artists have captured.

The reviewer for *The Herald* seemed more open to the modern but also simply compared the sister's approaches. He preferred Von's paintings for their '... touch of personal passion [which] places them one and all in sphere a higher than that of Valerie's faithful reportage.' However, he allowed that the best of Val's oils 'attain a charmingly broad, romantic quality in the Impressionistic style.'

The Australian tropics, tropical fruit and the brilliant tropical colour and light were then barely known to most Australians, who were more accustomed to grey-green foliage and dusty landscapes. Only *The Age* review picked up on the appeal of this tantalisingly unfamiliar subject matter:

> Exotically colorful oils of Dunk Island are making a vivid show in the cause of patriotic funds ... Though there is a strong vein of similarity running through their work, and both are preoccupied more with color than composition, there is more individuality and more imagination in Miss Yvonne Cohen's paintings. Mango trees bloom riotously from one canvas, another captures the light and shade of a banana grove, the tangled growth of the Jungle is contrasted with more spacious seascapes in a varied collection that visitors at the opening ceremony yesterday found a refreshing novelty for its tropical theme.

Possibly, Noel was in town to see the exhibition. The *Townsville Daily Bulletin* of 15 March revealed that he and Busst arrived in the north by 'yesterday's mail train after spending three months in Southern States'. During the exhibition, Val and Von gave a radio interview on 3LO-3WV, titled 'Escape to solitude'. They were billed as 'Two young Australian girls who have gone to live *alone* on an island in the Barrier Reef'. So much for their long-suffering companion, their mother, who, with the island bungalow completed, made the final payment on 12 March 1941, five months after the initial down payment, for a grand total of £340 (the equivalent of about $30,000 in 2022). She paid almost as much, £300, to insure the modest dwelling.

In April, the adventurous sisters again appeared in the newspapers, assisting at a hot dog and soup stall at the Royal Australian Air Force (RAAF) auxiliaries' ball with their friend Guelda Pyke. They were about to head north. Waiting for them at Dunk Island was a 'fine 16 foot clinker built runabout', with a six-HP clay engine from Sydney installed; ordered by Nugget. They were to name it the 'Valvon'. The *Townsville Bulletin* reported that 'Miss Cohen's newly painted boat should prove ideal for cruising among the islands'.

7

ISLAND RETREAT

Timana and South Yarra

(1941 – 1945)

'Our island was to be but a holiday retreat, but war changed all that,' Valerie wrote in 1979. Instead, it became a retreat from the war. By the winter of 1941, the bungalow on Timana was all but finished. This time, Viva chose not to accompany her daughters on their flight north. During her time on the islands, she had often been uncomfortable and bored, far from her friends. She particularly disliked the travel on bumpy roads and in little boats, Val recalled:

> … but she was game all the same and did her best to keep up. She loathed it when she had to stay in Tully at the pub, loathed riding in the back of trucks, loathed having to clean fish, and the sandflies.

On one trip to the mainland for supplies the three women had several hours to kill before the Dunk Island truck returned to pick them up. The sisters suggested a bus ride to fill the time, so they all boarded one that was about to leave for 'Paradise Park'. This was probably 'Paronella Park'—a fantastical, privately built pleasure garden and entertainment

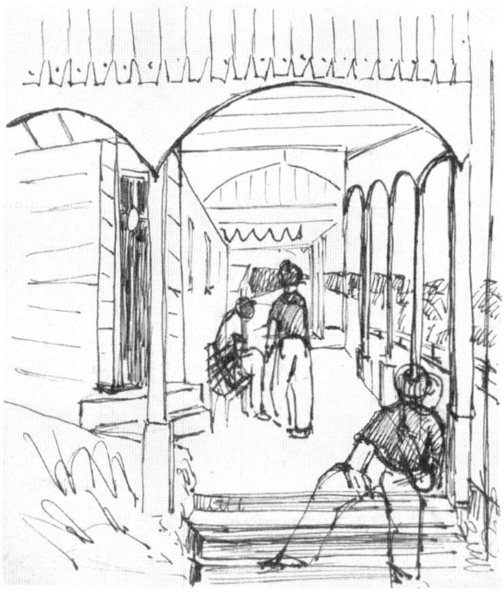

A typical pub veranda in Far North Queensland, sketched in pen and ink by Val. Travelling to and from the islands the sisters and their mother, Viva, often stayed the night at a pub, where the uncouthness and drunken behaviour dismayed Viva. Heide Museum of Modern Art, 2002.45, Melbourne. Gift of Valerie Albiston 2002 ©Estate of Valerie Albiston

centre, with cascades, swimming areas, fabulous gardens and ponds and, unusually for the time, multi-flavour ice cream for sale. After they had explored the park, they discovered there was no suitable return bus. The three began to walk back towards Tully, some forty-eight kilometres distant, expecting to catch a lift. Luckily, a passing logging truck driver recognised them. Viva climbed up beside him as he brushed beer bottles from the seat, and the sisters rode on the logs. At one point, they rocketed down a rough track in the scrub to pick up more timber from a bullock team. 'It was not Mother's idea of fun,' observed Val.

It hardly helped that on their journey back to Melbourne the previous year, washed out roads stranded the three overnight at one of Tully's pubs, '… where a dozen nationalities of sweating, blackened cane-cutters came to drink.' Viva was given a room that opened onto the veranda, where there was a bed for use by the inebriated. She lay awake all night, horrified by the coarse language that intermittently bounced through the walls and fearful that a drunkard might try to enter her room.

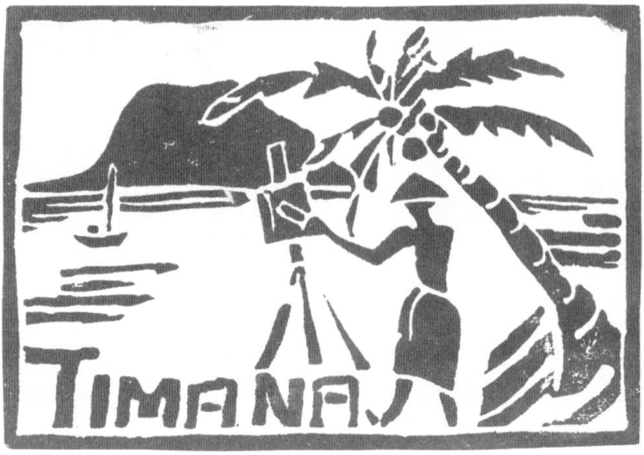

A small linocut print of Timana made by Val, complete with saronged man (likely Noel) in a paddy hat, painting at an easel beside coconut palm. Heide Museum of Modern Art, 2002.18, Melbourne. Gift of Valerie Albiston 2002 ©Estate of Valerie Albiston

On the islands, life continued more or less as usual for the sisters and their arty friends. At Dunk Island resort, tourist numbers were dwindling, but there were still a few honeymooners and holidaymakers. Bedarra, though, was a hive of building activity. John Busst had already built a temporary cabin. Greatrix and Huret, who bought the greater portion of Bedarra from the Colemans, had a sophisticated cottage, 'Les Tropiques', constructed alongside the sandspit facing the mainland. Huret, a retired French banker, embarked on their next major project: by employing Italian labourers to shift soil and boulders, he established a splendid, terraced tropical garden. Greatrix, who had been invalided out of the English balloon corps (military blimps), concentrated on setting up house.

Greatrix and Huret soon invited Charles (Chas) Martin and his partner Clifford Middleton to join them on Bedarra. Martin and Middleton, having done well in the book business (the Book Lover's Library at Sydney's King's Cross), sold up and drifted north before making the decision to move to the reef while they were still young enough to enjoy it. They took on the running of two resorts: one on

Heron Island, to the south of Bedarra, off Rockhampton; the other on Green Island, further north, off Cairns. For Chas and Cliff, along the spit at Bedarra, another cottage went up.

Nugget moved with Val and Von to Timana, building himself a shack at the far end of the little spit and filling it bowerbird-like with bric-a-brac. He was always there to assist as handyman and beat back the rainforest, relentless in its efforts to reclaim cleared ground. He rigged them up a shower, which could be heated by pouring sump oil into a container filled with the pumice which littered the island, lighting it and putting it into a tin heater. He installed tanks to hold the rainwater collected by the bungalow's roof or, in dry times, transported from the springs at Dunk or Bedarra. Not least, he caught fish for them all, smoking any excess in a chimney improvised from an old sail over a cool mangrove fire. For an additional source of food, he introduced a few pairs of brush-turkeys and chickens to roam free on the island.

Brassey's employee, 'Old Charlie', helped with supplies. Gathering a boatload of sprouting coconuts, he rowed them across from Dunk and planted the palms which still fringe Timana's shore. Charlie taught the city sisters to avoid deadly conus shells, stonefish and sea snakes and be wary of the Portuguese man-o-war and stinging bream. Noel too alerted them to the poisonous creatures of the reef, and '... how to open oysters as they fed, how to plait coconut fronds to line the walls of their bungalow and to use lawyer cane for fish traps.'

These few old-timers and new arrivals were Valerie and Yvonne's principal wartime neighbours. As well as Noel, the sisters particularly liked Chas and Cliff and often spent time with them. A shy man in his forties, Chas suffered from epilepsy; the result of injury during a battle off Heligoland during the First World War, when he was in the navy. Island life gave Chas some respite and Cliff, stocky and good-natured, kept an eye on him. According to the sisters, Chas was a 'Sunday painter', not a serious artist like themselves!

Through the 1940s, the sisters often stayed on Bedarra with Cliff

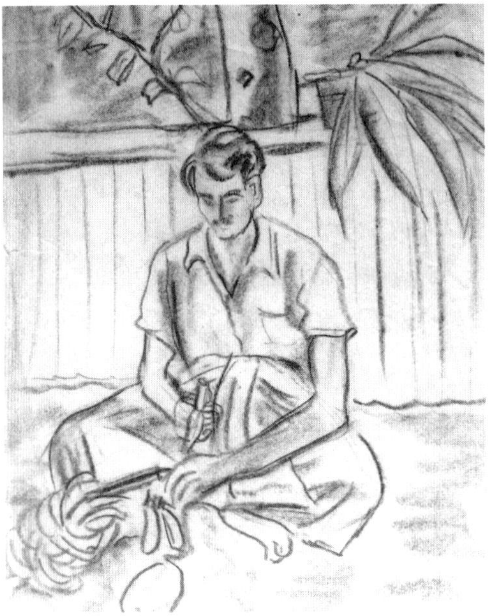

Noel, sketched in charcoal by Von, with some of his banana crop. Private collection

and Chas or with Noel, or Noel might stay with them. As Val recalled, 'Noel sometimes stayed to paint with us or we with him on Bedarra. An inventive cook, he'd wrap an old rooster in paw-paw leaves stowing it in our kerosene fridge to tenderise, then prepare it island style.'

Another night, Noel might cook them a coral trout fresh from his fish trap, cleaned and scaled on the rocks and washed in the sea, stuffed with oysters plucked from the reef, the whole wrapped in banana leaves and baked on hot stones. There was usually fresh fruit, straight from the tree, or dried or crystallised by Noel. In season, there were prawns from Lugger Bay and crayfish. Plates were disposable—green banana leaves placed on the round, red table under the sisters' small bungalow.

Noel was never short of conversation and he had a wicked, self-mocking sense of humour. Nor was he ever without an appropriate quote. Sitting on his veranda, on the edge of the moonlight ocean, looking across to the outline of Mount Tyson, in his deep, cultured voice, he might recite passages from a favourite book. Perhaps

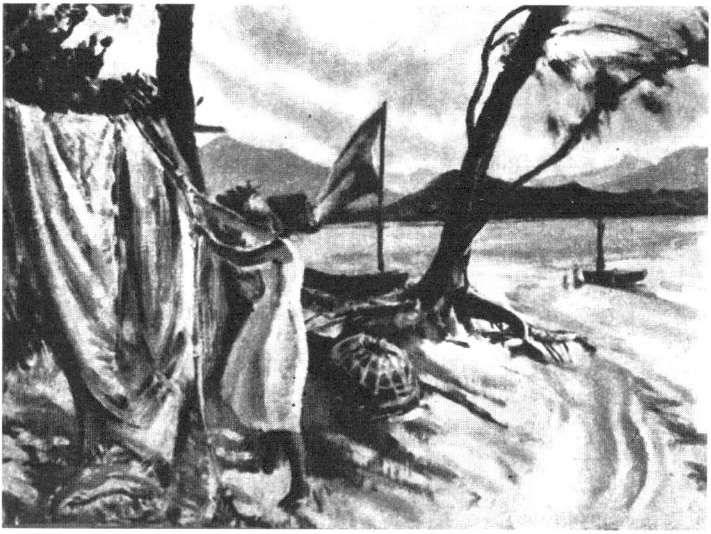

Reproduction of an oil painting by Noel of Val hanging out the fishing nets on Timana. *Pix* 8 June 1946, p.12

Thoreau's 'If a man does not keep pace with his companions, perhaps it is because he hears a different drummer'—a quote most famously associated with Banfield, but which could have applied to them all, far from the worries of civilisation, even with the war on their doorstep.

On one such perfect evening, Val recalled:

> Flying foxes squealed in the trees, the moon glistened silver on the banana leaves and the tide softly licked the sand. Far off the knock knock of the carpenter bird [a nightjar] was like the blows of a hammer, the mullet were leaping, a turtle poked up an enquiring head and the heavy perfume of Barringtonia filled the air.

Still, other evenings, they might make their way along the track Noel cut across Bedarra to Greatrix and Huret's relatively palatial home. 'Hip' and 'Hooray', as the sisters called them, were art-lovers and Huret filled the long, low bungalow with paintings. He was a quiet, withdrawn man; unlike Hip, who had been a theatre director and, Val

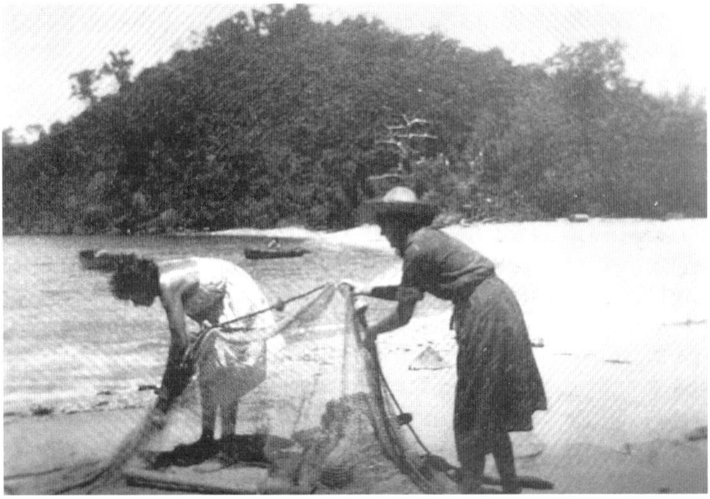

A photograph of Von (left) and Val pulling in the nets at Timana during wartime, illustrating an article by Val. *This Australia* vol. 7, Spring 1988, pp. 76–78

felt, was 'always conscious that he had been before the footlights' and 'fussed about the kitchen preparing gourmet meals which he served on ancestral china'.

Each morning on Timana the lamps had to be pumped and filled with Shellite, eggs gathered from among the grasses, the incoming tide watched in readiness for netting, the outgoing tide for oysters. If the tide was in, a morning dip was welcome. If the tide was right, the sisters would put in the nets to catch bait fish, or, best of all, deep-sea garfish:

> We'd take a lump of bread to the beach, attach it to a long piece of string and pick up a stone to use as an anchor. Casting our strung up bread, we'd wait until we saw the beaks of the fish pecking at the bread. Then one of us would wade out and run the net around the shoal. Often there were mullet, but they were quick and would leap over the net. Sometimes we'd pick up an old chisel and a billy and go for oysters. The oyster rocks near the house were kept for emergencies. Further away there were plenty.

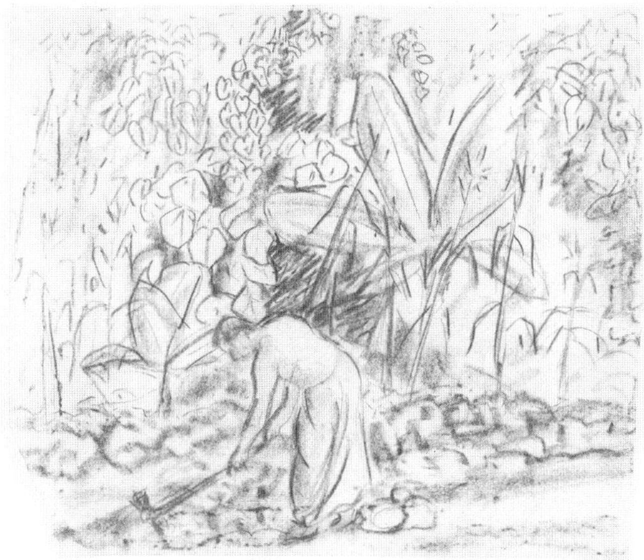

Noel, sketched by Von, working in the garden at Timana, 1940s or 1950s. 2004.116, Heide Museum of Modern Art, Melbourne. Gift of Valerie Albiston 2004 ©Estate of Yvonne Cohen

In 1998, Val recalled, 'When you had bad weather you couldn't fish or get oysters. If you were lucky enough to catch a fish a decision was made whether to paint it or eat it! ... but we also had wild turkeys and a wonderful garden with paw-paw and sweet potatoes.' In case of bad weather, there was a store of tinned food: canned peaches, along with the garfish, were a lifelong favourite.

The island dwellers all worked in their gardens. The rest of the day was free for fishing, painting and exploring. Cliff, though, studied marine molluscs. He collected their shells for museums and was always on the lookout for specimens. His main contact was Joyce Allan, conchologist and illustrator at the Australian Museum.

In October 1941, after six months on the islands and before the humid cyclone season blew in, the sisters flew home to Melbourne carrying frangipani blossoms, shells and other art and craftwork for sale by the Red Cross. The following month they were in Melbourne mode, manning stalls at fundraisers. With other artists and

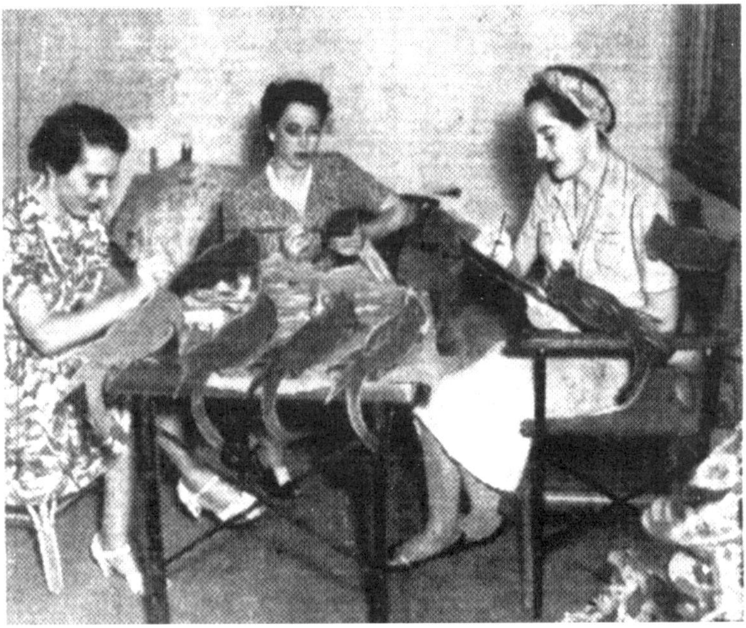

The sisters (Von at right, Val in the middle) painting some of the toys made from scrap materials to sell for Christmas to raise funds the war effort. The eight women involved were reported to have made over 200 'clever' toys and garments. *Weekly Times* (Melbourne) 9 December 1942, p. 22

craftspeople, they had made toys and other items for the Originality Shop, to be sold as Christmas gifts and add to the war funds; Yvonne won a special prize for her creative necklace of maize cobs. In December, they each donated £10 to the fund to replace the cruiser HMAS *Sydney*—controversially lost, with all her crew, in a gun battle off the Western Australian coast. Their mother must have been greatly pleased that they had taken on philanthropic work, as befitted young women of their station, and a world away from their island personas.

Occasionally the sisters used a studio: for a short time in the 1930s, in Collins Street—lent by Louis McCubbin—and then later in South Yarra. They considered themselves artists, had artistic friends and, often with Viva, attended wartime artistic and theatrical events. They were not alone, as Hal Porter observed of those times:

> Cheap rooms in the city are … easy to come by ... The attics and back rooms of Little Collins Street, Collins Street, and western Bourke Street are rented by young artists of every sort who use the places as studios, love-nests, pieds-a-terre away from mum and dad, or merely as settings for booze-ups.

Val and Von had planned to escape to Timana again in 1942 but, the previous December, Japan joined the war and began rapidly expanding its operations in the southwest Pacific. In January, Singapore fell. The Japanese occupied northern New Guinea and, in February, bombed Darwin. Consequently, the area north of Tully was declared a restricted zone and persons living in Cardwell Shire could enter only on production of an identity card. Voluntary evacuations of women and children were urged, and some packed up and left the district. Civilians were kept in the dark about military operations, but knew that something was afoot in early May, when planes began leaving Townsville in the build-up to the battle of the Coral Sea. At the same time, country rail services, especially to tourist destinations, were reduced to free trains for military purposes.

There were big changes on Dunk Island, which was annexed by the RAAF. On 5 October 1942, No. 27 Radar Station unit was formed in Townsville and secretly deployed to the island a month later. In preparation, at the top of a track that wound through the rainforest to the Mount Kootaloo, the highest point in the island, Cardwell Shire Council installed two powerful diesel generators, camouflaged in bunkers partly below ground. The RAAF unit camped at Brammo Bay in quarters that were part of the original resort, next to Banfield's bungalow. They extended the airstrip and installed a lightweight air warning radar on Mount Kootaloo. Intelligence was sent to Cairns by radio using coded Morse Code. The men also kept a flock of pigeons to carry messages to the mainland.

In about 1942, perhaps even earlier, the sisters bought a productive orchard, part of the old Glen Brae estate at Upper Beaconsfield. They hired a man to manage the orchard, mostly apple trees and summer fruits, and helped with the harvest. That year, stuck in Melbourne, the sisters tried to make themselves useful. Val signed up for the mobile canteen crews, which were manned by women trained in first aid and Air Raid Protection and tasked with helping to clean up after a raid. In the second half of the year, both re-enrolled at Melbourne Technical College, taking General Art, by which time Murray Griffin had left to become an official war artist. A report that year by Harold Herbert, artist and art critic, suggests that the tuition was still quite traditional and studio-based, but might have begun loosening up, thanks to the influence of well-travelled artists, concerned that Australia was behind the times. 'The drawings from life and from the cast are freely done, and show a painter's quality, rather than the snobbish pure line of the Slade School, which upset so many of our artists who studied abroad,' he wrote.

Come winter 1943, the sisters were determined to fight their way north. It seems that they called on their friends in Cardwell Shire: their Red Cross colleagues, including Charles Dickinson, mill owner and Chairman of Cardwell Shire Council. David Thomas, Shire Clerk, was Chair of the local Red Cross committee, and Mrs Dickinson was a prominent member. In March, Thomas signed a declaration that allowed the Cohens to travel in the shire, otherwise prohibited for non-residents:

> Mrs. Viva May Cohen and her two daughters, Valerie Frankel Cohen and Yvonne Frankel Cohen, have their permanent home and residence [on Timana] … until making their present visit to Melbourne they had and still have their permanent home on the said land at all times since early in the year 1939 AND THAT they have paid all Shire rates payable to this Council in respect of the said land at all times since the first day of January 1936.

With their somewhat broadly interpreted declaration in hand, the Cohens returned to their island in May, arriving in Tully just as John

Busst and Noel, having been called up for the Civil Construction Corps, left temporarily for Townsville. It had been a long haul by train from Melbourne—eighty-four hours and 3200 kilometres. Yet, the uniformed men who shared their carriage chivalrously looked out for the women, jumping off at stations to battle the mobs at the canteens and return with ginger beer, plum cake or a sandwich, 'steadily staler on each platform' according to Val. The train stopped at Townsville, where they killed time before continuing to Tully; as far north as civilians could travel. Townsville was bursting at the seams with US troops, 'black and white', one blocking the footpath to ask, 'How are you girls off for steady company?'

By mid-year, there were two troops to each civilian, their numbers swollen from 2000 the year before to 122,000. Food and water were stretched to the limit. Trenches, air-raid shelters, beaches and mudflats were covered in barbed wire and gun emplacements. Tully too had changed: the sisters' usual haunts were full of servicemen, their wives and girlfriends.

As they always did, the women bought stores in Tully, and, if they could, hitched a ride on the back of a truck down the dusty twenty-five kilometres of unsealed road to Mission Beach. Once they were settled on Timana, the RAAF 'boys' from Dunk often visited: 'As artists, we had little in common but they appreciated our hospitality and were always ready to help us out in any way.' The commanding officers changed every six months or so and all were young; one attracted Val, who enjoyed his company until his time on Dunk was up. Although access to Dunk was restricted, the sisters could slip across to see their resident artist friends. There, without tourists, 'It was a whole different set up, with all the unexplored rainforests, the untrodden beaches, the whole place was undisturbed.'

The sisters also shared their paw-paws, mangoes and bananas with the young radar operators and excess fruit produced on the islands went to the troops on the mainland. In their spare time, the radar men fished, sometimes using sticks of gelignite, which relieved their boredom and diet of Bully beef and army biscuits, marmalade and margarine, and made welcome gifts for their neighbours on Timana. Occasionally, the women's household orders were added to the list for Dunk, sent off by carrier pigeon, and the boys knew that they could row across to commandeer the *Valvon*—the sisters' reliable little boat—during emergencies.

There had been suspicious activity around the island in the early years of the war, even before the sisters saw Japanese 'sampans' supposedly harvesting Trochus. Once, Val wrote, she and Nugget witnessed an apparently clandestine meeting between two men arriving on the beach at Brammo Bay in separate boats, which they reported to police. A depth charge washed up at Timana, and a mine on the shores of Bedarra. Wartime censoring saw that Val and Von's mail was opened and the sisters worried about the intentions of the passengers on the odd trawler who might pass. Once, journeying back south on the train, a stranger attempted to question them about the RAAF men on Dunk Island.

During this period, according to Val, the standards of cleanliness in the resort's kitchen and dining hall had slipped. She implied that the fault lay with Minnie, a Chinese woman who worked at the resort. Maudie, Minnie's pretty teenaged niece, had helped them on Timana for a time but, perhaps not surprisingly, quickly become bored.

Von sketched Maudie and, many years later, Val wrote about Maudie and her aunt Minnie in an article for *The Sunday Mail Color Magazine*. Not only did Val criticise the state of the resort's kitchens and claim that Maudie had 'all the young bloods in hot pursuit as she wafted leisurely about like the green and blue butterflies', but she described Minnie thus:

> Minnie had long ago lost her slim Chinese figure. She had a piercing nasal drawl with a cutting Australian accent. She kept a garden going of Chinese cabbage, cherry tomatoes and a coarse kind of crinkly lettuce. When she wasn't working on it, she was trailing a broom behind her flaccid haunches in the most dilatory manner as she helped in the kitchen which cared for a handful of visitors.

The magazine received a stinging response from Minnie's daughter, Mrs Lyon. She had the support of the Morris family, who had run the resort when the RAAF was in occupation and hired Minnie to cook for the men. The editor forwarded Val a copy of Lyon's four-page letter, demanding an explanation. Lyon charged that 'the author' of the article was '… a writer of fantasy and very little in the article is fact. In fact she should be sued for defamation.' Among other things, Lyon defended her mother, Minnie, as an active person who kept the dining room 'spick and span' and set with starched white tablecloths. Nor was Minnie overweight, as evidenced by two enclosed photos.

Apparently, Val's response was less than satisfactory because the editor replied that as Val had presented the article as factual but was now admitting that some of the names were fictitious, which left 'other points in the article open to doubt'. Val's astonishing final response was: 'I never imagined what I wrote of Minnie (Mrs. Lyon's mother) could cause any distress. It was as I remembered her … I honestly can't comprehend Mrs. Lyon's attitude—unless she is hoping to make some monetary gain.' It would not be the last time that Val would be called to account for the veracity and insensitivity of her journalism, or her insistence on payment, and respond in fighting form.

One blustery day before the end of the war, a boat with one or two cane farmers and a 'young Aborigine' was wrecked against the rocks at the end of the island and the men struggled ashore with only a ration book, or a ration book and primus stove, depending on the telling. The sisters gave them a hot drink then lit a fire, piling it with green branches to make it smoke—the only way they could signal the mainland for help.

During another storm, the tail end of a cyclone, when 'the sea was mountainous, wind howled all night, bending the jungle backwards', the doors of the bungalow blew inwards and water rushed across the floor. The sisters swept and swept away the flow and worried about Phil, their new boatman, living in Nugget's little bamboo shack. At daylight, they were relieved when Phil picked his way through the wreckage to see whether they were alright. He told them the flattie, the

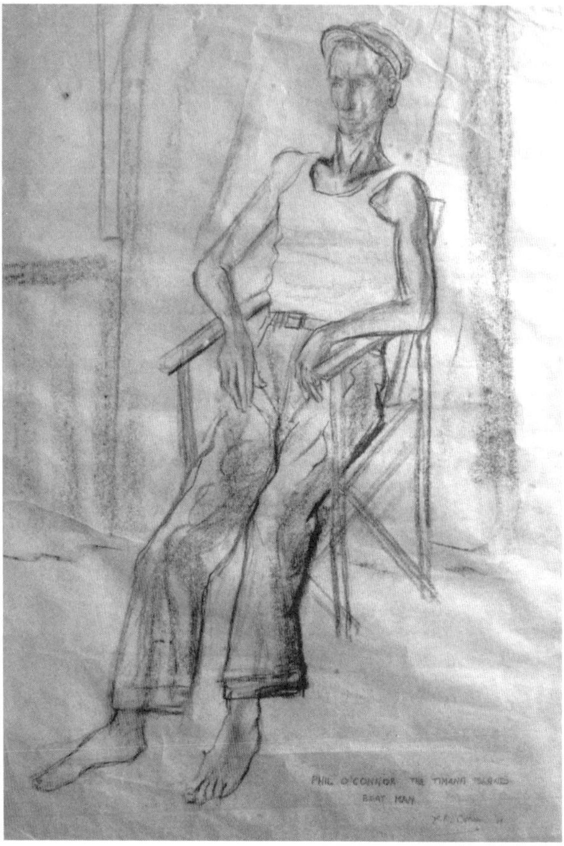

Phil O'Connor, one of the boatmen who delivered stores and mail to the islands, who later became the sisters' resident handyman, sketched by Von in 1939. Private collection

Valvon, had blown out of the boathouse. Searching with binoculars they spotted it bucking in the still choppy sea, its anchor snagged firm in the coral. They would retrieve it at low tide.

Help was never far away in the few other emergencies. When Val got a piece of oyster shell in her eye, Laurie, the laidback boatman from Dunk Island, took them to Tully to the doctor. Another year, both sisters succumbed to influenza and sweated away together upstairs in the bungalow. Their resident beachcomber tended them, building a fire so they could make tea.

There were the usual discomforts of the tropics. In October, the biting March flies would often arrive and the only escape was to sit under a mosquito net. In the rare wet season spent on the island (perhaps only in 1943), the sand flies descended to torment them, and they got batches of tropical ulcers on their legs, bandaging them and treating with Mag-Sulph and Epsom salts dried in the oven. The butcherbirds stole eggs from their open galley and cockroaches chewed their clothes. The sisters put poison around the poles supporting the house to deter the termites, yet one night a nest built in the ceiling collapsed on Val. *Uromys*, the giant white-tailed rat, ratted through the rubbish at night and toads and frogs lived in the toilet. The brush-turkeys Nugget brought to the island for food multiplied and became a nuisance, eating the chicken feed, flying up to pick at the bananas, and uprooting cassava, peanuts and sweet potatoes.

Sometime during the war, the useful Nugget became increasingly argumentative, and the sisters were relieved when he resigned as their resident beachcomber and moved back to his house of salvaged materials on Dunk Island. After Nugget, as Val was to write, '… we had a variety of beachcombers on the island, and they were a story in themselves! My goodness me! They had a little shack and we always kept somebody there.'

Phil, a tall Canadian and cheerful drinker with a gammy leg, was Nugget's first replacement. Then gentle Jiminy came to live in Nugget's shack on Timana. Wiry and patient, Jiminy turned out to be very capable in treating their brush-turkeys and hens for their various health problems. He smoked fish and taught them to attach coral to their green cotton fishing lines so that it would sink the line then fall off rather than snag.

The sisters were well-looked after. The laundry was even sent out. Ben—'willowy as a brolga and with as little memory', as Val described him—did the island run every ten days with mail and stores. His finest achievement, according to Val, was to absent-mindedly put their dirty linen on a train to Sydney: 'It took quite a while to get those things laundered,' she wrote in her unfinished autobiography. Such were the trials of island life!

Beachcomber-handymen aside, the sisters had plenty of company on Timana. Apart from their neighbours on Dunk and Bedarra, luggers, launches and fishermen sometimes dropped by. One day, half a dozen trochus-collecting Torres Strait Islanders called in for water and boiled blue lobster on the spit, singing as they cooked. Occasionally, overflying light planes might drop a newspaper. In Tully for stores, the sisters would visit Ann, the wife of the local agent and undertaker, and the postmistress: '… a tall, graceful woman with a long neck reminiscent of portraits I'd seen by English artist Augustus John,' Val recalled. Ann always had the kettle on and often sent them off with vegetables and other goodies. Laurie, who ferried tourists and stores to and from Dunk, had introduced these hospitable women to the sisters.

For variety, the sisters sometimes caught the 'Midnight Horror', which ran between Townsville and Cairns—a goods train with one uncomfortable passenger carriage. Once, Nugget organised a lift for them on a little coastal steamer going to Innisfail, some forty kilometres north, in the restricted zone. The captain anchored in the channel and turned a blind eye as the sisters clambered aboard for a free ride up the coast.

They made camouflage nets for the planes at Townsville and painted, socialised and explored with their friends on Bedarra. It was a happy, relaxed time:

> Sometimes we'd stay with Chas and Cliff on Bedarra, or with Noel, or he with us. We'd all paint. If we needed a change of scene we'd slip quietly into the restricted area up the coast in out boat, as far as Bingil Bay. There a friend from El Arish had a fishing shack. Nobody lived at the bay except the Alexanders, the remnants of that pioneering family, and [later] old Harry Plumb back in the scrub, growing illicit tobacco. The original homestead at the edge of the mango forest was in ruins. Their 3000 acres of beachfront where once coffee and pineapples grew for export was a sea of yellow bladdie grass seeping to the edge of the jungle. It was pure Gauguin country, its rich tomato coloured soil, wonderful subject matter.

Sometimes they sketched at Flying Fish Point, around and about Innisfail, and in the canefields at Lower Tully. Alternatively, they might stay in the little wayside pub at Lower Tully, where the owners were welcoming and the accommodation basic—'iron bedsteads, mattresses stuffed hard with coconut fibre and the dunny out the back'. During wartime, the rooms were free. In winter, the landscape beyond the pub was a visual delight for the artists: variegated patches of cane plumed pink, mauve and cream, colourful farmhouses and flaming tulip trees framed by a backdrop of lush mountainsides split by silvered streams, with clouds constantly claiming their peaks.

By the time the sisters returned south in 1943, Noel had completed enough paintings to stage another exhibition in Sydney. It opened in October at Macquarie Galleries and was attended by Lady Gowrie, Hugo's aunt. The art critic for the *Sydney Morning Herald* found Noel's work undisciplined but thoroughly likeable:

> Noel Wood is showing some very bright and cheerful landscapes of the Barrier Reef … He takes keen delight in the profusion of colour everywhere—the strong blues and greens of the sea, the yellow of the benches, and the red and pink of the soil. Yet his impatience to record his manifold impressions leads him often into chaos … A little more finesse and modulation in his too arbitrary tones, and, above all, more thought expended, should improve his work immeasurably without much loss of spontaneity … Despite his 'bull in the china shop' methods, however, these paintings have so engaging a quality of pure enjoyment … that one cannot help but like them with all their faults.

Many of the observations could just have easily applied to the man himself. In the autumn of 1944, Noel's art was on show again in Brisbane, three and a half years after he was first introduced, so successfully, to Queensland art-lovers. Apparently, his work held more resonance for people familiar with the tropics. *The Courier-Mail* wrote that there were forty-eight works …

> … nearly all of them splendid compositions … The colouring of the jungle vegetation is the striking feature: it hits you in the eye; you seem to feel and smell the tropic dankness, and close your eyes against the glare of a hard relentless light. Among the best pictures are 'Grey Day in the Cane Fields,' 'Bungalows on Dunk Island,' and 'Still-life,' all of them gems of tropic art.

The war years were rolling by and Val, Von and occasionally Viva (who wanted to be near her daughters) continued to travel to the islands each year. They may well have caught Noel's exhibition as they passed north through Brisbane in April 1944. After seven and a half months on and about Timana that year, they returned to Melbourne in December with Noel. The three were interviewed by a reporter for *The Argus*, who suggested that life on a tropical island must be idyllic. Val and Von agreed, but said they worked hard: when they were not painting, they tended the garden. This year, they said, they had had good crops of carrots, tropical beans, paw-paws, pineapples and bananas. Noel chipped in on his efforts, growing 5000 pineapples, among other fruits and vegetables, taken to Tully to be distributed among the troops. The reporter commented wryly that all that gardening did not seem to have interfered with their painting; for the three artists, with neighbour Charles Martin, were preparing for an exhibition in Georges' Gallery the following February:

> Yvonne and Valerie are not just lotus eaters, and their island is not simply a refuge on which to laze. They are artists, and both are considered among the most promising of our younger painters. Charming to look at, the sisters form an interesting contrast. Yvonne, dark, with perfect features, and smooth hair: Valerie, slight, fair, petite, and blue-eyed.

Von cautioned that painting in the tropics was not as idyllic as it might appear, the reporter wrote:

> … there were times when mosquitoes, sand flies, and particularly march flies, descended on them in hordes. This

> year had been particularly bad, and the reason, they were told, was the windstorms which had swept up from New South Wales. One of the most important questions that I almost forgot to ask her was what they wore in those parts. 'Sarongs,' she said, 'and play suits or shorts.' Nice, I thought, for the beach, but not so good during an insect plague.

The newspaper produced a cartoon to illustrate that final thought. Little did they know that the sisters often wore a lot less.

Noel, it seems, may have passed the summer down south. Not only did he have paintings in their joint exhibition in Melbourne in February 1945, but also in a solo show opening the same month in Adelaide. The latter was possibly organised by the loyal Eleanor, who continued to provide Noel with painting materials (and wine) and rallied her wealthy friends in support of his exhibitions. Sixty of Noel's works went to Adelaide and were tipped to have wide appeal. Some reviewers, such Esmond George of *The Mail*, found them too loose and abandoned:

> Palm-girt beaches, mountainous islets, peacock blue seas, and flower-decked jungle are pictured with facile brush and full palette. Wood's broad style is well known in Adelaide, but occasionally one wishes it was a little less broad. At times it borders on vagueness and calls for further definition. But the richness of color, even when exaggerated, is pleasantly stimulating, and there is some interest to be found in nearly every canvas.

The Melbourne exhibition, held over ten days, received attention from three respected art critics. Alan McCulloch, for *The Argus*, called it 'a gay and colourful exhibition' by the four young artists—'pride of place' going to Noel's painting 'Hibiscus'. The other works which particularly appealed to him, and he kindly nominated one from each artist, were Val's 'Wind in the Casuarinas'; 'Alananders' by Chas, 'attractive though perhaps a little obvious'; and 'Lilies and Leaves', 'a

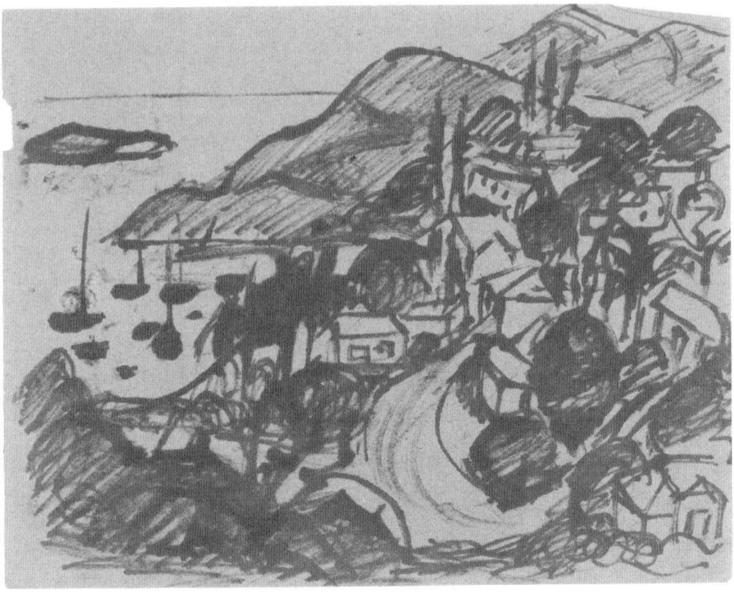

A Far North Queensland landscape in fibre-tipped pen by Val. Heide Museum of Modern Art, 2002.44, Melbourne. Gift of Valerie Albiston 2002 ©Estate of Valerie Albiston

tasteful work' by Von. Chas, the sisters' 'Sunday painter', was the odd one out, and not because of the standard of his flower paintings. As McCulloch observed, it was '… difficult to distinguish the difference between the work of the other three artists' because of 'their isolation from other influences, their close association and similarity of aim and outlook.'

George Bell, critic for *The Sun*, also liked Von's 'Lilies and Leaves'—calling it an 'arresting flower piece'—and he found her 'Canefields' and 'Blade Grass Country' were 'well stated', the latter showing carefully thought out rhythms. Of Val's, he picked 'Long Palms', with its 'individual colour sense', as her best. Bell would have intended no double entendre in observing that, 'A romantic interest attaches to the artists, who live on two small tropical islets off the coast and divide their time between painting and fruit cultivation.'

Like McCulloch, the third critic, Adrian Lawlor, found similarities among the works, particularly in regard to palette. He considered that '… the Misses Cohen themselves both lay generous hands on their colour tubes, and there is much bold orchestration evinced in their work.' Val and Von, it seems, were beginning to master colour, but form remained problematic. A fourth critic, from *The Age*, agreed:

> Optical report would give the impression that Yvonne and Valerie Cohen are pupils, or at least disciples, of Noel Wood. Their work is remindful of his but on a lower level. They, too, have color and the sense of design on the flat; with little consideration of depth or perspective other than diminution of forms.

After the Georges' exhibition, the sisters wintered on Timana. In mid-August, news of peace came through on the battery wireless. They took the *Valvon* to Mission Beach and walked along the deserted roads to Tully. 'The victory celebrations were a gay, but sad affair. There had been sacrifices in many families,' Val remembered.

With the fighting over, troops quickly dispersed from the north. In early September, the radar crew at Dunk Island was disbanded and the station dismantled. Later, the munitions were dumped at sea. In October, just before their regular migration south to Melbourne, Val and Von stayed at Green Island Resort, which Cliff was reopening, before spending a few days at Hides Hotel—the place to stay in Cairns, newly released from the restricted zone.

On return to Melbourne, they celebrated with friends; a cosmopolitan set, many from the art, theatre and literary world. The social pages of *The Argus* described a Sunday evening barbeque at the country house of the Wuttrich's, where, 'Luxuries in the way of food were there aplenty. Lashings of cream and homemade ice cream tempted everyone, and there were countless chickens, and altogether the supper had a pre-war flavour.' The article also mentioned, 'Yvonne and Valerie Frankel-Cohen, who are paying us a visit from their lotus-eating island off the Queensland coast' as being among the

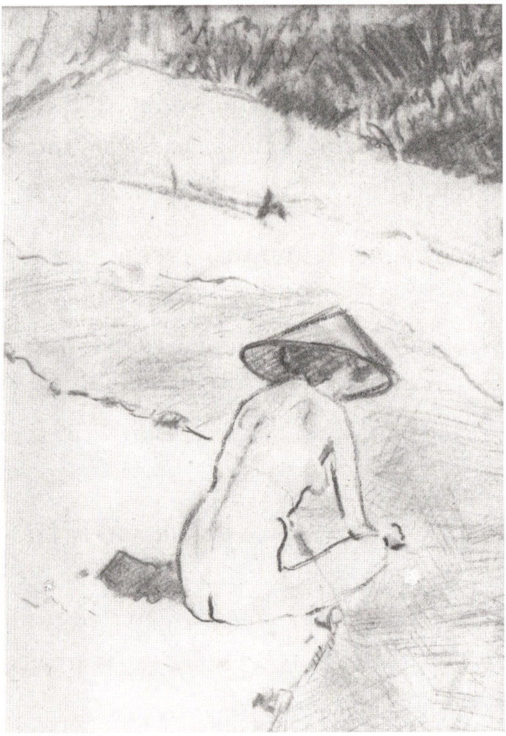

Von's charcoal sketch of Val on the beach at Timana wearing only the paddy hat that she brought home from Singapore in 1935

interesting array of guests, which included: painters and partners Lina Bryans and William (Jock) Frater; Dolia and Rosa Ribush, Russian émigrés and supporters of avantgarde theatre; writer Jean Campbell; actor-producer Keith Macartney; director Brett Randall; artists and designers Guelda and Mollie Pyke; and CSIRO geologist Dr Arthur Alderman. Many had been the subject of insightful portraits by Bryans.

That year, the final year of the war, Noel painted a relaxed portrait of Von reading on Timana. The warm brown tones of her skin and surroundings were a contrast to his more usual explosion of tropical greens. It was a loving portrait of the beautiful, gentle young woman. Also about this time, Pat Goldman painted Val's portrait, which she titled 'The Velvet Hat'. Goldman, the same age as Von, may have first met the sisters at Melbourne Technical College. She was among those

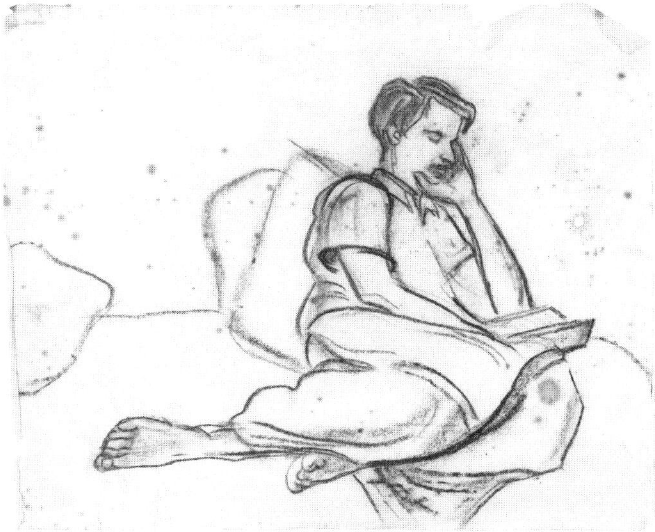

A sketch of Noel absorbed in a book, by Von, c.1945

who, a decade before, joined the sisters in painting landscapes with Rowell at Bayswater on Saturday afternoons.

Another Melbourne friend, 'Livo', on leave during the closing months of the war, visited them on Timana. In the wee hours of the morning, she arrived at a deserted Tully station and, while she was curled up asleep on a seat, a wandering dog lifted its leg, spraying her uniform. Livo regaled the sisters with tales of her adventures and faux pas as a driver for 'the Big Brass', an Admiral. As the three women sat naked on the steps of the bungalow looking at fashion magazines, she would tease Val, saying, 'You'd look good in this Porky.'

Back in sophisticated Melbourne, the women dressed to the nines in the latest fashion—complete with a hat angled just so, a fur over one shoulder and matching gloves and shoes—and headed into the city, to Bourke Street, hoping they might be noticed and photographed. Goldman painted 'Porky' in Melbourne mode: a fashionable beauty in blue and black.

8

LOVE AND LOSS

Timana and South Yarra

(1946–1951)

It was March 1946 and on the Family Islands nature had not heard that the war was over. Extreme winds and widespread floods cut off power and communications to Townsville. Later, an overflying pilot reported fowls stranded on rooftops and severe damage to buildings at Dunk Island: 'roofs appeared to be reposing on the airstrip and houses altogether damaged.' On Timana though, the little bungalow that Nugget built for the sisters stood fast.

On Bedarra, Noel's sheltered house also fared well. Noel was having yet another exhibition, this time at the Grosvenor Galleries in Sydney in April and the following month at Finney's Art Gallery in Brisbane. Perhaps he was pumping out the little paintings too fast. The critics were still suggesting that his work was fresh but undisciplined and that he was capable of more. The reviewer for the *Sydney Morning Herald* averred that '… vivid colours and a spirited, happy-go-lucky altitude may carry an artist quite some distance ... [but] We should like to see a more important work by him—beyond the definition of a sketch.' The art correspondent for *Pix* magazine agreed: 'Noel Wood may yet become one of the country's most important artists if he makes the effort. He certainly possesses the talent.' The reviewer for *Catholic Weekly* also found his work spontaneous but just a bit too free and easy. It was, '... for the most part quick studies of sunlight and color with form in some measure ... It will be interesting to see in further exhibitions the development of this island-versus-man contest. So far, the honors are even.'

In April, Val and Von were again receiving attention in Melbourne's social columns. With their friends the Pyke sisters and Lina Bryans, they attended an exhibition of modern art which '... gave the many people present at the opening day lots to talk about.' *The Bulletin* described the sisters as '... two artists ... who spend many months of each year on their island home, Timana, near Dunk Island.' By war's end, they had transitioned from fashionable, newsworthy young women about Melbourne town with a double-barrelled surname, to the *Cohen sisters*—artists with a bohemian lifestyle. Never again would Val be critical of women wearing bright colours and shorts, as she had been in her society days in the 1930s—far from it!

On 25 May, according to the *Townsville Bulletin*, Noel was in Sydney, frequently seen dining with his old friend Hugo, now a Lieutenant-Commander. Early that month, the sisters had also passed through 'the Harbour city' before flying to Townsville to spend the winter on Timana. Hugo also flew north to prepare his resort for the tourist season. Repairs and improvements were not finished until just before the official reopening in December. Glamorous guests began to return in small numbers—among them Mavis Ripper, who was designing dresses for the Australian adventure film 'Smithy', based on the life of aviator Sir Charles Kingsford-Smith, the founder of Qantas. In the meantime, Hugo, always a strong presence, and Noel, who typically took the easy road, were spending a lot of time together on and off island. They were rarely without a beautiful woman in tow, which would be the pattern for Noel for the remainder of his life. Many years later, Noel told his adult daughter Ann that Val had scolded him: 'You are just like a piece of flotsam, drifting on the tide.' When Ann asked whether he minded, he just shrugged.

Valerie and Yvonne gave their usual responses to reporters' queries about their 'idyllic isle': 'They grow their own fruit and vegetables, and with plenty of fish and a boat calling every ten days with stores, they find housekeeping fairly simple.' Other areas of their lives were complicated. In a weak moment, after drinking too much at a party, Val gave in to Hugo, and he immediately lost interest, having tried to bed her for years. He was 'one of those men', she told me, 'utterly charming but ruthless'. About 1946 or earlier, Von fell pregnant to Noel. Accounts of the outcome differ. She may have had an abortion; not hard to procure for well-to-do Melbournites at the time. Noel returned briefly to his family on Kangaroo Island, feeling upset for 'Vonnie', but, according to his nephew, grumbling that it had been 'another bloody girl', which suggests an alternative: that she may have given birth. Regardless, Von was deeply distressed and fled from the islands to Indonesia on a passing cargo ship.

Gradually, travel and transport became easier and although petrol rationing continued for some years, tourist cruises began plying the islands again. Before the war, as sometime-Dunk resident Ruby Haultain remembered, 'Artists who came to the island for a holiday were thrilled with the natural island beauty. Doctors on vacation found it a veritable haven.' Some of the artists never left and, immediately post-war, a doctor who was to change the sisters' lives stepped ashore on Timana.

The doctor, Norman Arthur Albiston, was a Melbourne psychiatrist escaping problems of his own: a difficult marriage to pianist-composer Margaret Sutherland and a difficult seventeen-year-old son, Mark, who was involved with a neighbour's young daughter. In August 1946, Norm flew to Townsville with eight other Collins Street doctors and three prominent businessmen who had charted a boat and crew for a three-week trip to the Barrier Reef, followed by a three-week tour to the historic Valley of Lagoons and scenic Hell's Gate on the Burdekin River. From Dunk Island, the group visited Timana, where the sisters were painting in the shade of their bungalow. For Val, 'It was, as the books write, love at first sight.' She determined to win him, starting right there and then in their island bungalow. In retrospect, there seems little doubt that they had met each other's match.

War's end brought big changes to the mix of residents on the islands and an end to the easy, close friendships and companionship that the sisters could expect on their return north each winter. Greatrix and Huret sold their portion of Bedarra Island to Busst and his sister Phyllis, another Montsalvat artist. In February 1947, still seeking the perfect, tax-free, mild-climate getaway, Greatrix and Huret took the mail train from Townsville to Sydney, where they embarked for Tahiti. The following year, *The Courier-Mail* reported, they had settled in New Guinea, at Wau, where Huret was again terracing the landscape and they had eight 'native boys' to cook, clean and help in the garden. With Greatrix and Huret moving on, the sisters' good friends Cliff and Chas also vacated Bedarra to divide their time between Green Island and Cairns.

Noel too was off. That January, he flew south on his way to England where he had been given a show at the prestigious Leicester Galleries in London. The celebrated artist Augustus John, who admired Noel's work, had agreed to open the exhibition, which may well have garnered Noel an international attention. But that wasn't to be. Noel crated up his best work and put it on the train before flying to Sydney to collect it and see it safely on the ship. It never arrived. Several people looked into the matter, but came up with nothing. His daughter Ann remembers him telling her about the loss:

> When people said: 'Can't you just paint some more pictures?', he would answer: 'If your babies died what would you think if someone said you could always make more?'. Over the years, people would send him catalogues from exhibitions all

> over Australia that showed some his works. Dad said he did not recognise some of the titles, so perhaps some were from the missing works?

Disheartened, in late March 1947, Noel sailed for England on the SS *Asturias*, arriving at Southampton on 26 April. The former troopship turned migrant ship ferried travellers from Australia to England and made the return voyage with English children as part of the now-infamous 'orphan' resettlement scheme. Noel travelled cattle class, sleeping in a tiny bunk-lined cabin in the hold, and suffering the queues for the most basic of food, but his companions made up for the discomfort. On board he met Alister Kershaw, bohemian poet and writer, and the Surrealist artist and writer, James Gleeson, both escaping Australia for the more progressive cultural arenas of England and Europe.

Kershaw, in his book *Hey Days*, recounted a conversation with Noel about the supposed isolation of his life on Bedarra: was he ever scared or lonely? Noel replied that he'd only been scared once, during the war. 'The Japanese army getting too close?' asked Kershaw. 'No, the Australian army' was Noel's wry reply. Noel had been on the mainland to pick up supplies when the first troops began arriving home from the Middle East. As he walked long-haired, bearded and sandaled down the main street, a convoy of rowdy troops came by. A roar went up from the men and Noel thought he was in for a beating. But the men were in good spirits: 'Look at that! A dinkum bloody civilian. Good on yer, mate!' It was a typically charming anecdote from Noel, who, for the next three years, would paint at Brassey's estates in Ireland and England, and spend time in London and France.

Hugo's return to Dunk Island was brief. Following the death of his father, he went back to his family home in Ireland and leased his section of the island to Gerald Caught, a former RAAF marine navigator from Adelaide who had stopped at the island during the war. By February 1948, Hugo had purchased a house in England, which, the papers claimed, he intended to make his home and, in

November, he married for the second time. He returned to Dunk only a couple more times, spending a belated honeymoon there in August 1949 with his new young wife, Barbara 'Bubbles' Peacock.

With the post-war dispersion of the old group, newcomers began to replace them. Arriving sometime in 1946, Raymond (Ray) Glass, a twenty-five-year-old artist and American GI, and his wife Rae (née Nuttins), spent a year on Bedarra with their infant son, 'rehabilitating' after the war. During that time, they stayed for a few days with the sisters on Timana and became friends. The Glasses had wed in Brisbane in 1944, where Raymond had been demobilised after serving with the psychological warfare section attached to General MacArthur's headquarters. After the Glasses brief post-war sojourn on the islands, they travelled to Mexico and the USA, where Ray was awarded a Fine Arts degree. In 1949, they returned to Australia and joined a small artists' colony at Mona Vale, just outside of Sydney. Glass began exhibiting in 1949 in the Sydney Society of Artists' August show, where his work was noted by a reviewer as 'promising'. Two solo exhibitions followed: in the David Jones Gallery, Sydney in June 1950, and Stanley Coe Galleries, Melbourne, that October. Mexico, not the Australian tropics, was the inspiration for his vividly patterned social realism and he was described as adventurous, but still developing as an artist. Val and Von bought four oils with Mexican themes: 'Los Ejidaleros' (communal farmers, fighting for land), 'The Burra' a donkey, and a woman's face, all dated 1949. Val also owned 'Island Dream', perhaps a gift, painted on Bedarra Island in 1946, which depicted the island as an Eden. In 1952, the Glasses returned to the USA and, apparently, to artistic obscurity.

On Bedarra, Busst began to build a cool, colour-washed pisé homestead on the headland above Hernandia Beach, looking across to Noel's fifteen acres at Doorila Bay. The U-shaped house and studio had wide shady verandas on the three sides and was lined with bamboo cut on the mainland. Val rarely mentions the Bussts in her writings. Apparently, John was often off-island and Phyl was an unhappy drinker. After the war, when Phyl decided to return to Melbourne, they split their block in two, selling off the northern sandspit. In 1950, John made a late marriage to Alison Pitchett, who joined him in the pisé house.

For the sisters, Noel's bungalow—the house of 'singing bamboo', so named for the music made when the wind gently whistled through—must have seemed very empty. Nugget's shack on Dunk Island was also abandoned. The beachcomber left early in 1947 to live at Argea, a station on the train line to Ingham, and in May he died. With his passing the islands lost a prominent island identity and his wide knowledge and generosity to visitors. Nugget's obituary revealed some things which Val said he had kept to himself—that his birth name was George Rivett, he was sixty-nine years old and had been born in Sydney.

Back in Melbourne, Val's mind was far from the islands. When the sisters returned from Queensland late in 1946, she visited Norm in his rooms in Collins Street, where they shared 'an intense moment' and then went to 'the Latin'—Café Latin—to meet some of his friends. From then on Norm spent as much time as he could with her. Val was hardly an innocent, having had a previous affair with another married man—they had trysts, she said, 'all around the countryside' in Victoria—and several other lovers on and off the islands and on and off Australia. Perhaps it was a sign of her desire to be interesting—to be a mistress, as well as an artist and published writer—that when the mother of one of Norm's women friends commented to him that 'she's been around', Val took it as a compliment.

According to Sutherland's biographer, Jillian Graham, and others, Norm was a 'handsome, witty, charming, urbane, cultured man'; indeed, one of his associates considered him to be among the best-looking men of his generation. At that period, medicos were highly revered and psychiatrists, of which there were very few, had the added allure of association with the new, sexually loaded Freudian thinking. In the 1930s, Norman was heavily involved in matters of child development and the trialling of child guidance clinics. He contributed

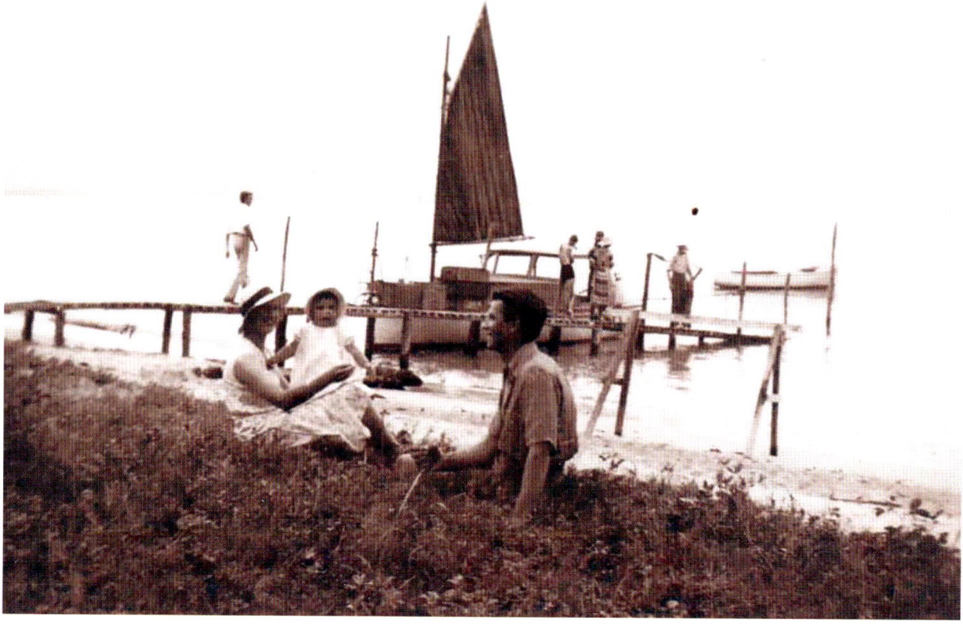

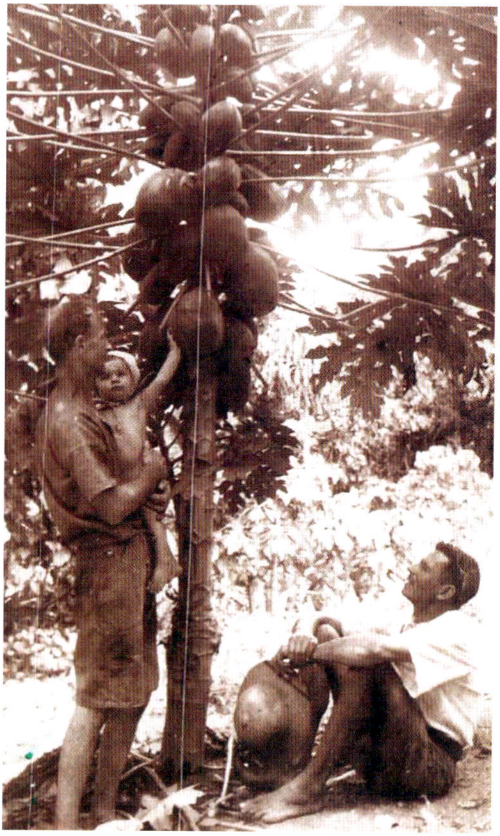

top: Eleanor, Gini and Noel Wood near the jetty on Dunk Island in September 1937, they year they bought land at Brammo Bay on neighbouring Bedarra Island. September 1937

right: Noel Wood and Dunk Island resort owner Hugo Brassey (holding Noel's daughter Gini) with an abundant crop of pawpaws. c.1938

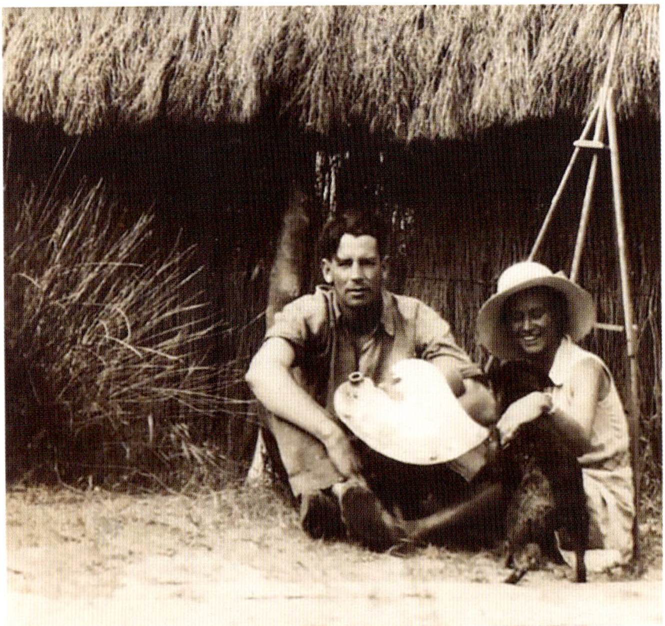

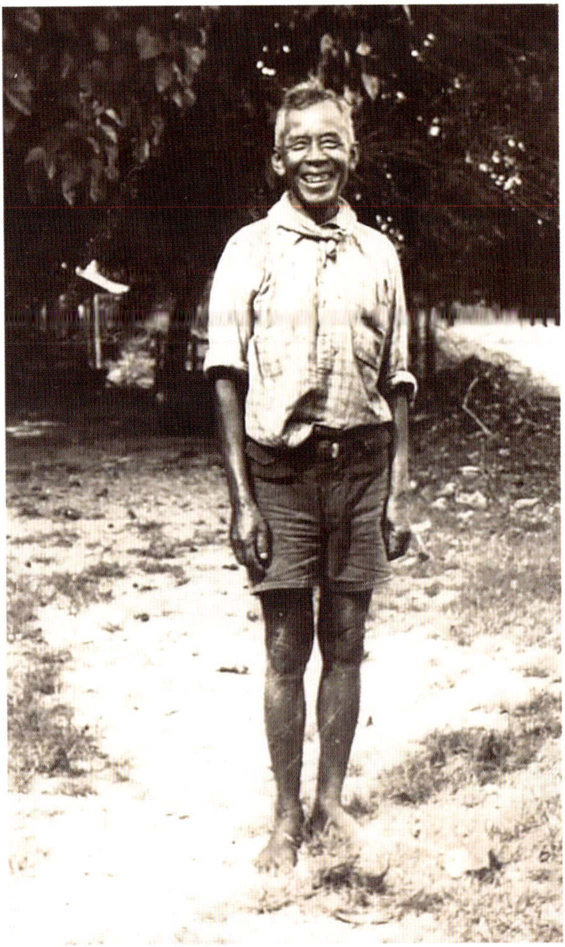

top: Noel and Eleanor on Kangaroo Island, South Australia, where they lived and painted for about two years until 1936, when they travelled north in search of a tropical island home. 1936

bottom: Charlie Nazan, Brassey's capable rouseabout on Dunk Island. c.1937

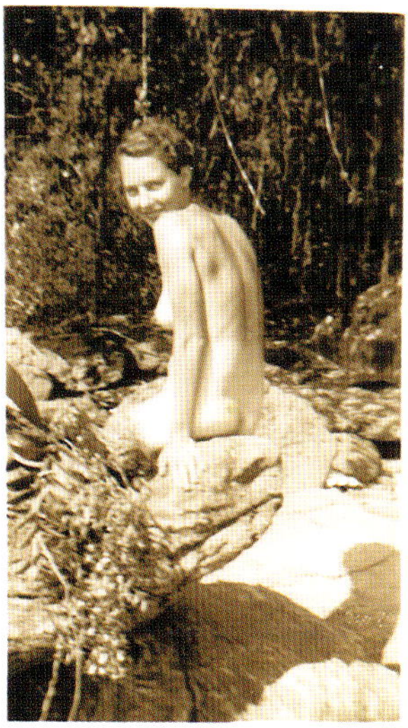

A Very
Happy
Birthday
Dear old Siss
Fun & Games &
Many Smiles
in The
Coming Year.
Big Love
V.

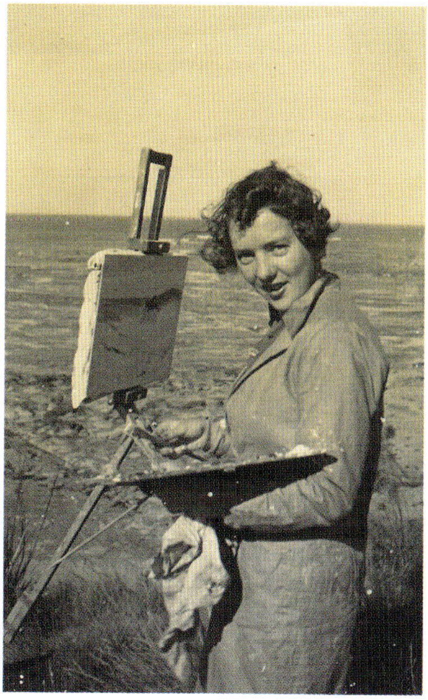

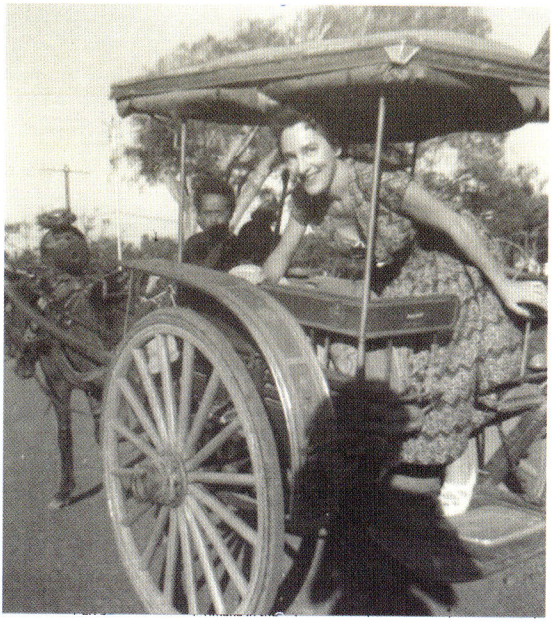

top: A typical creative card from Val to Von, including a photograph of Val in her birthday suit at the end of the spit on Timana Island. 1940s

bottom left: Val painting on the Victorian coast with an easel; something she later claimed they never used. 1940s

bottom right: Von alighting from a horse-drawn taxi in Bali during her visit with Guelda Pyke. 1954

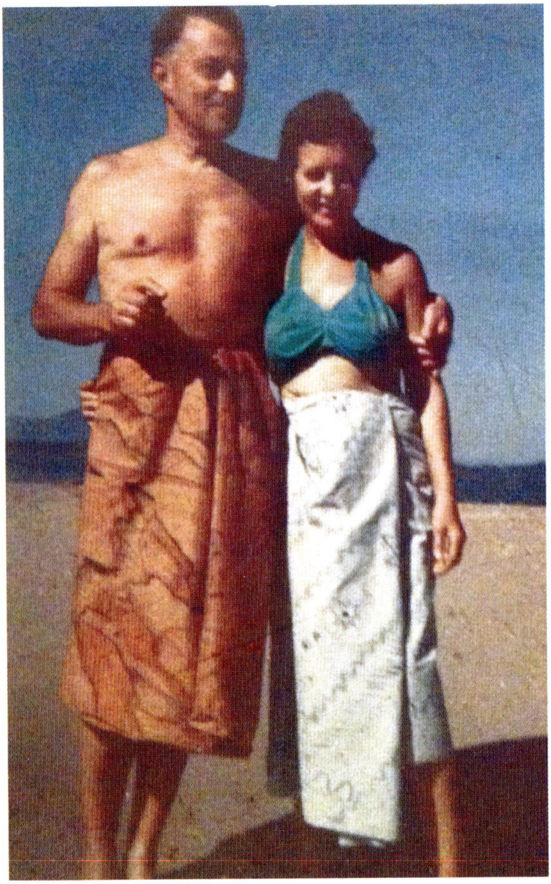

top: Val and Norm on the islands. c.1947

bottom: Val and Norm relaxing on Dunk Island. 1960s–70s

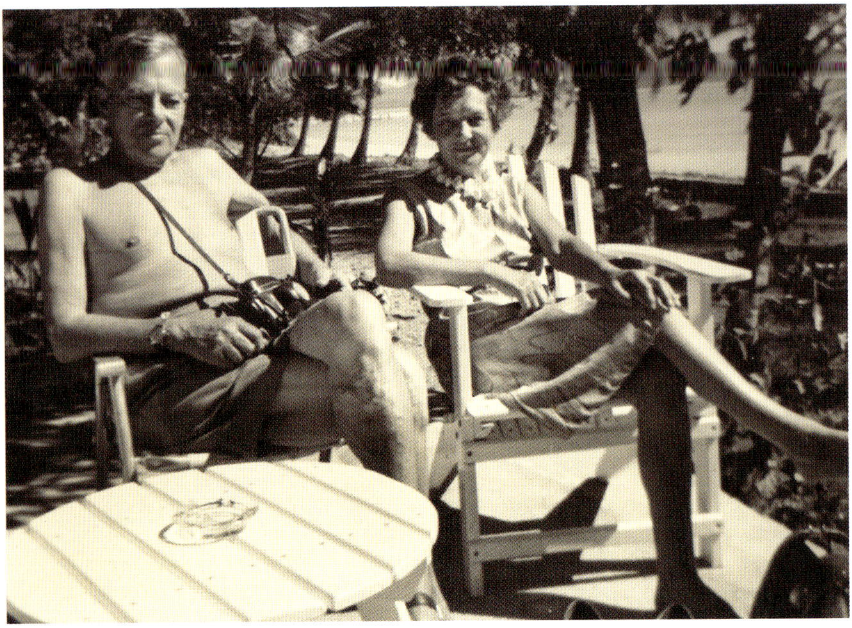

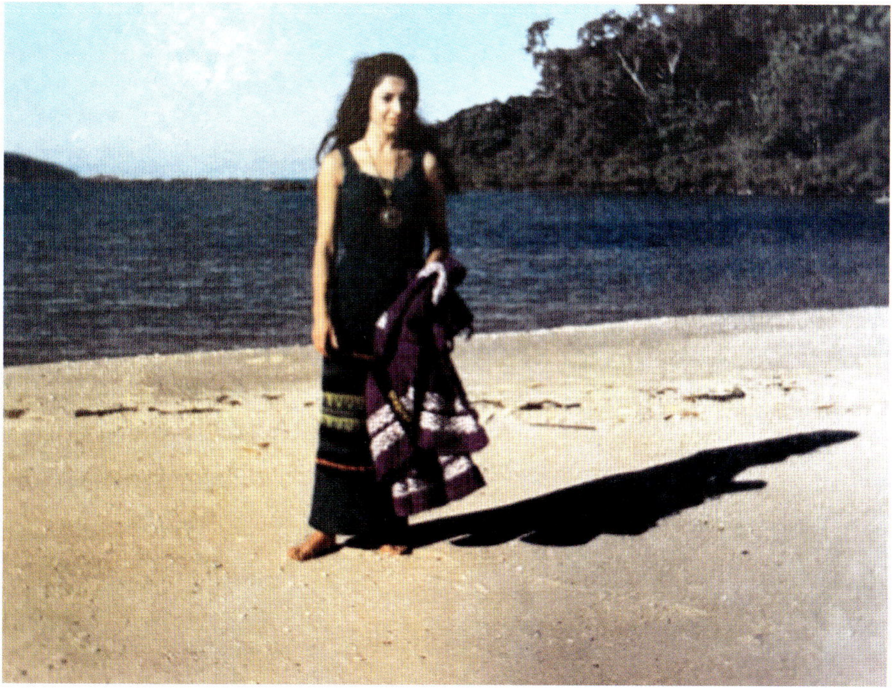

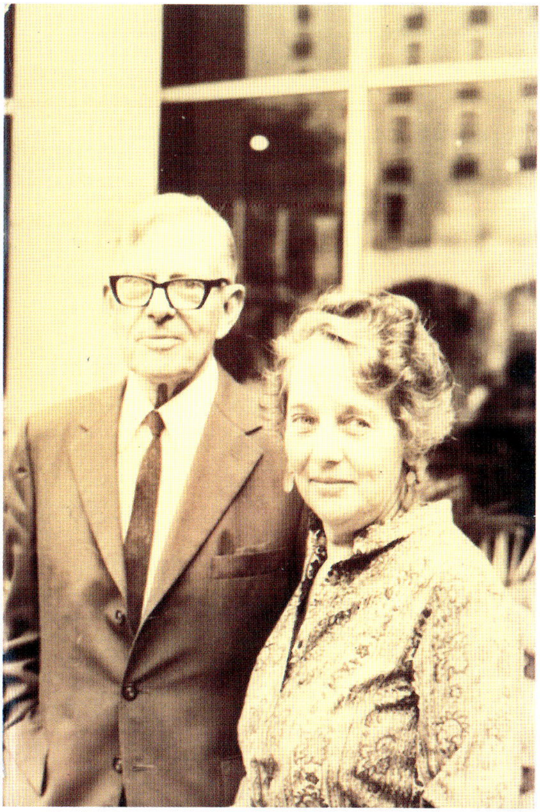

top: The sisters' tenant, weaver Deanna Conti, on the beach at Timana. 1960s

bottom: Val and Norm in Melbourne when Norm no longer travelled to Timana. 1970s

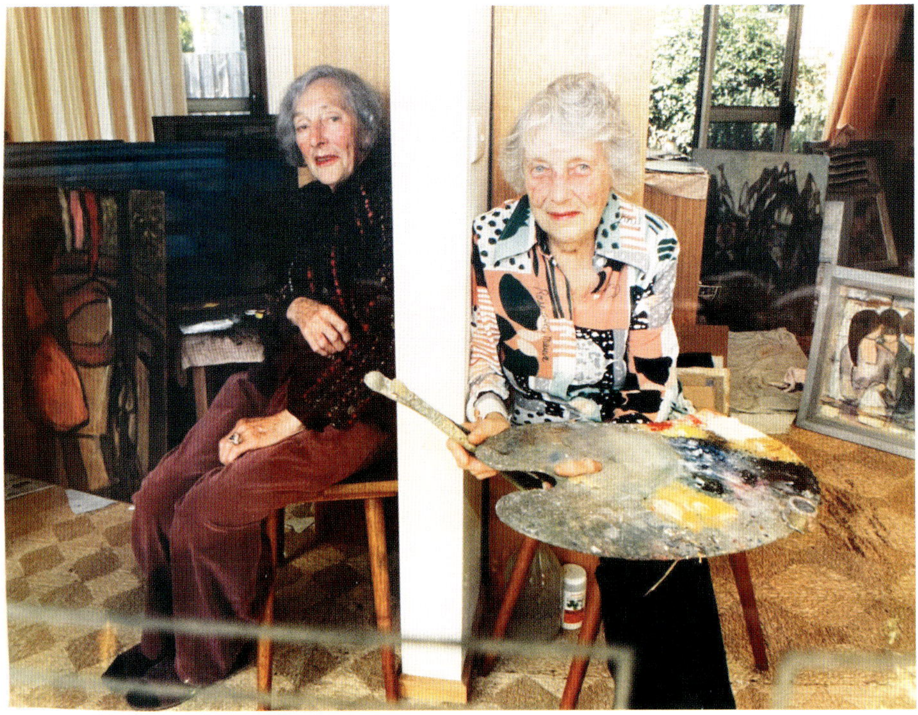

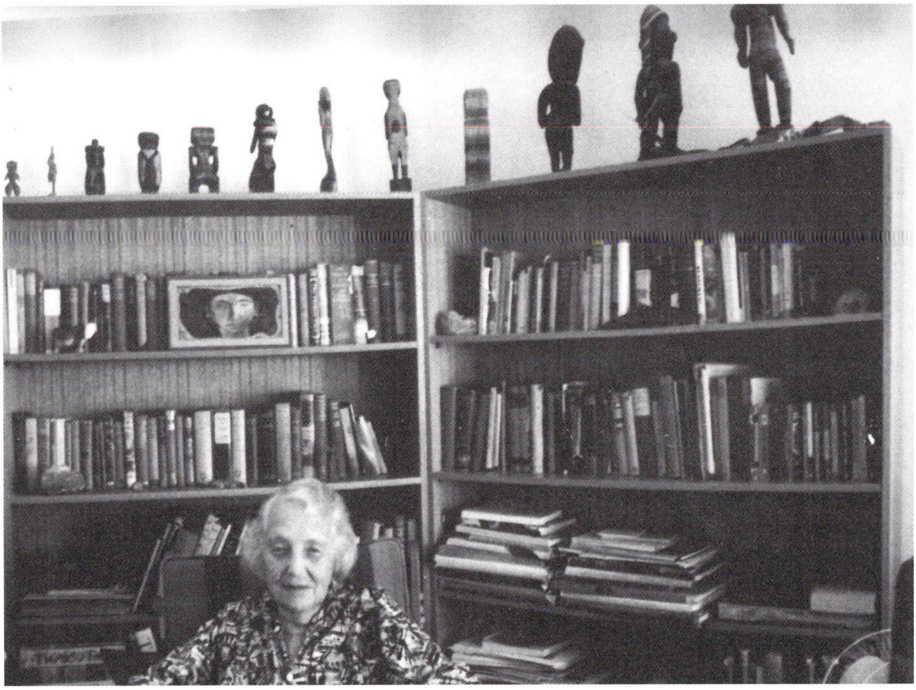

top: Val (right) and Von in their adjoining studios at Kew, aged eighty-eight and eighty-five. Some of their more recent work can be seen in the background. November 1999

bottom: Val alone at Kew in front of her well-stocked bookcase, wooden figures from New Guinea coyly faced towards the wall. Mid-2000s

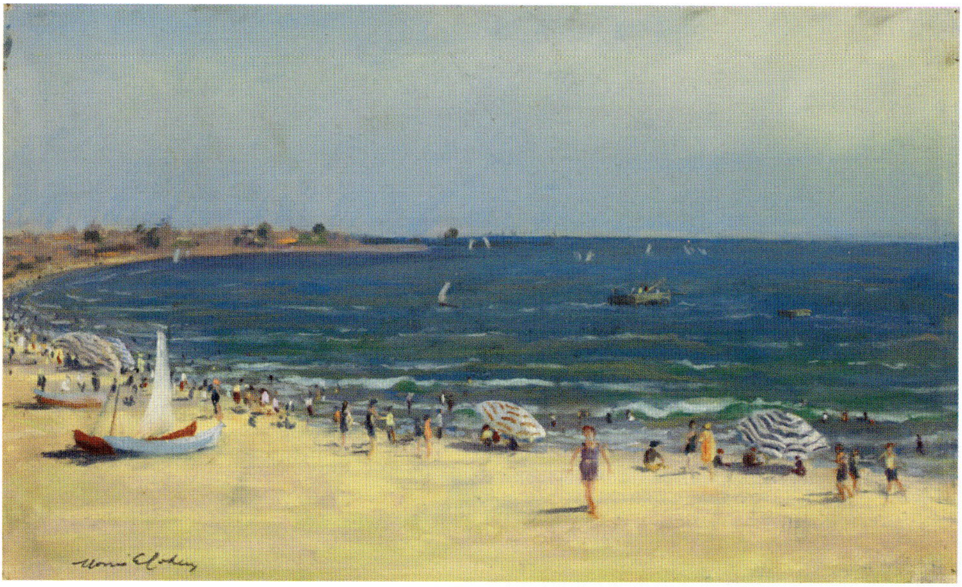

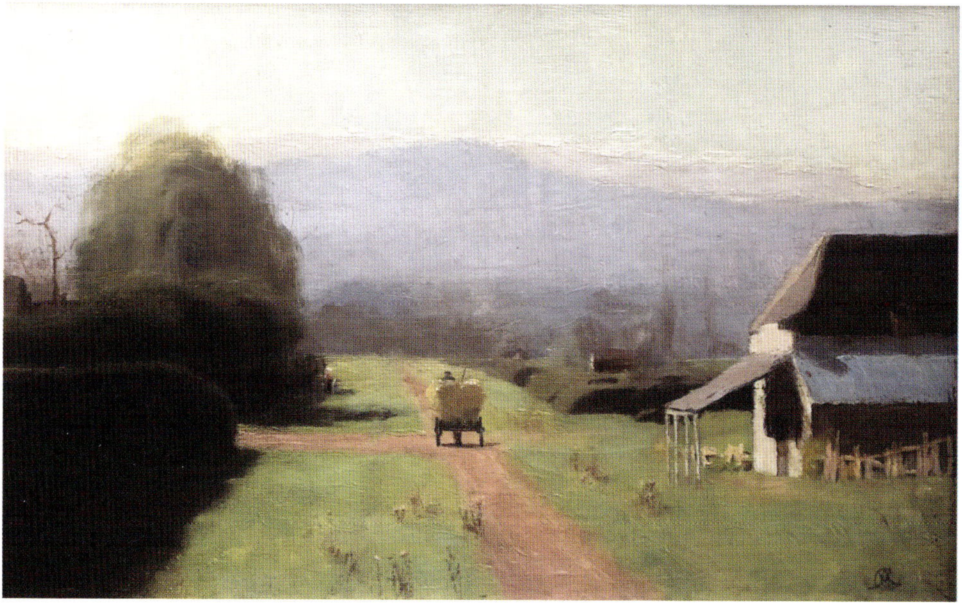

top: 'Elwood foreshore', the beach near the family home on the esplanade, which could be busy on summer weekends. Pastel on paper by Morris Cohen, c.1925

bottom: 'Victorian Farmland'; hung in Val's study at Templestowe. A rare example of Morris's early use of oil before switching to pastel. Painting by Morris Cohen, 1890s

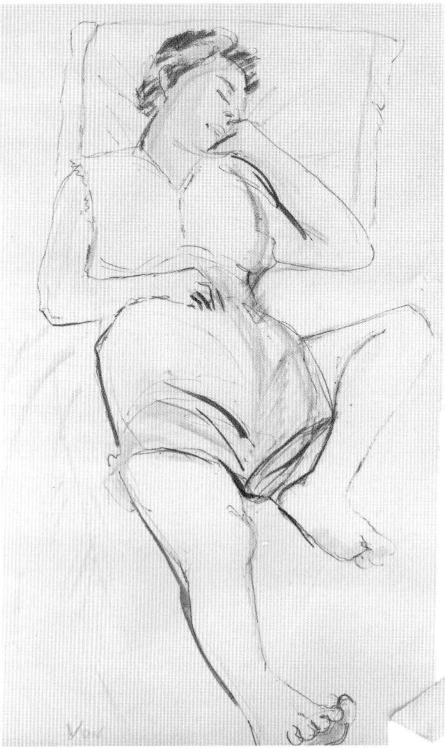

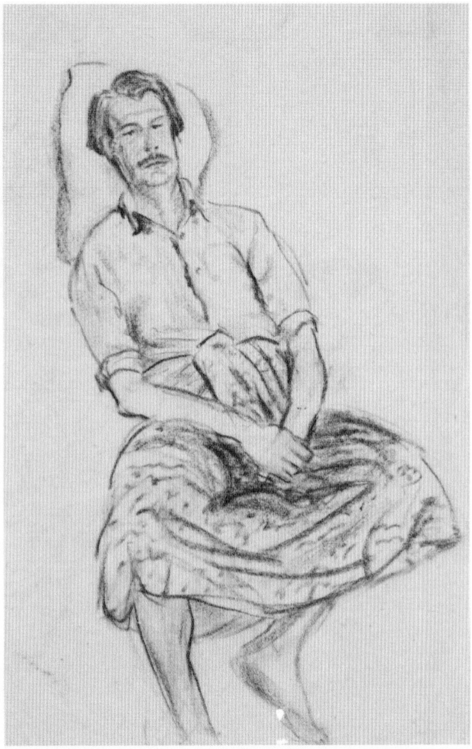

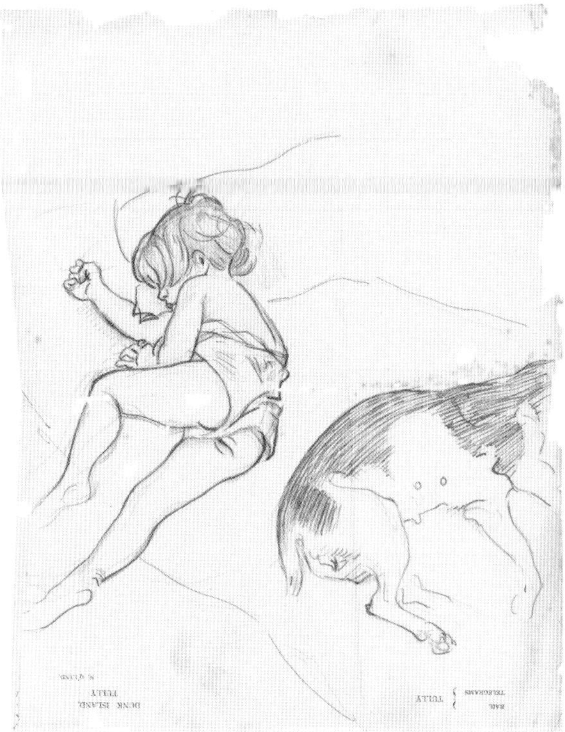

top left: Val captured sleeping in her playsuit on the islands. Charcoal sketch by Yvonne Cohen, 1940s

top right: Noel Wood, Von's great love. She kept this and several other sketches of him on the islands until the end of her life. Charcoal sketch by Yvonne Coen, 1940s

bottom: Gini Wood, Noel's daughter, and Louse, the Woods' terrier, asleep on the islands. Charcoal sketch by Noel Wood, c.1939, kept by Von top: Charlie Nazan, a personality on Dunk Island, who, with Brassey's permission, looked after the sisters and their mother, particularly during the war. Charcoal sketch by Yvonne Cohen, 1940s

bottom: 'Boatman', a relaxed portrait of Phil O'Connor, who Von sketched several times. Oil painting by Yvonne Cohen, 1940s

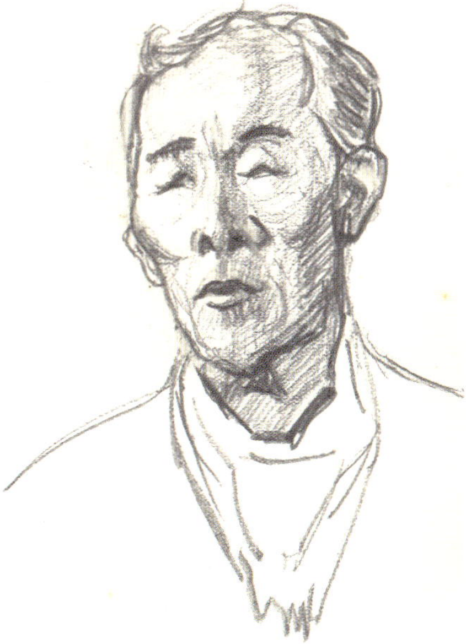

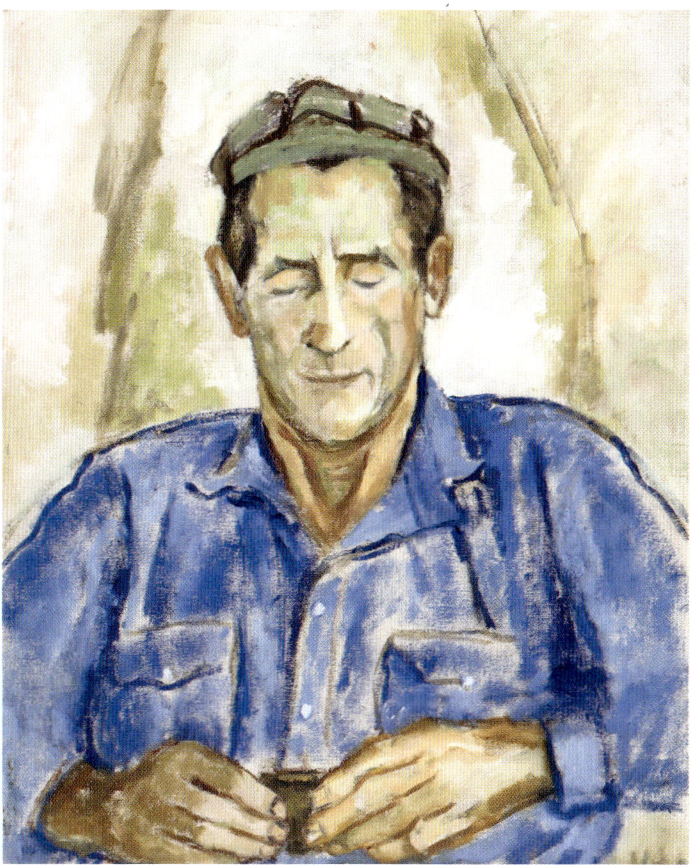

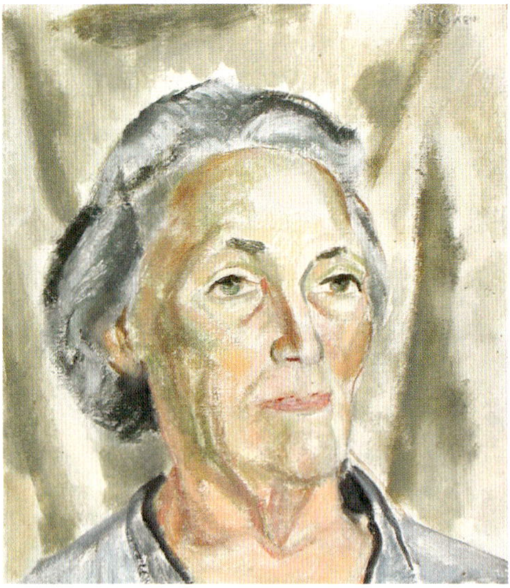

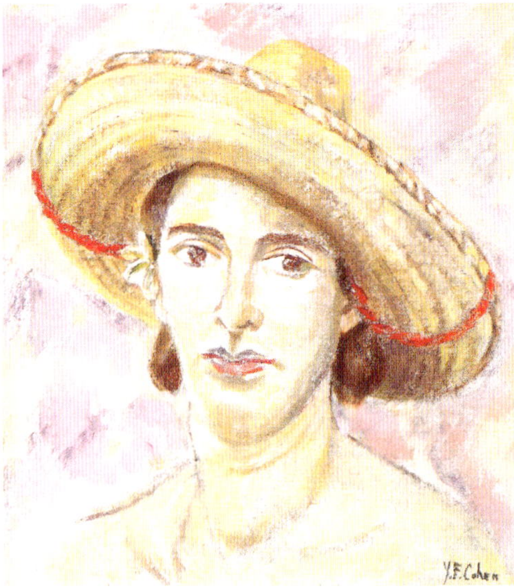

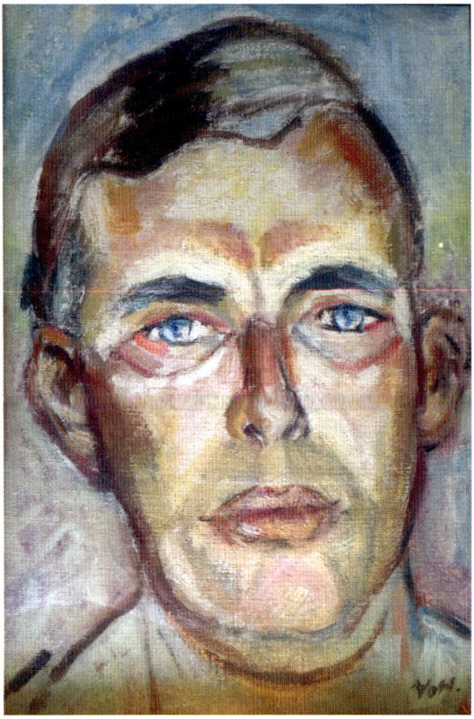

top left: Viva, the sisters' long-suffering mother. Oil painting by Yvonne Cohen, 1940s

top right: 'The Straw Hat'; Von's wistful self-portrait painted the year she turned thirty-two. She was still signing her work 'Y.F.K' for Yvonne-Frankel-Cohen. Oil painting by Yvonne Cohen, 1946

bottom: Portraitof Norman. On the verso it is titled 'Young man', with the note, 'Portrait of the artists' brother-in-law.' Oil painting by Yvonne Cohen, 1940s

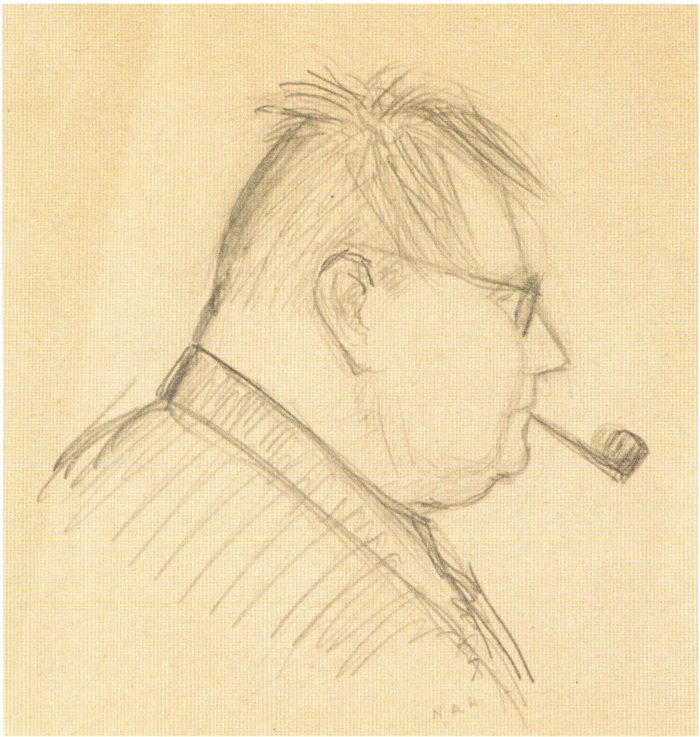

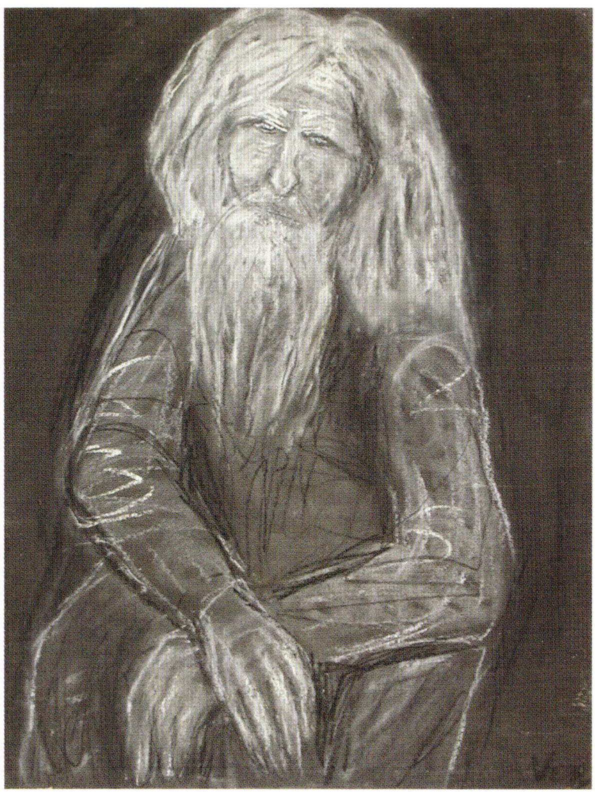

top: Study of George Bell; art critic, teacher, and mentor, whose life intersected with the sisters in many ways. Pencil sketch by Norman Albiston, 1950

bottom: Von was particularly fond of Neil Douglas, artist and founding gardener at Heide. Pastel by Yvonne Cohen, 1970s top: Deanne Conti, spinning wool on Timana Island. Watercolour and charcoal sketch by Yvonne Cohen, 1960s

bottom: Deanna and Bruce Arthur weaving on Timana, which they leased as a home and base for their weaving business. Watercolour and charcoal sketch by Yvonne Cohen, 1960s

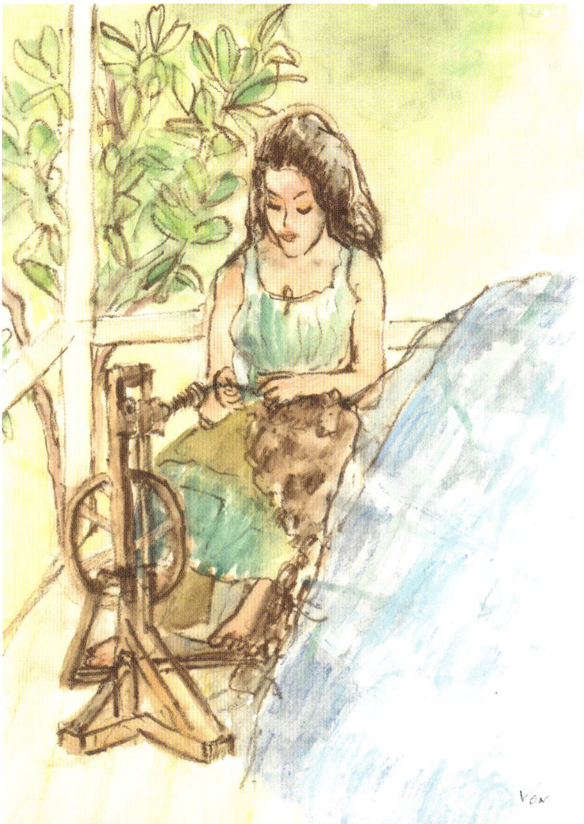

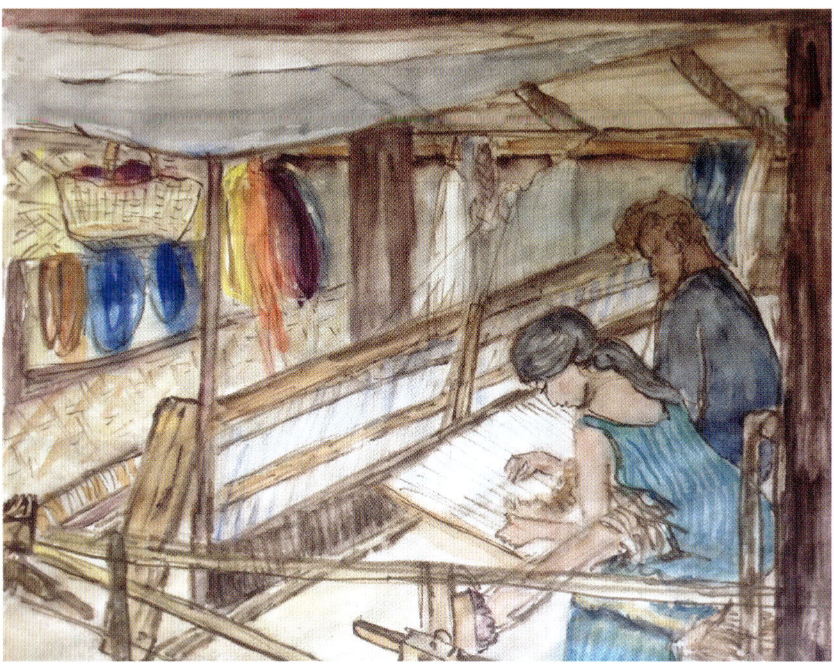

top: 'After the Bath'; the homework that was praised by Bell, much to Von's delight. Oil painting by Yvonne Cohen, c.1950

middle: 'Tropic Man', one of Norm's 'homeworks'; referencing Ian Fairweather's works. Oil painting by Norman Albiston, 1949–50

bottom: 'Grey After Gris' was painted by Von when she, Val, and Norm attended George Bell's art classes. It pays tribute to Gris's condensed forms and use of soft colours. Oil painting by Yvonne Cohen, c.1950

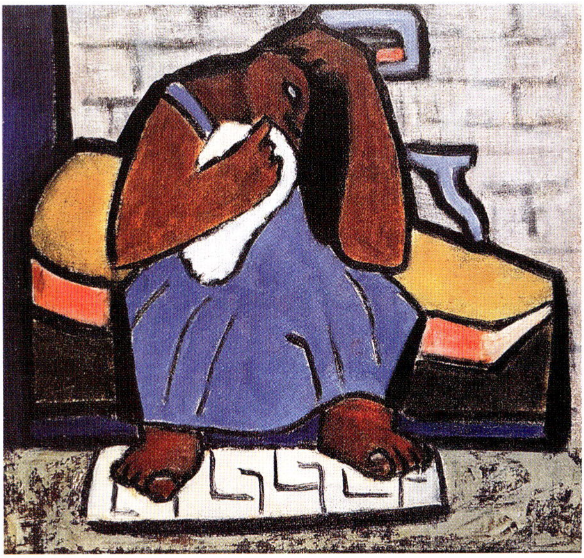

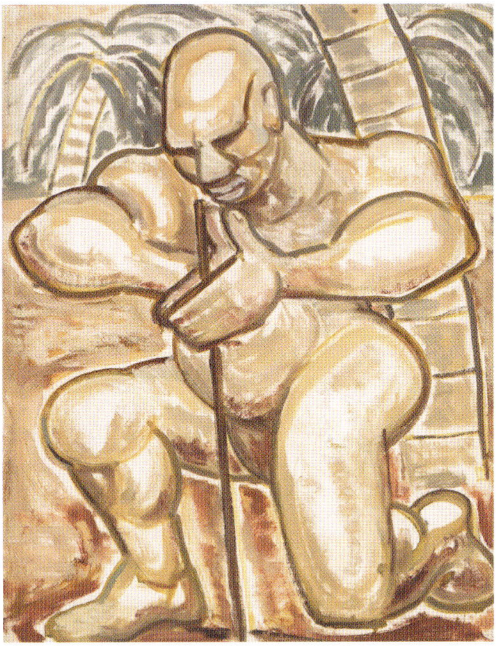

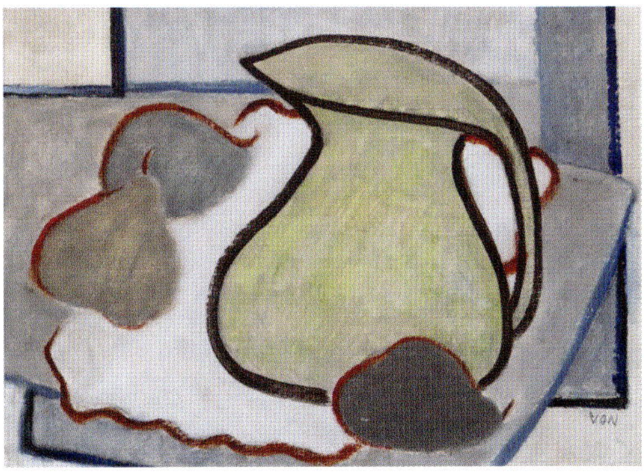

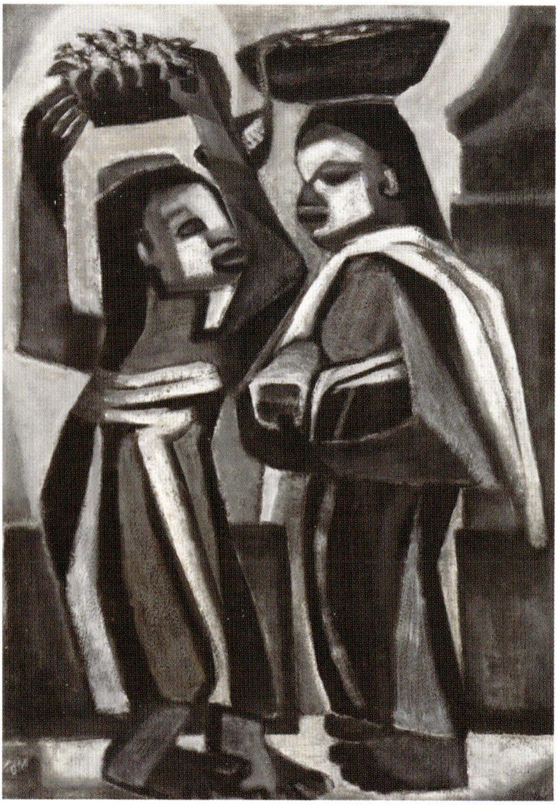

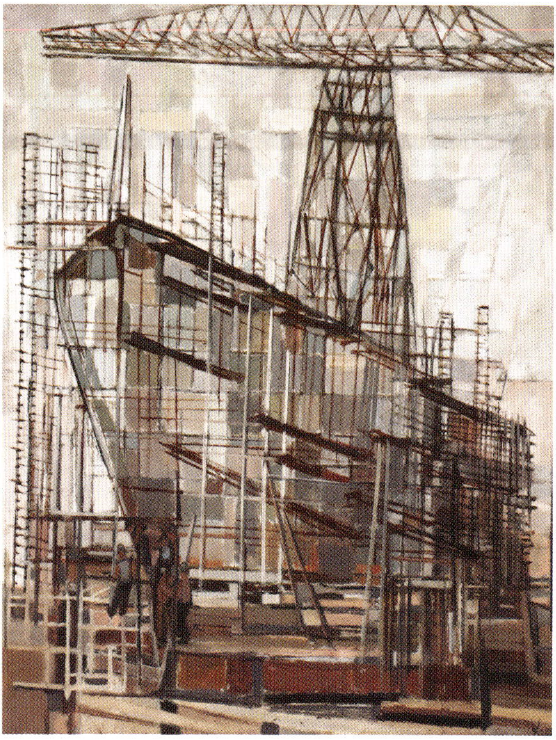

top: Going to market in Bali, presumably painted after Von's trip with friend and neighbour Guelda Pyke. Oil painting by Yvonne Cohen, 1954

bottom: Most likely based on Williamstown Docks in Melbourne, where the sisters visited occasionally to sketch, sometimes with their friend, artist Lina Bryans. Oil painting by Yvonne Cohen, 1954

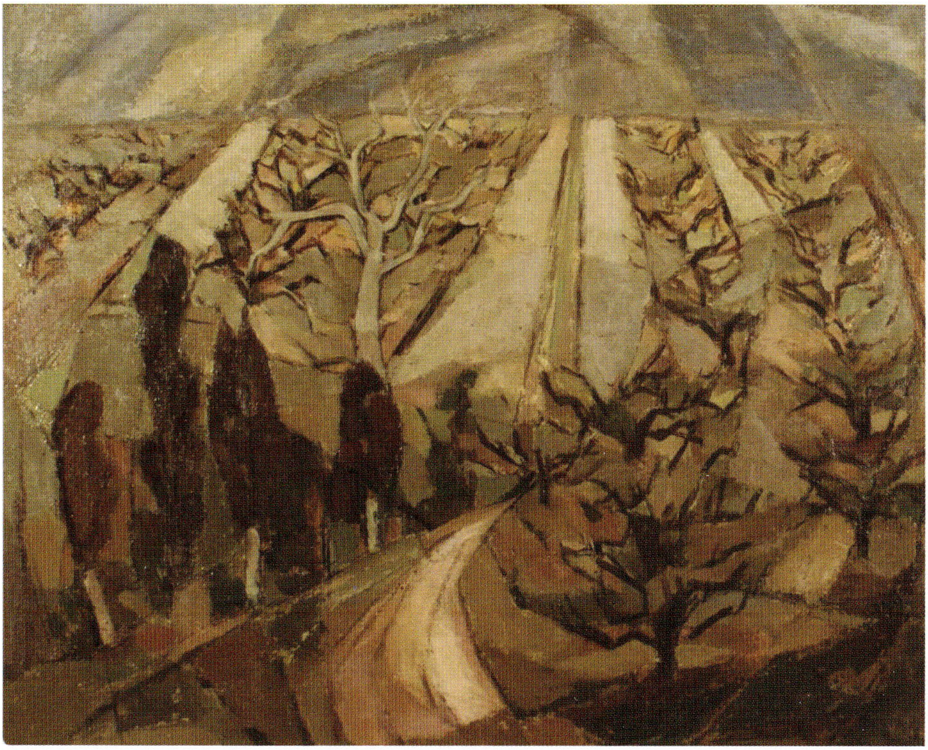

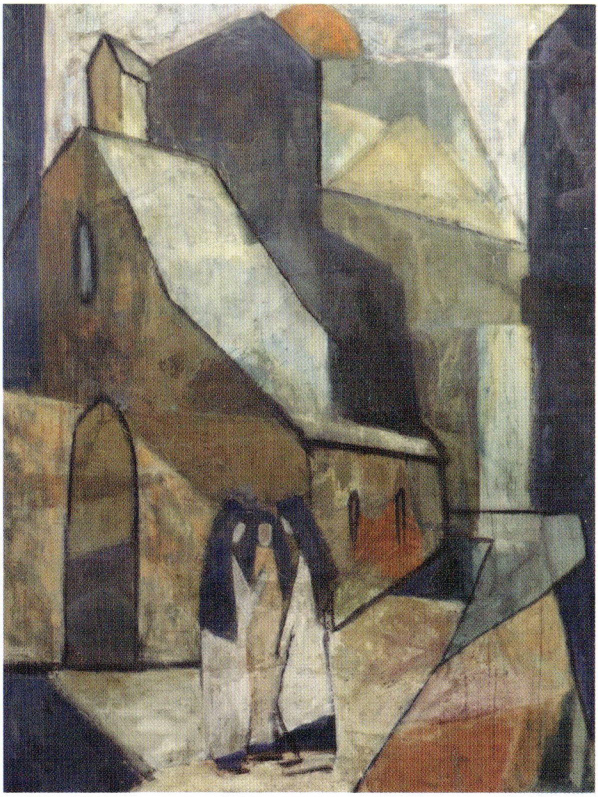

top: 'Orchard Country' inspired by the sisters' farm at Templestowe, shared first prize in the Victorian Artists Society Spring exhibition of 1958. Oil painting by Yvonne Cohen, 1958

bottom: 'Quiet Corner' hung on the wall of Val's studio and was exhibited in a George Bell tribute exhibition. Oil Painting by Valerie Albiston, 1950s

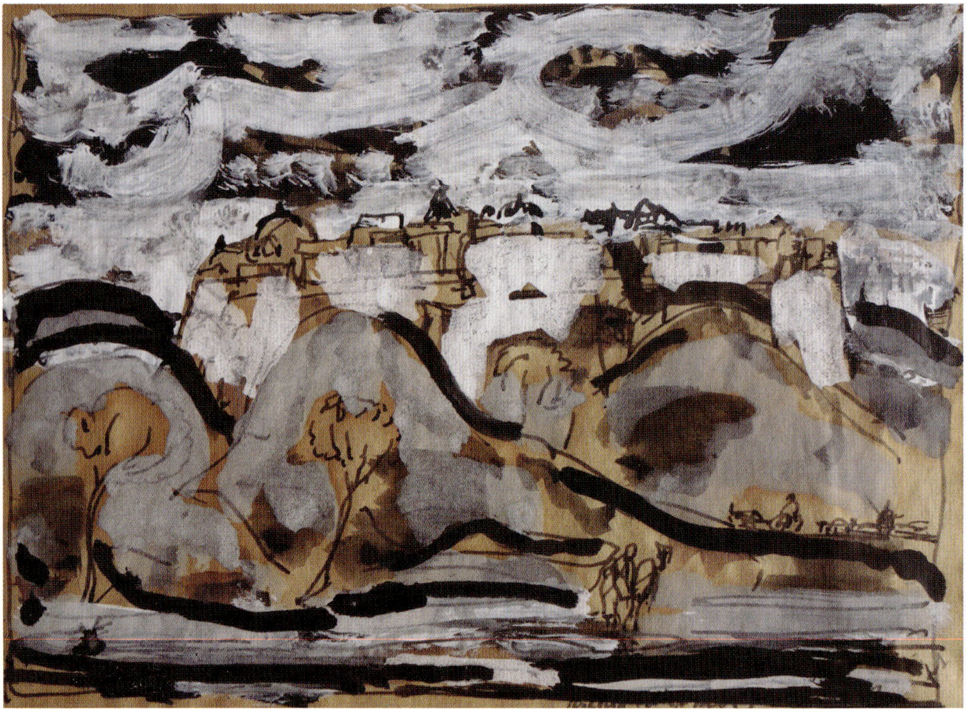

'Kulu Valley'; the most valuable of the small paintings stolen from Val in the move from Templestowe to Kew in 1990 and the only one recovered after her death. Oil painting by Ian Fairweather, 1949

a chapter to a lecture series, published in 1932, which put forward some of his beliefs. He argued that we are the sum of our habits—good and bad—and the best we can do for our children is to provide an environment where it is possible for them to 'maintain habits of a decent and refined life'. The results of our habits, he proposed, are our gift to posterity, whether 'building houses and cities, writing books, painting pictures or making laws'.

Neither of Norman's marriages had been a success, although the second and current one with Sutherland produced two children: Mark (born 1929) and Jennifer (1931) and lasted twenty-one years. The toxic Sutherland-Albiston partnership has been well-examined by Graham. The pair met when Margaret performed at Port Fairy, where Norman was working as a general practitioner and gave her a lift to her next concert venue. Norm's first wife, Rita, had just left him.

The first Mrs Albiston was Eleanor Margrethe (Rita) Stang, born in 1894, the same year as Norman: she in South Yarra, he in Mildura. In 1918, both graduated from Melbourne University as medical practitioners (he completed an MD and Batchelor of Surgery) and, the following January, they were married by Norman's father, a well-known Presbyterian minister. At the time Norman was serving as a Captain in the Royal Army Medical Corps and, with the war over, he was soon decommissioned.

The Stang-Albiston divorce in 1927 was widely reported, in great detail, under headings such as 'Doctor divorces doctor', 'Story of desertion' and 'Ruinous failure'. The details were not favourable to Norman. After four months in Tasmania, the couple moved to Port Fairy where Norman set up a practice. Evidence was presented that it was not long before he became cold and sarcastic 'to and about [Rita] in the presence of others'. The divorce was granted on the grounds of desertion—actual desertion by Norman and not just the required legal excuse. They had already been separated for a few years. Described as formidable, fair-minded and generous, in 1925, Rita found a position in Western Australia and went on to become a leading figure in child health and hygiene, significantly reducing child mortality in that State.

Part of Norman's problem was that he was unhappy in general practice. Before leaving for England in 1924 without telling Rita, he wrote to her:

> I have no plans for the future, save that I am not going to continue medicine any longer than is necessary. If I make you unhappy I make myself more so. It is nothing less than a ruinous tragedy which should never have occurred.

Norman's father, the respected Reverend Arthur Albiston—nicknamed the 'Prince of Preachers' and Professor of Theology at Melbourne University—gave his sons three career choices: the church, the law or medicine. Leslie, one of Norman's brothers, became a dermatologist. The other, Harold, was a prominent figure in veterinary medicine. If he had had his druthers, Norman, an accomplished pianist, believed that he would have chosen music.

Norman pursued a reluctant Sutherland, who was intent on her career. When she went to England to further her study, he followed, taking a job as a ship's doctor to pay his passage. He hoped to study music composition, but his teacher of choice—possibly the English composer Sir Charles Villiers Stanford—died, and he was unable to organise an alternative musical path. Instead, he stayed with medicine, but switched from surgery, which he described as 'glorified butchery', to the new field of psychiatry. He began work at Epsom Mental Hospital and, in 1926, gained a Diploma of Psychological Medicine from the Royal College of Physicians. His divorce from Rita came through in March 1927 and, in July, back in Australia, he and Sutherland were married by Norman's father in the Presbyterian Church at Camberwell.

Had Sutherland read the reports of Norman's divorce, she may have been even more cautious. Evidently, he treated her no better than Rita, taunting her privately and publicly, playing psychological games, withholding use of the car, or money (or hiding it so that

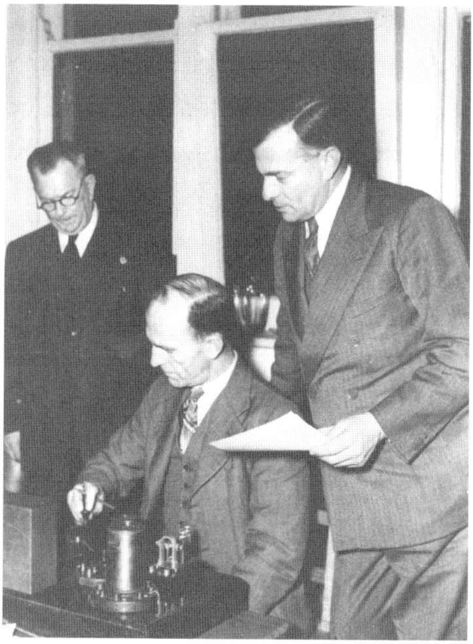

Norman (at right) was one of Victoria's leading chess players, representing the State in telegraphic chess competitions with NSW throughout the 1940s. National Library of Australia

she would have to search and find it) and refusing to recognise her financial contributions or exceptional musical talent. Soon he was involved with other women—his nurse, another nurse, and some of his patients. At a performance of one of Sutherland's new concertos, he turned up flaunting the attractive young woman on his arm. After a janitor reported that, in the evenings, Norman was using his shared professional rooms at Alcaston House to conduct affairs, he was asked to leave and had to move elsewhere on Collins Street.

By Sutherland's account, Norman was controlling; even cruel and sadistic. He apparently found it hard to cope with her burgeoning musical career, as a performer and composer, and reportedly asked composer and critic Felix Werder whether Sutherland's view that she had some talent as a composer meant that she was demented. Rather than using her well-recognised musical gifts, he expected her to devote all her time to him, the housekeeping and children. He might have written articles on child rearing (about which they differed) and the importance of family, but he spent little time with his own children, preferring the company of his women, or friends at the Masonic Club, where he played—reportedly very well—piano, chess, snooker and billiards. Sutherland had wanted to leave on and off for some years, but, like many women, stayed because the children were young and the divorce laws favoured men.

In 1947, Sutherland discovered two intimate letters from Val to Norman, which confirmed her suspicions. By Easter, she had confronted Norm, who admitted that he 'was desperately in love … they [he and Val] were spiritually suited to each other.' Sutherland asked him to choose but he wanted to stay with her and continue seeing Val, claiming he needed two women, a wife and a mistress, like one of his colleagues. He continued to have his cake and eat it, seeing Val and going home most nights to Sutherland and, as he told Sutherland's cousin, giving himself six months to make up his mind. When, in September or so, deciding among other things that at seventeen and nineteen years of age the children were old enough to cope, Sutherland took matters into her own hands and moved into the spare room. Norman's response was to tell her he had thrown all her compositions into the boot and was going to dump them in the river if she left. Finally, he accepted that it was over, packed his bags and left. Sutherland contacted her solicitor, who sent Norman a letter demanding that he return her music. Norm agreed provided Sutherland returned Val's letters. They made the exchange: he left Sutherland's music in the house and collected the letters but did not return to collect his belongings until the following year. Sutherland filed for divorce on the grounds of desertion.

In that eventful year of 1947, the sisters and their mother moved from their apartment to historic 'Mulberry Cottage' in Domain Street, South Yarra; a stone's throw from the Botanic Gardens. The glass-walled living room looked out onto a courtyard shaded by silver birches and crab apple trees. Perhaps, spending more time in Melbourne, they felt the need for a garden or a house more in touch with nature.

As ever, despite the turmoil in Val's life, the sisters made the most of their months in the city; attending the theatre, lectures and art shows. They also started visiting the potters at Murrumbeena, thirteen kilometres from Melbourne—Arthur Boyd, John Perceval, and, later, Aboriginal-inspired potter Carl Cooper. Arthur Merric Boyd Pottery operated from a former butcher's shop, initially making functional pieces for the domestic market, given the post-war austerity, then, as the economy improved, more creative, decorative, distinctly Australian pots, platters, and vases. About 1947, Arthur's brother David made Val an entire dinner-set and tea-set and the sisters bought teapots and platters by Arthur. The sisters befriended potter Katie Janeba, whose work they liked, and in the 1950s, Harold Randolph (HR) Hughan, buying several of Hughan's refined stonewares—typically subtle shapes combined with ancient Chinese glazes—made in the studio of his Glen Iris home.

Since the 1930s, Val, Von and their mother had been joining the 'artistic gatherings' at Margaret Maclean's studios in Collins Street. Maclean organised painting classes, poetry readings and art discussions as well as exhibitions by the likes of Hilda Rix Nicholas and Arthur Streeton. The events were 'the talk of the town', with speakers including Klytie Pate, Nora Gurdon, Madge Freeman, Jessie Traill, Elena Roach, John Rowell, Max Ragless, Dora Wilson and the Pykes. Maclean acted as an agent for several successful artists and painted herself. In November 1949, *The Argus* reported, the sisters were at Maclean's exhibition:

> Down on their annual visit from their island in Northern Australia, Misses Yvonne and Valerie Cohen called in to see Margaret Maclean's paintings at the Melbourne Book Club Gallery yesterday. Admirers of their tanned skin were quickly informed that it had paled since their trip south. But they are looking forward to seeing all their Melbourne friends, and are sure to be seen at most of the art exhibitions during their visit.

Val and Von had first painted with Maclean in the 1930s. In England in 1934, they had sketched with Madge Freeman and her friend Elena Roach. Earlier still, with their good friends Pat Goldman and Anne Montgomery, they painted at the studio of Blamire Young, regarded as the greatest Australian watercolourist of the day. Unlike several of these female colleagues, though, and later ones such as Lina Bryans, the sisters did not join the Melbourne Society of Women Painters and Sculptors, formed around the turn of the century to promote the acceptance of women as serious artists. Although they lived very free lives, they were by no means feminists; indeed they appeared not to see, or at least be fussed by, the inequality and marginalisation of women. They believed that women, if they so chose, could deal with what they called 'The Old Buggers' Club'. In reality, their financial independence freed them and allowed them indifference to such concerns.

Although Val was intimately involved with Norm, Von remained a big part of her life, and the three did most things together. In 1949 the trio enrolled in George Bell's art lessons, held at Bourke Street, where many renowned Australian Modernists had or were studying. Valerie wrote of Norman that from '1949 to 1952 he was to join my sister and myself at Geo Bell's art classes', but records suggest that he enrolled with Bell the previous year and he and Bell were already firm friends. Amongst his many talents, Norm was a capable draughtsman, especially when drawing the human figure, so he particularly enjoyed Bell's Thursday evening life drawing sessions. As a medical student in 1917, he had drawn the illustrations, described as 'first class', for George Horne's prescribed textbook *Practical Gynaecology.*

Val, Von and Norm all found in Bell a stimulating teacher and enjoyed the artistic environment. Along with other select, fee-paying students ('no beginners'), they attended Bell's classes on Saturday afternoons in the backyard studio of his modest Toorak house, in Selborne Road. In the 1950s, Barbara Blackman was one of Bell's preferred models for life classes.

Whereas Noel had influenced their palette, Bell pushed the sisters and made them think. Under Bell, their work became flatter and more abstract—bold shapes with a thick outline—and more formulaic. The latter was something that stayed with Val in particular. I recall her touting the 'Rule of Odds', for example. Von, a more intuitive painter, believed Bell's most valuable lesson was 'to start drawing from the inside, to scratch in the bones'—that is, to starting sketching at the core and work out, to understand form, rather than imitate. Beginning in the 1950s, Von ventured further than Val into abstraction.

The first two hours of a Bell class were spent life drawing in silence, the poses changing after twenty minutes with a ten-minute break between. During the final hour, Bell reviewed homework exercises set the previous week. Hushed and expectant, the students gathered around him as each anonymous work was discussed, hoping that it was theirs which made him smile and describe what excited him about the piece. He'd stress form and wasn't particularly interested in psychological or emotional meaning, nor in colour, except to serve form. Von never forgot Bell's delight in her little oil 'After the Bath', a homework assignment painted in about 1950.

Arguably, Bell was the most influential teacher of his era—certainly, the sisters often claimed that he was the painting master that they had been looking for. In 1950, Bell, then 'a bear of a man', turned seventy-two. Often unwell and grumpy, he remained dismissive of some of the directions that modern art was taking, railing against both the Angry Penguins led by John Reed—whose aim was to challenge entrenched traditions and modernise art and literature—and the social realists, often members of the Communist Party, who concerned themselves with matters of social equity. These ideologies and intolerances had caused a split in the Contemporary Art Society (CAS) in 1940, when Bell, its founder, and his supporters, including many of the society's patrons, resigned *en masse*. The society folded with the exodus of artists overseas post-war, but was revived by John Reed in 1954. Loyal to Bell, Val and Von became involved with the CAS only after Reed's five-year presidency ended.

Bell was among the few who recognised the unusual talent of Ian Fairweather when the eccentric Scottish-born artist first visited Melbourne in the 1930s. Fairweather returned for two years in 1945 to live at Lina Bryans's pink-painted house at Darebin, near Melbourne. The sisters did not actually meet Fairweather then, although Von well remembered glimpsing the reclusive artist as he retreated to his basement room when she visited the pink house in about 1946 to have her portrait painted by Jock Frater—the portrait didn't eventuate.

It was Frater who encouraged Macquarie Galleries in Sydney to exhibit Fairweather, then living in a hut on an abandoned goat farm at Hill's Creek among the mangroves near Cairns. In September 1949, the gallery staged his first solo show in Australia. His paintings proved too challenging for many, but Bryans, her lover Frater, and Bell and his students bought several. The *Sydney Morning Herald's* art critic's assessment was typical:

> The work of Ian Fairweather at the Macquarie Galleries is that of a decorator and a stylist. But it is much more than that; it is a fervent work, a tortured work, a mixture of sensuality and asceticism. It is an almost mystic work which regards the flesh with savagery; yet a work which at times can feel nothing but the flowing rhythm of nude bodies and the bleak exhilaration of the calligraphic line … He paints, not to relax, but to obey the imagery called from the deep recesses of his mind and to express the general rhythm which his sensibilities associate with life.

That November, Fairweather was again on the move. He left Cairns and headed further north, eventually to Darwin, where in 1952 he launched off on a raft, eventually drifting to Timor. Val recounted to us several times and to James Gleeson in interview that Fairweather told Charles Martin that he could have anything left at the campsite. Chas retrieved about a dozen unfinished, unsigned gouaches, which Val agreed to sell for him. She and Von 'picked the best out of them', and over a weekend sold the remainder to friends, for about £20 to £40 each. Chas, Val claimed, needed the cash and had little appreciation of the reclusive artist's work, indeed, she said, he burned the remaining material, including sketchbooks and notebooks. He was a 'Sunday painter', she explained to me, '… he did very sort of look and putters, you know, as we call them. He had no feeling for Fairweather's work at all, didn't understand it.'

In May 1950, Noel was back in Australia, staying in Cairns with Chas and Cliff and teaching art for a short while. Later in the year, he exhibited in a multi-art show with the Cairns Art Society and his paintings, and ten tropical scenes painted by Chas, were reportedly 'outstanding' among the one hundred hung. Back at Bedarra, there was much work to be done to reclaim his garden and repair his home. He was joined by his latest companion, Joyce Lambert, who he had met in Paris. The lady-like Lambert, a former society columnist for women's magazines, helped him manage the Dunk Island resort until it changed hands. Hugo had again asked Noel to oversee the resort because Caught, the lessee-manager, was in financial trouble. One of Noel's tasks was to remove Caught, who would eventually be declared bankrupt.

Early the next year, on Hugo's behalf, Noel advertised the sale of the resort through an agent in Tully. At that time there were eleven double and twenty-five single chalets with hot water and sewerage, as well as communal facilities. In August the sale went out to tender and, early in 1952, Eddie Doepel, a Ballarat businessman, bought the resort at much-reduced price. The semi-retired Doepel was keen to rebuild the business, but in another four years it would be back on the market.

All these changes among their island neighbours, painting buddies and lovers brought the idyll of the war years to an end for the sisters. No longer would the privileged little group of friends swim and fish and paint in the winter warmth. On a two-week Timana holiday with Norman in May 1951, the sisters decided to lease out the island long-term. They placed an advertisement in the *Cairns Post*: 'TROPICAL Island Paradise to let. Substantial bungalow, built-in furniture, septic, safe anchorage, fertile soil, long period. Apply letter Cohen, Timana Island, Tully.'

9

PAINTERS IN THE HIDDEN VALLEY

Timana and Templestowe

(1951 – 1959)

In 1949, a new group of artists had begun to assemble on the Family Islands, based on Bedarra. Neura Hall (née Harriet Zander) bought what had been Phyl Busst's portion of the island (owned in the interim two years by the Goldriches). Neura moved there with her third husband, Mike—a tall, elegant Canadian painter who had trained as a commercial artist. The exotically beautiful Neura was well-known in Melbourne for her work with the Council for the Encouragement of Music and Arts. Neura's most recent former husband was Guido Baracchi, wealthy Marxist intellectual and political activist, but Stalinism and Guido had disappointed her. With John Busst and Noel, the Halls formed a loose artists' colony: their houses out of sight of each other and with a bit of a tramp between if they wanted company. As Neura suggested in an interview with Keith Finley of *The Argus*, although sarongs and bikinis were the usual attire, to avoid surprises, it was best to sing or whistle when moving around the island. The people may have changed but the press played the same old tune.

How much interaction the sisters and Norman had with these newcomers during their winter holidays on Timana is unrecorded—they almost certainly socialised. Most winters, for a few weeks, Norm holidayed with the sisters on Timana. It must have been very different, especially for Von, who occasionally went up alone or stayed on alone, or holidayed there with a female friend. She always spent time with Noel when he was in residence.

Once, Von remembered in her later years, she was alone on the island with two workmen when three men arrived in a boat and asked if they could swim. Such impromptu visits were not uncommon and she agreed. However, the men proceeded to gather oysters near the house, which the sisters saved for emergencies. She asked them to take the oysters at the far end of the island, but they ignored her. The workers offered to get help, but Von took matters into her own hands. She went to the bungalow, got out their gun and fired it into the air a couple times. It had the desired effect, she said—'the interlopers were back in their boat in no time!'

Each year from 1951 to 1953, without the sisters, the Bedarra artists exhibited in the well-supported annual Spring exhibition of the Cairns Art Society, where the oils of Mike Hall and Noel attracted favourable comment. In March 1954, the Halls were ready to stage their own exhibition at Peter Bray Gallery in Melbourne: Neura's primitive paintings hanging alongside Mike's confidently designed, more picturesque work. Neura, described as tall, fresh and suntanned, blue-eyed and greying, told the reporter for *The Argus* that she looked relaxed because of their hassle-free existence on the island: '... life cut off from the world up there is paradise, and has had its effect on us.' Six months later, with Noel, the three very different portrayers of the tropics held a joint show at the Johnstone Gallery in Brisbane. A reviewer of that exhibition for the *Sunday Mail* also picked up on the romanticised, paradisiacal aspects of island life: 'Three painters, Neura and Michael Hall, and Noel Wood have found their Shangri-La on Bedarra.'

Yet, as ever, there were serpents in Eden and, not for the first or last time, the Bedarra artists' 'colony' collapsed into bitterness. When Noel went overseas for a few years late in 1954 to work in the USA, Busst attempted a coup—taking advantage of the fact that Noel's original purchase document was little more than a 'gentleman's agreement'. To the sisters' disgust, Busst staked a legal claim on Noel's corner of the island. Fortunately, Noel had a signed arrangement with Busst for first option if he ever wished to sell, which stood up in court as recognition of ownership. Around the same time, apparently, Busst also challenged Neura's title. When Clem Christesen journeyed north to stay with the Halls in 1954 to write and paint, the Halls were fighting Busst in the courts. If Busst had succeeded in his land grabs, he would have owned the whole island.

Noel had been lured from the island by Hollywood director Bernard Haskins. In 1952 the bespectacled Haskins had taken a deep-sea fishing holiday on Dunk Island, having finished shooting *His Majesty O'Keefe*, a film about the buccaneering history of Fiji. The director and his wife returned to Australia in 1954 to film *Long John Silver* on Sydney Harbour, Australia's first cinemascope colour feature. As filming wound down, in July the young, attractive Mrs. Haskins returned to Dunk Island to holiday for a week. Yet another of Noel's conquests, she convinced him to travel to Hollywood. In California, the Haskins organised work for Noel as an art director. Noel's companion, Joyce Lambert, also left the islands for New York.

After a year or so, Noel left the USA to stay with Brassey and to paint in England and Ireland. In a 1956 interview in *The New Yorker*, probably made during a visit to Lambert, it was clear that Noel had lost none of his appeal. He still had presence. The magazine described him as 'our new friend … a tall, dark-haired and charming man of forty-three'; an artist who had left his isolated island, where he was 'the sole inhabitant' (!). Noel was on the road, the article reported, looking up old friends in Hollywood, New York, London and Ireland. Lambert later joined him on a painting trip to Italy. Like Von and

Eleanor, she continued to carry a torch for him. Much later in life, Lambert asked Noel to move to New York so that they could spend their last years together, but he stayed in Queensland.

The Halls also left Bedarra in 1954 and moved to Ivanhoe, Melbourne, and— according to James Porter, Noel's biographer—later returned to Queensland to run a gallery at Southport on the Gold Coast. As for the litigious Busst, he stayed on until 1957, the year that Noel returned, when the Bussts moved to Bingil Bay on the mainland.

At their spacious mud and bamboo house on Bedarra, the Bussts had entertained sea-loving Harold Holt, then Commonwealth Minister for Immigration, and his wife Zara. Holt and Busst had been friends since their school days at Wesley College and Alison and Zara had known each other since childhood. From 1951–1955, the Holts enjoyed annual August getaways with the Bussts; sunbathing, swimming, diving and beachcombing and partying into the night. After the Bussts' move to the mainland, Holt, by then Treasurer, continued to holiday with them while he worked on his budgets, and eventually bought land in the area himself.

Although Busst's land grabs ultimately destroyed his island relationships, his intentions were to conserve Bedarra's natural environment, and he went on to play an important role in the environment movement. He was active in the Wildlife Preservation Society of Queensland, founding the Australian Conservation Foundation and, with Judith Wright and others, fighting to protect the Great Barrier Reef. Wright wrote of her friend that he was 'our indispensable spokesperson, contact with politicians, diplomat and tactician'. His ruthlessness and organisational and tactical skills served him well in a larger arena.

While in Europe, Noel visited his older brother Rex—a portrait painter and printmaker of note—who eventually settled in Portugal, where he taught art, exhibited and was able to live more freely as a homosexual than he could in conservative Adelaide. Rex became something of a Cubist, whereas Noel leaned to Impressionism.

It would be the last time Noel saw Rex, who was murdered under mysterious circumstances in 1970.

While turmoil tainted the 'laidback' lifestyles of the artists on the islands, on the outskirts of bustling Melbourne, the sisters set up their own artists' community. In the very late 1940s, Val and Von sold their Beaconsfield property and, with friends, bought another block of land at Templestowe, intending to live there as well as farm it. Post-war, the city had claimed the greater part of their lives, leaving Timana as a holiday destination for a few weeks a year at most. For Val, at least, 'The joy of being able to switch on a light, turn on a tap with indifference, revel in a fog, visit friends, galleries, theatres and art classes' had prevailed.

The sisters leased the island to a series of more or less successful tenants, from 'the Mayor of Tully to deep sea divers, cranks and black-marketeers', according to Val. Writer James Porter suggests that Ken Druitt, who later bought the sandspit portion of Bedarra, was the first lessee. The sisters' friend Charlie Dickinson, who had helped them with access during the war, was another. According to the local paper, the popular Chair of Cardwell Shite Council and his family and friends holidayed briefly on Timana in 1952 and 1953.

Perhaps the disputes over Bedarra prompted the sisters to tidy up their ownership of Timana. The history of European ownership of the little island is tied up with that of Bedarra, two of the very few freehold islands on the Great Barrier Reef. For a few years from 1913, Bedarra was the home of Captain Henry William Allason and his wife who, inspired by Banfield's *Confessions of a Beachcomber*, planned to plant coconuts commercially to make copra. Legend has it that Allason was a powerful swimmer and could cross the nearly three-kilometre-wide strait to Timana. With the First World War, Allason returned to England. While fighting in France, his health was damaged by gas and he never returned to Australia. Bedarra subsequently moved through a few other hands, including, according an unsubstantiated 1935 report in the *Sunday Mail*, Hugo Brassey's.

The sisters always claimed that they bought Timana in 1939 or 1940—in fact, it was much later. Records in the Queensland Titles Office (now Department of Natural Resources and Mines) show that Allason's purchase of Timana (then known as Thorpe Island) for £21.10s was registered in 1916. When Allason died in January 1935, at his home 'Villa Timana' in France, he left his Australian island to Barnardo's Homes National Incorporated, based in London. The idea behind the bequest, the sisters believed, was to use the island as a camp for homeless boys. If this was ever considered, issues with freshwater and access would have made it impractical. In May 1953, the sisters purchased the island from Barnardos for the princely sum of £50 (c. $2000 in 2022 values). However, there were issues with transfer of the title, in part because Allason's probate fees of £50 hadn't been paid. Documents show that following intervention by the sisters' solicitor, the title passed from Allason to Barnardos to the sisters all at once in 1955. Their Certificate of Title gives the date of registration in the sisters' names as 29 September 1955. They are described as spinsters, surname Cohen, suggesting that application for the title was actually made much earlier, before Val's marriage in 1951.

Immediately, the island paid for itself. In 1956, the sisters leased it out for a year, for a fee of £75 (plus agent's commission), to Mr and Mrs Frank Hanley. Retirement freed Hanley and his wife to pursue their dream of a simple life on a tropical island. Timana, with its little stilt house and caretaker's cottage, seemed ideal—not too far from civilisation. It wasn't long before reality hit. Shortly after Christmas, the sisters received a letter from Hanley, thanking them for their 'quaint' card and complaining about the 'dreary and depressing period we have been suffering since arrival on Timana'. The letter contained a litany of woes. Everything had gone wrong and he and his wife had not been able to take up occupancy until early November. Initially, there was no drinking water, they had to have new tanks installed, and they were stuck on the island because for various reasons they had not been able to bring their launch from the mainland, not least because the boatshed and slipway had collapsed since their inspection of the island's facilities in June. They had not had a food delivery for ten days.

Snakes, mosquitoes and a variety of flies besieged the Hanleys, seemingly oblivious to pesticides, and the sand flies had left them covered in sores. Parts of the stairs and veranda were missing, damaged either by termites or unauthorised visitors. Worst of all, it was summer, in the midst of a heat wave and cyclonic conditions, which was not only insufferable but added to their isolation from the mainland. They had spent most of their time clearing vegetation to open the house to the sea breezes. 'Unless you have lived here in the summer heat you could not appreciate the situation,' Hanley sniped. Not least, he confessed that they had been naïve about island living. He and his wife, who was unwell, would have to 'give up this dream venture'. It was a plea for permission to sublet.

Early the next year, Mrs Hanley was hospitalised and, at the end of April, Gilbert Hicks—a friend of artist Clifton (Clif) Pugh, and himself a sometime-artist—relieved the Hanleys of their lease and they immediately set off south. The steamy, uncomfortable summer was over and Hicks had a more positive experience of life on a tropical island. Yet he, too, was stranded for a time, in his case on the mainland, and he, too, soon discovered that his ideas about island life were unrealistic. He planned to bring his new wife and their baby to Timana. He wrote to the sisters enthusiastically about the fruit trees, in need of pruning but thriving despite the rainforest's attempt to strangle them. Most—pomelo, mandarin, lemon, custard apple, bananas—were fruiting and delicious, he said. Coconuts were everywhere and hibiscus and frangipani were flowering. To Hicks, at that early stage, there were only a few negatives. Some of the bamboo on the lower floor was rotting but otherwise the bungalow looked sturdy, despite evidence of past attack by white ants. Still, he wondered how to cope with the tides and the ever-growing grass and weeds.

The sisters had been happy to live simply and had always had the assistance of practical people like Nugget, as well as admirers, and access to the resort on Dunk. Mostly they were only there in the dry season. Apart from Nugget, nobody lasted long on Timana. There was the endless maintenance, the relentless vigour of the vegetation, and the isolation created not by distance but by the tides and the weather. By February 1959, Claude Riches and his friend Ed Trennick were in residence and doing a lot of replacements and repairs to the house. In a letter to the sisters, they said they had dumped six tea chests of tins, broken glass, a rusty stove and other rubbish out at sea. The tidal extremes had been a shock to them: at times the tide rose nearly four metres; at others they would be planning on going to the mainland and find the water unreachable, miles out from the shore. The following January Riches and Trennick were bailing out, citing the need to be close to medical attention.

Meanwhile in Melbourne, Valerie and Yvonne's French friend, Madam Didi Reddin, who shared their interest in the arts, had suggested the idea of co-owning a block of flats. They were joined by Guelda and Polly (also known as Mollie) Pyke, who were old friends from Toorak. For a couple of years, the women searched the Melbourne suburbs. Hoping to buy something suitable in these more avantgarde suburbs, with their artistic heritage going back to the Heidelberg School of painters, they eventually found their way to Doncaster-Eltham. As Val put it, there they could live among '… the ghosts of Conder, Roberts, Streeton, McCubbin, Withers, and Dave Davies, our father's friend, who's famous "Moonlight at Templestowe" hangs in the National Gallery.' The area was still semi-rural and there, as Alistair Knox, their architect-to-be, observed: 'Middle-class stigmas did not stick among its artistic community, which had always accepted personal freedom and personal licence as synonymous—a condition which was not to become the general standard elsewhere for at least another decade.'

One sparkling Sunday in about 1948, the six women were

disappointed yet again by the suburban offerings from the land agent and asked whether he had anything else. 'Only an orchard … the owner had an accident,' was his reply. It was not what they had in mind at the time, but they thought they might as well have a look. In the soft morning sunlight, the land, lined with neatly pruned trees, fell away in folds to the Yarra River. The gentle atmosphere charmed the two sets of sisters and they determine to buy. However, Madam Didi and her daughter Collette were not interested in buying a farm. In their place, Val and Yvonne invited Mabel and Norman Taylor, newly retired graziers from Far North Queensland.

The group bought the twenty-acre peach and apple orchard, in a 'hidden valley' above the river at Templestowe, with the aim of subdividing. Each tenant would have separate title but work the orchard as one. To realise the subdivision, they engaged Alistair Knox; quickly becoming the intellectual community's architect of the moment. The Taylors opted to live in the old wooden farmhouse, imported from England in the 1880s. The others also contracted Knox to build three houses. There would be one for Val and Norm, one for Von and their mother Viva, and a shared house with separate areas for each of the Pyke sisters. They tossed a coin to decide the order in which the houses would be built.

In his autobiography, Knox suggests that it was early as 1948 that an executive of the National Gallery of Victoria approached him on behalf of the sisters Cohen and Pyke. Regardless, the Templestowe project advanced slowly while Knox was finishing a mud-brick weekender at Eltham for composer Dorian Le Galliene and economist Professor Richard Downing.

In interview, Valerie told James Gleeson, 'This was Alistair's first big achievement over here. He had four houses to build and he left the bank and we really launched him on his career.' This was a bit of a stretch. As Knox himself recognised, he was already '… receiving considerable publicity in the press because earth-construction was beyond the imagination of most people.' The Templestowe contracts did, however, enable him to take leave from the bank that had employed him since he was a fifteen-year-old, then to resign. The sisters, he wrote:

> … had independent means, and this gave me my first opportunity to produce three sizeable houses amid the pink and white plum blossoms that covered the northern slope and looked over the river towards Eltham. It was an idyllic scene, particularly as these would be almost the first houses that could be seen from that direction. This was before any orchards had been subdivided, and the unbroken pattern of fruit trees separated by lines of ancient pines had remained unaltered since the land was first settled by a largely German community a hundred years earlier.

Knox decided that his alternative-style mud-brick houses '… would prove too great a strain on my elegant artistic lady clients, no matter how they thought about it before it all began.' Instead, for the sisters' homes he opted for conventional materials: timber construction on concrete slabs—both materials in reasonable supply for the first time since the war. The homes would be flat-roofed, long, low and light, designed to sit within and amidst the landscape. Each one was different, but influenced, via Knox, by the architecture of Frank Lloyd Wright.

Through his connections with the Montsalvat art community, Knox engaged Clif Pugh, on the brink of artistic recognition, to dig the ditches at Templestowe. Knox also employed artist Neil Douglas, who was living at Bayswater with his mother. Douglas was particularly fond of Von who, in the 1960s, painted his portrait. Douglas had green thumbs and Val remembered that when he visited the sisters at Mulberry Cottage in South Yarra, he would arrive 'with armfuls of vegetables that he'd grown on concrete'. On and off, the rugged individualist and bush-lover lived at Heide, John and Sunday Reed's property at Heidelberg on the Templestowe side of the Yarra River, having helped develop its gardens (notably, the wild garden) in the 1930s.

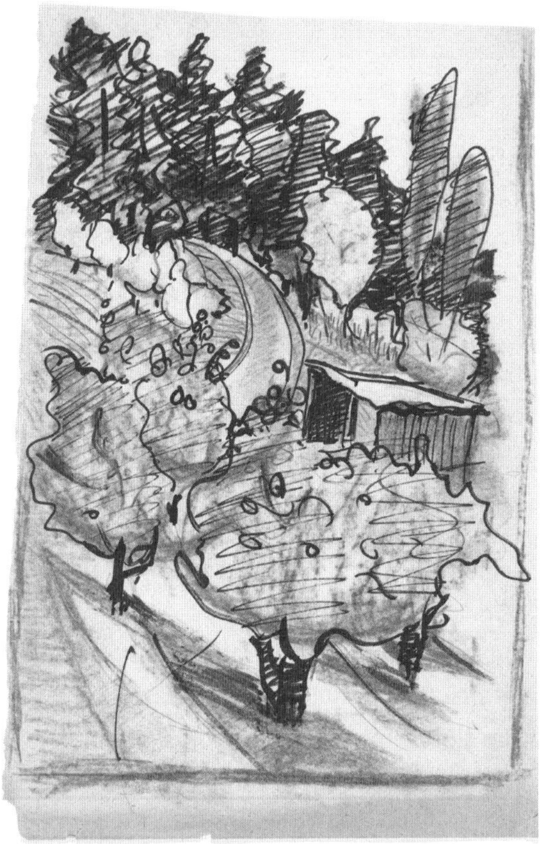

'Landscape' (orchard at Templestowe). Fibre-tipped pen and charcoal on paper, 39.6 x 25.2 cm. Heide Museum of Modern Art, Melbourne. Gift of Valerie Albiston 2004. ©Estate of Valerie Albiston

While the houses were being built, Val had a bumpy, three-year wait until she and Norm could marry. Norman's father tried to stop the marriage, and people snubbed the couple in cafes, but they went ahead and wed in the Melbourne Registry Office on 24 September 1951; a couple of months after Norm's divorce was finalised and three days after Norm's fifty-seventh birthday. Valerie was then forty.

Eventually, the Reverend Albiston, who was against divorce (a common view then), came to enjoy his latest daughter-in-law, Norm's adult children accepted her as a friend (not as a mother), and, against the odds, the marriage was happy and long. As Sutherland remarked bitterly: '... at the age of 53 [Norm] found his Indian summer.' There were, of course, awkward moments: such as when Norm's daughter,

Jenny, wed in 1953, and Valerie was not invited. In later years, Val developed a warm relationship, particularly with Jenny and her children, but also with Mark. She welcomed them at Templestowe, offering homemade lemonade while Norm amused the kids with magic tricks and playful antics.

Norman's three wives embodied his three great passions: psychiatry, music and art. Val was a painter, Sutherland a musician, and Stang a doctor. By the latter half of the 1940s, when he became involved with Val, he was a celebrity psychiatrist, called in to testify in a variety of high-profile court cases, ranging from whether certain artwork was obscene to questions of sanity and sexual obsession. Could a man slit his wife's throat while dreaming? Would an allegedly 'obscene' drawing corrupt children or teenagers? Could loss of nerve from a fall compromise a steeplejack's employment prospects? The latter was one of the first court cases admitting psychiatric evidence. It was also remarkable in that a claim for compensation on psychiatric grounds was unheard of in the history of the Workers' Compensation Board. Counsel for the employer played on the novelty: 'The introduction of psychiatry into this court creates a new terror ... Dr. Albiston spoke of "personality make-up". What a lovely phrase! It sounds like a cross between Max Factor and Freud.'

While Norm was sought after by barristers and judges, he was a loner among his professional colleges, only joining the Royal College of Psychiatrists in 1971. He rarely attended medical dinners or seminars, preferring the company of his less conservative, more creative friends.

He made a charming and challenging husband for Val, who could be feisty and, in some ways, just as unconventional. She would have spoken her mind and matched him in his stubbornness and game-playing. If she wanted to block, she would stand defiantly, hand on hip, and bluntly say 'nope'. Independent of mind and means, she had more options than her predecessor, Margaret. This left Norman with less scope to exert coercive control, as they call it these days. Val's painting and writing were serious hobbies rather than dedicated careers and her success in both solid but modest, leaving less scope for his inclination towards jealousy. It also helped that Val didn't want children (Norman arranged for her to have a hysterectomy). Both Val and Norm were casual and sociable and had similar interests in art and literature, and both liked to buck societal expectations. Their relationship was playful and sensual—Val described him as 'my lover'. Von complained to friends that she couldn't just walk into Val's house because she might happen upon them having sex, anywhere, anytime.

Von was a more modest soul, and still held a candle for Noel Wood, but Norm was family. We 'didn't interfere in each other's lives and he was good to Von', Val explained of the threesome. Risqué jokes and limericks were popular. Unquestionably, as Val often claimed, the three 'had a lot of fun'.

Norman, for his part, likened himself to a happy rooster with his two pretty hens. Although Val ruled the roost, she allowed Norm a great deal of freedom, quite likely relishing the unorthodox arrangement and possibly accepting that he was incorrigible—'a hard dog to keep on the porch', to borrow a phrase from Hillary Clinton. He continued to womanise. 'Helping his patient' or 'going to play the piano' were among the many euphemisms he and his relations used to explain his absences. He often 'stayed overnight at the Masonic Club', but eventually came home to Val and Von.

The Templestowe houses were ready in 1952. Val and Von had chosen a slightly elevated site at the end of a long drive and their houses, with the Pykes', were tucked into the north-facing slope. Val and Von began a search for an appropriate name:

> We wanted an aboriginal name … for those lost tribes who had lived for eons along this Yarra Valley. Our partners were satisfied with the late owner's choice of Stella Park, in memory of his mother. Thus half the property became Stella Park while we began our search for something aboriginal. We finally visited Dr Donald Thompson, the anthropologist

> at Melbourne Uni, asking his help. Half his property was one away from ours—the other half lay across the river. He would row over to his stone barn that was in construction—it was to be a resting place for his aboriginal artifacts. Its church-like frame remained unfinished all our years in Templestowe [and became a drawcard for artists]. We were unable to find a name that fitted our fruit growing area so we finally decided on The Wold—for the valley and rolling hills around us were reminiscent of the Cotswolds.

With the orchard came Pete, the horse, who went with a spring cart that they jogged along the empty roads to Mullens, the village blacksmith, who would shoe Pete in readiness for the picking season. Only fourteen miles from Melbourne GPO, Templestowe was still considered 'up the bush'. The first time that the sisters headed into town to attend a lecture with the Pykes, they discussed whether they had made a mistake choosing somewhere 'so far out'. But Val, always a reckless driver, came to use their country address to get out of speeding fines and the like—she was from the country, what would she know of road rules in the city, she would plead.

Two local brothers, Perc and Fred Chivers, were taken on to share farm—to manage the pruning, cultivating and pest control. When the fruit was ready, the group helped in the packing shed, where 'laughter bubbled' as they sorted and boxed the fruit. Their neighbours helped with spraying and were generous with produce—adding pears, plums and quinces to their own-grown fine apples and peaches—and, in return, the sisters dispensed homemade jams, chutneys and bottled fruits.

A dam stretched the width of the property and the group planted willows around it; their flock of three ducks suddenly grew to seventy, so they had a cull, setting up a roadside stall to dispose of the ducks for roasting. The plucking proved difficult and time consuming, so they co-opted Norm to help with the selling, but, after one of his Collins Street patients stopped to buy, he bolted.

Norm proved much more useful at social gatherings. He was never less than engaging and entertaining—even shocking. He could make guests feel special. After a dinner party he might tackle some tunes on the piano, wearing a monkey mask and smoking a fat cigar. Artists, writers and musicians came to their relaxed soirees, held in Val and Norm's house. The furniture was casual and contemporary with clean lines and solid colours, far from the formal floral sofas which were the norm. There were benches instead of dining room chairs and placemats rather than a conventional tablecloth. Tableware was from the Boyds' pottery studio. They served wine with dinner, at a time when spirits were standard. Books were in abundance and a modest collection of artwork—pottery, paintings and small carvings and sculptures, often by their friends—enlivened the walls and tables.

Val and Von liked to call the Templestowe subdivision an 'Artists' Community'. Certainly, the sisters were now considering themselves serious artists and each had a studio. The other artistically inclined members among the residents were the Pykes, who, like the Cohen sisters, were wealthy, interesting, well-travelled and great fun. Polly collected fine art and did charity work—'She should have been an actress with her crazy sense of humour,' Val thought. Guelda studied commercial art and then design and pottery. She also made jewellery, printed fabrics and fashion accessories which were sold in Harrods in London and Georges in Melbourne. Just as war was declared, Guelda arrived in Bali to stay with a woman who introduced her to Balian art and arranged for her to study with an important woodcarver. The experience made her want to know more about art, as opposed to craft, so she signed on with George Bell in 1948 and stayed for six years, retaining a feel for texture and colour but always, she felt, struggling with form. Nonetheless, she achieved some success and her paintings from the Templestowe period are in major galleries.

In 1954, Guelda wanted to return to Bali. Things were unsettled on the Family Islands, so Von decided to join her. They sailed on the *Nieuw Holland,* stayed for three weeks or so, and returned in July with mats, baskets, paintings, pottery, carvings and bamboo furniture for their new Templestowe houses and for friends. In Bali, they sketched on the beach and stayed in Ubud with Cokorda Agung; a Balinese Raja and patron of local arts who was introduced by Melbourne friends. The two attractive Australians must have made quite an impression: Yvonne, tall and serene, and Guelda, petite and vivacious. Von told a reporter from the *Sydney Morning Herald*:

> We were able to use his puri (palace) as headquarters, and from there we travelled round the villages by car or bus, or we walked through the rice fields. Every village is famous for something—weaving, painting, carving. And we saw the artists—of all kinds—at work.

Two years later, on Val's forty-fifth birthday, Viva died at Templestowe. Their mother had always preferred their South Yarra flat to Templestowe, which she found isolated and too far from her friends. But on 10 July 1956 she was staying with Val and Norman, unpacking a few things, when the phone rang. Val left her to answer the call. Norman was always very accessible to his patients, and it was a call from one of his most demanding. When Val finally returned to her mother, she found her on the floor. Viva had suffered a cerebral haemorrhage and died that night. It was a relatively easy passing for Viva, but not for Val and Von, who again lost a parent without warning. Viva's funeral was at Spring Vale Crematorium, one among several indications that she (and her daughters) had long moved on from her traditional Jewish upbringing and marriage.

In about 1959, Val, Von and Norm travelled together to New Caledonia—getting away, sketching and enjoying the culture. Valerie wrote an account of the trip in the first person and as though she had travelled alone, as she often did in her writings:

> Noumea, the capital, is colourful with the faded pinks and textured white shutters of the French houses beside strong mustards and oranges … a fleet of bright blue buses, some displaying 'Tout Les Routes' … Somewhere on the edge of

town I discovered a Russian-French artist, his studio crammed with paintings and a collection of Pacific arts and crafts.

The trio stayed with a French-Vietnamese family, in a house high over the bays and inlets of Noumea, against a backdrop of spectacular mountains. They tried to find music venues and were disappointed to be told that there was not much classical, but some jazz. In the countryside, they were delighted to come across many native musicians strumming and singing their Pacific melodies.

In a Citroen hire-car, they meandered along the east coast to where the people still lived in tribal communities. In the villages, sprinkled along the shore and inland in the valleys, the main saleable crops were coffee and copra. Outside the huts, mats were piled high with coffee beans at various stages of drying. At an old French farmhouse turned hotel, with a cellar, fretted woodwork and stone walls, the host served them a memorable meal of fried sardines and oysters.

A vast nickel mine, with deposits of cobalt, iron and copper, stood 3000 feet above the valley. Driving up an impossibly steep, winding red road to the mine, the engine of the little Citroen nearly boiled. Then, on a Sunday—the day for church and sport back down the valley—Val observed that while the men scrambled on the football field, the women played basketball in their gaily-patterned 'Mother-Hubbards'. A line of pink hibiscus flowers across a road marked the end of a bike race. They came across a 'tribal picnic' on the beach, boys with long fishing spears and canoes, and asked if they could make sketches. 'It was always the same, the laughter and interest wherever I wanted to draw,' Val wrote. She filled one sketchbook with colourful landscapes—less structured than her usual style, seemingly influenced by the early paintings of Ian Fairweather—while Von mostly sketched the people.

The '50s were particularly productive artistically for the sisters and, as the decade proceeded, modern Australian art became more and more marketable. With their tropical period more or less over, the sisters completed paintings at a variety of localities around Melbourne, several of which were included in mixed exhibitions.

Enjoying occasional sales of their own artwork, they (with Norm) invested in a handful of paintings by artists they admired. For works by artists which are now viewed as significant, they paid similar prices to those achieved by their own sales. Val purchased a small pale-blue and white abstract by Roger Kemp, their colleague from the National Gallery School. Dated 1952, it was possibly bought at a group exhibition at the Stanley Coe Gallery in Bourke Street that year.

The sisters frequently exhibited through the 1950s. As was their father before them, both sisters were accepted as members of the Victorian Artists Society (VAS), revived after the Second World War by their great friend: fine watercolourist and *bon vivant*, Len Annois. For several years during the 1950s, the sisters contributed one or two paintings each to the VAS Spring and/or Summer exhibition, which were hung alongside those of their colleagues Murray Griffin, Eric Thake, Lina Bryans, Jock Frater, Dorothy Braund, Mary Macqueen, Barbara Brash and Frank Werther.

Von's artwork in particular often garnered favourable attention. In 1954, for example, her entry in the inaugural AH Gibson Prize, supported by art patron and businessman, Aubrey Gibson, was well-received. She entered again in 1957, submitting four works which, a report of the judging recorded, were singled out for 'special attention ... All these, in their different ways, are excellent' and she was praised for her 'formal approach and intricacies of textures'. The following year, she was over the moon when her oil of Templestowe, 'Orchard Country', shared first prize with a George Mansell watercolour, from a record number of entries at the VAS Spring exhibition. Comments in the press included 'Woman wins art prize' and 'Orchard Country ... earns its honor by the taste and care of its cubistically organised color and forms.' Both sisters entered in the prestigious Crouch Prize for Contemporary Art at the Art Gallery of Ballarat in 1958 and again in 1960 and in the latter year Von received a 'Highly Recommended' in the oil section, won by Charles Blackman.

As loyal followers of Bell, who thought politics and art did not mix, the sisters were not involved with the Contemporary Art Society of Victoria until 1959, when the presidency of Bell's nemesis, John Reed, ended. Reed's reign had been unsupportive of women artists who were marginalised, particularly in the selection process for exhibitions. The year 1959 appears to be the first that the sisters exhibited with the group, showing two oils each, which a critic for *The Age* described as 'distinctive'. That year also, Von had work accepted for the substantial McCaughey Prize at the National Gallery, the third year of the acquisitive competition. Respected art critic Chris Wallace-Crabb made special mention of three works which he considered the pick of the show, including one by Fred Williams and one by Von:

> Among the paintings which suggested a deeper kind of involvement, the most immediately striking was Yvonne Cohen's 'Tugs at Work'. With a palette limited to blacks and yellows, this artist had created a world of swirling activity in which the black man-made structures were caught up in a forceful movement of water, smoke, and sky. Though the painting had a couple of awkward patches, the intelligence of its conception was undeniable.

The sisters also sent work interstate to a mixed exhibition of paintings and monotypes by Melbourne women—Val and Von, Guelda, Barbara Brash, Nancy Grant, Lesley Lawson—at John Martin's Art Gallery in central Adelaide in June 1956. Here again it was Von's work which stood out to reviewers, with her bold 'native-and-landscape studies'. Val's 'interesting pattern and composition in descending planes' were admired in her painting 'The Church Corner', but the reviewer considered that finest work belonged to Guelda.

Among the other painters in the sisters' milieu was Dorothy (Dot) Braund. Braund was like a younger sister to Val and Von and would often use Val's studio at Templestowe. Viva was also very fond of Braund, and Pat Goldman, another lifelong friend of the sisters, even remembering them in her will. Braund, born in 1926, studied at the National Gallery School with Bell from 1946–1949. Later, after studying in England, she joined Bell's regular Thursday night studio get-togethers. She was a popular art teacher at three girls' schools, drawing on Bell's teaching ideas. Instead of applying the tight, traditional academic approach, she gave the girls big pots of paint and large surfaces. With Val in particular, Braund shared an impish sense of humour and enjoyed risqué conversation, particularly when there was an audience—the first and only time I met Braund, she and Val discussed in detail the flashers they had encountered over the years. When Braund moved to the Mornington Peninsula, after visits to the trio at Templestowe, Norman would often 'drive her home'. The arrangement seemed to suit everyone. Val was understanding: 'Dot loved sex', she explained.

Other close artistic friends were gallery directors Laurence Thomas and Robert Haines, and influential art critic and art historian Alan McCulloch; the latter often visiting them at Templestowe and, later, at Kew. McCulloch had introduced the sisters to the Boyds in the 1940s. In 1959, after dinner at Templestowe, Arthur Boyd, Cliff Last and a few others were sitting around the fire. Val asked Boyd whether he had seen 'Cray-pas'—smooth-textured, bendable oil pastels intended for children:

> He said, 'No.' So my husband produced some and they all started scribbling with Craypas, sitting on the floor round the fire. Cliff said to Arthur, 'Oh, that's not a bad one of yours, old bloke.' He said, 'Put your name on it. I wouldn't mind that.' So he said, 'Well, we'll do a swap.' So, all the stuff that they left on the floor, all their scribbles, I threw in the fire.

Towards the end of 1959, Boyd and his young family moved to London. Within six months he was receiving great acclaim for his 'Brides' series, which launched him internationally. Later in life, Val wished that she had been more prescient.

10

TAPESTRY TENNANTS

Timana

(1960–1969)

The sisters struggled on with a series of more or less unsuitable tenants and caretakers on Timana. They no longer employed a resident beachcomber-handyman to maintain the 'garden' and protect the buildings from day-trippers, campers, drug-runners and other trespassers—and nature. A 1964 article in *The Bulletin* described Timana as neglected, yet its potential as an own-your-own topic isle still beckoned:

> Timana … carries exclusiveness a bit far, locals and envious visitors feel. The two Victorian sisters (the former Misses Val and Yvonne Cohen) who own it haven't set foot on it for years. White ants now are eating the sign on Timana's slim sandspit which warns trespassers they will be prosecuted. An idyllic isle where natural water has yet to be discovered, its tanks are rusted and its beach is eroding. Only the charm of its freehold, meanwhile, remains unchanged.

Most of Timana's lessees were escapees from stricter social norms of the south and out of sight of the Queensland authorities: homosexual couples and romantics, seekers of bohemia or arcadia. Others were simply unsettled souls. Some were handy, but all had over-expectations and little understanding of the practicalities of life year-round on a reef-fringed tropical island. It didn't help that the sisters were tight with funding for tools and materials for repairs and replacements.

Into the '60s, the Dingles of Tully held the keys to the bungalow and apparently acted for the sisters when asked, but tenants seemed mostly to deal directly with Val, or occasionally Von, in Melbourne. Surviving letters from contractors and lessees most often dealt with the buildings' state of repair and general cleaning up. Whenever they could, the sisters did a deal. Under one such arrangement, Roy Langley, from Tully, holidayed there for twelve days over Christmas 1962 in exchange for maintenance work.

In the early 1960s, Roy Cator and his wife took over the Timana lease from Riches and Trennick. The Cators had been living on Green Island but grew unhappy with the ever-increasing numbers of tourists, from which Timana offered some refuge. They sailed to Timana intermittently, as part-time caretakers. In June 1963, Cator, having had difficulties accessing the island for some time, reported that the cottage was in bad repair and the boatshed and slipway had been undermined by high tides. The stove had rusted away, everything was overgrown and '… everyone makes it their port of call, little fires have been made all along the beach from campers.' The sisters needed a tenant, not a caretaker, Cator suggested.

The sisters took his advice and found a Mr and Mrs Collins, who agreed to live full time on Timana. However, the Collinses were in the process of trucking up their boat and furniture when Val sent Cator an urgent telegram saying, 'On no account give up key.' Apparently, the sisters had been alerted that, without their blessing, Collins was intending to sublet and had placed an advertisement in *The Courier-Mail.* Several people had arrived in Tully in response—one, a Brisbane hairdresser with wife and son, who had plans to build tourist cottages in partnership with Collins from the bamboo he had been told grew on the island (there is none). Needless to say, the Collinses did not get the key.

In September 1963, Guelda and two other of the sisters' friends, Brita and Mimi, stayed for ten days on the island. Brita wrote thanking Val for 'the heavenly holiday'. They had found the place shabby, but not as a bad as feared. They had spent a day with Noel, who still had his charms. Brita reported to the sisters that he was:

> ... a remarkably well preserved man, both mentally and physically, who took us over to Bedarra and showed us the Scott place which he looks after and also his own Robinson Crusoe hut, and the vegetable garden and the white chickens who eat coconut and Chinese cabbage!

Early spring was a good time to visit Far North Queensland. The weather was perfect and, Brita's letter continued:

> You will be pleased to know that we have a charming dugong, blowing steam from his nostrils in the bay, a huge green lizard named Jack Spratt in the pantry and this nice Italian named Johnny, as pets around the house.

Johnny, apparently, had simply dropped in, with a fish dangling from his hand and 'head full of philosophical thoughts of original sin'.

Sometime during 1964, the sisters received a letter from Bruce Arthur in Perth, enquiring whether Timana was available. Bruce was about to leave for Queensland to set up a cottage weaving business in the Cairns/Tully area. 'My wife and I weave home spun cloths,' he explained. They would be passing through Melbourne in October and he hoped to receive a positive response.

Von must have written to Noel, for, in April 1965, he sent her a letter telling her that Bruce had contacted him some time ago about his interest in Timana, but that he (Noel) had been slow in replying.

Presumably, the men had met immediately post-war, when Bruce took 'a year off from society' on Dunk Island.

Noel encouraged Von to take full-time tenants: 'I would suggest that it is urgent that someone inhabits the place.' He was anxious about the state of facilities on Timana: the white ants had taken over, the water tanks were rusted through and 'every door and window swings wide to the trade winds'. He recommended Ed De Hagen as an ideal beachcomber-come-caretaker, to 'chase pilferers, slash back the vines & generally clean up'. Indeed, he proposed, De Hagen could help Bruce rebuild.

Von soon received a lengthy letter from De Hagen, who was working on Dunk Island and had been shown around Timana by Noel. De Hagen introduced himself as a forty-seven-year-old former teacher who had dropped out to live a simpler life. His outlook, he claimed, was much like Noel's, and his needs modest: 'a patch of grass, a hut, a stream, a goat, a flute'. He offered his services as a live-in caretaker, but would first have to give notice at Dunk. At month's end, he wrote again, rocked by the sisters' telegrammed 'No' to his request to buy some tools on their behalf. In May, he let them know that he was ready to move to Timana, but that he was dependent on Noel and his boat for access. A few weeks later he wrote again suggesting a salary, use of the hut, the fruit and oysters in return for his care of the same. The increasingly demanding letters from De Hagen soon ceased and Bruce took on the lease of Timana, without a caretaker.

In July 1965, after being stuck for a week with gear box trouble at Bangalow, forty-four-year-old Bruce arrived at Timana; not with his legal wife, but with Deanna Conti, a fellow weaver over twenty years his junior. Meanwhile, their intended business partners, Gerry and Dale, had left for Hawaii to escape the possibility of conscription for the Vietnam War.

Bruce and Deanna had prepared for life on the island. They wrote to the sisters on paper decorated with a spinning wheel and the letterhead 'Brudea Folkweave', with the address Timana Island, via Tully. They visited the sisters at Templestowe and, much later, Val wrote of that first meeting:

> Deanna and Bruce came to Templestowe one morning having heard about Timana. They were living at Dunmoochin on the acres at Cottlesloe that Clif Pugh had made into a retreat for potters and painters. They were willing to rent our place in the sun where they wanted to weave tapestries and hopefully start a tapestry workshop.

If Bruce and Deanna were concerned that the sisters might be shocked by their relationship, or unmarried status, they were in for a pleasant surprise. Val and Von immediately liked the lively, interesting, creative couple. Richard Bruce Arthur had enjoyed many years in the spotlight as a successful amateur wrestler. Melbourne born (1921) and raised, and encouraged by his father from an early age, Bruce was soon winning junior championships. Before World War Two, he supported himself by working in a women's underwear store—'but no sissy is he', according to an article in Perth's *Daily News*. When war came, he signed on as a physical training instructor in the Australian Army, just as his father had done in World War One. Then, after time out on Dunk Island in 1946, he ran a 'frock shop', selling dresses made in the workshop of a fellow wrestler.

Bruce went on to become Australian and Victorian amateur middleweight champion, representing Australia in the 1948 London Olympics and two Empire Games, and winning a silver medal in the 1950 Empire Games, held in Auckland. Adding to his somewhat heroic persona, frock shops aside, while in Vancouver preparing for the 1954 Empire Games, he was sunbathing on a beach when he noticed a teenage girl being swept out to sea, rushed into the water and saved her. In 1955, Bruce turned professional, and the next year was he was employed as assistant coach of the wrestling team for the Melbourne Olympics. He then toured Australia and the South Pacific as 'Snow White', wrestling in matches that required more showmanship than skill. In the 1950s, he ran Bruce Arthur Health Studios in Exhibition Street, then Swanston Street, Melbourne, which offered: physical conditioning (body building, slenderising, get-fit courses for businessmen; pre-season training for swimmers and athletes, et cetera); male and female instructors (some of them ex-Olympic and Empire Games contestants); male and female studios; and tanning lamps and heat boxes. Bruce's actual wife, Vera Rene, nicknamed Peg, was one of the lean, good-looking instructresses.

Deanna had studied art and sculpture at RMIT. She was also born in Melbourne, in St Kilda, to one of the city's oldest and most highly regarded Italian families—her mother was Josephine Canestra and her father Gaetano Conti. Coincidentally, as the sisters were to discover, Deanna's maternal grandfather, Bartolo Canestra, bought a block of four flats, one for each of his children, in Ormond Road, Elwood; only one street back from No. 45 Ormond Esplanade, the house in which Val and Von grew up.

Deanna and Bruce made a handsome pair: he athletic, bearded, with tousled reddish-blonde hair; she petite, exotic, with a luxurious fall of dark hair. With her golden skin, black hair and dark eyes, Deanna was often likened to a Tahitian beauty. Slim and vivacious, she dressed with care in fitted dresses and colourful sarongs, even on the island. Bruce, convivial and charismatic, generally wore only in a sarong, tied casually around his hips. They had a three-year-old son, Aurelio.

Unlike all of the sisters' previous tenants, Bruce and Deanna soon adjusted to life on the island. Bruce was practical and made the place more liveable. They baked their own bread and made good use of the island's chooks, vegetables, fruits and abundant seafood. They bought a trimaran to sail to Dunk Island for mail, newspapers and a few necessary store-bought supplies, such as milk and kerosene, or to the mainland every few months for stores. Once a year they or so they visited the mainland to see art shows and artists and stock up on the latest books and magazines, classical music and art supplies.

Several journalists got wind of the newly arrived couple and gave them welcome publicity, but Bruce and Deanna would quickly tire of the trite 'Tarzan and Jane' and 'naked as jays'-themed stories, and of the gawkers: 'sightseers coming to see the oddballs', as Bruce described it.

While living at 'Dunmoochin', Bruce and Deanna dabbled in weaving, developing an interest in texture and thread. The intersection of art and craft appealed to Deanna and the physicality of weaving suited Bruce. When Deanna's loom arrived, she made some small wall hangings, building on traditional flat tapestry by adding three-dimensional elements, textures, layers and strong colours. The little hangings did not sell well, so the sisters lowered the rent, allowing Bruce and Deanna more time to establish their business. Brudea got a start by sending hand-spun wool garments, knitted coats, woven bags and the like to the Craft Centre in Melbourne. Their hand-made cards, shell necklaces and plaited palm products were sold at Dunk Island Resort.

Val and Von were enjoying their new artistic tenants. Their letters contained suggestions for saleable items and contacts, and they sent dress lengths for Deanna to sew, gadgets to amuse Aurelio, and reading material. A copy of Rachel Carson's *Silent Spring* made Deanna feel glad that she had escaped to an island.

In 1967, a company chaired by Eric McIlree—founder of Avis Rent-A-Car—bought the Dunk Island Resort. McIlree proposed building a museum to commemorate Edmund James Banfield, the island's original beachcomber. He gathered an impressive museum committee—Sir Raphael Cilento, President of the Royal Historical Society of Queensland; Alec Chisholm, naturalist, journalist, and author (both of whom had known Banfield); Professor Colin Roderick, of Townsville University; and John Busst, described as a Queensland artist. The chosen gathered on the island to make plans. For the occasion, Jack Louttit, who was to be the resident curator, painted a portrait of Banfield from a photograph taken the year before his death in 1923. Other invitees included Harold and Zara Holt, on their last winter escape together. That December, Holt, then the Australian Prime Minister, was to disappear mysteriously while swimming in the Southern Ocean near Portsea.

In Cairns, Bruce and Deanna met Louttit in Cairns. Then in his sixties, Louttit had retired after three decades as a master weaver at the prestigious Gobelin Atelier in France. For a time, he lived on Dunk Island and stayed on Timana, teaching the couple about dyes and '… how to weave tapestries like Persian carpets, hanging on huge looms, with twenty different shuttles if we want them,' Deanna recalled. With Louttit's help, they began to develop their skills and distinctive style and to seek commissions.

Although Timana had no running water, there were tanks and with annual rainfall of about 320 centimetres, 'ample water for the weavers to dye their wool', as Val wrote in an unpublished manuscript about their resident weavers:

> Their days are filled with spinning the raw wool sent direct from a Queensland station, dyeing it, and weaving. Their bungalow is blaze of coloured wools piled into home-made cane baskets … Spinning wheels and looms of various sizes are scattered on rush mats and their finished products hang against plaited palm walls ... Like the musician, sculptor and the painter, this century is endeavouring to find different modes of expression in the arts. A freedom has been born, one that never before has been so unrestricted and varied. And absorbed and given away. This is a new era for tapestry and new methods are being employed.

Slowly, Brudea began to receive interest in their larger weaving work. Deanna and Bruce were hopeful when, in 1966, art dealer Rudy Komon visited Timana to see Deanna's work. They became frustrated when, a year later, Komon was still supposedly approaching known artists such as Russell Drysdale and Leonard French for designs and

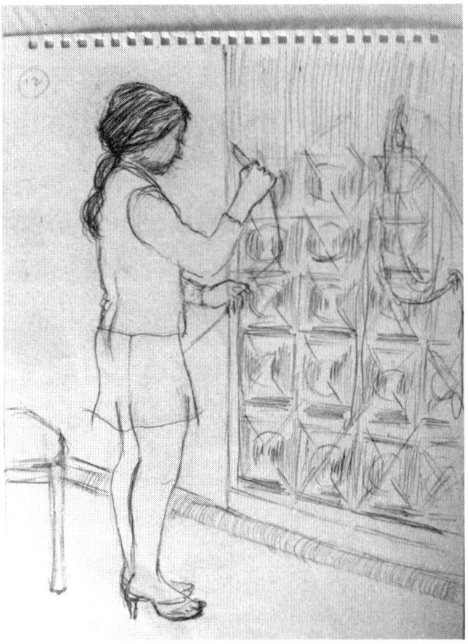

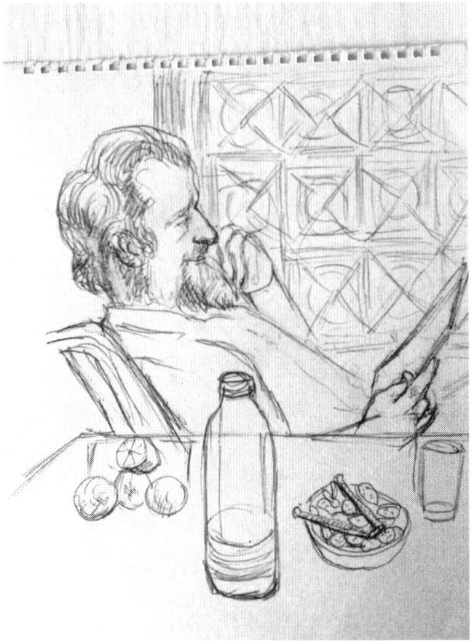

left: Deanna working on a large tapestry at Timana in the last half of the 1960s, sketched by Von

right: Bruce at the table, with Deanna's tapestry behind, sketched by Von. Private collection

planning an exhibition of the resulting tapestries. Deanna and Bruce needed income and worried that it was all too uncertain.

The news flowed south from Bruce, an entertaining and enthusiastic correspondent, when he found time: Timana's dire drinking water situation was unexpectedly relieved by an unsolicited, but very welcome delivery of 300 gallons by a navy survey boat, 'so we are saved'. Noel had stopped McIlree cutting down historic trees on Dunk island. Polly Pyke and friend made an 'untimely' visit to the island, causing chaos. The 'Marsh Flies, bloody dreadful things' had arrived and they had to live in 'little net tents' for a week. There was a glut of bananas, so they couldn't sell any, as the sisters had suggested. A Scot, one of the staff on Dunk, was helping them to spin wool, so they now had masses of wool hanging, 'all very gay'. Some of the locals had branded them communists for their political beliefs. And, to tease Norman, he averred that he, Bruce, was still chess 'champion' of the islands.

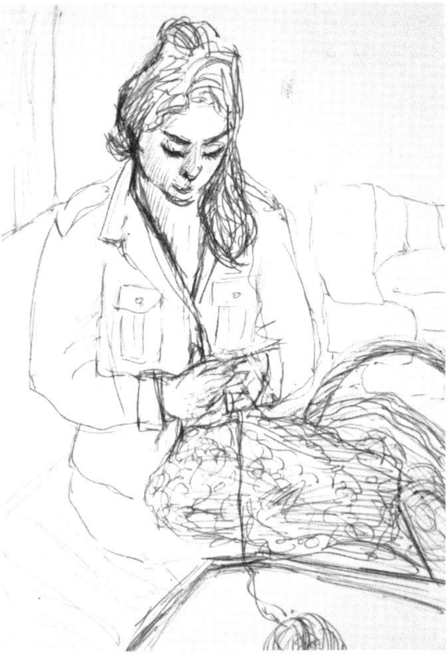
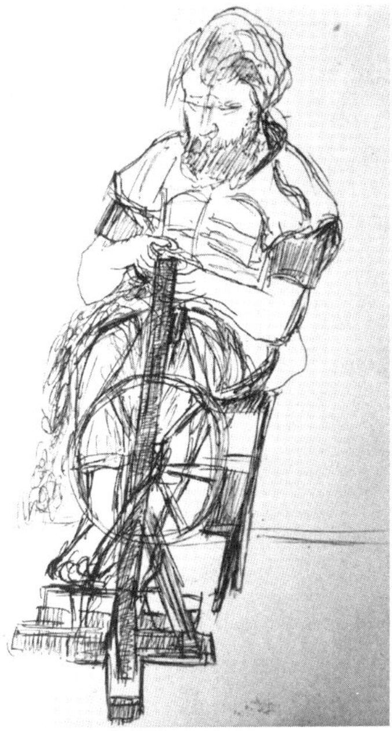

Sketches by Von of Deanna preparing wool and Bruce at the spinning wheel. Private collection

In 1967, a light plane crashed in the mangroves at the end of the spit. Hearing the engine, Bruce ran out to wave. For years, overflying planes had dropped a newspaper or bread, but this time the whole plane dropped, he blithely reported to the sisters—Aurelio couldn't believe his luck. The plane hit the water and bounced twice before overturning on the rocks. Three badly shaken men tumbled out. The pilot had given an incorrect location in his 'May Day' call, initially sending an armada of rescue boats and planes to the Barnard Islands to the north. Eventually, Timana's spit was alive with police, navy salvage personnel and locals intent on helping. Airforce Neptune and a dozen small planes buzzed overhead and boats sailed in from all over. The 'Timanians' salvaged some of the wreckage: '… engine cowling … nuts bolts … a high-powered sport rifle plus ammo from the pilot, one tomahawk and a fire extinguisher.' For once, visitors to the island were exciting, not unwelcome. By November, though,

Bruce was grateful for the 'dead quiet'. A cyclone was gathering off the Solomon Islands—'but let's not ponder on that issue, we couldn't cope with three major events: Polly, a crash and a cyclone,' he joked. They battened down in expectation of Cyclone Annie, but it passed them by.

By May 1968, Brudea had several large commissions underway. Bruce had constructed looms using water pipes, strung from the ceiling and attached to the floor. These horizontal looms allowed greater improvisation than was possible with more orthodox, vertical loom used by Aubusson, famous since the fourteenth century for its tapestries. The couple began to source special wool in Tasmania and to import dyes from Switzerland. They spun the wool unevenly, which added an unpredictable element to their designs.

They began to mentor young artists, including American Jerry Wallace, on a scholarship from Sweden, and Dale Beck, a Batik expert from Hawaii, who helped them dye and weave.

Bruce's letter of August 1968 carried excited news of the visit of 'Tass' (Russell) and Maisie Drysdale and plans for a big tapestry starting in the New Year, but only if Drysdale—a 'beaut bloke'—could get backing. Shortly after, under the watchful eye of the police, the new Prime Minister John Gorton and his wife Bettina visited Timana from the Dunk Island resort. Whatever Bruce and Deanna had hoped for, that meeting proved a 'dead loss'. Bruce wrote that he and Deanna were not long back from Sydney where they had confronted Komon, 'the monster', for too much talk and too little action, and Bruce thanked the 'dreadful girls' (quoting Val's own words) for doing likewise. He and Deanna had returned to the island, full of hope, to find a boatload of press arriving at the beach. They were covering the launch of the book *My Life and Harry* by Zara Holt—now Dame Zara—and demanded an interview. 'If you don't give us a story we'll invent one, or write local gossip,' they reportedly cajoled the tapestry makers.

As well as reporters, the allure of tropical landscapes, lifestyles and distance from southern restrictions continued to attract novelists,

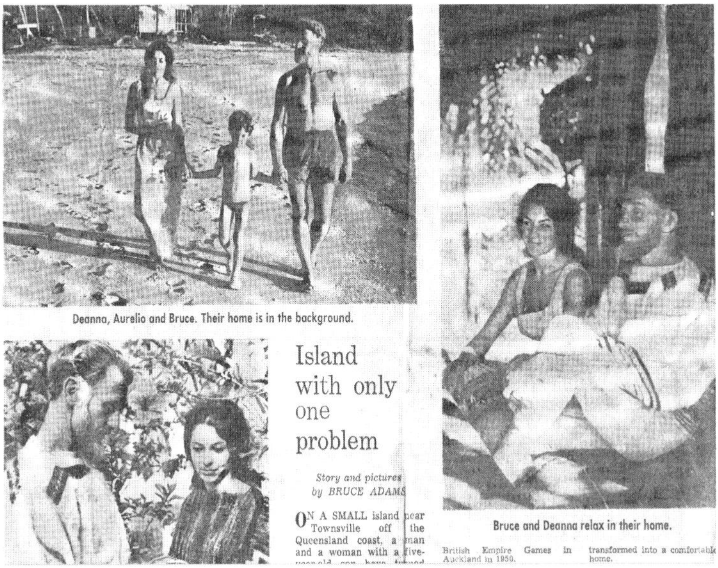
Deanna, Aurelio and Bruce. Their home is in the background.

Island with only one problem

Story and pictures by BRUCE ADAMS

ON A SMALL island near Townsville off the Queensland coast, a man and a woman with a five-

Bruce and Deanna relax in their home.

British Empire Games in Auckland in 1950.

transformed into a comfortable home.

Deanna and Bruce with their son Aurelio in 1967 and 1970, when interest in their unusual craft and lifestyle even reached London. *The Australian* 11 May 1967

artists and the occasional film-maker. Dunk Island was the setting for Maxwell Grant's 1980 book, *Barrier Reef*—a thriller that deals with the illicit trafficking of drugs into Australia and live birds out. Dunk, Grant wrote, was '... one of those idyllic places one is always longing to find.' In 1968, the island was the main setting for the film *Age of Consent*, directed by controversial UK film-maker Michael Powell. Powell's previous film, *Peeping Tom*, had caused a furore and *Age of Consent* had the coy 1960's censors demanding cuts. The film starred James Mason and introduced British ingénue, Helen Mirren. Mason played a jaded artist who retreats from New York to a tropical island. On the island, he finds Mirren, a nubile teen, who becomes his model and muse. Noel, a mature artist rarely without a younger woman in tow, could easily have been the inspiration for the film, but it was based on bohemian artist-writer Norman Lindsay's semi-autobiographical story of the same title. During filming, Mason, w co-producer as well as the lead actor, often escaped to th studio on Timana, where he found Bruce to be an entertaining and convivial host.

As ever, the peace-seeking people of the islands were embroiled in various human dramas. The islands were attracting more and more tourists and Bruce was only half serious with his statement to his landladies that they would soon have to 'barbwire the spit' to keep at bay uninvited visitors to Timana. There were plans which he and Deanna feared would overdevelop the Dunk Island resort. Noel too was claiming that it was all getting so crowded that he planned to sell his portion of Bedarra.

About that time, Noel was involved in a five-year relationship with Elizabeth (Betty) Kendall, a Sydney socialite and the daughter of a judge. Kendall wrote regular beauty and hostessing/entertainment columns for (English) *Vogue* magazine. For a year or two, Noel and Kendall lived across the island from Doorila Bay in the very comfortable, spacious mud-brick house and studio built by John Busst. They served as caretakers for the current owner, Colin Scott, a grazier from Gippsland. When Noel's daughter Ann visited with her husband, on leave from his job in Papua New Guinea, they met Kendall. Ann remembers that Kendall, who was probably in her late forties:

> [She] had a good skin and when she and Dad picked us up in Tully and we got on his boat, both of them smothered their faces in the placentas (of some animal—I think goats) which had been made into a skin cream by a friend of Dads.

In interviews, Noel almost never admitted that he had a family, so Ann was pleased when Kendall told her that Noel had proudly shown her some clippings of Ann which he had saved from *Australasian Post*. She was far from pleased with the magazine, though. Without her permission, they had made her the cover girl of the 17 March 1960 edition, and another photograph of her was used inside on 9 February 1961. Both issues described her as a seventeen-year-old

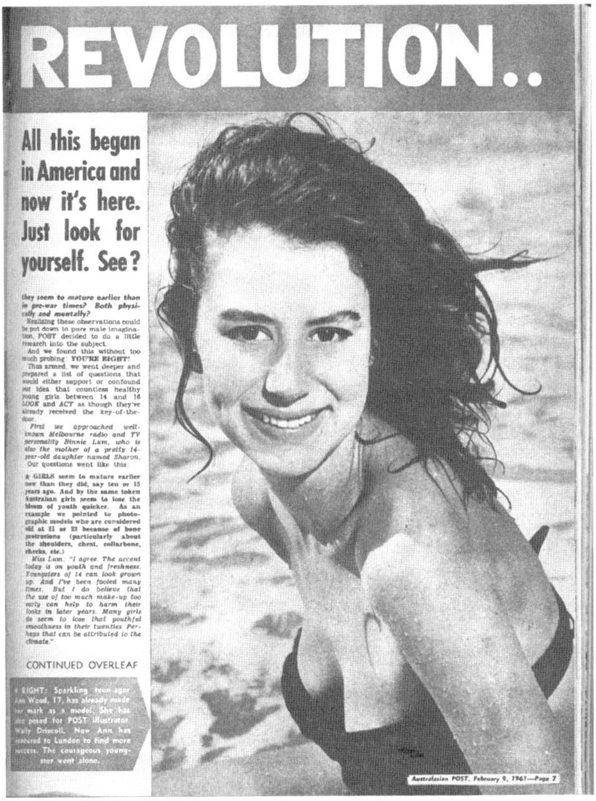

REVOLUTION..

All this began in America and now it's here. Just look for yourself. See?

they seem to mature earlier than in pre-war times? Both physically and mentally?

Realising these observations could be put down to pure male imagination, POST decided to do a little research into the subject.

And we found this without too much probing: **YOU'RE RIGHT!**

Thus armed, we went deeper and prepared a list of questions that would either support or confound our idea that countless healthy young girls between 14 and 16 *LOOK* and *ACT* as though they've already received the key-of-the-door.

First we approached well-known Melbourne radio and TV personality Binnie Lum, who is also the mother of a pretty 14-year-old daughter named Sharon.

Our questions went like this:

★ GIRLS seem to mature earlier now than they did, say ten or 15 years ago. And by the same token Australian girls seem to lose the bloom of youth quicker. As an example we pointed to photographic models who are considered old at 21 or 22 because of bone protrusions (particularly about the shoulders, chest, collarbone, cheeks, etc.)

Miss Lum: "I agree. The accent today is on youth and freshness. Youngsters of 14 can look grown up. And I've been fooled many times. But I do believe that the use of too much make-up too early can help to harm their looks in later years. Many girls do seem to lose that youthful smoothness in their twenties. Perhaps that can be attributed to the climate."

CONTINUED OVERLEAF

RIGHT: Sparkling teen-ager Ann Wood, 17, has already made her mark as a model. She has also posed for POST illustrator Wally Driscoll. Now Ann has ventured to London to find more success. The courageous youngster went alone.

Australasian POST, February 9, 1961—Page 7

Ann Wood, Noel's daughter, featured in an article on girls maturing earlier post-war. Described as a 'courageous youngster', seventeen and off to London alone, she was actually in her early twenties. *Australasian Post* 9 February 1961, p. 7

model—she was neither of those things and felt violated. Years later, she enjoyed hearing that '… a male schoolfriend of mine, who was in the highlands of New Guinea in 1960 … saw a local man roll his own cigarette and smoke me!'

A November 1968 note from Deanna to Val and Von, enclosed with a more fulsome letter from Bruce, revealed that they had been on the mainland again, staying with the Drysdales. Russell had lots of 'good tales' to share—and visiting mills and dye places and agents around Sydney. As well as a tapestry for Drysdale, Deanna was excited that she would soon be weaving one for Leonard French. Unlike the other dithering artists and agents, she wrote to the sisters, within ten minutes French had negotiated a price and details. The weavers returned to the island reinvigorated. Bruce's letter got down to the practicalities: they had returned to the island early because their temporary caretaker had taken off—'he couldn't stand it'. All their vegetables had died and half the chooks were gone, but, on the upside, they were home and had ample weaving work to tackle.

Previously, Australian artists had sent their designs overseas to be woven. Now John Olsen was expressing interest in engaging Brudea Studio. Initially, he had no money and, according to Bruce, he was a hopeless romantic with a phobia of hard edges. Nonetheless, Olsen came good with a commission. By March 1969, Deanna and Bruce had finished a 'very good' piece for him: 'Western World', a densely textured tapestry, with thick hanks and skeins of wool woven into and over the surface and twigs and other natural items incorporated. At the same time, they completed French's design, which had '20 colours, hard for the dyer, but beautifully set out'. French was working on a series for them to weave. Frank Werther, too, had been to Timana and 'did a great design whilst here'.

Brudea, the unlikely tropical tapestry workshop, was now producing substantial hangings. Each took about five or six months to weave and 120 to 130 pounds of wool. Their rugged, informal construction was in touch with the move in the 1960s and 1970s from traditional flat tapestries to more informal, organic craftwork; to soften the concrete walls and clean lines of the architecture of the period. For a time, as Australia's only tapestry workshop, Brudea became a hive of creative activity.

The workshop may have been busy, but business was still unpredictable. Olsen wanted to return to the island in May 1969 for four weeks to work on two large hangings, provided it fitted in with the sisters' planned trip north. Come July, when Rudy Komon notified the weavers that their long-promised exhibition would not be until 1970, Bruce railed that the dealer was '... a Bastard as well as a Vulture ... because he has been the main hold-up.' Then there was Drysdale, who telegrammed at the last minute to cancel a visit. 'You see what unreliable bastards we are dealing with,' Bruce wrote in annoyance to the sisters.

Bruce and Deanna's relationship with Val, Von and Norm continued to be warm and supportive. Bruce kept the sisters well-informed, often beginning his letters with 'Dear Three', and the three continued to holiday on Timana most years for as long as a month. They camped in Nugget's bamboo cottage, to which Bruce had added a small extension. Eventually, much to Von's delight, he replaced the hole in the ground with a flushing seawater toilet. Val, of course, would never admit to enjoying such creature comforts. Occasionally, Von stayed longer, and Bruce and Deanna ferried her across to visit Noel on Bedarra. They all enjoyed the lively discussions about society, sex, art, books, music and island life, and Bruce and Norm enjoyed their chess challenges.

The five friends all had a mischievous sense of humour; double-entendres and sexual innuendo ranked highly. 'Dear Frozen Ones', Bruce wrote fondly in August 1968, after the three had been up for their annual visit. He was missing Norm's '… perverted filthy yarns … which I absolutely hate intensely, but wish I could recall all the same.' Next year, Bruce promised, he would be sure to '[keep] Norm under control and … hide the muscat'. Von kept a little diary of quips and exchanges she particularly enjoyed, including Bruce warning her: 'Von, don't do what you did last time and fall off the back of the boat,' to which she had replied, 'No, I'll hang on to your thing.' 'What,' Bruce replied, 'all the way there and back?'

A Christmas letter from Bruce, thanking the sisters for their gifts, playfully enquired whether they had told Norman of their confessed '… drunken orgies, a disgrace to the "uptight" citizens of Templestowe. In fact it confirms the tales I have heard in this area over the years.' Most likely, Norm would have been well aware of and titillated by the sisters' earlier escapades.

For some years the happy arrangement worked well. Bruce maintained the main bungalows, kept everything in good order, gardened, fished and helped with the wool and looms, and Deanna did much of the actual weaving. The sisters and Norm were well-looked after on their annual holiday. Much later, Val wrote of those happy days:

> Soon they [Bruce and Deanna] were able to claim back the garden from the jungle. They placed a notice on the spit, which said 'PRIVATE KEEP OUT', because they didn't want callers, but undisturbed days to work ... In the old house Deanna created a curtain of shells that acted as the front door. The lower level of the house scintillated with the colored wools they hung from the rafters to dry in the sea breeze, or piled up on the floor, or in baskets woven from the island's lawyer cane. They worked from early morning until sunset, leaving little Aurelio to amuse himself with pencils and crayons. He was a self-sufficient and clever child, lonely in some ways, but rich in his love of the environment, something he never lost, even when he went to school in Townsville.
>
> Bruce helped with the dyeing of the wools. The dyes were all imported from Europe. The weight of the wet wool was far too heavy for Deanna to handle alone. Bruce also kept house in repair, oiled the verandahs, cleaned the strainers in the tanks and watched for white ants. He kept a patch cleared for vegetables. He rowed out to the coral caps and dived for fish.
>
> Our three weeks holiday often stretched longer. Both Bruce and Deanna made us most welcome ... Bruce built a stone fireplace under the house, around which we would all congregate for the evening meal, which consisted of endless varieties of fish which Deanna insisted on cooking.

Come Easter 1969, Aurelio was home from his first term at boarding school in Townsville—the Dunk Island pilot gave him a lift. He arrived 'shorn and in full rig including a felt hat', and unhappy about returning to school, which created some parental doubts. Bruce worried that he was being taught 'all the old Dogmas', so they considered finding a teacher nearby. Ultimately, however, they were too busy with commissions and Aurelio remained a boarder. The next school break, he came home with a friend and thereafter, he was settled at school and there was never any shortage of boys who were keen to spend their holidays on the island.

In October 1969, Bruce and Deanna were on the mainland in Sydney. One of Deanna's tapestries, 'Cycles of Life', had been accepted for the Transfield Prize and the couple were photographed for *The Australian* in front of the work. As ever, the attractive pair, with the 'idyllic' lifestyle, made good newspaper fodder. They were 'not utopian escapists or nut cases', a reporter for *The Australian* wrote. Rather, Deanna, told him, '… social anarchy is the only system that can survive on a little island.' As ever, Deanna was referred to coyly as Bruce's wife. The following September, Bruce was divorced from Peg, his legal wife of twenty years, after his father hired a private detective, who got evidence that *she* was in a relationship with someone else. Bruce and Deanna, however, had no plans to marry.

From the exhibition, Deanna travelled on from Sydney to Melbourne, where she saw friends and family and spent a day with Val, Von and Norm, who took her to see the sensational new musical *Hair*. In a thank-you note to the three, she wrote that she was keen to get back to Timana, away from the 'rat race', and the 'lonely people' with their 'anxious faces'.

11

TROUBLE ON TIMANA

Timana

(1970–2006)

More commissions flowed to Brudea Studio from leading artists, including Leonard French, Clif Pugh, Frank Werther, John Coburn and Tibor Hubay. Deanna worked from their cartoons—blown up designs, usually watercolours, with instructions on colours and textures—interpreting rather than imitating. Kenneth Baillieu Myer, arts patron and member of the Melbourne retailing family, and Henry Ford, the founder of Ford Motor Company, commissioned designs by Deanna herself. An international judge of the Transfield Prize, James Fitzsimmons had admired Deanna's entry, which helped her get solo exhibitions in Sydney and Melbourne. Brudea was buzzing.

In the first month of 1971, Cyclone Gertie blew in unexpectedly: the sirens woke Bruce at 4am and he and Deanna rushed about, battening down and securing the boat before huddling in their cyclone shelter. It was a relief when Gertie changed course, leaving them to deal with a fierce wind, but undamaged. About the same time, Ford's group, holidaying on Dunk Island, left Dunk with a tapestry—one of Deanna's own designs titled 'Pawn in their Game'—without paying.

However, Bruce wrote to the sisters, 'Brudea stole it back at Cairns airport', where Ford paid up and the tapestry left for the USA. Before leaving, Ford's group had also caused a storm at the resort, Bruce reported: 'After catching Henry rooting in the pool with a leading lady ... Bedlam! ... Mrs. Ford screaming ... it gets worse and worse.'

The occasional letter betrays that trouble was also brewing between the tapestry-makers and the sisters, initially over the cost of items to repair the house and, later, over rent. In April 1971, Val penned Bruce a terse 'business letter' voicing concern over their 'lax financial arrangements', claiming that the sisters viewed rental of the island as a business and threatening (bluffing) that there was a 'line-up' of people ready to take his place. Bruce responded that he too was worried about the unpredictability and was keen for a long lease. A full-blown storm was avoided, and Deanna and Bruce stayed on.

In June 1971, Bruce's letter to Templestowe opened: 'Dear People, Well—things go on. John Busst dies. Noel happy.' Noel had never forgiven Busst for his grab for Noel's land—nor had the sisters. The other news was that Pugh and his wife Judith had been on Timana for two weeks. Pugh had been commissioned to paint a portrait of McIlree, the owner of the Dunk Island resort—at that time world famous and attracting international celebrities such as Sean Connery, magnates like Henry Ford, and Australian Prime Ministers. While Pugh sketched and painted, he and the weavers worked together to turn one of his cartoons into a tapestry. Being a physical person, Pugh enjoyed weaving items into the wool to add texture. In Judith's autobiography, she recalled of the time:

> Timana was a peaceful place, precisely a tropical island: utterly white sand, jungle beyond, the waves hypnotic rhythm. The only incongruous element feral hens. When they'd arrived, as egg producers, they'd been normal sized, but had more than doubled as the generations fed on the rich tropical undergrowth.

Judith may have found the island getaway peaceful, but there were tensions, like tourists, everywhere. The relationship was cool between Timana's tenants and the manager of the luxury resort on Dunk Island. Still, Brudea was a business, so they opened the workshop to tourists once or twice a week.

That October, Deanna was in Sydney, photographed at an exhibition of her own work at Bonython Galleries. As was often the case, a reporter from *The Sydney Morning Herald* commented on her striking appearance: '[She] looked very much the island princess. In a simple, long white dress and copper slave jewellery, she wore a wreath of pink flowers in her curly black hair.' Just previously, the tapestries had been shown at Deanna's first 'one-man show', in the Joseph Brown Gallery in her hometown of Melbourne. The fourteen pieces ranged in size up to two metres in length and were promoted as being made from Australian wool. All were coloured with fast and fadeless Swiss dyes, with moth and silverfish repellent incorporated during the dyeing. A reviewer for *The Australian* described them as:

> … gay with three-dimensional geometric variations in brilliant colours of yellow, purple, hot pink, orange, green and red played against overlays of copper and dangling clusters of plaited and stranded wool which combine to make decorative and imaginative contemporary designs.

In that winter of 1972, Keith Willey, a writer for *Walkabout*, stayed at the resort, reporting that '… even though today the tourists are everywhere … it is still a paradise, but it has yielded to the tourists' demand to be castaways—with luxury on tap.' He described a memorable visit to Brudea. Entering the bungalow through a curtain of linked shells, surrounded by looms and tapestries. he found Bruce, the '… muscular ex-wrestler with a blond beard and surprisingly … the pale skin of one who spends much time indoors.' Bruce, who distrusted reporters, looked put out. Deana didn't appear. Apparently, she preferred the company of 'selected friends, mostly artists and chess-players'.

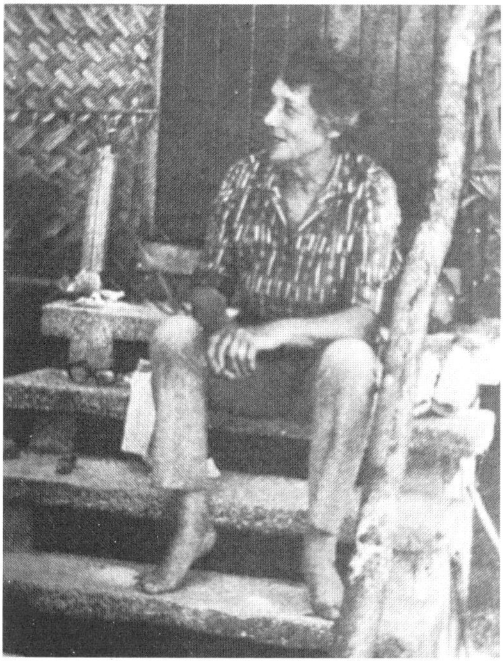

Val on the steps of Nugget's renovated bungalow on Timana in 1972, talking to a reporter from *Walkabout* magazine; her statements regarding Dunk Island caused a stir. *Walkabout* 1 October 1972, p. 24

Willey discovered that Val and Von were holidaying on their island, 'living in a native-style thatched hut they had helped to build', nestled among the trees. Von proudly stated: 'We don't cut anything down. We just plant. There were no coconut trees here until we came.' Val added, 'The Torres Strait pigeons come back each year. We have metallic starlings and white cockatoos here all the time.' *They* looked after their island; the neighbours, however, were a problem. Val launched into a tirade about the rubbish she believed drifted across from Dunk Island; tins and bottles which, she claimed, took up to two hours to pick up each morning. She was on a roll, continuing:

> The coral around here used to be so beautiful, but now it's all dead. I blame the pollution from mainland rivers. When the resort people extended the airstrip on Dunk they put the bulldozers through an Aboriginal burial ground. It's revolting, quite unforgiveable. We used to be thrilled when we saw a boat, but now they're always whizzing about. The

> privacy is gone. Having this island is like owning a beautiful jewel which you can never replace, never want to lose. We have made it a sanctuary so at least something from the past can be kept.

Asked what she thought Edmund Banfield would say if he returned to his beloved beaches, Val replied, 'I think he would be horrified.'

Straight after the article appeared, Bruce Smee, the Director of Resort, sent *Walkabout* a strong rebuttal. He stated that they had a robust rubbish disposal service at the resort and there was no evidence of any burial grounds near the airstrip. Nor did he think Banfield would be horrified. He had a witness, none other than writer Alec Chisholm: '... unquestionably one of Australia's leading conservationists and lifelong friend of Edmund Banfield, has regularly visited Dunk and has had nothing but praise for the way in which we have developed and are operating the island.'

After their visit to the islands, the sisters must have known that the relationship between Deanna and Bruce was in peril. Bruce was easy-going, but he had a short fuse and a wandering eye. He had fallen in love with Joanne Sivyer and, in late 1971, while Deanna was on the mainland, she moved in with Bruce and Deanna shifted to Nugget's bungalow. The little island had suddenly become very crowded.

The following year, Bruce and Deanna were trying to work together and Bruce, who acted as their agent, portrayed Deanna as 'an independent tapestry weaver, who works for her own shows'. Some of her work was hung in Adelaide, at the Festival of the Arts held at the Art Gallery. Bruce's letter south in October 1972 was, as usual, full of news, but not of their personal issues. John Olsen had just left the island, where he worked on appliqués to his latest tapestries, including one called 'Timana' that was about to be sent to Komon for sale, and the ABC had been there filming Olsen in the rainforest.

Olsen, Bruce reported to the Templestowe three, had given them a new recipe for pickled eggs and they had finally been able to introduce him to Noel: 'bloody good—a wonderful meeting, sunk much red, etc., under the palms'. There had been no rain and they were carting water. Not least, world-famous photographer Wolfgang Sievers was staying on Bedarra with Noel. Sievers had arrived from New Caledonia on an outrigger with 'two Red Setters & bird', the latter not of the feathered kind. His selfies show that he was happy conforming to the naked, island-loving, bohemian stereotype that Bruce and Deanna had sought to avoid.

Bruce enclosed two eighteen-dollar cheques (about $220 each in 2023 values), covering the rent for September and October 1972. But all remained unsettled on Timana and Bruce's letters to Templestowe became less frequent. Val remembered:

> After one serious disagreement Deanna landed at Templestowe with nothing more than what she was wearing. Their reconciliation wasn't to last. With the next upset, Bruce tipped Deanna out of the house, and threw all her tapestries into the rain. She was forced to retire to Nugget's shack. Bruce then refused her food. It was an appalling period for her. Finally Bruce slunk over to Dunk, rowing off in their flattie, leaving Deanna destitute. She was used to the island, so she managed for the next few weeks until a cheerful young German called Bert, who was working as a carpenter on Dunk, happened to call in. Eventually he moved in. He had a large boat in which he intended sailing the world—instead he stayed.

In fact, it was Deanna who fled Timana in about mid-1973. She was surprised to be rebuffed when she sought refuge at her friend Colin Scott's house on Bedarra and moved to the mainland, where Bert—who the weavers had actually known for some time—came to her rescue. Bert, Herbert Eichblatt, was kind, down-to-earth and practical. He built Deanna a temporary hut so that she could complete tapestries for her forthcoming Melbourne exhibition, due in September 1973, but delayed until March 1974. He also acted on her behalf, visiting

Timana to collect her half of the wools and dyes, with limited success. Joanne, backed by Bruce, claimed that they were keeping them to cover Deanna's share of expenses.

The sisters took Deanna's side, sending instructions for Bruce to vacate Timana by 1 August 1973. Bruce argued that he had several large commissioned tapestries on the loom that he needed to finish before he could move and, reluctantly, Val extended the lease until Christmas. Val suspected he was stalling and looked into increasing the rent to put pressure on him. Come November 1973, Bruce was still living on Timana, but soon after, with a strong push from Melbourne, he vacated.

In the meantime, June 1973, Fred Williams, a highly successful artist and etcher, arrived to holiday with his family on Bedarra. Williams was immediately seduced by the sun, sand, sea and rainforest, writing in his diary:

> We are dropped on a superb beach and walk up this track to our cabin. It is a simply magnificent island and my eyes are about to drop out, just looking at the different shapes and so on … I had no idea the island could be so perfect.

The lush landscapes of the Family Islands inspired Williams and he painted several goaches of both Bedarra and Timana, including a serene strip triptych of Timana rising gently from the sea. In the midst of the turmoil on Timana, perhaps unaware of it, Williams organised for one of his gouaches of Bedarra's rich rainforest to be interpreted in tapestry, deciding to highlight the vibrant vegetation by placing it against a black background. Bruce completed the weaving in 1974, after he had left Timana and Deanna for Dunk and Joanne. On Dunk, he set up a new atelier, 'The Good Shepherd', taking with him Brudea's outstanding commissions. When Jill Gray, a reporter for *The Age*, dined with Bruce and Joanne on Dunk that June, an Olsen and a Werther were on the loom.

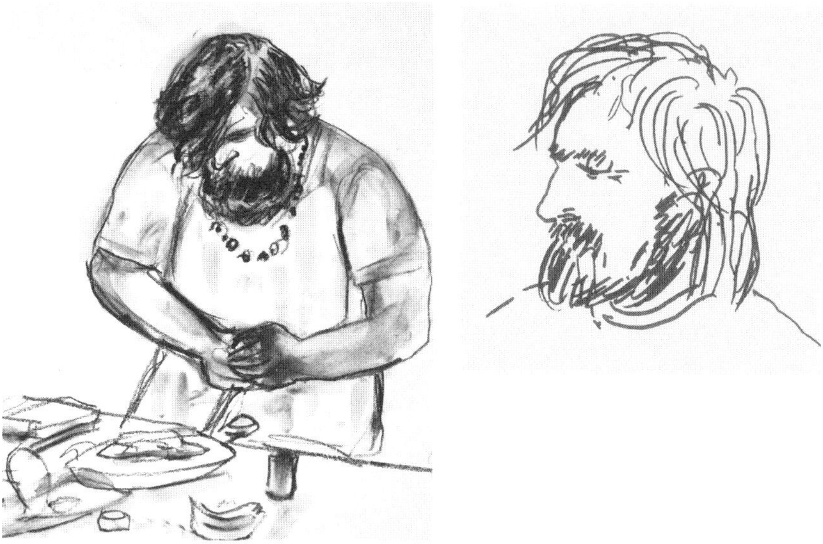

Charcoal sketches by Von of Bruce, who vacated Timana for Dunk Island in 1973, and Bert, Deanna's new partner after she took on the lease of Timana. Private collection and Heide Museum of Modern Art, 2004.141, Melbourne. Gift of Valerie Albiston 2004 ©Estate of Yvonne Cohen

Deanna took on the lease of Timana and Bert again stepped in to help. As Bruce had, he made looms and assisted Deanna to dye the heavy wet wool, boiled over a driftwood or coconut-shell fire. But Deanna now had to take on responsibility for the other aspects of the business which Bruce had managed, such as sales, ordering materials and preparing the wool. With his strong promotional skills, Bruce had better success setting up and promoting his own workshop, which the *Australasian Post* erroneously reported was 'the original and first tapestry weaving workshop in Australia'!

Perhaps Brudea was doomed regardless. It was not long—1976—before the Victorian Tapestry Workshop (now Australian Tapestry Workshop) opened and interest in the northern workshops waned. Bruce and Deanna's heyday, working with the big artists, was all but over. It was more convenient for prominent artists to deal with weavers in Melbourne.

Still, Deanna exhibited her own designs again in 1975, at Manyung Gallery, Mount Eliza. She had commissions from architects and institutions and was invited to compete in the Swiss Biennale, but her income was meagre. As Val remembered of the late 1970s:

> Bruce by then had found himself a corner of Dunk where like the old guru with his long white beard and endless stream of willing females he set up a rival tapestry centre. Deanna had arranged for interested tourists from Dunk to drop in and look at her work—she made small pieces especially for that market.

On the southern end of Dunk Island, in a bay just across the water from Timana, Bruce built a mud-brick house and eventually drew a small group of artists—a painter, glass artist, sculptor and jeweller—around him. As Val had observed, he always had a young woman to weave for him. After Deanna, it was Joanne and, by 1979, seventeen-year-old Robin Laver, known as Robin Lighthouse, because she had grown up in one. Then in his late fifties, Bruce was still in good shape physically and presented a relaxed, easy-going charm. Nancy Lowe, from Mission Beach Water Taxi, whose mother looked after the Dunk Island resort manager's children and whose father was the chef, remembers him as a loveable tease, a bit of a rogue, who would fill her with horror with his teasing prediction that when she grew up, she would be 'a weaver's moll'.

Val's first article for the new arts magazine, *Artlook*, in December 1978, was an attempt to promote Deanna and her weaving. It was written as though they had just met, even though they had known each other well for thirteen years. Tapestry was making a comeback, Val wrote—an exhibition of the work of the late, inspirational Jean Lurcat, leader in the revival of contemporary tapestry, had toured Australia in 1973 and institutions were buying large tapestries to grace their halls. As Deanna explained, '... wool is a sound absorbing material which all helps in today's concrete and steel constructions.'

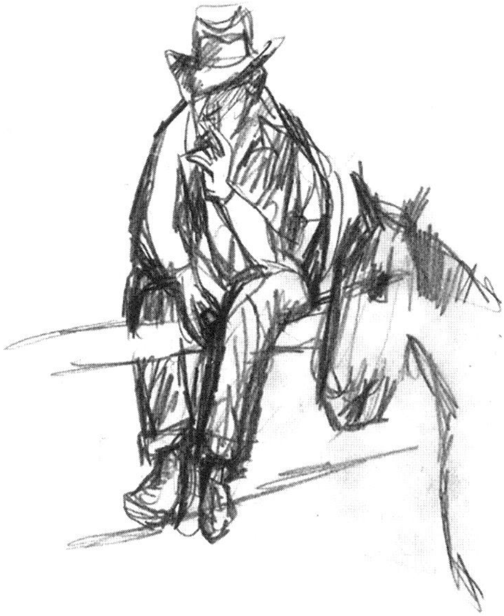

One of several charcoal sketches by Von at Mareeba rodeo, a fertile ground for colourful subjects. Private collection

Deanna's greatest concern, according to Val, was getting a finished tapestry safely off the island: '… the weather can be very tricky, so it has to be well packed.' In reality, Deanna had more than that to contend with, with a rival workshop a few kilometres across the water and another in Melbourne.

As the 1970s progressed, the sisters still occasionally made the winter trip to the islands. They were beginning to feel their age and Norm no longer accompanied them. In the latter half of the 1970s, on the return journey, they had time to fill at Townsville. They found a dilapidated old boat tied up at a dock and began sketching it. After a while, the owner, an old salt, came over to see what they were doing. According to Val, the conversation went as follows:

> 'I don't go out in her much these days … I used to go up those islands around Dunk in here. Once I dropped off a boat to an island there near Dunk where two young girls lived', he told us. We looked at each other, wrinkled and white-haired, unable to admit it was us.

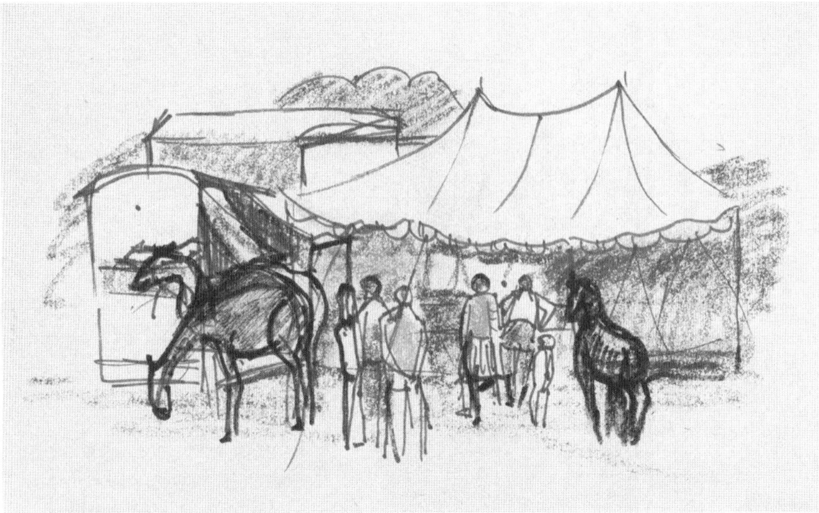

A sketch by Val at Mareeba rodeo, or similar event, enjoyed by the sisters during their winter trips north. Fibre-tipped pen and pastel, Heide Museum of Modern Art, 2002.43, Melbourne. Gift of Valerie Albiston 2002 ©Estate of Valerie Albiston

While they were in the north, Val and Von sometimes headed to Mareeba for the annual rodeo; a highlight for many in the region. They liked the colour and diversity, the stalls and rides, and the excitement of the competition. Von enjoyed sketching the Aboriginal peoples. They attended one last time:

> Mareeba rodeo took place once more, with its colourful crowds … My sister and I had been discussing disposing of the island because of the enormous changes … The journey north each year was becoming arduous, especially for my elderly husband. I had no desire to visit without him.

In about 1977 or 1978, Val and Von put Timana on the market, leaving it with an agent in Townsville and offering a five-year settlement with access rights for their annual holiday, just in case things changed and they decided to head to the winter sun. They weren't quite ready to let go.

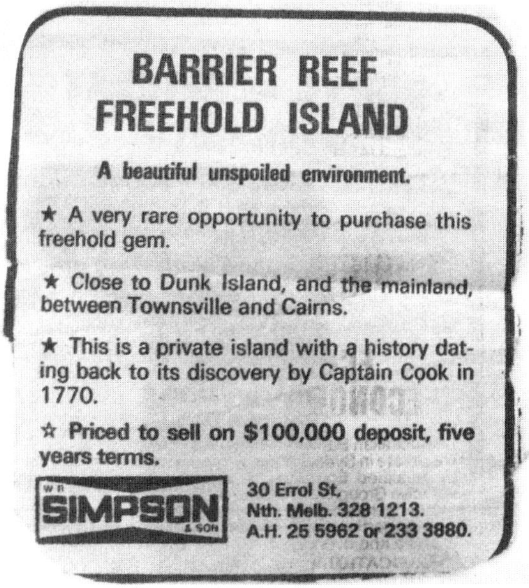

An unlabelled cutting kept by Val advertising the sale of Timana. Curiously, it turned out to have been placed in *The Australian Jewish News* and appears to have been published only once, on 2 November 1979 (p. 35), but presumably resulted in the sale to a Melbourne businessman. Private collection

In May 1978, in an occasional letter to the sisters, Deanna reported that their agent had been on Timana showing potential buyers around, 'looking over everything with a fine tooth comb'. Dunk Island, she continued, was about to 'turn into a hell of a place'. It could now cater for some 300 people. Marcus, as her son now called himself, was working there. Noel was visiting Timana once a week with books and vegetables and in return she and Bert were collecting supplies and mail for him in Tully. In June, they had all been invited to Dunk Island for dinner and to hear American pop sensations, 'The Supremes'. The night was not a success:

> Well the dinner was terrible and we were blasted out of our minds by the noise from the … group. Noel tells me never again … the Supremes will last him a lifetime. Our ears are still ringing. We all left early back to the peace of Timana and Bedarra.

That winter, only Von made the trip north, with Elizabeth, a friend—her final visit to their island. At Templestowe, Norman's health was failing rapidly. A letter from Deanna to Val, dated April 1979, expresses her sorrow that he was unwell. She missed their company on Timana: 'all those beaut jokes and laughs we had together'.

In 1980, Timana sold outright—Val said for half a million dollars. A tourist boat script from the 1990s gives a figure of 1.1 million. Regardless, although the sisters lost their holiday home of four decades and a key contributor to their personas, they made a tidy gain on their £50 investment.

The little island was bought by Ian Veall, a Melbourne businessman, sight unseen. Veall engaged Bert, who had been trained in Germany, to build him a holiday home on the island. Bert built on the site of the sisters' very first bungalow, which had long since succumbed to weather and white ants. As a memento, he left the remains of the sisters' old tank stand under the shelter of the raised building. He built the house to last, with heavy timbers and a shingle roof, each shingle secured with three nails—the idea being that a cyclone would loosen a few shingles rather that lift off the entire roof. Inside the robust construction, to divide the rooms, he shaped concrete formwork to resemble the inner spiral of a shell and, at the apex, installed a beautiful stained-glass skylight made by Deanna. Outside, the shape of the external stairs echoed the buttress roots of the island's giant milkwood trees. These functional and creative elements were completed, but the house was only built to lock-up stage and was never occupied. Veall went off the idea, and when he and his family visited the islands, they stayed in resorts.

When Bruce died on Dunk Island in 1998, Olsen remembered him fondly:

> The genial, good-natured Arthur, a wrestler-turned artist-bohemian with worldly tales from his upside-down career fascinated us, as well as his moon-and-sixpence lifestyle in the tropics at the edge of the Pacific Ocean … [he and Denna were] among the most innovative Australian tapestry weavers of the 1960s and 70s … Clifton Pugh, Fred Williams,

> Frank Werther, myself and art dealer Rudy Komon were fascinated by their achievements and we designed many tapestries woven by them.

Deanna and Bert managed to maintain their own 'moon-and-sixpence' lifestyle for several more years, renting from Veall. Severe cyclones, Larry in 2006 and Yasi in 2011, tested Bert's roof, which held fast, but Larry felled the bungalows. Following Larry, perhaps concerned about legal responsibilities for tenants, Veall refused to renew Deanna's lease. After four decades on Timana, she moved to the mainland with Bert, leaving Timana again deserted—nearly seventy years since two young Melbourne artists chose it as their winter escape from the cold and conservatism of the south.

12

STORIES AND STONES

Templestowe

(1960–1979)

The 'co-operative' at Templestowe worked well until their share farmers, the Chivers brothers, decided to concentrate on their own properties and Norman Taylor recruited Johnny, who had worked for him in Queensland, to manage the orchard. The group had a house built for Johnny on Taylor's land. Taylor, however, began to expect payment for what he saw as extra time and effort spent running the orchard, which split the group. Val's Norman '… had no time for home politics; and his spare hours were for art and music,' leaving the two sets of sisters, the Pykes and Cohens, to handle the matter alone. There was a resolution of sorts when Taylor died suddenly while travelling overseas and the two houses on his block were sold: the old house to a medical friend of the Pykes, the other to a young couple.

Val and Von met Italian migrants Pasquale Finicelli and his wife Rosa, and offered them the land at 'The Wold' to grow seasonal crops. The Italians cleared most of the remaining fruit trees, which were ageing, a lot of work and not particularly profitable. The old fruit trees were felled and provided many years of wood for the sisters' open fires. They were replaced by tomatoes 'growing in precise rows in their thousands'. The Finicellis' son, Amelia, brought his brides from Italy. The first died in childbirth and he remarried. In 1978, Pasquale and his growing family were still bringing the sisters 'armfuls of broccoli, sweet corn, strawberries and tomatoes', but eventually they took up their own market garden block almost next door, leased from the Melbourne and Metropolitan Works Board.

By the end of the 1960s, from their hillside, Val and Von could see the unwelcome suburbs creeping ever closer. On Bribie Island, Ian Fairweather, whose paintings they and the Pykes had bought when he was regarded as an oddity by much of the art world, was also worried about encroaching development. In August 1962, Fairweather had his most successful exhibition, the majority of the paintings going into public collections. Critics hailed him as Australia's greatest painter—a master. Meanwhile, living (as ever) in a makeshift hut, the artist had been bitten on the ear by one of his tame goannas and spent three weeks in Brisbane Hospital having the resulting infection treated. He emerged distressed by the human suffering he had witnessed and depressed about his slow-healing ear and failure to secure a cowshed as a studio.

Whether it was the media attention or Lina Bryans alerting them to Fairweather's struggles, the sisters wrote to him and offered him refuge on Timana. They received a most gracious reply, declining but hoping the offer would stay open:

> I have been so long here that I have grown into my humpy like a snail—However I am only squatting here—housing developments may soon displace me—Till then I haven't the energy to move— but I like to keep it in mind—in case—and thanks.

About five years after their brief correspondence, Val and Von (and perhaps Norman) joined the many artists who travelled north to pay their respects to the great artist, then seventy-six and in poor health. They had letters of introduction and notes for him from Lina and Frater. By then Bribie Island had been connected to the mainland by a bridge.

Fairweather, who eschewed the western world to live a Buddhist-like, aesthetic existence, was living in a substantial shambling hut, open to the weather, tucked away in a glade of Casuarinas and Boronias. He had built it himself from old timber and thatched its roof with reeds and bark. His bed was a little palliasse (straw mattress) raised from the ground; his paintings, at various stages of progress, were propped or hung around the walls. The sisters spent only a short time with him and were struck by his impeccable manners and 'marvellous voice'. Val's impression was: 'He was getting very old and sick and he looked pretty sick when we saw him then. But he was still the English gentleman.' Von told me, '… those eyes, those deep blue eyes sort of pierced you.'

When Norman and the sisters holidayed on Timana, their sketchbooks were always in hand. Back at Templestowe, the sisters painted in their studios and took part in group exhibitions, particularly with the Melbourne Contemporary Artists Society (MCAS), founded by Bell. Occasionally, Norm showed a painting, but for him art was a hobby. Critic Arnold Shore reviewed MCAS's November 1960 exhibition at the Argus Gallery in La Trobe Street, making note of portraits by Drysdale and work by Bell, Sali Herman, Mary Macqueen, Anne Montgomery and Von. He concluded that '… texture and design are well related by Yvonne Cohen in her semi-abstracts "Dockside" and "Industrial Landscape".' Allan McCulloch, too, found Von's paintings 'worthy of note'.

Both sisters garnered a special mention in the MCAS 1963 exhibition. A critic for *The Sun* named Val's 'Deserted Mining Scene' and Von's 'Sentimental Journey' among the standouts. The 1965 exhibition was judged to be generally depressing by a reviewer for *The Age*, '… because so few of the painters understand that paintings must have interesting shape. So many are lost with raw texture and crude colour.' He excepted only Von, whose 'nude drawings were light and sensitive'.

There were also invitations to take part in a few mixed exhibitions outside the Bell group. Both sisters contributed to an exhibition by women for the Pan-Pacific and South-East Asian Women's conference in Canberra in 1961; part of a push to give women artists more prominence. It was a national event—co-exhibitors included Margaret Olley, Grace Cossington Smith and Elizabeth Durak. Von sent 'Fishing Boat and Gulls' and 'Dockside', and Val 'Out Beyond'. When Melbourne's Leveson Street Gallery held a 'Homage to the Horse', with John Brack, Eric Thake, Len Annois, Septimus Power and Dorothy Braund among the exhibitors, Von contributed an oil—'Preliminary Canter'. Leveson also included both sisters in their Christmas exhibition of 1962 and again in a showing of new stock in February-March 1964.

In March 1965, with their friends Edith Wall and Mary Macqueen, Val and Von took part in a group show at Barry Stern Galleries—their first in Sydney. Titled '4 Melbourne Artists', each was represented by eight or nine works. Sydney reviewers were scathing, and worse, sexist. The *Sunday Telegraph's* Daniel Thomas decided that the sisters' paintings made them '... look like the art teachers one supposes they are with dull academic exercises in semi-abstraction—Valerie Albiston does Fairweatherish figure groups, Yvonne Cohen does angular flocks of birds.' Mary Macqueen fared better, but Thomas suggested that her '... feeling for comforting matt surfaces might well derive from the instinctive womanly problems of tending babies' skins.' Critic WT contended that the '... collection of works by four Melbourne artists brings nothing more than the effect of superficial student fumblings in art' and that the sisters' work was '... on the fringe of any useful attempt to express a more substantial and coherent development of semi-abstracted forms and remains arid in design and equally dry and mannered in the use of pigment.'

John Ogburn from *The Sun* was only a little kinder: 'ambitions are modest and so are the prices'. He continued:

> Yvonne Cohen limits herself to the movement of birds ... [she] manages to contain movement by keeping it rather to the centre of her canvas, but in doing so loses something of the all-over vitality of the canvas ... Valerie Albiston paints in a manner which assures that the colour will work harmoniously, and leaves the drawing to do most of the work. The drawing is satisfactory but limited.

Through much of the 1960s, the sisters entered the occasional art competition—including the 1961 Bendigo Art Prize, to which Von submitted 'Myall' and Val 'Desolate Country'. The same year, the acquisitive Portland Prize was begun to build an art collection for the Victorian city, and in 1966 Von won the oil section with her northern-themed painting 'Banana Grower'. Val entered her little painting, 'To the Islands'; the title borrowed from a 1958 novel she admired by Randolph Stow. She also sent a watercolour, 'Northern landscape', to the 'Watercolour, Drawing and Print Exhibition' at the Argus Gallery in 1966 and an oil, 'Havoc, High Noon', to an Anti-Vietnam War exhibition in 1967.

Neither Val nor Von complained of sexism, but into the 1960s, as in the previous two decades, women artists continued to be neglected, if not discriminated against. According to Christopher Heathcote, the sisters' younger friend Dorothy Braund was among those 'unjustly neglected' women whose art came to maturity in the 1950s. Edith Wall, born in 1904, interviewed in the 1980s, commented that in that earlier period, women artists were regarded as lightweights, if not freaks. This seems particularly regrettable for Von, who was more devoted to art than Val, and whose work mostly pleased critics.

Perhaps the turgid reactions to their Sydney show dampened the sisters' enthusiasm. The panning coincided timewise with their reduced involvement in exhibitions, but so too did the death of George

Bell in 1966, not long after being awarded an OBE. A great supporter of his students and friends, Bell had always included Val and Von in his group exhibitions. After his death, the sisters had something of a hiatus until the 1980s, when interest in the Bell School was reawakened.

If not painting and exhibiting as much, Val and Von still greatly enjoyed the art scene. During this time, Val said, she became 'very fond' of jewellery-maker and sculptor Matcham Skipper, who had an open marriage. Sculptors Clifford Last, Marc Clark and Berliner Inge King, as well as King's Australian printmaker husband Grahame, joined the Templestowe guest list. Inge King had been in Australia nearly a decade; a period she described as a sculptural desert. In 1959, she had started welding large pieces inspired by the vastness of the landscape, which found success. Gareth Jones-Roberts, a young winner of the 1966 Archibald Prize for his portrait of Alan Marshall, was also a visitor to The Wold, as were gallery directors Ron Radford and James Mollison. Radford arrived with a hole in his trousers, which the sisters mended. After Lina left Jock Frater, their neighbour Guelda became his confidante, so they saw quite a lot of him.

In 1967, Val and Von met thirty-five-year-old artist William (Bill) Ferguson and his wife Nancy when Bill won the Doncaster Festival Art Prize. Bill taught art in a secondary school and would later become a senior lecturer at RMIT. As she often did when they met interesting creative people, Val asked the couple to one of their dinners and they became firm friends. They would discuss art and literature. Bill shared their sense of fun and passed on art tips. He was inspired by Aboriginal Australian art, a culture that appealed to Von.

The Templestowe soirees mixed young and old; regular invitees were the daughters of their great friend Pat Goldman. Among the young guests was my brother, Peter, who had been driven to Templestowe by our gorgeous grandmother, Viva; and the sisters' cousin, in her stylish Borgward Isabella Coupé 2-door 1960 convertible. In many ways, our grandmother was the complete opposite of the sisters—if they fancied themselves bohemians, she fancied herself a Toorak princess.

For several reasons, the drive and dinner were memorable to Peter, a fifteen-year-old Canberra boy. He was in Melbourne during school holidays for work experience at the family business, Ormiston Rubber Company. Our grandmother put Peter up at the St Kilda Road Travelodge and the company manager picked him up each morning. At the dinner Norm left the table and reappeared at the piano in his (in)famous monkey mask, a fat Havana cigar clamped between his teeth. He played beautifully. Peter was told 'That's just Norman'. Peter later discovered another eccentricity: the toilet had several layers of doors, presumably to provide extra soundproofing.

On arrival, guests were offered the mandatory vermouth and stale crackers spread with fish paste (which Bill Ferguson referred to fondly as 'bloater fish pate'). Often, with a wry grin, Norm would ask of whoever he sat beside, 'How is God today', or similar—an intimidating experience for newcomers. He liked to unsettle—to see who he was dealing with. Among his advice to Ferguson, he said, 'If you ever have an affair, lie like a lizard.' For Ferguson, a music-lover, the music at these soirees was sublime. Norman was passionate about the moody classics of Alan Hovhaness and Tom Lehrer, and his tears would flow at Mahler's Resurrection Symphony. Overall, though, there was lots of laughter.

Many years later, when Val was giving away some of her art material, Ferguson said he would like their pigments. He was particularly interested in the new and unusual colours which Norm had collected, and he received a big box full of tins. Val, however, had forgotten that she had hidden a one-kilogram silver bar among the tints. Reminded by my brother, she sent him to alert Ferguson. Some of the pigments were metal-based, hence some of the tins were heavy even without the bar, so it took some time to probe with a stick for the hidden treasure.

With a lessening of enthusiasm for painting, Val pursued journalism more earnestly again and Von took up lapidary, then enjoying an increase in popularity. Von began to spend at least half her creative time making chunky jewellery using stones set in silver.

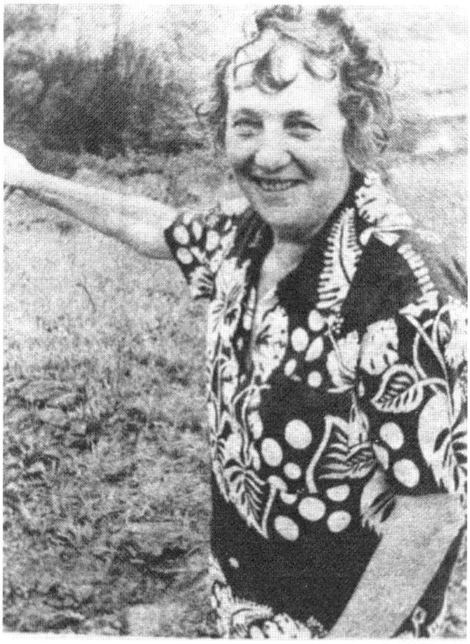

Val at 'Stella Park', Templestowe, a photo taken to illustrate her 1978 newspaper article on their orchard home in what was once a 'hidden valley.' *The Mirror* 7 June 1978, p. 29

She crafted rings, pendants and brooches, which she sold to friends and through exhibitions at the Nunawading and District Lapidary Club (some fifteen minutes from Templestowe). Together, the sisters caught the bus to Coober Pedy and Andamooka in search of opals and other semi-precious stones. The outback towns, in the centre of South Australia, north of Adelaide, was just the sort of place they used to seek out in the north on trips to Mareeba, Cooktown and the like—chock full of character and characters. Inspired by the colours and sparseness of the outback, apposite to the riotous vegetation of the north, Von painted a large oil of an open cut mine at Andamooka, and several of traditional Aboriginal peoples.

Norman continued to practice psychiatry, always somewhat casually but increasingly more so. He was often paid in wine, music or other goods and 'services', or not at all. Now and then he was called to court, as in the 1967 case of the abstract black and white drawing by Ron Upton called 'Oops', which, it was claimed, 'would tend to corrupt or deprave anyone who saw it'. Norman was among those who successfully defended the work.

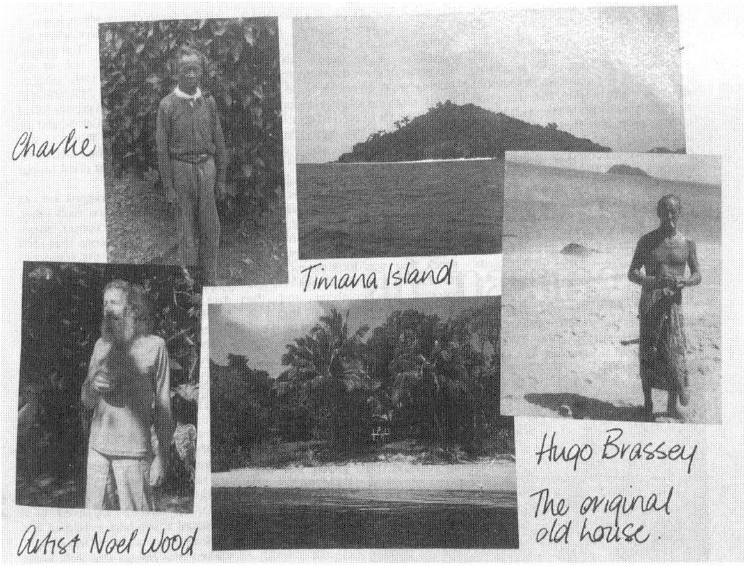

Photos of Noel, Charlie, Hugo, Timana Island and its bungalow, taken at various times since 1939, reproduced in an article by Val on wartime on the islands. *This Australia* vol. 7, Spring 1988, pp. 76–78

In the late 1970s, Val took up the pen with a vengeance, writing and rewriting several articles about their time on the islands and the old identities and pioneers they had met. She described herself as a painter and freelance journalist. Several of her articles found a place in newspapers and magazines. Her descriptions of the people tended to be slight, written from the viewpoint of a privileged visitor, but they were intended for a popular audience. Indeed, three times she won story of the month in *Parade* magazine.

Nevertheless, at least one reader questioned the accuracy of the information in her prize-winning article on Cooktown, written following a visit in 1974. *Parade*'s editor, Colin Pura, sent her an advisory letter:

> It is imperative that we be absolutely accurate with our copy and I would ask that you please check all such information in your current piece and in any other stories you may do

> for us. … [and] it is always important to double check what people tell you.

Thus scolded, for her 1977 article, the 'Old timers of the north', Val did indeed check with Les, one her subjects, but still promulgated hearsay, presumably thinking it added interest. Les reportedly told her, '… now there was a real character. "Hats and boots" we called Fenby. Always wore a pith helmet and a shirt, nothing else.' The accompanying photograph shows Fenby as a wiry man wearing only shorts—no shirt and neither hat nor boots. According to Val, Jim—another of her old-timers—characterised Fenby as, '… a dreamer. He had no idea how to cope with our primitive conditions … He owned a big block too, 160 acres at least, and left it all to the Aboriginals. None of them have ever come near it.'

Other authors, Dorothy Jones and their friend Constance (Connie) Mackaness, both locals, have written a little about Rupert Fenby. They describe him quite differently: as a nature lover, living cleverly and self-sufficiently—growing fruits and vegetables, making butter from coconut cream, grinding his own flour substitutes, growing cassava, arrowroot, yams and other unusual vegetables and selling just enough for his other needs. If Val had done her research, she may have discovered that, in 1933, Fenby had his property, Clump Mountain Farm, declared a sanctuary under the Animals and Birds Act and in the 1940s. He negotiated with the North Queensland Naturalists Club to act as trustee of his land after his death. Later still, he hoped the 'Aborigines' might take on that role—but nothing came of it, and he died in 1960.

Val also wrote about the spoiling of the Family Islands by expanding tourism; a process that began in the 1930s but took off post-war. Once, she wrote, in the evenings, there may have been 'a glimmer of light from a fisherman's humpy on the mainland', but by the end of the 1970s, from Timana, the mainland was '… a glittering ribbon, the lights shining from hotels, houses and caravan parks.' Her concerns were more social, even personal, than environmental.

On the islands, she wrote, too often noise, people or their detritus disturbed their peace. Boaters felt they could call in or stop to fish, or simply gawk.

In the 1970s, the resort at Dunk Island began tours around the surrounding islands. From the back of the garden at Timana, Val would hear a voice rumbling through a megaphone: 'this is the island where the two old eccentric sisters live'. Even in the 1990s, when the sisters no longer owned the island, they were still remembered, if somewhat inaccurately, in a tour script from the ferry based at Clump Point. The ferry serviced Dunk Island and also took passengers on a tour of the coast and islands off Mission Beach, during which the following text was read over the loudspeaker:

> Welcome aboard the Lawrence Kavanagh … Coming up on the lefthand side is Timana Island … one of the very few privately owned islands on the east coast of Australia, most other islands are freehold, perpetual lease or national park … it was bought by two sisters from Melbourne, Von and Val Coen.

On Bedarra, Noel, too, was annoyed by the impositions. Once when a tourist boat entered Doorila Bay, announcing from the deck that it was the home of a hermit, he put on a show. Stark naked, he stood on his head in the shallows, his feet in the air. 'He swore he could hear the cameras clicking,' Val reported. Mostly, the sisters simply hid in the jungle until the intruders moved on. Occasionally, though, Val claimed, they didn't disappoint the sightseers, and emerged from the tangle of vegetation unclad. But they were younger then. Now, in the late 1970s, Val wrote of Noel, '… his appearance … is of an apostle, with long greying beard and matching knotted hair.'

Like Noel, Val and Norm were great readers and both enjoyed contemporary Australian writers and more avantgarde writers in general. From her wall of books at Templestowe, she introduced me to the work of Marguerite Duras and Lillian Hellman. Several well-known authors were part of the Templestowe three's wider circle of acquaintances, among them: Clem Christesen, John Morrison, Alan Marshall, and Vance and Nettie Palmer. Particularly at Lina Bryan's get-togethers, they socialised with many creative thinkers. Lina was at the centre of a Melbourne circle of academics, writers, theatre producers, artists and musicians, who questioned contemporary Australian attitudes, which they saw as staid.

Norman, the psychiatrist, with his intelligent, entertaining and lateral take on the world, was a welcome addition, and could offer his services to the troubled. He once helped Lina's then-partner, Alex Jelinek, a visionary architect, when Alex suffered some sort of anxiety attack on an aircraft. He continued to offer his support when, more than once, Alex became suicidal and Lina called Norm in desperation in the middle of the night. Possibly in gratitude, Lina gifted Norm a painting by Ian Fairweather—which Macquarie Galleries had given the title 'Bioscope'—of an Aboriginal father, mother and child attending a film screening.

In 1971, the worst happened. Norman's daughter Jenny was killed in an horrific car accident, broadsided by a drunken driver running a red light as she arrived to collect her children from school. Norm was distraught and, Val observed, the shock aged him.

Eight years later, he was admitted to hospital and wanted Val to stay with him, but she went home to get some fresh clothes. To her regret, he passed away while she was gone, on 17 July 1979 at the age of eighty-five. Val believed that he knew he was gravely ill and chose not to tell her. They had been together for three decades and she would be alone for another three. Over the years, she had shared him with her sister and friends. His death left them all bereft.

Above all, Val had treasured his '... extraordinary personality ... I found his talents astonishing: his understanding of music and art and his skills at chess.' In 1980, on her misbehaving old typewriter, she typed out a three-page biographical note on Norm and lodged it with the National Library of Australia. She concluded her summary of his professional career with a few loving lines on his personal gifts and beliefs:

> He had a keen memory for faces and could get remarkable likenesses without a sitter. As a draftsman he could portray the human body with ease and as a musician his touch on the piano was sensitive. Music was a strong element in his life. He was no believer in organized religion but his beliefs on the continuedness of mind, personality, call it what you will, was a faith he strongly clung to. He could not believe that the aspirations of man, his creations, were something that didn't continue in some form. Altogether he was a unique and much admired man.

13

FROM TEMPLESTOWE TO KEW

Templestowe and Kew

(1980–1990)

Following Norman's death and the sale of Timana, both major life events, the resilient sisters embraced the next stage of their lives. They decided they should see more of Australia, which, in turn, triggered a burst of creativity. About 1980, they travelled northwest to the diverse mallee country of Victoria's Little Desert. They stayed at a lodge that Ray 'Whimpey' Reichelt and his wife Maureen had established a decade before, near Nhil, close to the South Australian border. Whimpey ran four-wheel-drive tours of the area to promote its natural values and encourage the protection of the endangered mound-building malleefowl; one of its many bird species. Thanks to Whimpey and others, the area is now a National Park. Val interviewed Whimpey and wrote two versions of an article entitled 'Whimpey's wilderness', which was basically an advertorial, covering a little of the background to the retreat's establishment, tariffs and similar details. She failed to find a publisher.

In the autumn of 1982, having never been west of Adelaide, the sisters determined to explore the Flinders Ranges for a fortnight. With my brother Peter as driver, they hired a roomy car and, assisted by their trusty Royal Automobile Club of Victoria (RACV) guidebook, made their way from Melbourne, motoring from town to town. They stayed where they could mostly, at the sisters' insistence, in cheaper places. The first night, they slept at a beautiful old stone house at Kapunda on the edge of the Barossa Valley, then headed north to Blinman and Parachilna. According to Val, they fully realised that they were in the outback while eating at a pub-restaurant. A 'fat lady' waddled in with two kids in tow, one whining. 'Shut up,' the woman said, whacking the complaining boy so hard that he was knocked flat on his back.

At Wilpena Pound, the trio heard the whispers of the spirits of the pound. While the sisters pottered around and sketched, Peter made the six-hour climb to the top of St Mary's Peak, where kites circled. They had brought a pad and crayons for Peter, but he preferred walking. He was 'up everything he could find', Val remembered in one her many risqué double entendres, recorded in a little scarlet book that Von kept of any of her sister's utterances that tickled her—most of which are of the better-if-you-had-been-there kind.

The sisters' suitcases were full of biscuits and sardines. Everything was counted out: so many per person per day. Morning and afternoon tea had to be taken at the right, Eastern Australian, time—even when, a few years later, they travelled together to north-western Australia with its different time zone.

From the pound, they drove to Arkaroola, then home through Mildura; Norman's birthplace. It was a wet trip and on the many unpaved roads they passed several cars bogged on the verges. The hire-car was plastered with mud. Along the way Von collected rocks, mostly cutting stones left by the early Aboriginal peoples. By the time they got to Parachilna, the back of the car was so weighed down that Peter made Von throw out one stone for every new one found. At Templestowe, she added the stones to the rows lining the track between their houses.

In the winter of 1986, Peter braved their company again. With his wife Artemis, they explored the Top End and northern Western Australia. Again, they stayed at pubs picked from an RACV travel book. Artemis took leave from her job at Shell and her time was limited, so this trip they booked ahead. They flew to Darwin, hired a car and drove to Tennant Creek, Hall's Creek and the Bungle Bungles, reaching as far west as Tunnel Creek before driving on to Wyndham, Kakadu and Katherine. In preparation for the celebration of Australia's bicentenary in 1988, several major highways had been upgraded, which removed the need for a four-wheel-drive.

At Fitzroy Crossing, Peter swam while the women worried about crocodiles. Whereas, at Tunnel Creek, fear of crocodiles, claustrophobia and the threat of flood meant that they all waded only fifty of the 750 metres of icy creek that would have taken them through the tunnel to the far side of the Napier Range. Wyndham, with the stench from its abattoir, ugly mudflats and yet more crocs, was a disappointment and they moved on. Despite the sisters' preference for budget hotels, all proved adequate except one, which was too rough even for Val and Von. They drove on and, notwithstanding Val's usual bravado, it was Peter who had to ring and cancel their booking. The only double bedroom available at the replacement hotel was the honeymoon suite, where the waterbed provided an interesting challenge for the petite Artemis and much heavier Peter; a story Val and Von greatly enjoyed retelling.

Both sisters sketched but, apparently, few finished paintings resulted. Whenever the opportunity arose Val interviewed Aboriginal peoples and local characters. Notebook in hand, she would bowl up to someone lying outside a pub in the segregated area that was hosed down at the end of each day. At Lake Argyle, she questioned Roy, a stockman-come-poet. At Hall's Creek, where they enjoyed a flight over the Bungle Bungles, it was Jim—'a full blood'.

These trips to parts of the country previously unknown to the sisters probably inspired two of Val's published articles from this period: 'The wide, brown land' and 'Our Top End … A vast red land'. The first seems to be fictional; the description of a coach trip to an unnamed destination where the 'roads run straight to the horizon in hypnotic flatness'. The passengers include a Frenchwoman, complete with diamond earrings and pearl necklace, travelling with 'her gross elderly husband', who, after a fellow traveller informs her that she might expect a rise in the landscape during the next 150 kilometres, replies 'the Australian has the humour very funny'. Val's disdain for overweight people is evident in several characters: the cocky Fred tightens his belt 'over an extended stomach' and his spouse, Alice, 'is all bulge overflowing her seat'. Herb, though, is rotund and jolly. In the partly imagined 'Our Top End', where '… the traffic is sparse as tyres grip and spin on the bicentennial surfaces', a truckie, 'a bulging mountain of flesh' in a filthy singlet intrigues a busload of German tourists by pulling out his swag and squeezing under his vehicle to sleep. Peter recalls that, at a rest house on the Hall's Creek Road, they (sans tourists) had indeed watched a semi-trailer driver eat an ice cream, wipe his mouth on his stained stop and crawl under his truck to sleep.

Throughout the 1980s, Val regularly wrote. Beginning in December 1978, she contributed a monthly column to *Artlook*—Australia's first arts magazine. When the editor of the newish Perth-based magazine, began soliciting regular columns on happenings in the other States, presumably to increase the reach of the magazine, Val needed little encouragement to put up her hand. For 'Melbourne Scene', she drew on her many friends; fellow creatives, individuals and couples—sculptors, painters, craftspeople, jewellers, printmakers, ballet dancers, collectors, glass artists and graphic designers. Her first article was on Deanna and the tapestry studio on Timana. Others followed on painters Bill Ferguson, and Neil and Abbie Douglas, art dealer Chris Deutscher, curator Rowena Clark, sculptor Clifford Last, potter HR Hughan and theatre designer Kenneth Rowell. Her last column, on the gallery at Heide—where she was a voluntary guide—appeared in August 1983. Just three months later, what must have been a dream 'job' for that stage of her life, ended when *Artlook* ceased publication. The magazine was produced by a progressive not-for-profit and funding had always been a struggle.

Val's publishing history was not without controversy. Over the years, she was accused of plagiarism, inaccuracy and even fabrication. One editor responded to her submitted article outlining a newly arrived migrant's story, thus:

> I found your story of great interest—there were parts of it I enjoyed immensely! One reason I did not print it was I couldn't quite believe it in parts—I mean I'm not saying you were 'lying' or something ... Some of what the characters said didn't seem quite right to my ears & I wonder why that is.

This may have been her article on 'Emma' and 'Sam', a young couple newly arrived at the Victorian gold diggings, which was first published in a 1979 issue of *Australian Family Circle* and five years later in *The Weekly Times*. The earlier article, described as the 'true-life story' of Emma and Sam, claimed to quote from Emma's diary:

> With only a tent for shelter and eggs at 13 shillings a dozen, life on the diggings in north-eastern Victoria was a daily struggle for survival. The diary of a young wife and mother describes the ups and downs of living in Australia more than 120 years ago.

Without acknowledging it, Val had drawn on the lives of Emily and William Skinner, as recorded by Emily. Emily arrived in Australia in 1854 to marry her fiancée William before the couple took their chances on the Victorian goldfields. Their descendants deposited a transcript of Emily's writings at the Burke Museum, Beechworth, in June 1979, three months before Val's article appeared in print, but copies had been circulating before that, and Val somehow came by one. Despite claiming her article was biographical, for some reason,

Val renamed the couple 'Emma' and 'Sam' and also tampered with Emily's words. She got away with it. On republication a few years later, she presented the same narrative as a short story.

Adding to uncertainty over her absolute veracity, Val wrote personal accounts—presented as factual, solo experiences—when her sister and, often, her mother, were present, and she changed names without alerting the reader. Always stroppy, particularly when it came to money, she tended to argue with editors over payment, whether late or unforthcoming. In a reply to a November 1977 letter from the editor of the *Townsville Bulletin*, politely thanking her for a 'most interesting piece' on Timana and advising her that they were not able to pay for copy, she replied: 'I am amazed that a paper like the *Bulletin* established for over 100 years has no funds for contributors.' After pointing out that she had been published in '... six Australian leading newspapers and odd magazines and never been confronted with such a policy', she demanded that they return the article. A not atypical comment from Val, made when she was nearing her eightieth birthday, was that the editor of *Tirra Lirra* kept asking her out to lunch. He seemed to be 'a sex maniac', she said, 'but only gave me one article'! Perhaps, he found her tales of the two sisters' seemingly hedonistic, earlier lifestyle intriguing.

Always a great reader, as well as a writer of factual articles, Val tried her hand at short fiction, even a script for a play, but with little success. Of her many short stories (at least thirty), few seem to have found favour with an editor. 'The wide, brown land' (1983), 'Emily's Cake—a new short story' (1983) and 'The cage' (1987) appear to be the only exceptions. 'Emily's Cake' was accepted after Val made the 'minor changes re language' requested by the editor. Presumably these were to tone down the exchanges between the warring married couple over the husband's beloved cockatoos. Some of the characters reappear in Val's half-hour play, 'Emily's Darling Daughter', possibly penned around the same time. In both play and story, the main character, Emily, is a vibrant older woman who has lived a very full life, outshines other women, and adores men who adore her back. Rex, a homosexual artist, could be based on Noel Wood's brother of the same name, occupation and inclination; a head-on collision that takes the life of the daughter, Jen, echoes the fate of Val's step-daughter Jennifer. Indeed, Emily could be Val. Val's description of her older doppelganger was: 'A small old lady of ninety. Gay. Delightful sense of humour. Shines in male company. Determined, self-centred.'

In 1985, when Val submitted an article on their time on Timana to *Family Circle*, the features editor remembered her previous unsuccessful submission, replying that she was '... still feel[ing] that while it may not be right for the pages of *Family Circle*, you still have a story that needs to be told.' She recommended that Val tell the whole story in a book or as a TV or film script and suggested that there might be funding opportunities. As it happens, in August 1977 Val had offered 'Early days on our Barrier Reef islands' to ABC radio, who apparently weren't interested.

During the '80s, the sisters volunteered as guides at Heide Park and Art Gallery (now Heide Museum of Modern Art)—the former home of John and Sunday Reed, then recently sold to the Victorian Government. Under the first director, Maudie Palmer, a superb gallery was built and a sculpture garden begun next to the river. Volunteering her journalistic services, Val wrote a couple of articles promoting the new gallery. One, for a local paper, publicised an exhibition of paintings on cigar box lids in celebration of the landmark 1889 exhibition on cedar by the avantgarde Impressionists of Heidelberg School.

Not only were the sisters travelling again and actively involved in the art scene, but from the early 1980s they also enjoyed a resurgence of interest in their own artwork, particularly that from the 1940s and 1950s, associated with a new appreciation of the Bell School. Even after his death, George Bell was looking after them. Val acknowledged the sisters' debt to Bell in her 1982 article in *Artlook*, 'Tribute to a teacher'.

The revival began in 1981 when Deutscher Fine Art held an exhibition of Bell 'homeworks', gathered from some of his 1000 or so students. At the opening, Mary Eagle and Jan Minchin's book—*The George Bell School: Students, Friends and Influences*—was launched, and brought the school firmly back into the public eye. The exhibition travelled from the Georges Gallery to regional Victoria and the National Trust in Sydney. Val contributed two Bell 'homework pieces' from about 1950: 'Conversation' and 'Play', which illustrate her broadening from landscape to portraits of everyday people; always faceless, yet somehow intimate. Von still had 'After the Bath'—the exercise 'that surprised and delighted Bell'—and 'Grey after Gris', with flat areas of colour outlined simply in black, as was typical of the Spanish artist. Val also dug out three of Norman's exercises, painted in 1949 or 1950. His 'Monday Wash' and 'Cubic Exercise' showed the influence of Cubism and 'Tropic Man' illustrated his strong interest in the human figure.

A number of other Bell School exhibitions followed through the 1980s and 1990s and the sisters were usually included. Now in their ninth decade, they enjoyed the late recognition, having spent a decade or two with few exhibitions and receiving little interest in their artwork. It was a chance for early work, saved for sentimental reasons or left unsold, and more recent work, to get an airing. During the lean years, they shared the not uncommon view of artists of their generation that galleries were focussing on younger experimental and conceptual artists. Once thought too modern, their paintings were now considered somewhat old hat.

In 1986, the National Trust of Australia (NSW) staged a recreation of the early years of the Contemporary Art Society, which Bell had founded (in 1938). Also, that year an Australian Academy of Art exhibition titled 'Counterclaims: Presenting Australian Art 1938–1941', was shown at the SH Ervin Gallery at The Rocks in Sydney. The organisers had done their research and hoped that Von might know the whereabouts of four particular paintings from that era. From her own collection, she was able to send them 'Garden at Coonanglelbah', soon after sold by gallery owner Charles Nodrum for $1200.

Later in the year, Allyn Fisher contacted the sisters from Bendigo. She was organising a tribute to George Bell on the twentieth anniversary of Bell's death. Both sent examples of their work and attended the August opening in Bendigo's National Trust Building. Bell and twelve of his students were represented, including Russell Drysdale, Alan Sumner, Mary Macqueen and Guelda Pyke. Bendigo Art Gallery bought some of the sisters' paintings, including small still-lifes by Val, and Von's 'Woeful Women' (also known as 'Balinese Women'), painted after her trip to Bali with Guelda over three decades before.

Two years on, yet another Bell tribute titled 'George Bell Students and Friends: A Major Collection of Fine Art of the 30's, 40's & 50's', was held at Alex Holland's galleries in Double Bay, Sydney. Val contributed 'The Spit, Timana. 1952'. Fellow exhibitors were George Bell, Lina Bryans, Eric Thake, Adrian Lawlor, Drysdale, Dorothy Braund, Sali Herman and Fred Williams. Once again, Val was in good company for someone who, as the catalogue quoted from Eagle and Minchin, 'never regarded herself as a professional painter'. As for Von, Charles Nodrum exhibited her admired little homework for Bell, 'After the Bath', in a group show titled 'Modern Australian Paintings'.

The sisters were still living on the farm at Templestowe. They and the other two creative sisters—the remaining original residents of the loose 'artists' cooperative'—had lived happily at Templestowe for four decades. Both pairs of sisters began to think about scaling down, simplifying their lives. As the 1980s drew to a close, Val and Von were well into their seventies and the Pyke sisters older still: Guelda would soon be eighty-four and Polly eighty-two. The suburbs were closing in on their once-tranquil rural retreat. Explaining their decision to move, Val wrote that the large houses of 'migrants made good' threatened to swallow them up: '… houses of vulgar proportions were beginning to surround us on rural lands lost forever.' Increasingly, there were disputes over fences, privacy (they felt overlooked by 'McMansions'), light and noise pollution.

Not least, in the lead-up to Christmas 1985, Von had had the first of several strokes and was admitted to the Austin Hospital in Heidelberg. On return home, with her sister's encouragement, she recorded an account of her experience—a rare example of her own words, typed on Val's old Adler:

> I awoke in a heavy sweat in ward 2A. With festive season almost upon me I was trying to finish a commissioned ring … and had set the flashing opal in its silver setting, when my right hand went limp … and I slumped to the floor. It was some months since I had been in Coober Pedy and had visited the young Yugoslav miner who was just about to take off for Europe with his superb collection of stones … The one I bought was left over. Lucky me for, he was most generous. I had noodled on various dumps without great success, but the lure of the elusive gem fired my blood.

In a manner reminiscent of Val's writing, Von goes on to mock her fellow 'inmates': 'three crumpled and contorted old paper bags opposite', whose antics the sisters found amusing. One staged midnight raids to collect anything she coveted; another, with a nose drip, liked showing her breasts to male visitors; a third, who they nicknamed 'I'm sorry Sister', was repeatedly making extravagant apologies for wetting her bed. 'Their unnatural behaviour took my mind off my own medical problems. I was assured of early release, while Ivy, Edi and Edna had no such prospects,' Von concluded.

The sisters always tried to keep track of Noel, the love of Von's life. Never much of a correspondent, he wrote occasionally, but after Von's death, Val burned his letters. In December 1985, about the time that Von was in hospital, a friend sent the sisters a copy of the Brisbane *Sunday Mail* colour feature on seventy-three-year-old Noel. Not unusually, Noel was described as a hermit, a Crusoe (an image he promoted—romantic but inaccurate). The article did, however, capture something of the attraction and elegance of the man and his actual lifestyle. The reporter saw him as 'a tall, impressive, Messiah-like figure'. Noel had shown the reporter, a woman, pictures of himself modelling for *Vogue* magazine in the late 1920s and early 1930s—a dapper, dark-haired young man about town with a Clark Gable moustache. He surprised her with his courtliness and the comfort of his home. 'He drinks beer from a glass, not from a stubby or can, and offers you some white wine in a proper wine glass,' she wrote. 'Shafts of sunlight pour through the heavily perfumed vines that clamber over this lovely rustic cottage.' The kitchen was well-ordered and well-stocked, she noted. Big cooking pots hung over the huge stone fireplace and baskets full of vegetables, fruit and flowers harvested from the terraces behind the house or plucked from the rainforest were strung from the ceiling.

Over the years, Noel's bungalow, 'Singing Bamboo', evolved and was given a new name. He told the reporter that the Japanese characters painted on the outside meant 'Peace and Tranquillity by the Seashore'—a legacy from a Japanese woman who lived with him for a time. The sheltered half-moon beach in the cove below, fringed with coconut palms, was his 'million-dollar swimming pool'. Now, it was time, he told her, to put his slice of Bedarra on the market.

Noel's daughters were also sent a cutting on Noel, written by the same reporter and published in the *Sunday Mail* a month before. They were surprised and delighted that Noel mentioned that he had a family: 'Wood was once married and speaks fondly of his two daughters, Ann, an artist and author of children's books, and Virginia'—the latter who inherited his love of gardening. He even produced photographs of his grandchildren. Over the decades, in countless interviews, there had never been mention of a wife and children.

Noel's children, Gini and Ann, only got to know him as adults when they began visiting him on Bedarra in the 1970s. He and Ann discussed art, enjoyed the same books and laughed a lot. Indeed, Ann found him totally disarming:

> He told me women were always turning up: I'd be painting and look up and there—behind the rocks—was a female

> who just couldn't wait to take off her clothes', he'd say. When I asked what he did about it, he'd invariably say: 'Oh well, it was a nuisance to stop what I was doing, but, as they threw themselves on me, I didn't want to hurt their feelings!'.
>
> Once, I found a mattress hidden in a cave-like rock formation. He said it was for assignations with a married woman who used to visit him when she needed sex—her husband was impotent. As if I wanted to know this!

On one visit from Gini, Noel was living with Michelle, a lovely girl, younger than his daughters. He had a furious argument with Gini when Michelle went off exploring the island with Hamish, Gini's son and his grandson. 'She was mine,' he complained to Gini.

Amongst the many women infatuated with Noel was Frances Shand Kydd, the estranged mother of Diana, Princess of Wales, who, while holidaying on Dunk Island, enjoyed a brief flirtation with him. Dame Zara Bate (previously Holt), lonely after her third husband died in 1984, motored across the water in her boat to visit him, bringing a generous supply of gin in square blue bottles (Bombay Sapphire). The bottles ended up in the window that Noel created from empty rum, whisky, gin and champagne bottles, all consumed on the island. Cemented with their round bases facing the interior, when the sun shone through, as it often did, his house glowed with the rainbow hues of a stained-glass window.

If Noel was careless with women, he was just a bad at managing his financial affairs. He simply shoved incoming cheques into a hessian sack until someone else banked them, or not. As he explained to an interviewer in 1940: 'I'm hopeless with money, and I had to find some way of living where the rent man didn't call.' On a visit by Gini and her husband Geoff from Melbourne in 1977, Noel told them he was thinking about selling his whole entitlement to cover what he owed. Gini paid his back rates so that he could stay on unhindered. After her visit, Noel decided to leave a portion of his section of the island to his daughters.

However, the following year, his tenure on Bedarra was threatened. As Deanna conveyed to the sisters, Noel had come Timana in 'a hell of a state'. Colin Scott and Ken Druitt, with whom Noel had shared Bedarra in a collaborative way for two decades, and their solicitor, had visited him and demanded that he sign papers of sale for his corner as part of a deal with an American company to purchase the whole island. Never one to hold firm in a conflict, Noel was wavering. Deanna and Bert advised him to warn Gini, and Bert ran him across to the mainland to ring her. Gini said she would handle it and did: without Noel's land, the deal fell through.

In 1986 or 1987, although Noel had not painted for many years, he was still a good story. An ABC TV crew visited Bedarra to film him for a documentary, titled *The Island and The Painter*. In 1988, he also featured in the ABC series *A Big Country*, hosted by Jim Downes. In 1991, he was still living on his corner of the island. To mark the tenth anniversary of Townsville's Perc Tucker Gallery, his work was hung in a ground-breaking exhibition titled 'Artist in the Tropics; 200 Years of Art in North Queensland', curated by Ross Searle. The exhibition was accompanied by Searle's book of the same name, which tracks how artists had responded to the Queensland tropics historically, since 1790, thereby contributing to the State's cultural heritage. Of course, Val and Von's work was represented, including 'Timana Island', painted by Val in 1945. Searle's assessment of their work ended on a romantic note, which would likely have pleased them. During that period of their lives, there was plenty of romance to be found in their relationships and their surroundings. Searle wrote:

> Albiston's work in particular was marked by a strong analytical approach in rendering form and, like Margaret Preston, she was concerned with recording the essentials of structures in the landscape by use of line and mass without the distraction of colour. Cohen's painting, like that of her contemporary, Noel Wood, was more intuitive in conception and showed more vigorous use of colour and feeling for

> design in its treatment of the luscious vegetation. They were after all living in the most idyllic of circumstances and were profoundly influenced by the environment.

The year after the exhibition, when Noel turned eighty, he moved to the mainland to live with Barbara Reid near Mission Beach. Eventually, the rent-man had come to call. Noel's corner of Bedarra—most of his three hills, two bays and a spring—was subdivided into six or seven quarter-acre blocks and sold off in part to pay for rates (much escalated from the early days), maintenance and other expenses, which again had built up. Noel had promised his daughters a slice of his corner of Bedarra, but all his land was sold without their knowledge.

When Noel died in 2001, Reid and her daughter got everything, including three of his paintings. His health had been failing for a while, but his daughters, Gini and Ann, were kept from him. They believe that all was not above board and wanted an inquest, but Noel's body had already been cremated. They also believe that between Reid, a dodgy lawyer and the local real estate agent, Noel had been swindled on the sale of his land. There was little left in his estate but the daughters would have liked his artwork to keep for the family. They took the matter to court, eventually to Queensland's Supreme Court—without success. Later they saw that the paintings had been sold. It was a sad, litigious postscript to a free-spirited life and doubtfully something Noel would really have wanted for his island home and his daughters. But he had always taken the easy road and was easily swayed.

With Noel's move to the mainland, Val and Von lost their last connection on the Family Islands. In Melbourne, they were about to make a big move. In 1989, the two pairs of sisters, Cohens and Pykes, put their properties on the market together, just as they had bought it together forty years before. 'The Wold' was sold and, the following year, Val and Von moved to Kew, which, like Templestowe, boasted a fine artistic pedigree. The sisters' mentor, George Bell, was born there in 1878 and Louis Buvelot had been buried there in 1888. For Val and Von the location held extra significance: 'The site we found was where the river flowed through the city, the same river which passed Templestowe, winding its way towards the sea of our Elwood childhood, far from the sea which had surrounded Timana.'

They bought a modest, two-storey house in Blythswood Court, a quiet street on the escarpment immediately above the Yarra River, looking out over central Melbourne. The backyard met common land above the river and was large enough for a vegetable patch. On one side, in season, a wonderful old apricot tree needed protection from hungry birds. In the front yard, Val planted little lemon trees and the odd pumpkin, which eventually scrambled over the brush fence.

They had the house altered to suit two people and two painters. Entry was through a generous foyer, hung with paintings by Ada Plante and Bill Ferguson, and finished with a long table strewn with shells, Aboriginal flints, driftwood and other souvenirs from the sisters' well-lived lives. The upstairs bedroom, an existing addition, had an ensuite and the best view in the house, but went unused—although Val used its landing as a study. Beyond the entry, the remainder of the ground floor was rearranged to make a bedroom each, with shared bathroom and toilet between; two modest living-come dining rooms looking out to the garden; two little kitchens; a laundry; and, between the house and garage, two open studios, Von's entered through Val's.

The removalist came to Templestowe in June 1990. But the move was not as smooth as they hoped. Six small paintings went missing: 'Kulu Valley', a 1949 gouache by Fairweather; an untitled 1952 blue and white abstract by Roger Kemp; two oil paintings by Raymond Glass ('Island Dream' and 'Mexican Farmers'); and two tiny oils by Val. The items they were packed with, as listed in the removalist's inventory, arrived, but the paintings did not. The police and insurance company were notified and the sisters telephoned their gallery contacts to alert them in case any of the works came on the market. Pat Hillcoat, a friend who wrote for *Women's Art Register Bulletin,* organised a full-page notice headed 'Stolen Paintings'. It was illustrated, somewhat incongruously, by a photograph of the sisters happily sunbathing in their earlier years.

STOLEN PAINTINGS

Two sisters, artists who were students of the George Bell School in the 1930s moved from their Templestowe artists' community to Kew on the 18th June 1990. On the day of the move six paintings from their collection disappeared. The missing paintings were listed in the mover's inventory and other items with the paintings were unpacked at Kew that day. The police and insurance company are investigating. Would members please be alert to the possibility that these pictures might be in the market place.

Please contact:

Valerie Albeston 853-0644
Yvonne Cohen 853-0655

1 **Kulu Valley**. Ian Fairweather. gouche and pencil. 1949
15cm by 22cm. Sandy colours with blacks and ochres.
Signed and framed.

2 **Untitled**. Roger Kemp. Oil. 1952.
appros, 15cm by 22cm. Abstract in pale blues and whites.
Signed and framed.

3 **"Mexican Farmers"**. Raymond Glass. oil. 1949.
approx. 18" by 24". Father and 3 sons wearing hats.
Distinctive because of the black eyes in a horizontal line.
Framed and signed.

4 **Island Dream**. Raymond Glass. Oil. 1949.
approx. 12" by 14". Figure over a rock playing a mandolin, little red fish in water, girl half submerged in water.

5 **Untitled**. Valerie Albeston. oil. 1940s.
approx. 3" by 2". Semi-abstract rocks and landscape.
Unframed and probably unsigned.

6 **Untitled**. Valerie Albeston. oil. 1989-1990.
approx. 3" by 2". semi-abstract figures and trees in aboriginal colours, blacks, ochres, reds and whites.
unframed and probably unsigned.

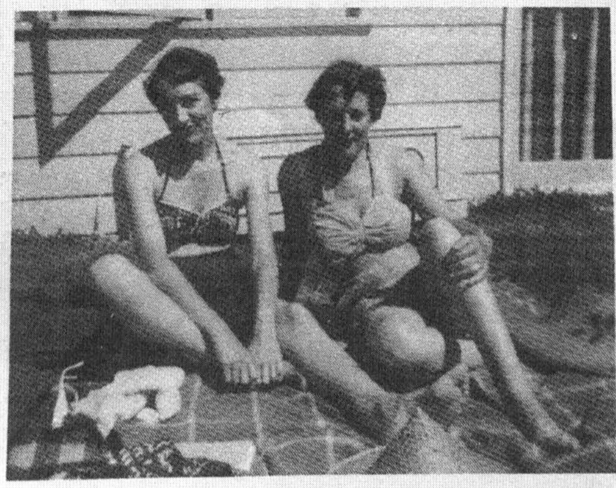

18

The article aimed alerting the art world to the theft of several paintings during the sisters' move from Templestowe to Kew in 1990. The accompanying photograph is of the sisters (Von at left) in the 1960s. *Women's Art Register Bulletin*, vol. 2, no. 2, p. 18

14

LAST YEARS

Kew

(1990–2008)

Settled in their peaceful house at Kew, the sisters only occasionally painted. Every now and then, they were invited to contribute to significant exhibitions. In 1992, the National Gallery of Victoria held a show of earlier paintings by George Bell and his circle, honouring what had segued from Modernism to 'Classical Modernism'. Von again dug out 'After the Bath', her little homework for Bell, and Val, 'Boat Builders'. In the catalogue, the curator, Felicity St John Moore, analysed the works; perhaps suggesting both were a bit derivative. She observed that 'After the Bath's …

> … single eye is reminiscent of [Moise] Kisling's 'La Petite grace', of which Bell had a postcard. Cohen relates the pattern of the bathmat to the wall behind and uses heavy outlines to flatten the volumes suggested by the curved lines.

And, in Val's seaside composition, perhaps painted at Timana:

> The fishing boats and boat shed are used to structure the composition in the manner of Braque's 'Fishing boats' 1909.

> Angled and tilted, the boats lead the eye across the sand to the boat shed and then back to the two simplified figures in the foreground.

Six years later, the sisters were among only five women selected by independent curator Gavin Wilson for inclusion in a well-reviewed exhibition of art created in North Queensland, held at Cairns Art Gallery, and touring to other regional galleries. The twenty-four artists represented in 'Escape Artists: Modernists of the Tropics' included Russell Drysdale, Donald Friend, John Olsen, Margaret Olley, Sidney Nolan, Brett Whiteley and Ian Fairweather. Val's 'Timana Island' (1945) and 'To the Islands' (1950), and Von's 'Garden on Dunk Island' (1943), 'Mango Trees' (1945), and 'The Catch' (1945) had all been donated by the sisters to the Cairns Art Gallery or City of Townsville Art Collection in 1990. The exhibition catalogue includes a beautiful portrait of Von, painted by Noel in about 1945 and donated by Val, and Noel's 'Brammo Bay (Dunk Island) 1946'. In assessing the artwork of the three friends, Wilson made a telling comment about Noel, who in art and life was usually characterised as charismatic and undisciplined:

> Noel Wood's 'Dunk Island' c. 1946 and Yvonne Cohen's 'Mango Trees' 1945, both exhibit a passion for the pure use of colour. This direct intuitive approach reveals an affinity for the work of the Fauves. But the great difference between the two artists is temperament. There is an edge to Wood's work. ... One gets the impression that in all this profusion of life and apparent sense of freedom, is a doubting, troubled individual.
>
> On the other hand, Yvonne Cohen displays a bright optimistic temperament that revels in the elements on offer. Her vigorous use of colour reflects the joy of living in the most idyllic of circumstances. Cohen's effective use of colour prevents the work from tottering into the facile. In the best of Valerie Albiston's painting we see a reductive process at work.

> Albiston shows an interest in cubism, particularly the work of George Braque. Her probing, analytical approach to the problem of eliciting meaning from the tropical landscape, as in 'Timana Island', 1945, derives from her skill in deploying line and mass all within a narrow colour range.

Val and Von were pleased to be sent the catalogue but were not up to travel to view it.

Beginning in the late 1970s, the sisters donated most of their father's work, with caricatures going to the State Library of Victoria and the Australian National Gallery, and sketches and pastels to Australian National Gallery, National Gallery of Victoria, Art Gallery of Ballarat and Mornington Peninsula Regional Gallery. At Kew, Val began dispersing some of their own, Norman's and their friends' works which hung on the walls or sat in corners of their studios. Von's health was failing and Val had trouble getting her to sign her unsigned work before she offered it for exhibition and to galleries.

Towards the end of 2000, Von had a near-death encounter with pneumonia, coupled with strokes, which left her with diminished cognitive ability. Val was left struggling to care for her. The following year, Von entered an aged-care facility on Riversdale Road and later moved to their brand-new facility, Camberwell Green, in the same suburb. Without fail, Val telephoned Von every evening to say goodnight. Still driving (as recklessly as ever), Val visited whenever she could, and Jan Tracy, Sigrid Warne and other mutual friends also ferried her to see Von. Although Von seemed accepting of her situation, mercifully, she had little understanding of it. For Val, who had looked out for Von for the whole of her life, it was a miserable time—she had begged the hospital to let Von die.

With Von no longer living at home, Val took in a series of more or less suitable lodgers, found through various agencies, who received board in exchange for a few hours of practical assistance, such as with shopping. Val was still sociable and often had friends and family for tea or lunch and the lodgers were company at night and kept an eye on her. She eventually fell out with most. One of the longer lasting carers abused her situation by setting up a home business, with an office in Von's studio, even inviting her lover to live in. Scared to lose her, Val agreed to the latter after a promise that he would not use the bathroom!

Although she must have been feeling vulnerable, at ninety years of age, Val was still spirited and on the ball. Vigorously, she kept up the pretence of being penniless. At the supermarket, she bought items on sale because their use-by-date was up. She did deals with the dentist, choosing the least expensive option, even when it meant she could only eat soft food, and gave him her own paintings as payment. She had always been frugal with heating, claiming that she was not cold, when she clearly was, and arguing with Von about it. The house had central heating, but instead of using that Val bought a cheap two-bar radiator—one of the lightweight, concave variety that can easily be tipped over—and sat in front of it. We wished it gone, given the dangers, but many times Val argued that she was careful—until the day we returned from a lunch outing to discover a damp towel thrown over the heater. A nervously grinning Val knew she had been caught out. It was turned off, she argued. Furious, my brother ripped the heater from the wall socket and confiscated it.

A few years before, when Val had trouble with her accountant, my brother Peter and his accountant had, with input from Val, begun managing her financial affairs. The only way that Peter could convince Val to let the accountant pay Von's aged-care fees was by telling her that it would come out of Von's estate. Val approached several gallery owners, offering them the silver and jewellery left to Von in their mother's will. She also offered Von's Fairweather, 'Dervish' (plate sixty-nine in Bail's *Fairweather*) to gallery owner Charles Nodrum—all allegedly to raise money because she could not afford the fees for Von's care. Nodrum was about to go on holiday and while he was away Val became impatient. She approached Paulette Calhoun (now Clouseau), who had handled the estate of Val's friend, artist Mary Macqueen. Paulette quickly sold the watercolour, in dubious

Progress Press **November 29, 1999 - 25**

Sisters' dreams on show

"IF YOU were lucky enough to catch a fish, a decision was made whether to paint it or eat it."

Such was the life for Kew artists and sisters Valerie Albiston and Yvonne Cohen, who not only lived on but owned their own tropical island for more than 40 years.

The island was Timana on the Great Barrier Reef and the time was the 1930s.

Ms Albiston, "the adventurous one", had packed her bags and headed to Queensland to the newly-opened Dunk Island.

Upon arrival, she persuaded her sister to join her and in 1939 they bought Timana Island — 12ha of tropical paradise between Bederra and Dunk islands.

Their island had no telephone, no electricity and no radio. During the war years, Timana became a haven for off-duty soldiers and the two sisters contributed to the war effort by growing fruit for the troops and making camouflage nets.

In between catching fish, finding oysters and ridding their house of white ants, they honed their painting skills, passed on from their father, a talented "Sunday artist".

"He used to take us with him while he painted but it was only after he died we started painting," Ms Albiston said.

And paint they did.

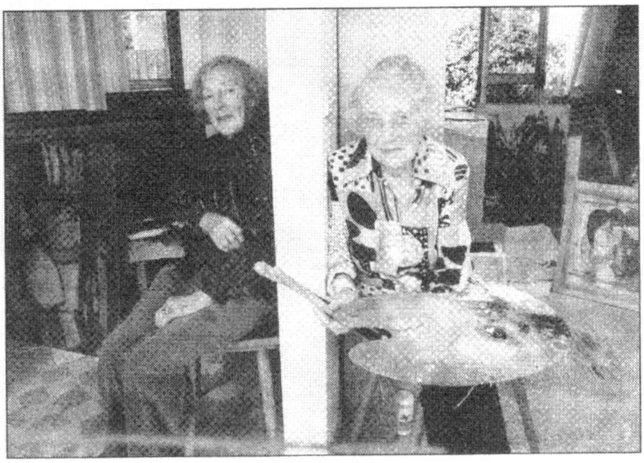

Together in art: *sisters Yvonne Cohen and Valerie Albiston.* 023TG306

Now, at 88 and 85 respectively, Ms Albiston and Ms Cohen are about to unveil their latest works at Barkers Gallery, Hawthorn.

The pieces are mainly abstract — over the years Ms Albiston's paintings have come to focus on images of people and Ms Cohen's are mainly scenic.

But the vibrant modernist pieces also reflect a sense of the lush tropical vegetation of the island paradise they shared for so long.

Although they no longer share their own island, the two sisters are still painting together — in a studio separated only by a thin partition.

And they still share the same thoughts about painting — it is what dreams are made of.

"I can go into my studio for an hour's painting and come out six hours later," Ms Cohen said.

"It is the most relaxing and entertaining of pursuits. It can transport you anywhere."

The sisters' work can be seen at a mixed exhibition of paintings and sculpture from December 5-19 at Barkers Gallery, 72 Barkers Rd, Hawthorn. Inquiries: 9853 1957.

— LAETA ANTONYSEN

In the late 1990s the sisters, well into their eighties, were trying to empty their very full studios. In December 1999 they were part of a multi-artist exhibition at Barkers' Gallery, Hawthorn. *Progress Press* 29 November 1999, p. 25

condition, for $30,000, to Bill Nuttall of Niagara Galleries and Aman Siddique; the latter then a respected conservator. The restored work ended up in Brisbane. Although these quirky Val moments brought us some amusement, it was a sad and trying time for all.

When the sisters moved to Kew, they met and befriended Catherine (Cathie) and Jules Stocky; the owners of a small, nearby gallery and framing shop. Cathie in particular enjoyed their tales and little eccentricities, beginning an essay she later wrote on them with a quote from Thoreau: 'If a man does not keep pace with his companions, perhaps it is because he hears the music of a different drummer. Let him step to the music he hears.' Edmund Banfield's grave on Dunk Island bears the same inscription.

Their studios were still very full. On the top of the bookshelf of Val's studio stood a framed collection of tiny collages of erotically posed figures—a gift to Norman by the sisters' lifetime friend Dorothy Braund. Propped beside it was a portrait of their mother Viva, by Von. Here and there in the house were a few other paintings by their friends Bill Ferguson, Roger Kemp, Roger Juniper, Elaine Haxton, Hughan and Boyd pottery, little Marcus Clarke sculptures, and a small painting by Donald Friend. The latter, Val claimed, was a gift from the artist, painted with a brush she made for him when they met in Bali.

Cathie helped Val to sell the sisters' own artworks to galleries or donate them under the Australian Government's Cultural Gifts Program. Cairns Regional Gallery, City of Townsville Art Collection, Rockhampton Art Gallery, Warrnambool Art Gallery, and Bendigo Art Gallery accepted the gift. In addition, in the early noughties, at their gallery on Cotham Road, the Stockys held an exhibition-sale for each of the sisters—their only solo shows. Pre-publicity photos in the local papers show Val alone, separated from her sister after a lifetime together. She is surrounded by twenty-three of Von's paintings and fifteen works on paper, including 'Orchard Country', for which Von won the Gibson Prize in 1958, and a very early work, 'Street Scene in Bruges 1934', painted during the family's travels in the 1930s.

In an interview, Val told Cathie, 'We have never had a competitive

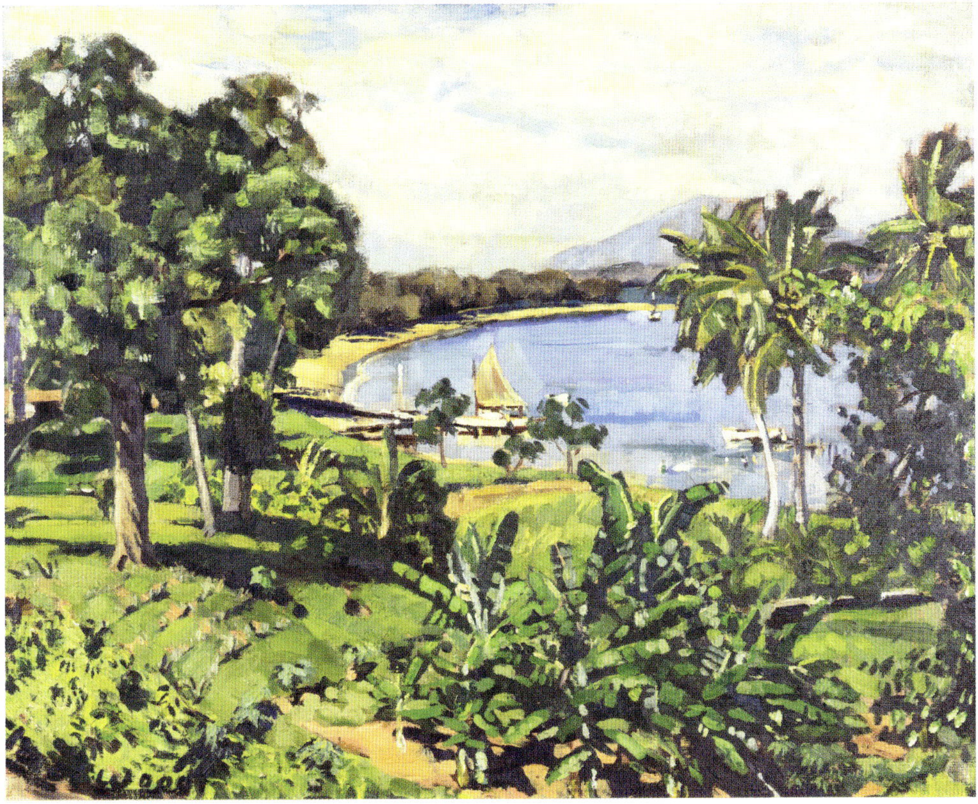

'Brammo Bay'. Painting by Noel Wood, 1946

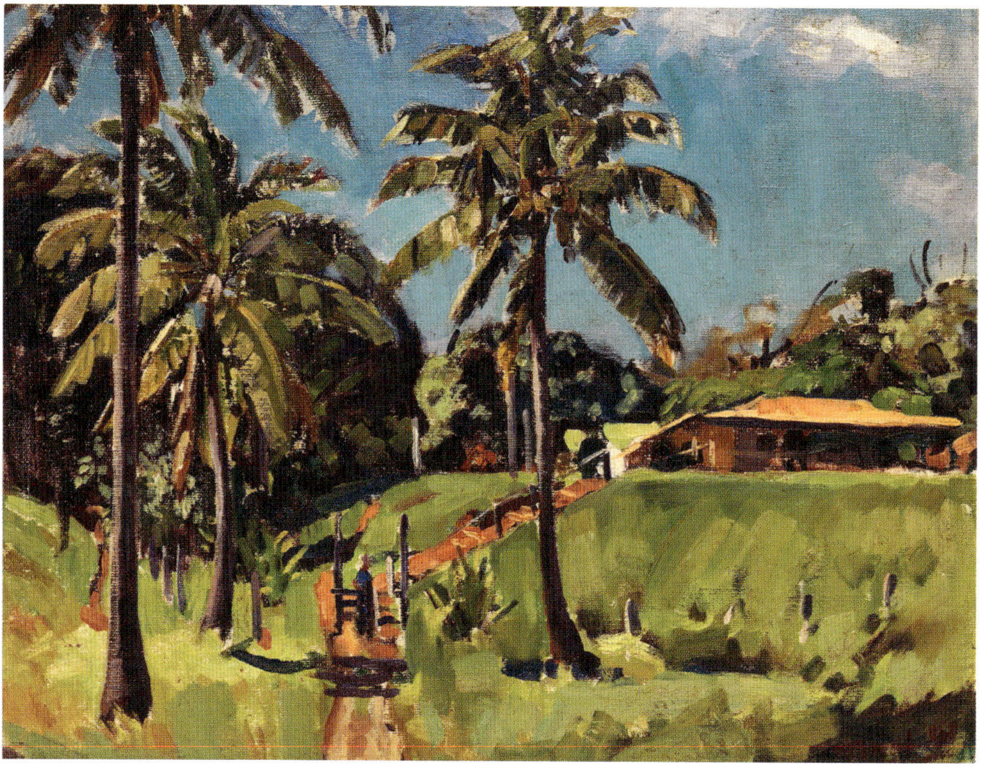

'The Pathway to Banfield's Old Home (Dunk Island)'. Painting by Noel Wood, c.1940

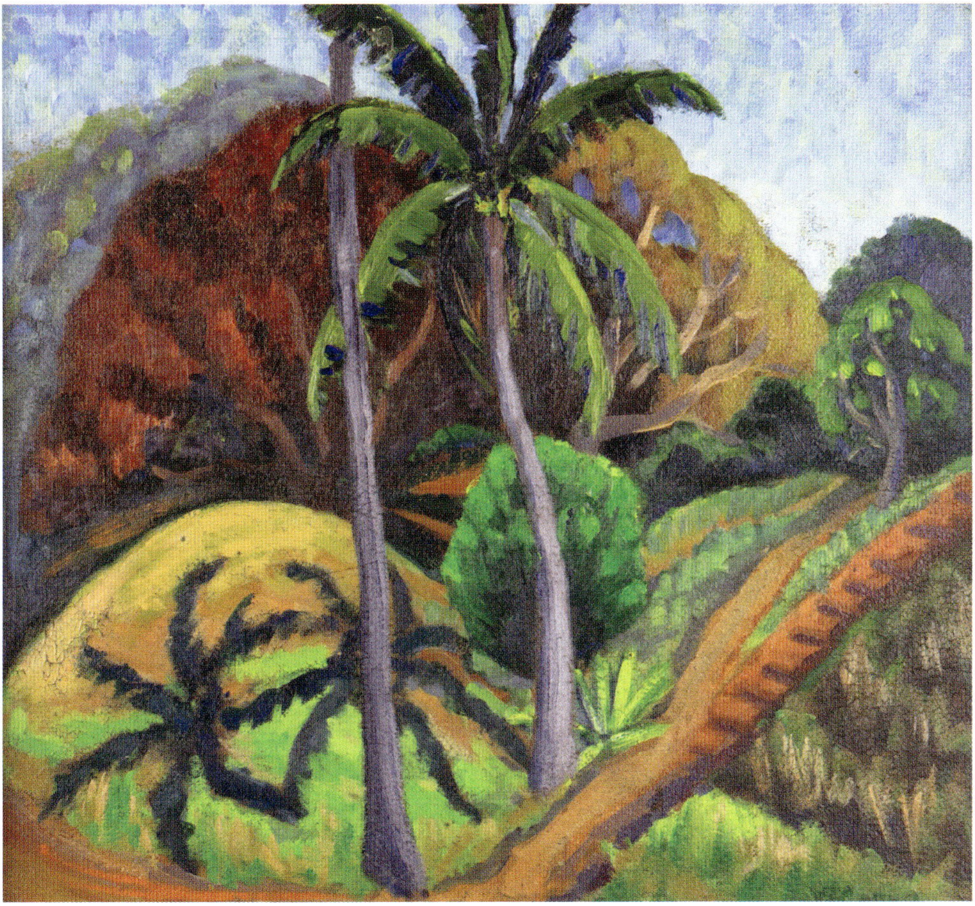

'Mango Trees'. Painting by Yvonne Cohen, c.1940

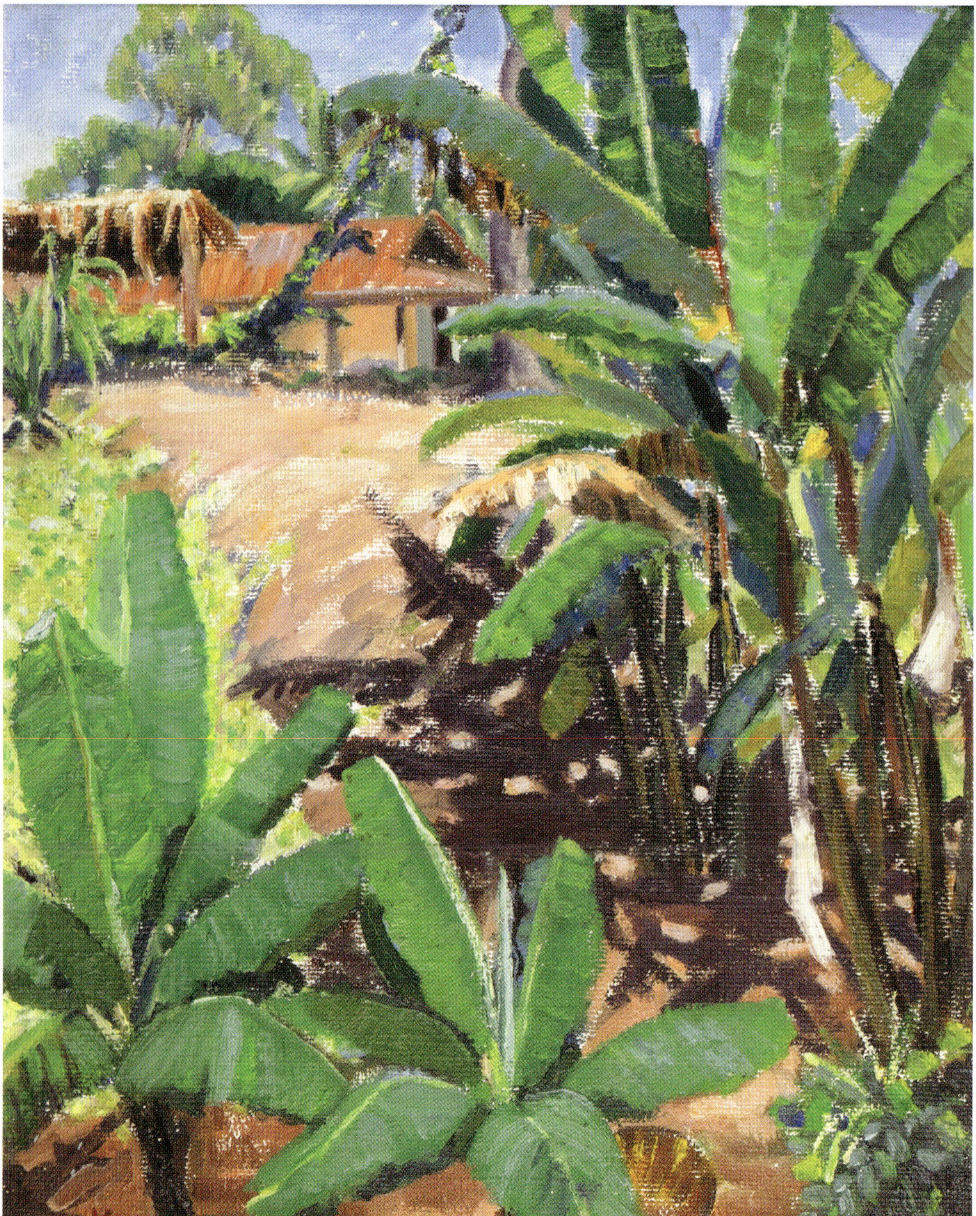

'Garden on Dunk Island'. Painting by Yvonne Cohen, 1943

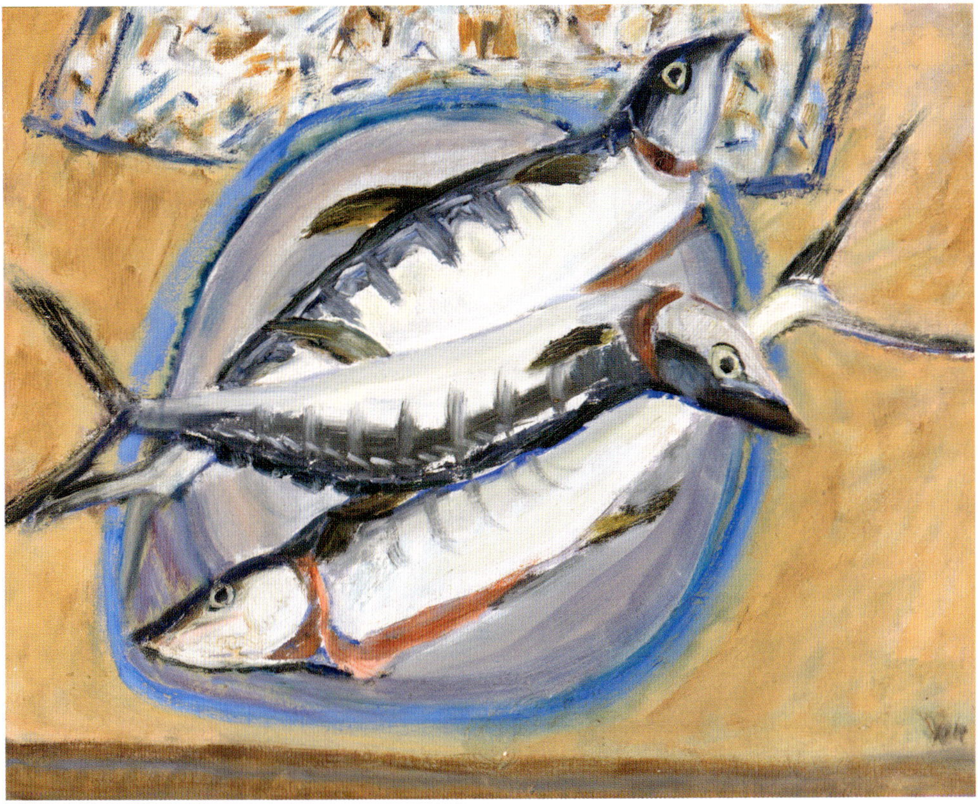

'The Catch'. Painting by Yvonne Cohen, 1945

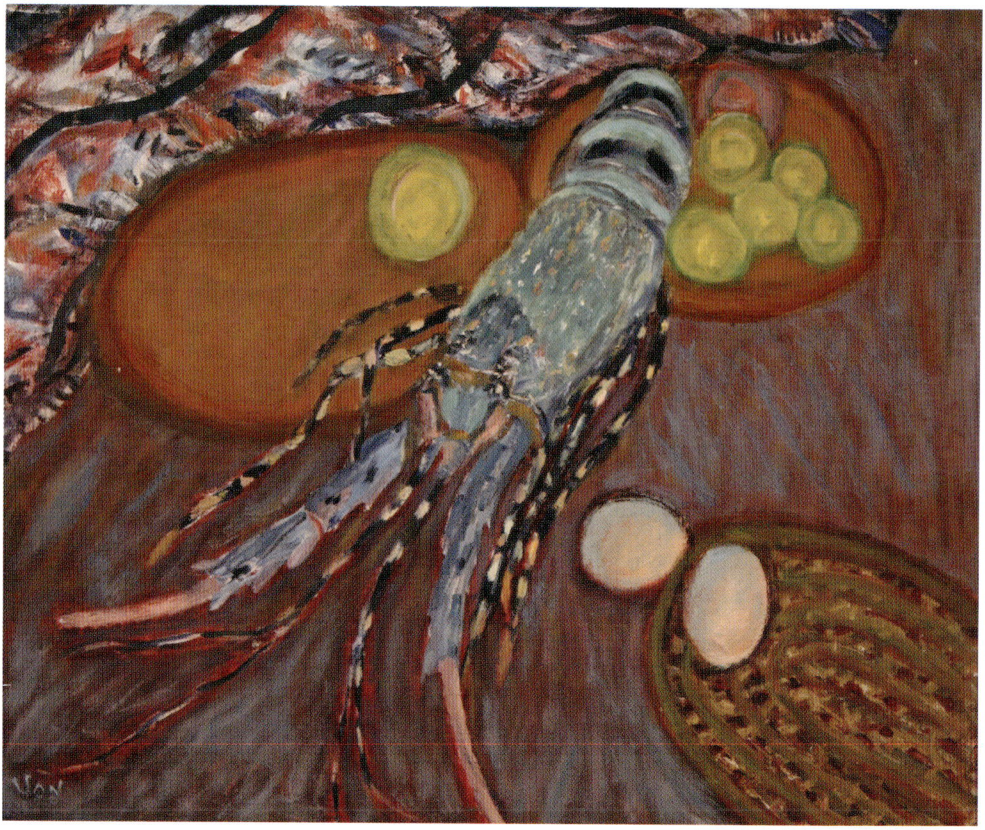

'The Blue Crayfish'. Painting by Yvonne Cohen, 1945

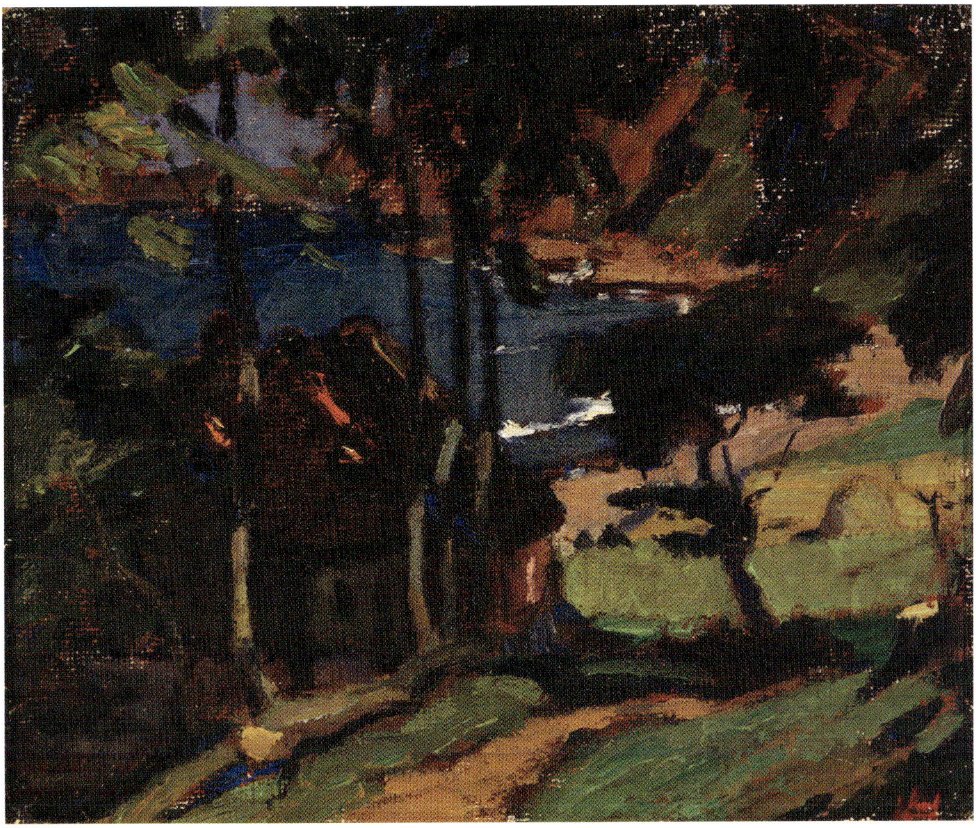

'Untitled (Bedarra Island Hut)'. Painting by Yvonne Cohen, 1940s

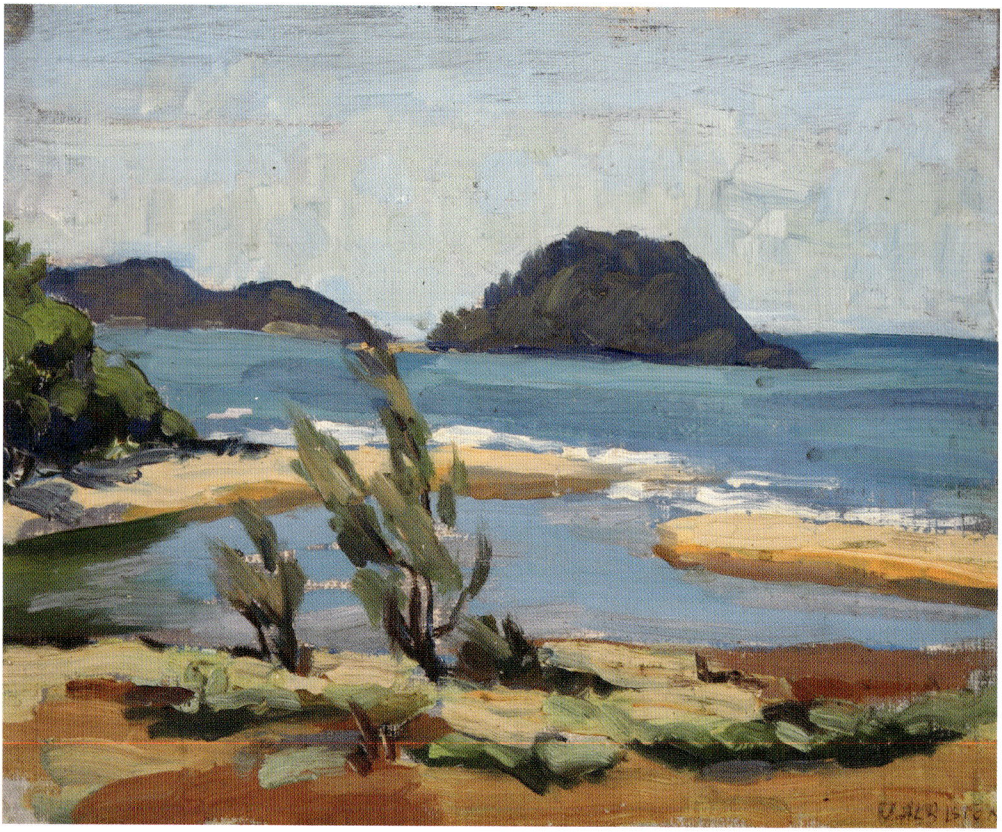

'To the Islands, Timana'. Painting by Valerie Albiston, 1950

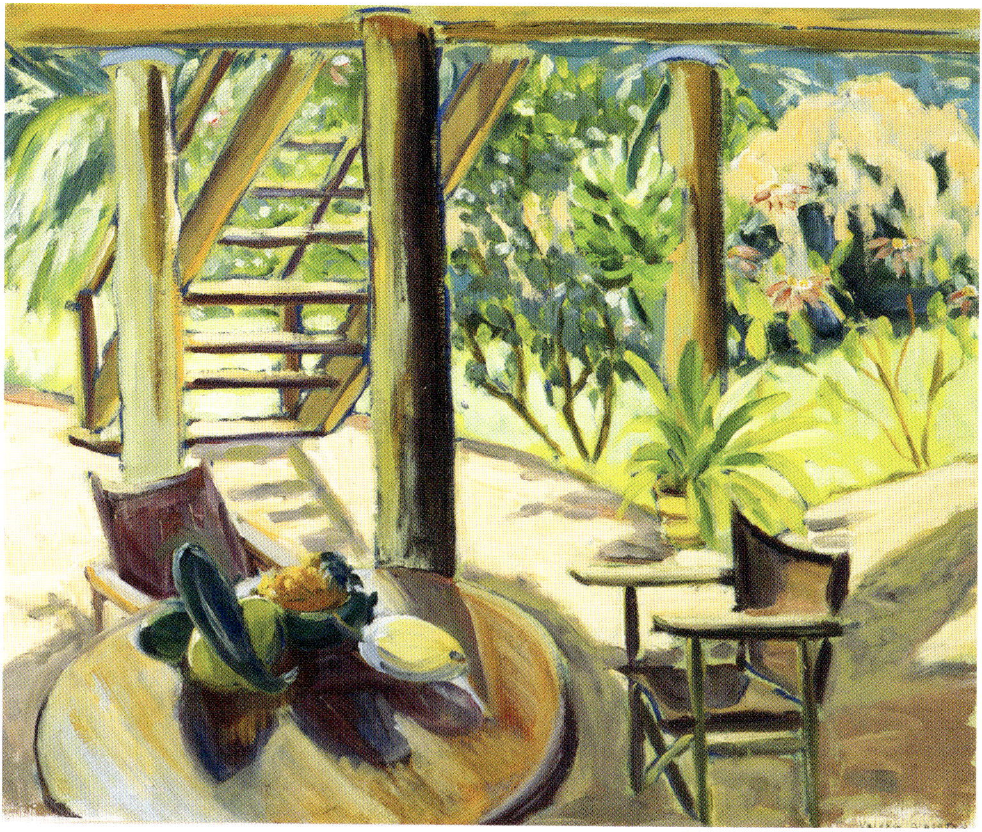

'Timana Island, Under the House'. Painting by Valerie Albiston, 1950

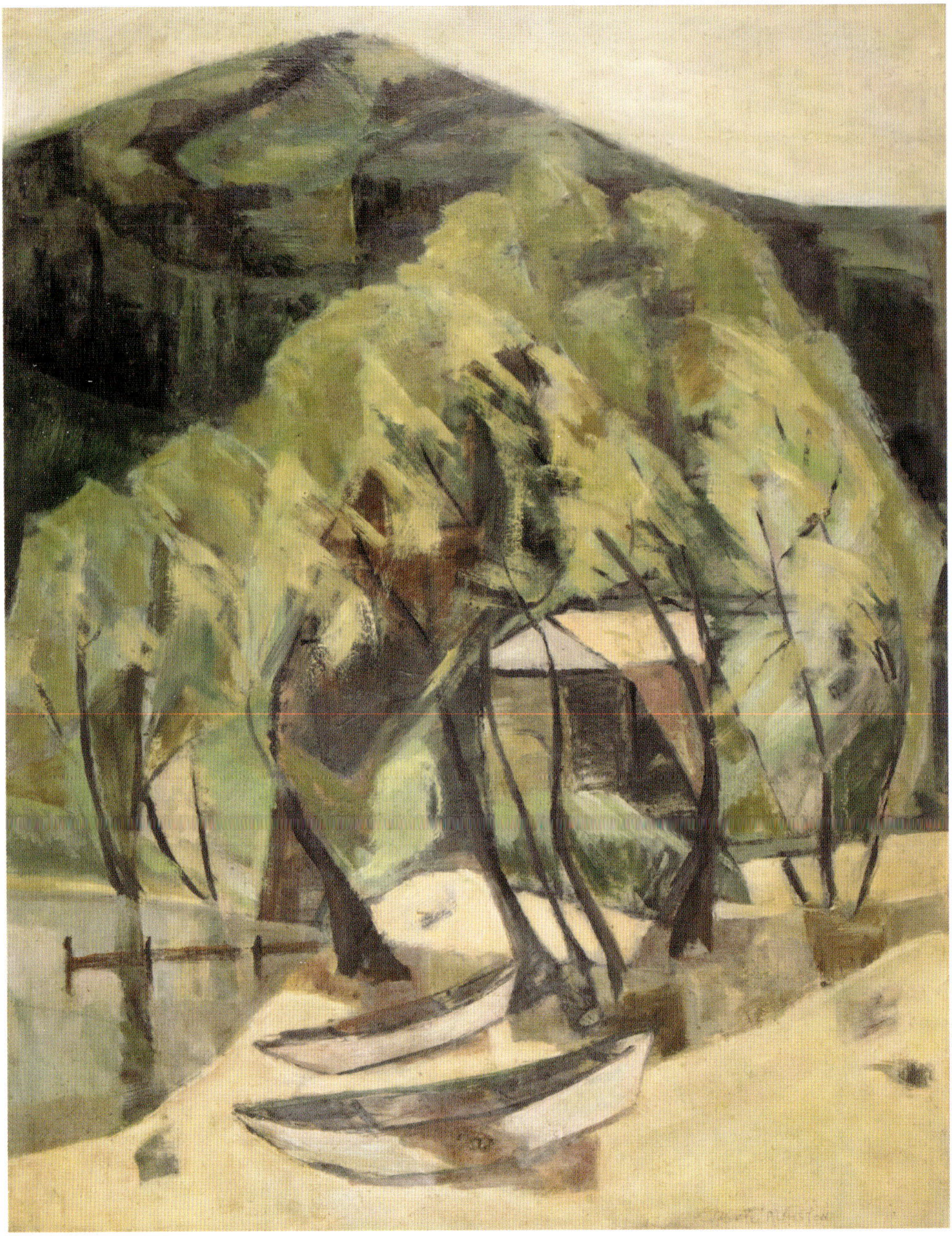

'Timana Island'. Painting by Valerie Albiston, 1945

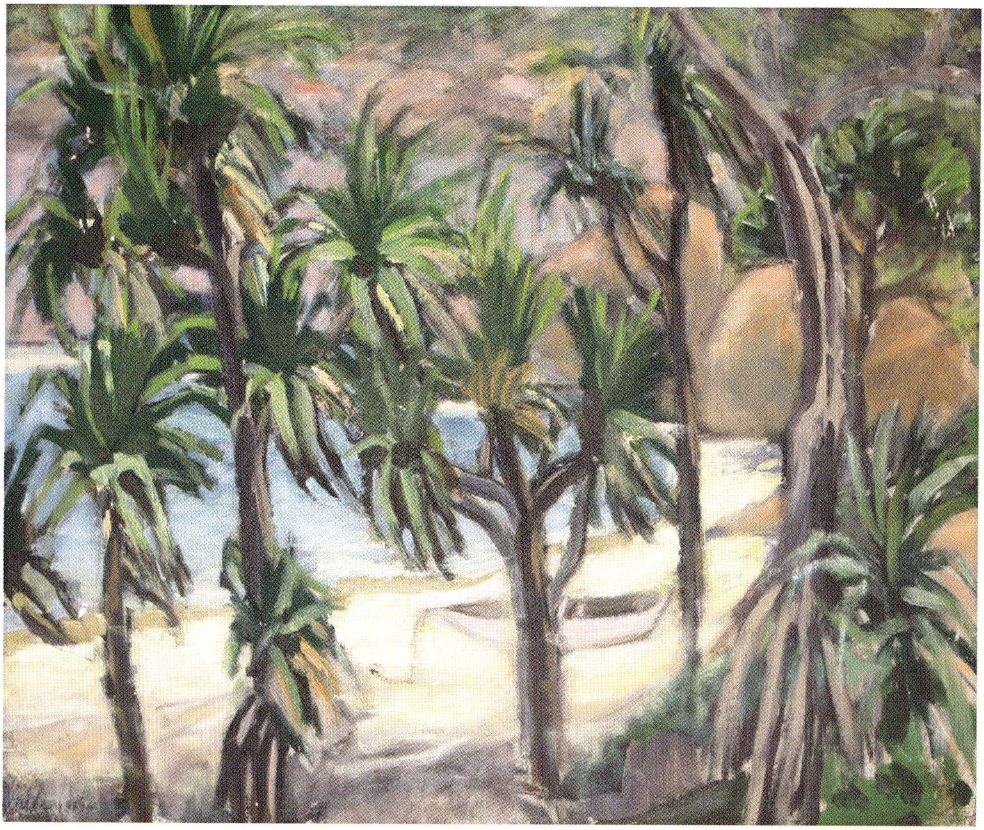

'Bedarra Island'. Painting by Valerie Albiston, 1940s

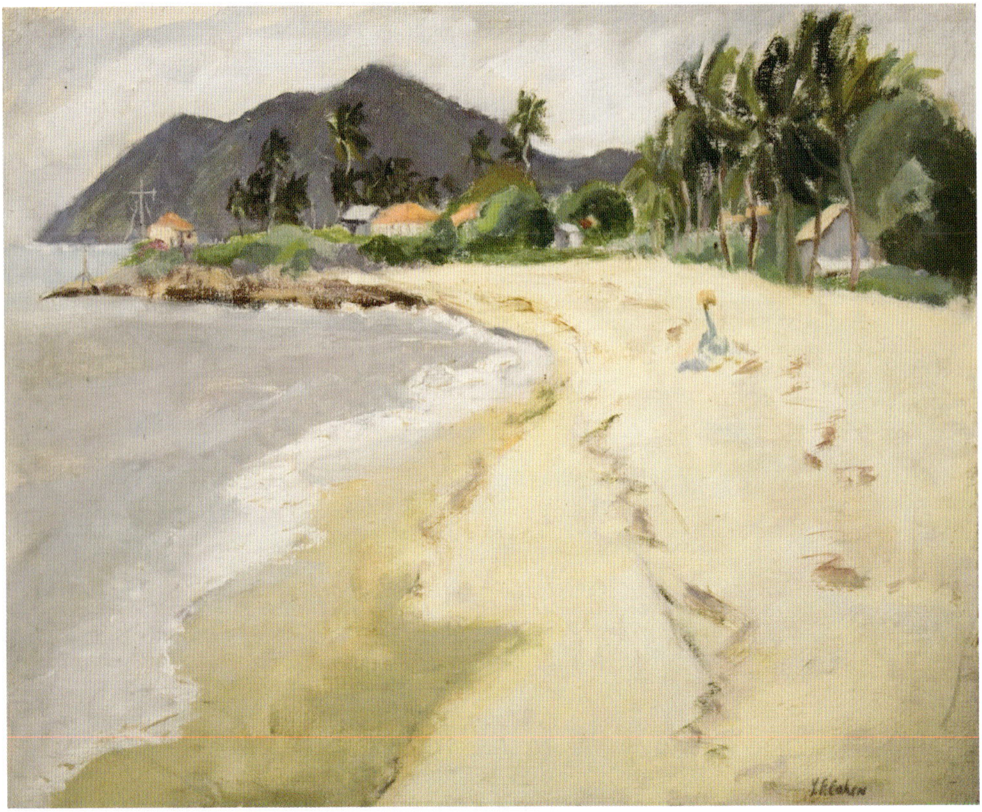

'Queensland Beach'. Painting by Yvonne Cohen, 1945

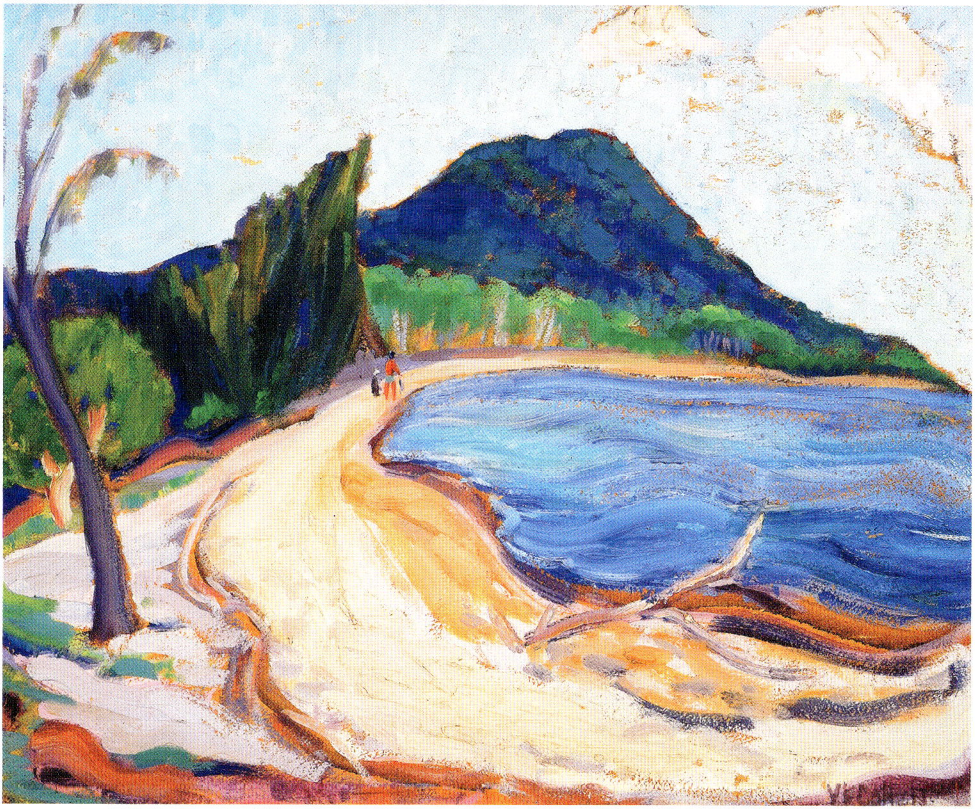

Beach at Dunk Island'. Painting by Yvonne Cohen, c.1950

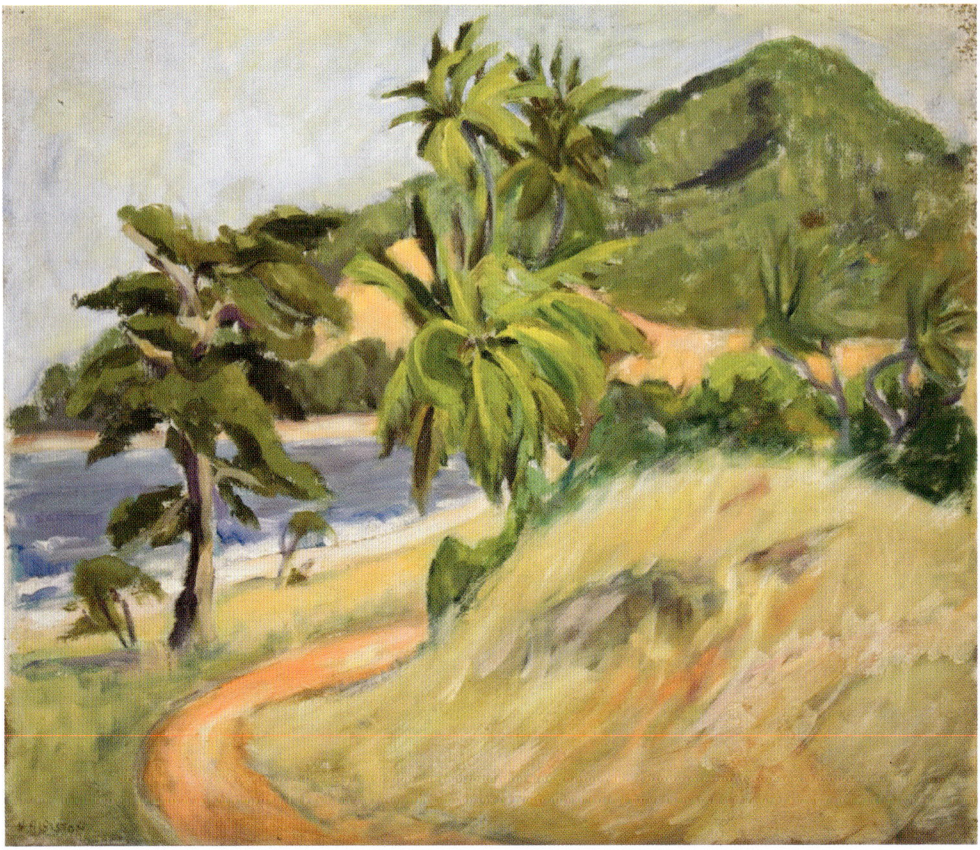

'Windy Morning, Bingil Bay'. Painting by Valerie Albiston, 1950

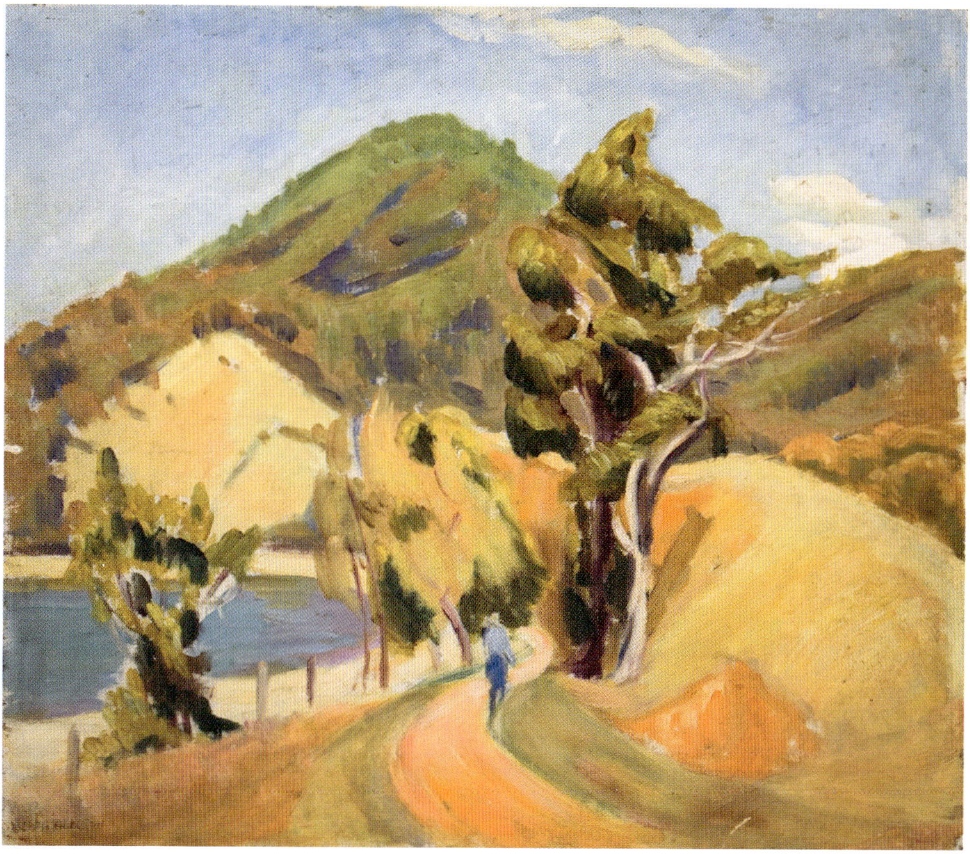

'Along the Track, Bingil Bay'. Painting by Valerie Albiston, 1950

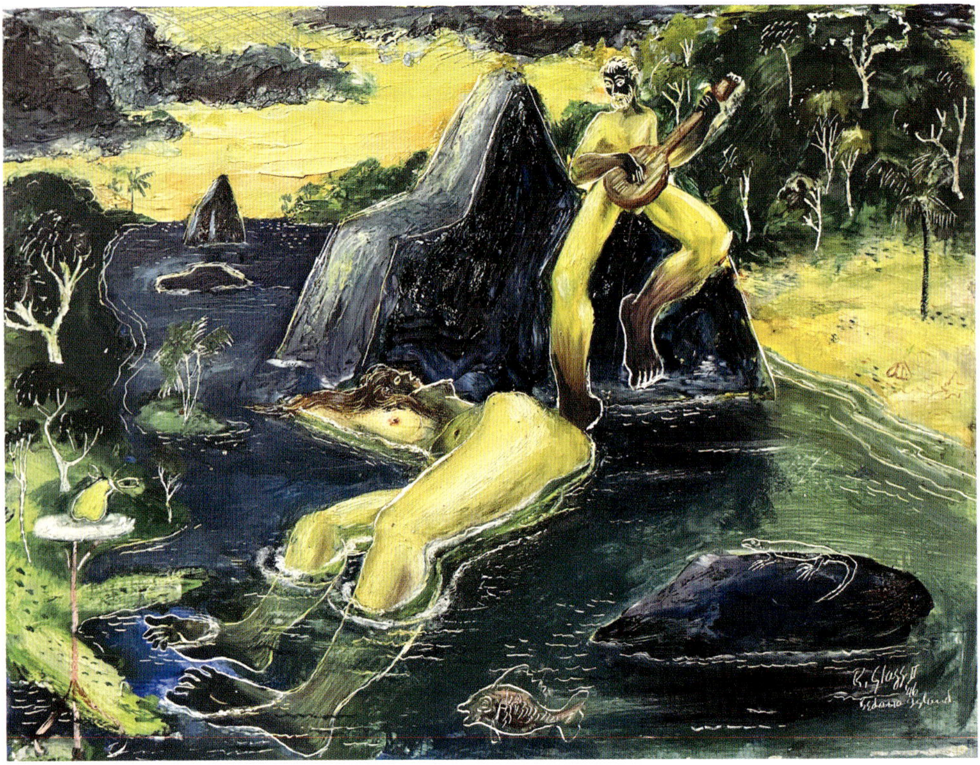

'Island Dream, Bedarra Island'. Painting by Raymond Glass, 1946

relationship. If Von was asked to show some paintings and got good reviews, I was happy for her, just as she was for me when I had an exhibition.' Without doubt, Val was absolutely devoted to her sister, and they enjoyed each other's company and sense of humour, yet it is doubtful that she ever had a totally non-competitive relationship with *any* woman, and it was most unusual for the sisters to exhibit separately, anyway. For Val, the details varied with the day: to Cathie she said that she and Von were 'each other's best critic', but told an interviewer for the *Manningham Leader* that '... we both had studios at home next to each other, but we didn't really take much notice of each other.' They could, in fact, be quite harsh about each other's work. A 2009 interviewer asked the question, 'Did you influence each other's work?', to which Val replied, 'No, I don't think so. I used to say to Von, that's all out of kilter, she'd say that drawing is terrible.'

It would have rankled Val when the reporter for the *Manningham Leader* observed, 'Valerie Albiston doesn't strike you as the bohemian type.' Despite their efforts to live and style themselves as unconventional, impoverished artists, she and Von had indeed remained essentially genteel bourgeoisie. That is not to say that their lives had been entirely conventional or unexceptional—quite the contrary.

Von's solo exhibition, 'Timana Island and Beyond', opened on 6 May 2001. As arranged, Von arrived by taxi from the aged-care facility. The staff had done her hair up, as she often wore it when she was younger, and finished it with a frangipani. She was still lovely. Touchingly, she spent the occasion in a wheelchair, transfixed on one of her island paintings.

In September, it was Val's turn, with 'South of Capricornia': oils and watercolours from the 1950s and 1960s, including several of New Caledonia which Val had kept tucked away since their inspirational holiday there in 1959. In an article promoting the exhibition, Cathie described the watercolours thus:

> ... the New Caledonian native spirit of 'laissez faire and bon vivant' [is] beautifully captured in these paintings. Her

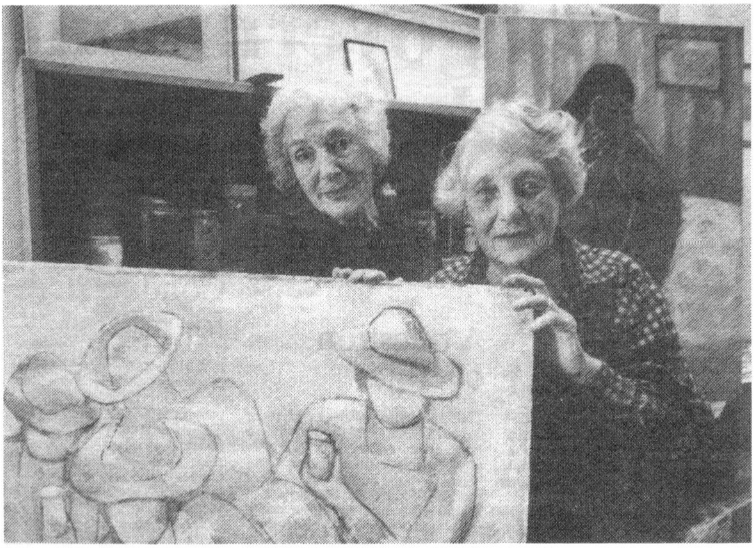

Von (left) and Val in the late 1990s, holding one of Val's many oils of faceless people in hats and with one of Von's paintings behind. *Leader Community News* date unknown

> palette of rich tropical colours, faded pinks and textured whites, so typical of the French colonial presence, contrasts wonderfully with her use of strong mustards and oranges to portray the east coast country.

Val told Cathie that in 1965, Anne Purves of Australian Galleries had invited her to exhibit the watercolours, but they had a falling out and Val buried them in her studio. We wondered at this, not because of the altercation, but because Val was a vigorous non-hoarder, nor was she sentimental. Many times, she told us that she was ruthless, unlike Von, who accumulated sketches on scraps of paper, backs of envelopes and in sketchbooks, and amusing cartoons and caricatures from newspapers. They were also unlike any of Val's other work that we had seen at the time, but it transpired that they were in a style she briefly adopted into the 1960s.

In 2002, the Stockys included the sisters in an exhibition of selected works from the 'George Bell Circle and other Modernists':

four of Val's recent oils, mostly of outback drinkers at the pub ($4500–$4950), and two of Von's groups of Aboriginal figures ($2500–$4000). A selling point was always that the artist's fee would go to charity, or so Val told Cathie Stocky—which certainly did not happen, at least while Val was living.

In 2002, under the Cultural Gifts Program, the Heide Museum of Modern Art took a selection of Val's artbooks for their reference library. Through Leonard Joel's auction house, Val sold off Von's paintings, including a couple by Noel: a landscape and 'Xmas' (a Christmas gift?). Also, small works by Martin Collocot (who, in 1989, had become Michelle Frances Collocot); a 1978 painting by fellow Bell School member, Ailsa O'Connor; and 'Rainbow Serpent', by the sisters' friend Bill Ferguson.

Von died quietly in 2004 on the last day of February, four months short of ninety. She left the bulk of her estate to Val, who was also her executor, with a few small bequests for friends and family. She intended that a significant sum of money was to be used to set up a scholarship for Aboriginal artists. Val was resistant to the idea—'they'll only waste it', she argued. Regardless, with a big push from the other executors, a trust was set up and the inaugural Yvonne Cohen Award for Creative Indigenous Australian Youth was awarded in 2005. The annual award, of about $5000, assists artists aged thirty and under to advance their career and has found some worthy recipients. Von's other wishes were ignored.

Von's death certificate lists her occupation as 'Artist'—information presumably provided by Val. A common comment by Val was that she, Val, never considered herself a 'professional artist'. That may be true of her, but I believe that Von, at least for a time, was determined to be successful artist. She told me this was why she never married—she wanted to dedicate her life to art. Certainly, both sisters were keen to be recognised as working artists and they made solid sales. As their friend and fellow artist Bill Ferguson pointed out, at times their work sold for more than that of the likes Ian Fairweather.

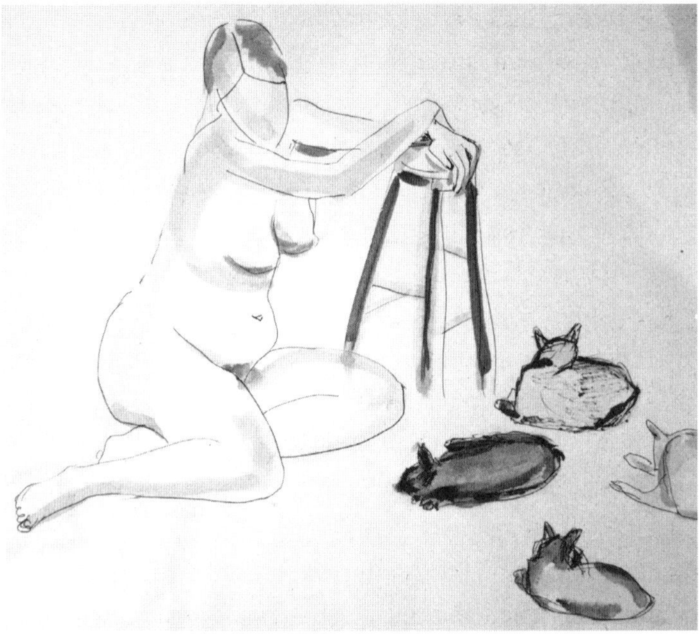

Von always loved cats and fed several strays at Kew. Over the years, she even included them in several figure studies. Private collection

After Von's death, Val donated a batch of Von's artwork to Heide Museum of Modern Art: thirty-three drawings and paintings, including the oil of their mother, Viva, and of Neil Douglas. There were several drawings of Noel, one of Noel drawing Val, and one by Noel of Gini and the Woods' terrier sleeping that was most likely drawn in late 1939. Von had a soft spot for cats, and they feature in several of her early life class sketches and on various scraps of paper left in her studio. Further work went through the Cultural Gifts Program that year: 'Dockside', an oil by Von from the early 1960s; and an oil by Val, 'Albert Park', painted in 1955. Whatever her tax savings from the gift, some of it went back to the gallery. Val is listed in Heide's annual report as a donor each year from 2004 to 2007.

Towards the end of 2006, Val fell and broke her femur, which required an operation, a pin and a further period in hospital undergoing vigorously resisted rehabilitation, during which she claimed several times not to have been fed. She had been at home alone. Contrary to her agreement with my brother and sister-in-law that she would not leave the house without her walking stick, she headed outside empty-handed and immediately fell heavily against the back step. She was lucky that a friend, Jan Tracy, had been invited for tea and found her. She healed remarkably well for a ninety-five-year-old and was soon scooting about the house with the aid of a walking frame, cooking for herself and socialising. No longer able to drive, though, she reluctantly gave up her battered car and sent my brother to get a refund on the balance of her driver's licence.

My brother was already managing Val's financial affairs through an unofficial arrangement with her accountant, and with Val's tacit approval. After her fall, he quietly took on her formal guardianship so that she was allowed to return home. Because Val had repeatedly told hospital staff that she was going to kill herself, as well as taking responsibility for her, Peter was required to remove all sharp knives and poisons from Kew, for which she chastised him. He had also taken her valuable paintings home to keep them more secure while she was in hospital and was accused of their theft! With agreement from the accountant, Peter and Artemis organised full-time carers, without revealing the cost to Val.

In January 2008, on what turned out to be my last visit, she was bedridden and told me to go away. I was devastated—we were losing her. There would be no more 'Alright, duckie', her usual farewell. Still mentally alert but with her body failing, she died a fortnight later.

Val's death certificate gives her occupation as 'Widow', which seems antiquated in 2008. She worked hard to be recognised as a freelance journalist and artist, although she may not have minded 'widow' as an addition. She was proud to have been married to a medico, especially such an interesting one. Partly for security, she was always listed in the phonebook under his name. Being a doctor's wife could also come in handy. When the sisters moved to Kew more than a decade after Norman's death, Val successfully argued that his professional needs required that the phone be connected pronto.

In memory of the sisters, Chris Deighton, Val's step-grandnephew (the grandson of Norman's sister, Marianne), funded two scholarships at the University of Melbourne. The Valerie Albiston Painting Scholarship and the Yvonne Cohen Sculpture Scholarship are each awarded biennially to a student entering their second year, through nomination by the School of Art. Approximately $5500 is awarded per annum, for two years, intended to go towards fees, and has assisted several worthy young creatives.

The sisters' memory will also live on in their artwork. They would be pleased but not surprised to know that it is still in circulation and still exhibited. As they told an interviewer in the 1990s, the journey some of the paintings took to 'pop up where least expected' was part of the magic of painting. In May 2012, their work was among that of several fine artists at 'Australian Artists of Influence', held at Gecko Studio Gallery in Geelong.

They would have been especially delighted to know that they featured with old friends Noel Wood, Deanna Conti, Fred Williams and Bruce Arthur in 'To the Islands'; an exhibition that focused on the artists who worked on Dunk and surrounding islands from the 1930s to the 1990s. Curated by Ross Searle, the exhibition opened at the Perc Tucker Regional Gallery in Townsville on 18 October 2013 and ran for six weeks before moving to the Cairns Regional Gallery from January to March 2014. The comprehensive catalogue, with essays and full-page reproductions of the sisters' seventeen paintings held by those two galleries—seven of Val's and ten of Von's— contains two portraits of Von: the warm portrait painted by her lover Noel in 1946 and a charmingly fresh self-portrait made the following year.

In a review of the show for *The Australian,* Nicolas Rothwell commented on the '... delightful exhibition... The works are modest records of an encounter ... presented here without a single false note.' He singled out Von's 'Into the Blue' as 'the most striking piece ... a vortex maelstrom'. Kenneth Wilkinson of *The Herald* also preferred Von's paintings, *because he felt that '... their touch of passion places them in a sphere higher than that of Valerie's faithful reportage.'*

The artwork the sisters made on the islands was as radical for its time as their lifestyle during that period of their lives. It was a shame that their work was rarely fully appreciated while they were living. It took Searle to place it in context:

> While not all of the artists associated with this exhibition are household names, they produced highly original works of art in what is a little known period of Australian art history. ... the creative energy of Wood, Cohen, Albiston and Conti remains unparalleled and little appreciated in the national context. For decades these artists produced strikingly original works of art ... indeed the work of Noel Wood and the Cohen sisters is quite remarkable and their reputations as pioneers of the Modernist Australian painting movement remain underappreciated.

15

FINDING FAIRWEATHER

It was left to my brother, Peter, and his wife, Artemis, who were Val's executors, to clean up and dispense with what remained in the house at Kew. Paintings still graced the walls of the living rooms, including the changing display of Val's own small works. The studios were hung with a few old favourites and packed with canvases, sketchbooks, pigments and other typical artist's paraphernalia, including easels—despite Val telling reporters that the latter were too expensive and that they always painted kneeling. Even on Timana, as Von's sketches show, they had an easel.

It was not an easy will to administer. Val left her most significant artworks to friends and family, but several beneficiaries were given the choice of one of Val's paintings, to be distributed in the order of people specified in the will. Thankfully for Peter, some of the recipients asked him to choose for them. The actual extent of Val's wealth—well over twenty-five million— was a surprise, as was the main beneficiary. We expected her to leave the bulk of her estate for some artistic or literary purpose. Instead, 99 per cent went to the Salvation Army to build a men's wing at one of their aged-care facilities, in memory of her parents, Morris and Viva. Certainly, Viva would have been pleased by the act of philanthropy. Curiously, Val had shopped at the Salvo's op shops, among others, but otherwise had shown no interest in the organisation. On hearing of the main beneficiary, Jan Tracy, one of Val's close friends late in life, was particularly hurt because several times she had told Val of her experiences as a young social worker with the Salvation Army. She'd reported the abuse she had witnessed of girls in care, but it had fallen on deaf ears.

The most important artworks among Val's estate were five paintings by Ian Fairweather. After we had taken the sisters' ashes back to Timana in 2013, I began research for their biography. Val had always told us, as she and Von implied in a 1978 interview with James Gleeson, that their Fairweathers had been among twelve or so unsigned works left behind when the artist departed Cairns in 1949, and sent to Melbourne by their mutual friend Chas Martin. We had always been slightly suspicious of the story, which varied in its detail and was sometimes accompanied by a lot of winking between the sisters. Once, she and Von even told me that they went to the upturned boat where he was living and helped themselves to the paintings (he actually lived in the hull of boat in Darwin, not Cairns!). Another time, Val told me that 'Bioscope' had been a gift from Lina and that they kept one each of the unsigned works from Chas, which *was*, it seems, the case. Von's Fairweather was sold to help fund her care. The five listed in Val's will were: 'Bioscope', 'Composition', 'Water Carriers', and two untitled works; one of a young woman seated at a dressing table and the other of three girls kneeling with musical instruments.

After Val's death, I had the opportunity to closely inspect the four paintings, which I'd been led to believe had been collected by Chas and were unsigned. Afterwards, I began trawling through catalogues and books on Fairweather. From the information in Murray Bail's books, I quickly realised that two works—'Composition', and 'Water Carriers'—were indeed signed, with the somewhat cryptic monogram that Fairweather used in the years 1957–1959 and 1961. I contacted Bail, who was able to identify them and the date they were exhibited by Macquarie Galleries in 1957. Bail recognised a third painting, 'Seated Woman', as among those exhibited at Macquarie Galleries in 1949, with the stolen work, 'Kulu Valley'. Perhaps it was on the way home from Timana in September 1949 that Norman and the sisters stopped in Sydney to see the exhibition. Certainly, Norm and Val bought two: a lyrical landscape of Kulu Valley, India, dated 1949, for seven guineas, and the sensuous image of a naked young Indian woman grooming herself before a mirror ('Seated Woman' in 1948).

It became obvious that Chas could only have collected one of the five remaining Fairweathers in Val's estate: an unsigned work on paper of three girls kneeling with musical instruments, which Fairweather must have painted in 1949 or earlier. Nor, as Val had told me and Gleeson, could Chas have burnt the remnants of Fairweather's material left in Cairns. Bail relates that, in 1951, Jock Frater—in company with Clem Christesen—journeyed to Cairns to visit the shack Fairweather abandoned in 1949, where they found paintings still scattered about, on bits of cardboard and pages torn from the *Women's Weekly*. Tragically, the tropical climate had left only one salvageable.

By some extraordinary twist of fate, in December 2013 I learnt that 'Kulu Valley', the Fairweather stolen in 1990 when the sisters moved from Templestowe to Kew, had recently come on the market as part of a 'builder's estate'. I rang my brother and we decided to try to recover the little painting. Peter contacted a friend in the Victorian Police who put him in touch with Detective Mark Rippon, a Senior Constable with the Boroondara Criminal Investigation Unit. I sent Rippon the information I had dug up, most critically the report of the theft of the Fairweather, along with five other paintings, published in the *Women's Art Register Bulletin*. Also, extracts from Bail's two tomes on Fairweather, published 1981 and 1990, in which 'Kulu Valley' is reproduced. In the first, the provenance is given in the caption as 'Collection Dr and Mrs N. Albiston' and in the second, in the catalogue, as 'Mrs N. Albiston, Melbourne. Stolen, June 1990; whereabouts unknown'.

Fortunately, we already had an idea who might have stolen the paintings: Chris Georgiou, the builder who had renovated Kew (on the cheap, at Val's insistence) and helped the sisters move. My brother had always considered him a fast-talking, slippery character, quite capable of the heist. In 1990, Von also slightly suspected the builder, but Val, who had hired him, wouldn't hear of it, and, as ever, prevailed.

A search of obituaries revealed that Georgiou had died in 2008, not long after Val. In the meantime, I was told that it was Peter Gant who had been offering 'Kulu Valley' to galleries. Sue Hewitt, of Mosman Galleries in Sydney, and another, minor, gallery had been approached. So, too, had Tim Abdullah of the auction house Deutsche-Menzies. Peter contacted Abdullah, who suggested that Clayfoot was involved, or so Peter thought he heard. That turned out to be John Playfoot, who had a gallery in Prahran.

It did not take much time on the internet to discover that Gant had been implicated in many art world forgeries. In August 2014, Victorian Police charged him with fraud offences relating to three dodgy Brett Whiteley paintings. In 2016, he was found guilty of fraud and jailed. Also tangled up in the Whiteley case was crack conservator Aman Siddique, who had been charged with creating the forgeries which Gant allegedly sold on.

Playfoot was also connected. In 1998, he had lost his licence in a London court for selling Lalique glass alleged to have been irradiated to turn it purple, making it more valuable; he named Gant as the supplier. We couldn't believe it: Playfoot and Gant. Neither was squeaky clean and Gant was possibly the most notorious art dealer in Australia!

In early 2014, Rippon applied for a warrant to search the Georgious' house. We all worried that, while there was good evidence that there had been a theft, we only had suspicions about where the paintings might be. Still, the magistrate approved Rippon's application. Once the warrant came through, Rippon knew he had to use it wisely so that the paintings did not go underground.

In March, I spoke to Val's friend Paulette Clouseau, who had sold Von's Fairweather, and she contacted her former colleagues in the art sales business. Miraculously, she discovered that 'Kulu Valley' was in Perth and had been sold for $15,000 'to a QC who was about to become a judge'. With this important information, Rippon felt it was time to move. Late in the month, with search warrant in hand, he visited the Georgious' premises and was shown paintings hanging in various rooms of the house and a few stacked in the garage. The Fairweather had been stolen, along with five other paintings: one by Roger Kemp, two by Raymond Glass and two by Val. From the Georgious' garage, Rippon recovered two, both by Raymond Glass: one of Bedarra Island and the other, 'Los Ejidaleros', of Mexican farmers demonstrating for land rights.

By April, the Perth barrister had requested and been shown evidence that 'Kulu Valley' was stolen property and he returned the painting to Victoria, where it was in police custody. Rippon sat the little abstract on his desk for a while and quickly came to enjoy it—when it was wrapped and moved to a controlled temperature storage facility for safe-keeping, he missed it. Meanwhile, the Georgious continued to insist it was a gift from Val.

On 22 May 2014, Peter went to the Victorian Magistrate's Court to establish the painting's provenance. Georgiou's son, Thomas, testified that the painting was a gift, that Val had given them other paintings and $30,000 towards their house, and that she had seen the Fairweather hanging on their wall. Georgiou asked for representation and was told twice by the magistrate that we had evidence and he had only hearsay. Still, Thomas wanted to proceed, so the hearing was rescheduled for the following Tuesday.

At the next hearing, 27 May, Thomas produced affidavits from himself and from his mother, which, as he had been warned, were inadmissible. The judge found against the Georgious and asked to see

Val's will. The Magistrate quickly read it, deciding that the painting should go to the Salvation Army. Peter argued successfully that we would approach the Salvation Army and sort it out and/or be back in court in two weeks to contest the meaning of the will.

Nothing, it seemed, was straightforward. However, our solicitor wrote to the Salvation Army, and, happily, their lawyers agreed that the painting should stay with the family. A final appearance in court on 8 July saw the Magistrate inspect the papers and mutter and mumble before announcing; 'Okay, it should go to Miss Georgiades.' He agreed with Salvation Army's interpretation of the will: the residue of Val's estate had been left to Artemis, so the painting was hers.

Finally, twenty-four years after its theft, 'Kulu Valley' was back in the family and looking radiant. It had been beautifully restored and framed (by Siddique, we wondered). In 2015, Artemis donated it to the National Gallery of Australia under the Cultural Gifts Program, where it joined another small Fairweather ('Karaun', 1949), executed the same year in Cairns from Fairweather's memories of India.

16

RAKING THROUGH THE EMBERS

I have unpacked the sisters' history and put it back together, hopefully not introducing too many new errors, distortions or dramatisations. My sources—newspaper reports, letter, books, Val's autobiographical accounts and interviews with the sisters, their family, friends and acquaintances—might be flawed and, of course, misinterpreted. So too memories. Still, it seems the sisters, Val especially, were never concerned with verisimilitude when it compromised a good story.

Perhaps, where I have tried to sift fact from fiction, I will appear critical or judgemental. That was not my purpose. As a scientist, I seek facts—the truth, whatever that may be. In truth, the sisters' inventions made them all the more intriguing. They had fun, they were never dull; their lives were most fortunate and full. They mixed with some of the most significant cultural figures of the twentieth century. As Val once wrote, 'there was a lot of living'.

As I was to discover, Val and Von began as more or less typical, wealthy young women, seen at the races and cocktail parties, involved in charitable events, somewhat aimless in their studies. They travelled widely overseas during the Great Depression—something only the well-to-do could easily manage but also during a time when money would have gone further. A pair of studio photographs of them at this time, young and beautiful, perfectly made-up and coiffed, their shoulders draped with furs, were tucked away in their Templestowe house and later 'vanished', edited from their lives. With the tragic death of their father, and with their travels, they gradually shed their socialite skins and determined to pursue their enthusiasms and live interesting lives among interesting people.

For most of their adult lives, they attempted to hide or play down their wealth. Their house at Kew had a fine address but was modest; their clothing was Salvation Army; their private Barrier Reef island, another fine address, was bought opportunistically for a song. They shopped for food on sale, got it free whenever they could, and kept it far too long—unabashedly serving stale cake and biscuits to their guests. Val, at least, the 'boss' of the family, paid tradespeople what she decided.

The sisters fudged reality to suggest that all of their most valuable paintings, the Fairweathers, had been salvaged from the dirt floor of his hut. They stuck to the tale that they had to struggle north by train every winter to live self-sufficiently, isolated and with few creature comforts. Once they settled on Timana, the living was indeed basic, but they always hired a resident beachcomber. In Far North Queensland, women were something of a rarity and the sisters were not only young and gorgeous, but also lively and in great fun. There was no shortage of men, of all ages, eager to ferry them to the island, help with chores, become their resident odd-job man, or drop by with gifts of fruit or seafood. On the neighbouring islands, there were friends to visit and to come visit them. On Dunk Island, they could eat at the resort. A boatman delivered supplies and their laundry from Tully on his regular island run.

As for the difficulties of access to the north, these were real, but wealth allowed occasional respite. Val began her published accounts of her first visit to the resort on Dunk Island with the journey from Townsville: rattling along for the five hours it took to reach Tully, just ninety miles (200 kilometres) south, followed by the variously long, or even longer, wait for the boatman to ferry them to Dunk Island, and a treacherous crossing. In her unfinished autobiography, which I found in the box of papers she left me, she writes that when it came time for her to leave after that first visit to Dunk Island, presumably to bypass this painfully slow leg on the train, the resort's owner Hugo Brassey told her, 'You must fly down to Townsville.' Her response, 'But I've never flown. If I get killed, I'll never be forgiven!', made them all laugh. Bravely, she took the light plane, climbing aboard with sandy feet, excited as the pilot swept low over the Whitsundays. She does indeed appear among the passengers listed in the *Townsville Daily Bulletin*, picked up from the hard sand airstrip at Mission Beach by the Dragon airliner *Cairns*, enroute to Townsville on 22 July 1938, where she could catch the train south. In 1940, the Airlines of Australia return fare from Brisbane to Townsville alone was £16.10—expensive considering that the average annual wage for a male at the managerial level was about £380. Except during wartime, when the train was obligatory, flying was one of their few financial indulgences, and they kept it quiet.

That first meeting with Noel, Val told me and indicated many times in print that he was alone, divorced, and they never met his wife. However, my research uncovered that the sisters did indeed know Eleanor, Noel's wife, and were at the very least contributors to her leaving Noel and the islands two years later—for good.

And what of their fantastic story about how they came to buy Timana, their very own island? It turned out to be substantially true. They simply paid the back fees owed by its previous owners. But all was not straightforward: Timana was purchased in 1953, not in 1939 or 1940, as they claimed or perhaps believed. Incredibly, in the interim they were simply squatting.

Perhaps unwittingly, given that children often don't know the extent of their parents' activities and interests, the sisters characterised their father, Morris, as an untrained weekend painter, but he was far more than that. Although he was a busy, successful businessman, he had been involved in the Victorian art world since studying art in Ballarat as a youth, and invited to exhibit alongside many famous names. Not long after his retirement from the family company, he held a well-received solo exhibition of pastels and was accumulating more for another show when he drowned.

Art was firmly in the sisters' background. Not only did their father take them out when he painted on weekends, but his best friends were painters, and the family attended cultural and artistic events in Melbourne. Many times, both sisters asserted to interviewers that Morris did not teach them and that they did not paint on the outings. Nor, they claimed, did they begin to study art when he was alive; but enrolment records show that they were indeed studying with William McInnes at the National Gallery Art School (NGAS) in 1930, the year before Morris died.

In 1999, having just read *Stravinsky's Lunch*, I asked Val and Von whether they ever felt disadvantaged as women, particularly as female artists: they weren't interested. When pressed, Val agreed that sexism existed: 'yes, yes, the Old Bastard's Club'—dismissing me along with the old bastards. Yet, the sisters must inevitably have suffered from some prejudice, particularly following World War Two, when women were expected to go back into the home to procreate. Von, especially, was hitting her stride then, winning prizes in the 1950s.

Still, the sisters were not driven to make a living from their art and enjoyed the milieu as much as the practice. In 1940s and 1950s Melbourne, the artistic and literary scene was vibrant, modern, and exciting. The sisters mixed with artists, writers, musicians, academics and architects who questioned the old ways of living. They had the courage to fight convention, to a point, and their wealth gave them freedom to do so—to make choices not open to most.

On a day-to-day basis, the sisters lived relatively frugally and they enjoyed the beauty and artistic possibilities of nature, but they never took up the environmental cause of the Barrier Reef, as did some of their friends. Although Val wrote several articles in which she bemoans the change in the Family Islands by the 1960s and 1970s—for her, it was too many people, too much activity, a breaking of the peace. It seems that, like feminism, environmentalism was barely on the sisters' radars. Nor did there seem to be any awareness that Val's own articles romanticising the islands might have contributed to increased interest in the area.

In discovering Timana Island, where rainforest meets reef, Val and Von found an alternative lifestyle; an escape which could be indulged during the welcoming winter months. When the girls returned south, looking tanned and fit, their romantic island existence captured imaginations and gave the young artists a certain cachet. Their joyful paintings of the tropics mainly date from that earliest period, the 1940s, when they were young, carefree and seeking love.

On the islands, they could fish and swim and sketch. That life may have had particular resonance for them, perhaps unconsciously. Their father, who they had last seen beleaguered, clinging to a dinghy, loved all three activities. Not infrequently the sisters painted coastal scenes and, Val especially, upturned boats. There were other echoes from the past. The Chinese man, with his baskets strung from a shoulder yolk, who so frightened a young Val, was echoed in one of her Fairweather paintings. And, more obviously, like her father's, Val's writings romanticised exotic localities and people.

As in every life, there were symmetries; forty years visiting Timana, and forty at Templestowe; three decades with Norman, and three after his death. The Yarra River was a strong thread. Their father holidayed on a riverside farm, and the family took refuge there after his death. The river sweeps past Templestowe and Kew, linking it to their childhood home at Elwood. Although neither father nor daughters were movers and shakers, they embraced and contributed to the progressive trends of their times. Their father was active in the art world during the Melbourne-based movement to professionalise, modernise and nationalise. He would have seen the paintings exhibited by George Bell, who was soon to become a leader in the push for Modernism, taken up by the sisters.

I thought about ending the book on the high of the 1980s and 1990s, when then sisters received the attention they deserved for their paintings in the 1940s and 1950s—arguably, when they were at their artistic peak. However, I decided to write about their declining years, simply because that is life—part of the sweep of their long lives, through most of the twentieth century, two world wars, and charging on into the twenty-first century. The sisters lived well beyond the Cohen family expectation of fifty-odd years. Their longevity apparently came from the Frankel side. Modern medicine assisted Von; Val, though, had sturdy genes.

Even a richly lived, privileged life can have its bumps. Both sisters loved creative, sexually profligate men who flaunted societal norms, which made them interesting and seemingly progressive, yet ultimately their 'free-thinking' was self-serving. Noel was Von's great love; he remained very fond of her but flitted from woman to woman throughout his life. Val's dominance of Von's life was, perhaps, not always appreciated, but mostly welcome—a lifelong constant.

Val, on the other hand, was stubbornly determined to live life on her terms. She had little luck controlling Norman's pursuit of women, but seemingly he made up for his dalliances with an abundance of intelligence, humour and charm. Val presented herself as sexually liberated and enjoyed the shock value that she could have, yet, after marriage, apparently never (rarely?) took lovers herself. She was competitive and, to my mind, that must have caused some jealousy or concern about his other women, but she would have been too perverse to admit that to me or anyone else. Perhaps she was sure enough of herself to accept that she had the most important role, as wife, and his mistresses and flings were ephemeral.

Behind Von's good humour, we always felt a wistfulness—even

melancholy. Whether it was for the absence of a lover or a child, we can't be sure. At the far end of life, alone and somewhat irritable, Val seemed more fulfilled. For us, both were significant figures in the family—at once warm, wicked and wonderful. We were rapt audiences for their remarkable tales and enjoyed their youthful playfulness.

In one of Val's early articles, written in the 1930s as a twenty-four-year-old travelling the world, I discovered a sentiment that seemed to capture something of the sisters' philosophy: 'Romance is in all of us. We long to fashion romantic careers for ourselves. We yearn to read those of others, whether they be of love, life, wealth.' Val was determined to be interesting, to *live*. She yearned to tell her story and succeeded in recording large portions of it, some published, for others to read. A handwritten note and one of many homemade greeting cards, made decades later, suggest that her credo remained basically unchanged:

> Old people regret most not what they have done but what they have failed to do—experiences never known. This eager appetite for experience[,] the discontent of wanting more of life however much one has[,] is the very stuff of being human.

As do her playful wishes for Von's seventy-third birthday:

> Happy Day
> Happy Year
> A belch. A yawn. A pot of beer.
> Lots of health
> A little wealth
> The lot all in top gear.

If Von's voice is less in evidence in this biography, it was also so in life. Val set their course, and Von followed. To me, Von can be found most visibly in her sensitive portraits of Val, Noel, Norm and island personalities and in her intuitive paintings, in which she took more risks than her headstrong sister. Together, their lives were a true romance in both senses of the word—the quest for love and a fulfilling life, and an escape from the everyday.

On our visit to Timana Island with the sisters' ashes in November 2013, the mangroves at the western end of the spit, sheared off by cyclone Yasi two years before, were re-establishing. The house that Bert built, never occupied, stood strong, with only a few shingles missing; the greatest insults to it inflicted by human hands. Protected underneath were the remains of the tank—all that was left of Val and Von's bungalow. We swam in the warm shallows of the fringing reef, scattering shoals of small fish in the crystal water. On Dunk Island, we hiked from the jetty along the beach of Brammo Bay, past the airstrip and the broken and twisted remnants of the once-popular, cyclone-ravaged resort. At beach's end we began the climb to the top of Mount Kootaloo—a two-hour return walk to the jetty. Up we went until we could look across at Timana and, beyond, to Bedarra; both seemingly untouched, still looking luxuriant, still beckoning. Yasi took the resort and Noel's house, and all three islands had long been abandoned by artists.

For the moment, nature was winning against 'progress'. At Templestowe, though, houses smothered the rolling hills.

List of artworks in the colour sections

Sketches

Note: Unsourced sketches in the text are from the collection of the author.

Charlie, c.1940s, Yvonne Cohen. Charcoal on paper. Collection of the author

Deanna, c.1960s, Yvonne Cohen. Watercolour on paper. Collection of the author

Deanna and Bruce, c.1960s, Yvonne Cohen. Watercolour and charcoal on paper. Collection of the author

Portrait of Gini and Louse, c.1939, Noel Wood. Charcoal on paper. Heide Museum of Modern Art, 2004.120, Melbourne. Gift of Valerie Albiston 2004 ©Estate of Yvonne Cohen

Noel, c.1940s, Yvonne Cohen. Charcoal on paper. Collection of the author

Study of George Bell, c.1950, Norman Albiston. Pencil on paper, 17.5 x 17.3 cm. National Library of Australia (ANL) R9208

'Val Sleeping', c.1940s, Yvonne Cohen. Charcoal on paper. Collection of the author

Paintings

'After the Bath', c.1950, Yvonne Cohen. Oil on canvas on board, 35.5 x 37.2 cm. Private collection

'Along the Track, Bingil Bay', 1950, Valerie Albiston. Oil on canvas on board, 45 x 53.5 cm. Cairns Art Gallery Collection, 1999.06, Cairns. Gift of Valerie Albiston and Yvonne cohen under the Australian Government's Cultural Gifts program, 1999

'Bali Market', 1954, Yvonne Cohen. Oil on board, 75 x 54.7 cm. Art Gallery of Ballarat, 2002.25, Ballarat. Gift of Valerie Albiston under the Cultural Gifts Program 2002, courtesy of the artist's estate

'Bedarra Island', c.1940s, Valerie Albiston. Oil on board, 38 x 46.5 cm. City of Townsville Art Collection, 2005.25, Townsville. Gift of the artist under the Australian Government's Cultural Gifts program, 2005

'Boatman', c.1940s, Yvonne Cohen. Oil on canvas, 58 x 49 cm. Warrnambool Art Gallery, 1510.2002, Warrnambool. Gift of Valerie Albiston through the Australian Government's Cultural Gifts program, 2002

'Brammo Bay', 1946, Noel Wood. Oil on board, 46 x 58. City of Townsville Art Collection, 1995.102, Townsville. Purchased, 1995

'Elwood Foreshore', c.1925, Morris Cohen. Pastel on paper, 18.9 x 31.9 cm. Art Gallery of Ballarat, 1977.162, Ballarat. Gift of Valerie Albiston and Yvonne Cohen, 1977

'Garden on Dunk Island'/'Garden on Coonanglebah', 1943, Yvonne Cohen. Oil on canvas on board, 50.1 x 40.9 cm. City of Townsville Art Collection, 1993.37, Townsville. Purchased, 1993

'Grey After Gris', c.1950, Yvonne Cohen. Oil on board, 25 x 35.4 cm. Private collection

'Island Dream, Bedarra Island', 1946, Raymond Glass. Oil on board, 22.5 x 29.8 cm. Private collection

'Kulu Valley', 1949, Ian Fairweather. Gouache and pencil on board, 15.7 x 22 cm. National Gallery of Australia, 2015.1171, Canberra. Gift of Artemis Georgiades 2015, donated through the Australian Government's Cultural Gifts Program

'Mango Trees', c.1940, Yvonne Cohen. Oil on board, 45.5 x 50.5 cm. City of Townsville Art Collection, 1986.9, Townsville. Purchased, 1986

'Orchard Country', 1958, Yvonne Cohen. Oil on board, 60 x 75 cm. Private collection

Portrait of Viva, c.1940s, Yvonne Cohen. Oil on canvas on plywood, 38.3 x 48.5 cm. Heide Museum of Modern Art, 2004.145, Melbourne.

'Queensland Beach', 1945, Yvonne Cohen. Oil on canvas on board, 45.5 x 57 cm. Cairns Art Gallery Collection, 1999.08, Cairns. Gift of Yvonne Cohen and Valerie Albiston under the Australian Government's Cultural Gifts program

'Quiet Corner', c.1950s, Valerie Albiston. Oil on board, 41 x 33.5 cm. Private collection

'Ship Building', 1954, Yvonne Cohen. Oil on board, 74 x 59 cm. Courtesy of Charles Nodrum Gallery

Study of Neil Douglas, c.1970s, Yvonne Cohen. Pastel on cardboard, 62.2 x 47 cm. Heide Museum of Modern Art, 2004.109, Melbourne. Gift of Valerie Albiston 2004 ©Estate of Yvonne Cohen

'The Blue Crayfish', 1945, Yvonne Cohen. Oil on canvas on board, 46 x 56 cm. Cairns Art Gallery Colletion, 1999.09, Cairns. Gift of Yvonne Cohen and Valerie Albiston under the Australian Government's Cultural Gifts program, 1999

'The Catch', 1945, Yvonne Cohen. Oil on canvas on board, 38.7 x 48.7 cm. Cairns Art Gallery, 1999.10, Cairns. Gift of Yvonne Cohen and Valerie Albiston under the Australian Government's Cultural gifts program, 1999

'The Pathway to Banfield's Old Home (Dunk Island)', c.1940, Noel Wood. Oil on canvas on board, 46 x 59.8 cm. Queensland Art Gallery | Gallery of Modern Art, 1.0283, Brisbane

'The Straw Hat' (self-portrait), 1946, Yvonne Cohen. Oil on canvas on board, 43.6 x 39.3 cm. Rockhampton Museum of Art, 2002.052, Rockhampton. Purchased, 2002

'Timana Island, Under the House', 1950, Valerie Albiston. Oil on canvas on plywood, 44 x 53.3 cm. Collection of the University of Queensland, 1999.04, Brisbane

'Timana Island', 1945, Valerie Albiston. Oil on board, 86.6 x 69 cm. City of Townsville Art Collection, 1986.008, Townsville

'To the Islands, Timana', 1950, Valerie Albiston. Oil on canvas on board, 20 x 25 cm. Cairns Art Gallery Collection, 1999.05, Cairns. Gift of Valerie Albiston and Yvonne Cohen under the Australian Government's Cultural Gifts program, 1999

'Tropic Man', 1949–50, Norman Albiston. Oil on paper on board, 59.2 x 45.9 cm. Warrnambool Art Gallery, 856.1986, Warrnambool. Purchased, 1986

'Untitled (Bedarra Island Hut)', 1950, Yvonne Cohen. Oil on canvas on board, 25 x 30 cm. Cairns Art Gallery, 2010.23, Cairns. Purchased, 2010

'Victorian Farmland', c.1890s, Morris Cohen. Oil on board, 24.3 x 39.5 cm. Private collection
'Windy Morning, Bingil Bay', 1950, Valerie Albiston. Oil on canvas on board, 45 x 53.5 cm. Cairns Art Gallery Collection, 1999.06, Cairns. Gift of Valerie Albiston through the Australian Government's Cultural Gifts program, 2002
'Young Man', c.1940s, Yvonne Cohen. Oil on canvas on board. Private collection

Photographs

Birthday card of Valerie in her birthday suit, c.1940s. Collection of the author
Brassey, Gini, and Noel with pawpaws, 1938. Courtesy of Gini Thompson
Charlie Nazan, c.1937. Courtesy of Gini Thompson
Cohen family at Sevilla, November 1916. Collection of the author
Cohen family, November 1930. Collection of the author
Deanna, c.1960s. Collection of the author
Eleanor, Gini, and Noel, September 1937. Courtesy of Gini Thompson
Noel and Eleanor on Kangaroo Island, 1936. Courtesy of Gini Thompson
Val and Norm in Melbourne, c.1970s. Collection of the author
Val and Von in Kew, November 1999. Collection of the author
Val painting, c.1940s. Collection of the author
Val's bookcase in Kew, c.2000s. Collection of the author
Von in Bali, 1954. Collection of the author

BIBLIOGRAPHY

General Bibliography

Australian Dictionary of Biography; http://adb.anu.edu.au

Design and Art Australia Online; http://www.daao.org.au

Germaine, Max (ed.) (1979). *Artists and Galleries of Australia and New Zealand.* Sydney: Lansdowne.

Germaine, Max (1984). *Artists and Galleries of Australia.* Sydney: Boolarong Publications.

Germaine, Max (1990). *Artists and Galleries of Australia.* Roseville: Craftsman House.

Germaine, Max (1991). *A Dictionary of Women Artists of Australia.* Roseville: Craftsman House.

McCulloch, Alan (1977). *Encyclopedia of Australian Artists.* Richmond: Hutchinson.

McCulloch, Alan, McCulloch, Susan and McCulloch Childs, Emily (2006). *The New McCulloch's Encyclopedia of Australian Art.* Carlton: Meigunyah.

Reserve Bank of Australia: Pre-Decimal Inflation Calculator; http://www.rba.gov.au/calculator/annualPreDecimal.html

1. THE ESPLANADE
Elwood (1911–1930)

'Advertising', *The Horsham Times* 10 December 1920, p. 5.

'Advertising', *The Argus* 7 October 1933, p. 2.

Albiston, Valerie (undated manuscripts, c. 1990s). 'Time to tell', or 'Raking through the embers'.

'An argument', *The Michaelian* vol. XV, no. 1, July 1926, pp. 34-35.

'Anzacs welcomed home. Melbourne's hearty greeting. Heroes cheered through crowded streets. Touching family reunions', *The Argus* 25 November 1918, p. 7.

'Classified Advertising', *The Argus* 6 December 1915, p. 13.

'Classified Advertising', *The Argus* 26 August 1916, p. 13.

'Classified Advertising', *The Argus* 2 February 1918, p. 13.

Cooper, John Butler (1931). *History of St Kilda: From its First Settlement to a City and After, 1840 to 1930, Volume 1.* Melbourne: Printers Proprietary Limited.

'Dance at Fawkner Park: Five young hostesses', *Table Talk* 10 October 1929, p. 68.

Eagle, Mary and Minchin, Jan (1981). *The George Bell School: Students, Friends and Influences.* Melbourne: Deutscher Art Publications.

Eidelsen, Meyer (2006). *The History of Elwood: Flood, Fire and Fever.* St Kilda Historical Series Number 9. Melbourne: St Kilda Historical Society; http://melbournewalks.com.au/the-history-of-elwood/

'Emily McPherson College. Duchess receives first diploma', *The Australasian* (Metropolitan edition) 30 April 1927, p. 49.

'Firbank Church of England Girls' School, Brighton', *The Argus* 17 December 1920, p. 1.

'Firbank Church of England Girls' Grammar School', *The Argus* 21 December 1921, p. 18.

Firbank Old Grammarians' Association (1960) *Life at Firbank 1909–1959*. Melbourne: Firbank Old Grammarians' Association.

'Firbank wins challenge cup', *The Australasian* (Metropolitan edition) 7 May 1927, p. 64.

Gleeson, James (1978). 'James Gleeson Interviews: Valerie Albiston and Yvonne Cohen, 29 November 1978'; http://nga.gov.au/Research/Gleeson/pdf/Cohen_Albiston.pdf

Haese, Richard (1986).' McInnes, William Beckwith (Billy)', *Australian Dictionary of Biography Vol. 10*. Melbourne: Melbourne University Press. http://adb.anu.edu.au/biography/mcinnes-william-beckwith-billy-7371

Heathcote, Christopher (2007) .*A Quest for Enlightenment: The Art of Roger Kemp.* Melbourne: Macmillan.

'Isabel Ramsay meets many Australians who follow spring to Europe. News and doings of our folks abroad.' *Sunday Times* 7 June 1925, social and magazine section, p. 1.

'Leaving by R.M.S. Orama', *The Sydney Morning Herald* 9 January 1925, p. 12.

Macnaughtan, Jacqueline (2004). *From Life: Works by Early Generations of Students at the National Gallery School.* Southbank: Victorian College of the Arts.

'Measles in Victoria. A mild epidemic', *The Advertiser* 4 May 1920, p. 7.

Newsome, Mary 'Interview with Yvonne Cohen, 26 April 1988', Victoria College, Prahran Campus, Victoria.

'Nude models. Few in Australia. Plaster cast studies', *News* (Adelaide)(Home edition) 30 January 1930, p. 9.

Peel, Victoria (1999). *St Michael's Grammar School: A Study in Educational Change.* St Leonards: Allen & Unwin.

Penrose, Helen (2009). *She Who Conquers: A Centenary History of Firbank Grammar.* Melbourne: Utber & Patullo Publishing.

'Personal', *The Argus* 12 January 1925, p. 10.

Series VPRS 5843 Students Attendance Register – National Gallery Art School Ver.1. Record Cards – Art Students National Gallery of Victoria VPRS 10348 Public Records Office of Victoria.

Shiels, Julie and Eidelson, Meyer (2006). *Voices from Elwood; A Guide to Recording Personal Histories.* St Kilda Historical Series Number 11. Melbourne: St Kilda Historical Society.

'St Michael's C.E.G.G.S .Sports', *The Argus* 26 April 1926, p. 4,

'St. Michael's C.E.G.G.S. Women's Influence in the World', *The Argus* 17 December 1924, p. 26.

'The British Fleet', *Gippsland Times* 20 March 1924, p. 4.

The Magazine of the Emily McPherson College of Domestic Economy (1927–1938). Melbourne: Emily McPherson College.

The Michaelian vol. XIV, No. 3 December 1925, p. 9; https://www.stmichaels.vic.edu.au/news/publications/the-michaelian-yearbook/

The Michaelian vol. XV, No. 2, December 1926, p. 1; https://www.stmichaels.vic.edu.au/news/publications/the-michaelian-yearbook/

The Michaelian vol. XVI, No. 1, June 1927, pp. 11, 13; https://www.stmichaels.vic.edu.au/news/publications/the-michaelian-yearbook/
The Michaelian vol. XV,I No. 2, December 1927. p. 11; https://www.stmichaels.vic.edu.au/news/publications/the-michaelian-yearbook/
The Michaelian vol. XVII, No. 1, May 1928, pp. 11, 12, 27; https://www.stmichaels.vic.edu.au/news/publications/the-michaelian-yearbook/
The Michaelian vol. XVII, No. 2, December 1928, p. 10; https://www.stmichaels.vic.edu.au/news/publications/the-michaelian-yearbook/
The Michaelian vol. XVIII, No. 1, May 1929, pp. 10, 11; https://www.stmichaels.vic.edu.au/news/publications/the-michaelian-yearbook/
'Victorian vignettes', *The Hebrew Standard of Australasia* 16 January 1925, p. 15.

2. 'FATHER': MORRIS E. COHEN
Ballarat and Melbourne 1854–1906

Albiston, Valerie (undated manuscript, c. 1990s). 'Time to tell', or 'Raking through the embers'.
'Advertising', *The Bacchus Marsh Express* 5 May 1888, p. 2.
'Advertising', *The Argus* 4 October 1890, p. 11.
'Advertising', *The Argus* 26 October 1897, p. 3.
'Advertising', *Examiner* 5 December 1931, daily edition, p. 5.
'Birth', *The Ballarat Star* 27 May 1865, p. 2.
Blee, Jill and Roberts, Phil (Eds) (2010). *Under Minerva's Gaze: 150 Years at Ballaarat Mechanics' Institute*. Ballarat: Ballarat Mechanics Institute.
Bowers, D.H. (Ed.) (1970). *Ballarat School of Mines Retrospect 1870–1970* Ballarat: Waller & Chester.
Catalogue of the Ballarat Fine Art Exhibition, 1884. Ballarat: James Curtis; http://handle.slv.vic.gov.au/10381/109153
Catalogue of the Commonwealth Exhibition of Australian Art, Sydney 1901. Sydney: Society of Artists.
Champion of the Seas (clipper); http://en.wikipedia.org/wiki/Champion_of_the_Seas_(clipper)
Cohen, Morris E. (1898–1915). Correspondence to Victorian Artists' Society. Records of the Victorian Artists' Society, 1856-1995. State Library of Victoria MS 7593; 583/4 b MSM 481.
Cohen, Morris E. (1905) .Types and tips of waiters', *The Australasian Traveller* 7 December 1905, pp. 21, 50.
Cohen, Morris E. (1906). 'The C.T. in the provinces (England)', *The Australasian Traveller* 10 January 1906, p. 44.
Cohen, Morris E. (1906) .'Some current British types', *The Australasian Traveller* 10 January 1906, p. 53.
Cohen, Morris E. (1906).'Everyday street types in Paris', *The Australasian Traveller* 7 February 1906, p. 1.
Cohen, Morris E. (1906) .'French military types' and 'Coming from the baker's', *The Australasian Traveller* 7 February 1906, p. 3.

Cohen, Morris E. (1906) .'Market types at Harlem – Holland', *The Australasian Traveller* 7 March 1906, p. 11.
Cohen, Morris E. (1906) .'Wanderings in Spain'. *The Australasian Traveller* 4 May 1906, pp. 5, 7.
Cohen, Morris E. (1906).'A railway porter and a railway guard. How they do it in Spain', *The Australasian Traveller* 4 May 1906, p. 37.
Cohen, Morris E. (1906) 'Wanderings through Egypt and the Holy Land', *The Australasian Traveller* 2 June 1906, pp. 5, 60.
Cohen, Morris E. (1906) .'The land of the Pharoahs', *The Australasian Traveller* 2 June 1906, p. 43.
Cohen, Morris E. (1906) .'America at work', *The Australasian Traveller* 7 December 1906, pp. 50.
Cohen, Morris E. (1930). 'Cruising around tropical islands', *The Australian Traveller* 10 December 1930, pp. 3, 35.
'Family Notices', *The Ballarat Star* 23 June 1865, p. 2.
'Family notices', *The Argus* 22 February 1890, p. 1.
'Family notices', *The Argus* 5 June 1890, p. 1.
'Family notices', *The Argus* 18 November 1897, p. 1.
'Family notices', *The Australasian* 17 February 1906, p. 60.
Gleeson, James (1978). James Gleeson Interviews: Valerie Albiston and Yvonne Cohen, 29 November 1978; http://nga.gov.au/Research/Gleeson/pdf/Cohen_Albiston.pdf
'History of the Commercial Travellers' Association of Victoria 1881–1899'. *The Traveller* June 1899, supplement, pp. 1–12.
'Mechanics Institute', *Ballarat Courier* 14 July 1870, p. 2.
Mein, W. Gordon (1965?). *History of Ballarat College 1864–1964*. Ballarat: Ballarat College Council.
'Mining meetings', *The Argus* 28 October 1904, p. 10.
National Archives series A712 (control symbol Z1856/10057 and Z1856/10229 and 1871/Y6050) Naturalisation documents 1856.
'Notes and news', *Jewish Herald* 30 June 1905, p. 8.
'Passengers by the Manuka', *Evening News* (Sydney) 8 July 1905, p. 3.
Perry, Warren (1984). *A History of the School of Mines and Industries Ballarat 1870–1982*. Ballarat: The School of Mines and Industries.
'Pleasures to seek. Holidays within easy reach wide range of attractions in the north. Surfing, angling, and sporting facilities', *Examiner* 19 December 1931, Daily edition, p. 6.
Powell, J.A. (1886). *Progress of the Ballarat Fine Arts Public Gallery and Art Museum*. Ballarat: James Curtis.
Punch 28 June 1906, p. 16.
'Sailing by Marsina', *The Sydney Morning Herald* 9 August 1930, p. 19.
'Shipping intelligence. Arrived, *The Argus* 29 December 1854, p. 4.
'Shipping intelligence. Hobson's Bay', *The Argus* 7 July 1891, p. 4
'Shipping. Sun, moon, tide', *Examiner* 30 March 1931, daily edition, p. 6.
'Social. All about the people you know: Current happenings', *Table Talk* 2 April 1931, p. 39.
'Tackra' (1901). 'Society of Artists. Commonwealth Show. Critique II'. *Evening News* 5 January 1901, p. 3.

'The Art Gallery', *Bendigo Advertiser* 6 March 1888, p. 2.
'The Ballarat fine-art exhibition', *The Argus* 16 June 1884, p. 6.
The Victorian Artists' Society Catalogue of Winter Exhibition, Eastern Hill, Melbourne March 1890. Melbourne: Victorian Artists' Society.
The Victorian Artists' Society Catalogue of Painting, Sculpture & Drawings: Illustrated Catalogue, May 1892. Melbourne: Victorian Artists' Society.
Will and probate records of Simon Cohen, Alma Road, St Kilda, Colony of Victoria 17/7/1890. Public Record Office Victoria: VPRS 28/P0, unit 534; VPRS 28/P2, unit 290; VPRS 7591/P2, unit 164.

3. MORRIS AND MARRIAGE
Melbourne, 1909–1931

Albiston, Valerie (undated manuscripts, c. 1990s). 'Time to tell', or 'Raking through the embers'.
'Advertising', *Examiner* 5 December 1931, daily edition, p. 5.
'Amusements', *Evening News* 4 August 1900, p. 3.
'Amusements', *Evening News* 1 July 1905, p. 2.
'Art exhibitions. Landscapes in pastel. Mr. Morris E. Cohen's Work', *The Argus* 1 August 1929, p. 15.
Bell, George (1929). 'Quiet charm. Amateur painter's work praised', *The Sun News-Pictorial* 1 August 1929, p. ?
Blee, Jill and Roberts, Phil (Eds) (2010) *Under Minerva's Gaze: 150 Years at Ballaarat Mechanics' Institute*. Ballarat: Ballarat Mechanics Institute.
'Boating accident. Melbourne visitor missing. Tragedy feared', *Advocate* 31 March 1931, p. 4.
'Boating fatality. Tourist drowned accident at Scamander', *Examiner* 31 March 1931 Edition: Daily, p. 6.
Bowers, D.H. (Ed.) (1970). *Ballarat School of Mines Retrospect 1870–1970* Ballarat: Waller & Chester.
'Burglars at St. Kilda. Tragic ending to search. Woman's death from shock', *The Argus* 4 September 1924, p. 8.
'Business merger', *The Brisbane Courier* 18 July 1928, p. 10.
'Classified advertising', *The Argus* 11 June 1929, p. 18.
Cohen, Morris E. (1908).'On the Gordon River', *The Australasian Traveller* 3 February 1908, p. 3.
Cohen, Morris E. (1900).'The Apollo Bay Pier. To the Editor of The Argus', *The Argus* 12 February 1900, p. 3.
Cohen, Morris E. (1909) .'Gentlemen of the lake', *The Australasian Traveller* 6 March 1909, p. 11.
Cohen, Morris E. (1909). 'In mystic New Zealand', *The Australasian Traveller* 6 March 1909, pp. 41–42.
Cohen, Morris E. (1909) .'The C.T. and the sandiflies', *The Australasian Traveller* 6 March 1909, p. 47.
Cohen, Morris E. (1912) .'David Davies. To the Editor of The Argus', *The Argus* 17 July 1912, p. 10.

Cohen, Morris E. (1916). 'The late T.P. Isaacs'. *The Australasian Traveller* 3 May 1916, p. 37.
Cohen, Morris E. (1925) .'Wanderings in Sicily', *The Australian Traveller* 6 June 1925, p. 5.
Cohen, Morris E. (1925) .'On the ocean, Jany 1925', *The Australian Traveller* 4 April 1925, p. 9.
Cohen, Morris E. (1925).'Types on an ocean liner (No. 2)', *The Australian Traveller* 6 May 1925, p. 25.
Cohen, Morris E. (1925). 'Wanderings through Norway', *The Australian Traveller* 4 November 1925, pp. 3–4.
Cohen, Morris E. (1925)..Doings in Germany', *The Australian Traveller* 5 December 1925, p. 35.
Cohen, Morris E. (1926).'European types', *The Australian Traveller* 7 January 1926, p. 3.
Cohen, Morris E. (1930) .Cruising around tropical islands', *The Australian Traveller* 10 December 1930, pp. 3, 35.
'Country news. Ballarat and district', *The Argus* 5 February 1924, p. 15.
Danglow, Minister Jacob, St. Kilda Hebrew Congregation, letter to Morris Cohen, 11 May 1922
'Death of Mr. M. E. Cohen', *Hardware and Machinery* vol. xivi, no. 6, p. 147.
'Elwood', *The Prahran Telegraph* 22 December 1917, p. 7.
'Elwood and South St. Kilda Progress Association', *Malvern Standard* 1 June 1912, p. 3.
'Elwood and Sth. St. Kilda Progress Association', *Prahran Chronicle* January 1915, p. 3.
'Faithful lover's suicide. Tragic count of days', *The Braidwood Dispatch and Mining Journal* 20 October 1909, p. 4.
'Family notices', *The Argus* 25 September 1920, p. 13.
'Family notices', *The Argus* 25 July 1922, p. 1.
'Family notices', *The Argus* July 1926, p. 1.
Gadsden, Jennifer (1995). *Robert Eagar Taylor-Ghee (1869–1951): A Retrospective Essay*. Melbourne: Melbourne Fine Art Gallery.
Gleeson James (1979). 'James Gleeson Interviews: Valerie Albiston and Yvonne Cohen, 29 November 1978'; http://nga.gov.au/Research/Gleeson/pdf/Cohen_Albiston.pdf
'Isabel Ramsay meets many Australians who follow Spring to Europe: News and doings of our folks abroad', *Sunday Times* 7 June 1925, social and magazine section, p. 1.
'Jewish Girls' Guild', *Evening News* 29 May 1906, p. 6.
'Leaving by R.M.S. Orama', *The Sydney Morning Herald* 9 January 1925, p. 12.
'Mails Inward', *The Argus* 3 August 1929, p. 22.
'Missing. Boating accident. Carried out of the Scamander', *The Mercury* 31 March 1931, p. 7.
Mein, W. Gordon (1965?). *History of Ballarat College 1864–1964*. Ballarat: Ballarat College Council.
'Melbourne crime burglar under bed causes woman's death', *Singleton Argus* 6 September 1924, p. 1.
'Nature in pastels', *The Age* 1 August 1929, p. 13.
'News and views', *The Hebrew Standard of Australasia* 15 July 1910, p. 7.
'News and views', *The Hebrew Standard of Australasia* 19 August 1910, p. 9.
'Obituary', *The Australian Traveller* 10 April 1931, p. 27.

'Obituary. Mr. Arthur Phillips', *Healesville and Yarra Glen Guardian* 30 November 1940, p. 3.
'Ormond Esplanade. Complaints of misconduct', *Prahran Chronicle* 26 June 1915, p. 5.
Perry, Warren (1984). *A History of the School of Mines and Industries Ballarat 1870–1982*. Ballarat: The School of Mines and Industries.
'Personal', *The Argus* August 1919, p. 6.
'Personal', *The Argus* 15 September 1920, p. 14.
'Personal', *The Australasian* 29 July 1922, p. 39.
'Personal', *The Argus* 12 January 1925, p. 10.
'Pleasures to seek. Holidays within easy reach wide range of attractions in the north. Surfing, angling, and sporting facilities', *Examiner* 19 December 1931, Daily edition, p. 6.
'Sailing by Marsina', *The Sydney Morning Herald* 9 August 1930, p. 19.
'Sydney', *The Jewish Herald* 2 September 1910, p. 3.
'Sydney Comedy Club', *Evening News* 2 December 1908, p. 11.
'The Ballarat Courier', *The Ballarat Courier* 17 March 1916, daily edition, p. 2.
'The studio. Landscapes in pastel', *The Australasian* 10 August 1929, metropolitan edition, p. 19. Article
'Traffic along Ormond Road. A citizen's complaint', *Prahran Chronicle* February 1915, p. 5.
'When we were twenty-one', *Evening News* May 1909, p. 8.
Young, Blamire (1929). 'Pastel exhibition', *The Herald* (Melbourne) 31 July 1929, p. ?

4. DEPRESSION TIME TRAVEL
Melbourne and overseas (1931–1937)

'Advertising', *The Argus* 7 October 1933, p. 2.
'Advertising', *The Argus* 14 October 1933, p. 2.
'Advertising', *The Argus* 27 November 1935, p. 5.
Albiston, Valerie (undated manuscripts, c. 1990s). 'Time to tell', or 'Raking through the embers'.
'Art. British Contemporary Art', *The Australasian* 18 March 1933, p. 16.
'Australians abroad London', *The Australasian* 23 April 1932, p. 12.
'Boating accident. Carried out of the Scamander. Elderly visitor missing', *The Mercury* 31 March 1931, p. 7.
'Boating accident. Melbourne visitor missing. Tragedy feared', *Advocate* 31 March 1931, p. 4.
'Boating fatality. Tourist drowned. Accident at Scamander', *Examiner* 31 March 1931, daily edition, p. 6.
'Boating tragedy. Scamander victim. Death presumed', *Advocate* 24 July 1931, p. 7.
Burdett, Basil (1933) 'Mrs. Zander's Exhibition of British Contemporary Art', *Art in Australia* 15 April 1933, pp. 6–9.
'Caught in current. Man drowned. Daughters swim to land. Launceston, March 30', *Queensland Times* 31 March 1931, daily edition, p. 8.
'Classified Advertising', *The Argus* 9 November 1931, p. 2.

'Coming by Oronsay', *The Sydney Morning Herald* 4 April 1933, p. 13.
'Current topics', *Examiner* 12 June 1931, daily edition, p. 8.
'Decorative art', *The Argus* 23 October 1935, p. 16.
'Drowning fatality. Mr. E. Cohen, of Melbourne. Verdict of accidental death', *The Mercury* 9 July 1931, p. 5.
Eagle, Mary, and Minchin, Jan (1981). *The George Bell School: Students Friends, Influences*. Melbourne: Deutscher Art Publications.
'Easy for Germans to travel', *The Argus* 14 September 1937, p. 7.
Fitzpatrick, Sheila (2008). Foreigners observed: Moscow visitors in the 1930s under the gaze of their Soviet guides. *Russian History/Histoire Russe*, 35, pp. 215-234.
Frankel-Cohen, Valerie (1935). 'The leisured paradise. Bali—land of content', *The Herald* (Melbourne) 2 November 1935, p. 28.
Frankel-Cohen, Valerie (1936). 'Fairy village; along the Zuyder Zee', *The Herald* (Melbourne) 2 January 1936, p. 32.
Frankel-Cohen, Valerie (1936) .'In a medieval village', *The Herald* (Melbourne) 15 February 1936, p. 33.
Frankel Cohen, Valerie (1936) .'On top of Europe: 11,300 feet up by train', *The Herald* (Melbourne) 7 March 1936, p. 33.
Frankel-Cohen, Valerie (1937). 'A note-book in Sweden', *The Herald* (Melbourne) 27 March 1937, p. 2.
Frankel-Cohen, Valerie (1938). 'Where the telephone can't ring. The islands of the Barrier Reef', *The Age Literary Supplement* 15 October 1938, p. 2.
'George Russell Limited to close to-day. Sale of stock and freehold', *The Argus* 3 April 1937, p. 17.
'Human remains on beach', *The Argus* 12 June 1931, p. 7.
'Human remains. Discovery at Scamander. Fate of Melbourne visitor', *The Mercury* 12 June 1931, p. 7.
'Human remains on beach. Echo of Scamander fatality', *Advocate* 12 June 1931, p. 2.
'Informal leap-year party', *Table Talk* 20 February 1936, p. 42.
'In England. These hotels will make your stay enjoyable', *The Straits Times* 5 August 1934, p. 3.
'In social news', *The Herald* (Melbourne) 3 June 1933, p. 12.
Kerr , Joan (Ed.) (1995). *Heritage: The National Women's Art Book*. Roseville East : Craftsman House.
Knapp, Florence, as told to Mustapha., Gaël (1930). 'Brown Derby was a hot spot for Hollywood's elite'; http://www.reminisce.com/1930s/brown-derby-was-a-hot-spot-for-hollywoods-elite/#ixzz3LUiLo800
'Late Mr. Cohen. The Scamander tragedy application for probate. Melbourne, July 12', *The Mercury* 15 July 1931, p. 5.
Legge-Wilkinson, L. C. (1936). 'Letters to the Editor: Progress in the Alps', *The Herald* (Melbourne) 10 March 1936, p. 33.
'Luxury fashions at Caulfield. Chilly weather brings forth new winter styles', *Table Talk* 19 April 1934, p. 43.
'Man believed drowned. Rowing boat mishap. (Australian Cable Service.) Auckland, March 31', *The Northern Miner* 1 April 1931, p. 5.
'Melbourne chatter', *The Bulletin* v. 56, no. 2896, 13 August 1935, p. 40.

'Melbourne chatter', *The Bulletin* vol. 57, no. 2936, 20 May 1936, p. 43.
'Melbourne chatter', *The Bulletin* vol. 57, no. 2947, 5 August 1936, p. 43.
'Melbourne chatter', *The Bulletin* vol. 58, no. 2976, 24 February 1937, p. 36.
'Melbourne chatter', *The Bulletin* vol. 58, no. 2982, 7 April 1937, p. 36.
'Melbourne chatter', *The Bulletin* vol. 58, no. 3006, 22 September 1937, p. 35.
'Mining Aberfoyle Tin', *Examiner* 1 May 1931, daily edition, p. 11.
'Mr. M. E. Cohen's death. Probate of will to be granted', *The Argus* 24 July 1931, p. 10.
'News of special interest to women about people and parties', *The Argus* 7 April 1936, p. 5.
Newsome, Mary, interview with Yvonne Cohen, 26 April 1988. Victoria College, Prahran Campus, Victoria.
'Notes from the capitals Melbourne. Gala matinee', *The Australasian* 26 August 1933, p. 12.
Olsen, Penny, interviews with Valerie Albiston and Yvonne Cohen, Kew, 1997.
Rees, Anne (2010). 'Mary Cecil Allen: Modernism and modernity in Melbourne 1935–1960'; emaj issue 5 2010; www.melbourneartjournal.unimelb.edu.au/E-MAJ
'Round about London Town with Stanley Parker', *Table Talk* 27 August 1936, p. 7.
'Sailing inside coral reef: Liner's cruise to New Guinea', *The Herald* (Melbourne) 21 June 1933, p. 10.
'Scamander fatality. Unavailing search for body', *Advocate* 1 April 1931, p. 6.
'Scamander fatality. Damaged boat found', *Advocate* 21 April 1931, p. 6.
'Shipping', The Argus 20 May 1933, p. 1.
'Social. All about people you know: arrivals and departures', *Table Talk* 2 January 1936, p. 34.
'Social. All about the people you know: current happenings', *Table Talk* 8 June 1933, p. 37.
'Social. All about the people you know: current happenings', *Table Talk* 26 April 1934, p. 29.
'Social notes', *The Argus* 13 September 1937, p. 10.
'Swept out to sea. Man believed drowned. Launceston, March 31', *Townsville Daily Bulletin* 1 April 1931, p. 6.
'Swept out to sea. Sad end to holiday. Father drowned. Daughters swim to shore. Launceston, March 30', *Morning Bulletin* 31 March 1931, p. 6.
'Swept out to sea. Sad end to holiday. Launceston, March 30', *The Central Queensland Herald* 2 April 1931, p. 3.
'Tasmanian tragedy. Death of Mr. M. E. Cohen. Life lost while boating', *The Argus* 15 July 1931, p. 10.
'The letters of Letty', *Table Talk* 9 April 1936, p. 14.
'The Scamander tragedy. No trace of body. Search being continued', *The Mercury* 1 April 1931, p. 10.
'The world of women. Talking of...this and that. Modern art puzzles', *The Argus* 14 September 1937, p. 8.
'The world of women: Talking of... this and that. Novel trimming', *The Argus* 15 September 1937, p. 9.
'To paint coronation pictures', *The Argus* 15 May 1937, p. 17.
'To write book about celebrities', *The Advertiser* 17 April 1936, p. 29.

'Tourist's death. Circumstances related. Scamander fatality. Melbourne, Tuesday', *Examiner* 15 July 1931, daily edition, p. 6.
'Travelled travellers', *Table Talk* 10 January 1935, p 14.
V.F.C. (Valerie Frankel Cohen) (1939). 'Tropical vignettes. Glimpses of North Queensland', *The Herald* (Melbourne) 11 November 1939, p. 13.

5. TO THE ISLANDS AND WAR
St Kilda and Dunk Island (1938–1939)

'Academy of Art paintings to be seen here', *News* (Adelaide) 12 May 1939, p. 4.
'Advertising. Dunk Island for the ideal and perfect holiday', *Cairns Post* 14 June 1939, p. 2.
'Aerodrome for Dunk Island. Open for Easter', *The Courier-Mail* 13 January 1939, p. 3.
Albiston, Valerie (1976). 'War years on our Barrier Reef island', *The Canberra Times* 11 September 1976, p. 11.
Albiston, Valerie (1979). 'The Dunk Island story', *The Cairns Post* 11 June 1979, p. 12.
Albiston, Valerie, unpublished manuscript, c. late 1980s. 'Early neighbours on a Barrier Reef Island'
Albiston, Valerie (undated manuscripts, c. 1990s). 'Time to tell', or 'Raking through the embers'.
Albiston, Valerie (undated, unpublished ms; 1970–1990s) 'Once upon an island'.
Albiston, Valerie (1995). 'Early neighbours on Bedarra Island'. *Griffith University, Queensland Studies Centre Newsletter* 3/95, pp. 3, 6.
'Artist lives on lonely island', *Pix* 4 March 1939, pp. 36–37.
'Art exhibitions. Mr. Louis McCubbin's work. A tropical tour', *The Argus* 1 March 1932, p. 3.
'Art of Robert Campbell. Pictures of the north', *The Courier-Mail* 21 August 1934, p. 19.
'Artist-hermit turns back on money, cities', *Smith's Weekly* 22 July 1939, p. 17.
'Artist's improved work', *The Advertiser* 14 November 1935, p. 9.
'Barrier Reef paintings', *The Courier-Mail* 2 March 1939, Second Section, p. 1.
Barrymore, Freda (1933). 'Let's Buy a Queensland Tropic Isle', *The Home* 3 January 1933, pp. 31–33, 54–55.
Barrymore, Freda (1933). 'The romantic isle', *The Home* 1 November 1933, pp. 38–39, 62, 66, 74.
'Beachcomber the second. Mr, and Mrs, Crusoe happy on tropic isle', *Sunday Mail* 1 January 1939, p. 22.
The Contemporary Art Society Inaugural Exhibition, 1939. National Gallery, Melbourne, June 6–25 1939.
Cottrell, Dorothy (1928). *The Singing Gold*. Sydney: Angus & Robertson.
Edquist, Harriet and Grierson, Elizabeth (2008). 'Artwork 1940s–50s'. *A Skilled Hand and Cultivated Mind: A Guide to the Architecture and Art of RMIT University*. Melbourne; RMIT University, p. 53–57.
'Delights of Dunk Island regular air service from Townsville', *Sydney Morning Herald* 8 July 1939, p. 13.
'Doings on Dunk. July 11', *Cairns Post* 14 July 1939, p. 13.

'Dunk Island', *Cairns Post* 29 October 1938, p. 4.
'Dunk Island to be sold. Company may purchase. Tully, Friday', *The Courier-Mail* 11 December 1937, p. 16.
Eagle, Mary, and Minchin, Jan (1981). *The George Bell School: Students Friends, Influences*. Melbourne: Deutscher Art Publications.
'Enchanted days on islands of Barrier Reef', *Johnstone River Advocate,* 6 November 1936, p. 4.
'Family Notices', *The Advertiser* 16 January 1937, p. 16.
'For sale: island of dreams. Tropic spot of poignant memory', *Sunday Mail* (Brisbane) 15 May 1938 Magazine section, p. 2.
Fuller, H. E. (1935). 'Society of arts Exhibition. Standard much higher. Opening today', *The Advertiser* 26 September 1935, p. 11.
Frankel-Cohen, Valerie (1938). 'Where the telephone can't ring. The islands of the Barrier Reef', *The Age* 15 October 1938, p. 2.
Frankel-Cohen, Valerie (1938). 'Mustaf and the mummy hawk', *Jargon* 1938, p. 33–37 (31–35 in some issues).
George, Elisabeth (1936). 'Tuesday topics', *The Advertiser* 1 December 1936, p. 8.
Gray, Ken (2021). Our Own Gatsby: Hugo Brassey of Dunk Island. Mission Beach Historical Society. https://nla.gov.au/nla.obj-3085624279/view
Haultain, Ruby (1939). 'Halcyon days on Dunk Island. Calm shattered by war', *The Sydney Morning Herald* 4 December 1939, p. 8.
Herbert, Harold (1939). 'Art shows. Noel Wood's work', *The Argus* 30 May 1939, p. 4.

Herbert, Harold (1939). 'Art Exhibitions. "Lost" among moderns', *The Argus* 6 June 1939, p. 11.
'Interested in paintings', *Sydney Morning Herald* 1 March 1939, p. 7.
'Let's talk of interesting people', *Australian Women's Weekly* 2 April 1938 p. 2 .
'Life on Dunk Island. An artist experiences beachcombing', *The Courier-Mail* 22 August 1934, p. 13.
'Lady Gowrie at exhibition', *The Sydney Morning Herald* 1 March 1939, p. 7.
Lord Gowrie at Dunk Island', *The Sydney Morning Herald* 22 July 1937, p. 8.
MacIntyre, Peggy (1939). 'Noel Wood and the Barrier Reef', *Art in Australia: Art and Architecture,* 15 May 1939, pp. 42–45. Sydney: John Fairfax & Sons.
Mackay, R. D. (1936). 'The Dunk Island of 1936. Now luxury resort for tourists', *The Advertiser* 22 February 1936, p. 11.
'Melbourne Chatter', *The Bulletin* vol. 59, no. 3042, 1 June 1938, p. 38.
'Melbourne chatter', *The Bulletin* vol. 60, no. 3073, 4 January 1939, p. 32.
'Melbourne Chatter', *The Bulletin* vol. 60, no. 3088, 19 April 1939, p. 38.
'Mr. Hugo Brassey joins navy', *The Sydney Morning Herald* 9 December 1939, p. 19.
Newsome, Mary, interview with Yvonne Cohen, 26 April 1988. Victoria College, Prahran Campus, //Victoria.
No title. *Townsville Daily Bulletin* 5 January 1938, p. 4.
Noonan, Michael (1983) *A Different Drummer: The Story of E. J. Banfield, the Beachcomber of Dunk Island*. St Lucia: University of Queensland Press.
'Oils exhibited by Noel Wood. Oneness of vision in some pictures', *News* (Adelaide) 13 November 1935, p. 4.

Palmer, Vance (1935). 'People of the reef', *Walkabout* 1 March 1935, p. 26.
'Personal Vice-Regal', *The Canberra Times* 22 November 1939, p. 4.
'Personal Vice-Regal', *The Canberra Times* 4 December 1939, p. 2.
'Plane at Dunk Island', *Cairns Post* 11 July 1939, p. 6.
Porter, James G. (2000). *A Family of Islands: Dunk and Bedarra Island Group, North Queensland*. Brisbane: Boolarong Press.
'Romance ended', *The World's News* 16 February 1938, p. 25.
'Social notes', *The Courier-Mail* 28 January 1936, p. 17.
'Social sphere: Gossip', *Townsville Daily Bulletin* 11 October 1938, p. 8.
'Southern letter, Brisbane, October 25', *Townsville Daily Bulletin* 27 October 1939, p. 8.
'The air services', *Townsville Daily Bulletin* 23 July 1938, p. 6.
'The Barrier Reef. Brilliant paintings', *The Sydney Morning Herald* 1 March 1939, p. 8.
'The brighter side', *The Sydney Morning Herald* 9 October 1939, p. 4.
'The man with the open door', *The Mail* 13 May 1939, p. 27.
'"Trade Wind," Noel Wood's oil painting which has been bought by the National Gallery from the Society of Arts exhibition', *The Advertiser* 16 September 1939, p. 24.
Trezise, Percy. & Wright, Richard (1966) The durability of rock paintings on Dunk Island, Northern Queensland. *Mankind* 6, pp. 320–324.
V.F.V. [i.e., V.F.C.](1939). 'Tropical vignettes: Glimpses of North Queensland', *The Age* 11 November 1939, p. 12.
'Weds baroness. Couple to live on Barrier Reef island. London July 27', *The Advertiser* 29 July 1935, p. 15.
'Week's social happenings. Unusual trip', *The Mail* 7 December 1935, women's section, p. 5.
'What women are doing', *The Australian Women's Weekly* 19 February 1938, p. 13.
Wilson, Gavin (1998). Interview with Valerie and Yvonne in August 1997. *Escape Artists: Modernists in the Tropics*. Cairns: Cairns Regional Gallery.
Wood , Eleanor (1937). 'Touring in north Queensland: from Tully to the tableland', *The Advertiser* 11 March 1937, p. 54.
Wood, Eleanor (1937). 'Summer comes to Bedarra', *The Advertiser* 13 November 1937, p. 11.
'World of women', *The Argus* 27 October 1939, p. 8.

6. CRUISING THE ISLANDS
Timana and St Kilda (1940–1941)

'A Melbourne letter. Spotlight on society', *The Australasian* 3 May 1941, p. 32.
Albiston, Valerie (undated, unpublished ms; 1970s) 'Early days on our Barrier Reef island'.
Albiston, Valerie (1974). 'Where shadows linger', *The Sunday Mail Color Magazine* 10 March 1974, p. 13.
Albiston, Valerie (1976). 'Faded footprints', *Parade* June 1976, pp. 18–19.
Albiston, Valerie (1976). 'War years on our Barrier Reef island', *The Canberra Times* 11 September 1976, p. 11.
Albiston, Valerie (1977). 'Pioneers of Bingil Bay', *The North Queensland Register* 15 January 1977, p. 20.

Albiston (, Valerie 1977). 'Where time stood still', *The Advertiser* 13 July 1977, p. 24.
Albiston, Valerie (1977). 'Where time stood still', *The Sydney Morning Herald* 18 July 1977, p. 15.
Albiston, Valerie (1978). 'Timana's toehold in history', *The Cairns Post Weekend Magazine* 14 January 1978, p. 1.
Albiston, Valerie (1978). 'Timana's toehold in history', *The Canberra Times* 5 August 1978, p. 11.
Albiston, Valerie (1979). 'The Dunk Island story', *The Cairns Post* 11 June 1979, p. 12.
Albiston, Valerie (1988). 'Wartime on a tropical island', *This Australia* vol. 7, Spring 1988, pp. 76–78.
Albiston, Valerie (undated manuscripts, c. 1990s). 'Time to tell', or 'Raking through the embers'.
Albiston, Valerie (undated, unpublished manuscript). Untitled autobiography.
Albiston, Valerie (undated, unpublished manuscript; 1970–1990s) 'Once upon an island'.
Anon. Transcript of interview with Valerie Albiston in Von Cohen's studio, 30 April 2009, possibly by a representative of Heide Museum of Modern Art.
'Art exhibitions. Dunk Island in oils', *The Argus* 18 February 1941, p. 4.
'Art exhibitions. "Lost" among moderns', *The Argus* 6 June 1939, p. 11.
'Art show opening', *Cairns Post* 14 December 1940, p. 10.
'Bach and bananas', *The New Yorker* 26 May 1956, pp. 25–26.
Banfield, Edmund J. (1933). *Confessions of a Beachcomber.* Sydney: Australasian Publishing Co.
'Beach idyll', *The Courier-Mail* 7 December 1940, p. 6.
'Bushland beauty captured on canvas', *Queensland Country Life* 7 November 1940, p. 6.
'Comforts Fund', *The Argus* 11 July 1940, p. 2.
Devanny, Jean (1944). 'Debunking Dunk', pp. 29–35 in *By Tropic Sea and Jungle: Adventures in North Queensland.* Sydney: Angus & Robertson.
'Display of art. Fine exhibition', *Townsville Daily Bulletin* 27 September 1940, p. 2.
'Doctor sues for divorce. Gippsland and Melbourne interest', *Gippsland Times* 31 July 1933, p. 5.
'Exhibition for Funds', *The Argus* 19 February 1941, p. 7.
'Escape to solitude', *Barrier Daily Truth* 24 February 1941, p. 5.
Ferrier, Carole (1999). *Jean Devanny: Romantic Revolutionary.* Melbourne: Melbourne University Press.
'Flood damage at Home Hill set at £100,000. Burdekin River now falling. Brisbane, April 9', *Morning Bulletin* 10 April 1940, p. 7.
'Gladys Hain reviews the novels'. *The Argus* 22 December 1951, p. 15.
Harcourt, John (1940). 'Art exhibition. Fine show for Red Cross', *The Argus* 19 March 1940, p. 3.
'Hugo Brassey wounded', *The Courier-Mail* 19 September 1940 , p 2.
Huxley, Julian (ed.) (1935). *Thomas Henry Huxley's Diary of the Voyage of H.M.S. Rattlesnake*. London: Chatto & Windus.
'Life of Melbourne. Hot dog and soup stall'. *The Argus* 17 April 1941, p. 8.
'Life on a Barrier Reef island'. *The Advertiser* 8 December 1951, p. 6.

Mackness, Constance (compiler) (1983). *Clump Point and District: An Historical Record of Tam O'Shanter Beach, Mission Beach, Bingil Bay, Garner's Beach and Kurrimine.* Cairns: Clump Point-Mission Beach Progress Association.
'Melbourne divorce case. Society and art concerned', *Townsville Daily Bulletin* 31 July 1933, p. 5.
'Modern art show again extended'. *The Daily Telegraph* 26 October 1940. P. 6
Morrison, Guy (1951). *We Shared An Island.* London: Phoenix House.
No title. *The Argus* 13 March 1941, p. 8.
Olsen, Penny, interviews with Valerie Albiston and Yvonne Cohen, Kew: 23 January 2000; 19 February 2000; 18 February 2000; 13 May 2000; 9 April 2000; 9 April 2000; 13 May 2000; 2 May 2004.
'Out among the people. They had their revenge', *The Advertiser* 10 May 1940, p. 23.
'Painters blazing artistic trail on tropic coast', *The Courier-Mail* 29 November 1940, p. 10.
'Painting tropics. Queensland artists', *Cairns Post* 5 December 1940, p. 3.
'Paintings of Dunk Island', *The Age* 19 February 1941, p. 5.
Parker King, Phillip (1825). *Narrative of a Survey of the Intertropical and Western Coasts of Australia. Performed Between the Years 1818 and 1822.* London: John Murray.
'Personal', *Townsville Daily Bulletin* 26 September 1940, p. 4.
'Petition fails. Society divorce suit', *Newcastle Morning Herald & Miners' Advocate* 12 August 1933, p. 7.
Pierce, Peter (2004). 'Tropic Days: Literature and Art of North Queensland'. *Etropic: Electronic Journal of Studies in the Tropics*, vol. 3, no. 1; http://www.jcu.edu.au/etropic
'Pictures of Dunk Island', *The Bulletin* vol. 62, no. 3185, 26 February 1941, p. 33.
'Popular art show extended'. *The Daily Telegraph* (23 October , p. 8.
Porter, James G. (2000). *A Family of Islands: Dunk and Bedarra Island Group, North Queensland.* Brisbane: Boolarong Press.
'Record crowd at art show'. *The Daily Telegraph* 28 September 1940, p. 6.
'Sheltered two days in bombarded cave. Lieutenant Hugo Brassey missed death by inches in Norwegian fiord battle', *The Australian Women's Weekly* 8 June 1940, p. 12.
'Social gossip', *Townsville Daily Bulletin* 21 November 1940, p. 6.
'Spotlight on society', *The Australasian* 15 February 1941, p. 26.
'Spotlight on society. Building home on island'. *The Australasian* 26 April 1941, p. 37.
Symons, Sandra (2007). 'A passion for justice and women: Guy Morrison 1917–2007'. 23 October 2007: http://www.smh.com.au/news/obituaries/a-passion-for-justice-and-women/2007/10/22/1192940983554.html
'The air services', *Townsville Daily Bulletin* 11 April 1940, p. 6.
'The Contemporary Art Society Exhibition, 1940'. David Jones Gallery, September-October.
'The Townsville daily bulletin. Thursday March 20, 1941'. *Townsville Daily Bulletin* 20 March 1941, p. 4.
'Their tropic isle was crowded'. *The Sydney Morning Herald* 5 January 1952, p. 7.
'To-day's wireless programmes', *Advocate* 24 February 1941, p. 6.
'Town and country', *Cairns Post* 19 August 1940, p. 3.
'Tropic oils bought for art gallery', *The Courier-Mail* 18 December 1940, p. 4.

'Tropic north in art', *Sunday Mail* (Brisbane) 8 December 1940, p. 15.
'Tully notes', *Cairns Post* 27 June 1940, p. 11.
'Tully notes', *Townsville Daily Bulletin* 15 March 1941, p. 3.
'Visitors throng art show', *The Courier-Mail* 6 December 1940, p. 14.
'Waded 12 miles. Northern tourists. Tully, March 27', *Queensland Times (Ipswich)* 28 March 1940, daily edition, p. 6.
Wilkinson, Kenneth 'Artists react differently to tropic isle', *The Herald* (Melbourne) 17 February,1941, p. 8.

7. ISLAND RETREAT
Timana and St Kilda (1941–1945)

A. L. (1945) 'Exhibition by four', *The Herald* (Melbourne) 12 February 1945, p. 5.
Albiston, Valerie (undated, unpublished ms). Untitled biography.
Albiston, Valerie (undated, unpublished ms; 1970–1990s). 'Once upon an island'.
Albiston, Valerie (undated, unpublished ms; 1970s). 'Early days on our Barrier Reef island'.
Albiston, Valerie (1974). 'Where shadows linger', *The Sunday Mail Color Magazine* 10 March 1974, p. 13.
Albiston, Valerie, post 4 June 1974, draft letter to Herbert G. Turner, Editor, *The Sunday Mail*, Brisbane.
Albiston , Valerie (1976). 'Faded footprints', *Parade* June 1976, no. 307, pp. 18–19.
Albiston, Valerie (1976). 'War years on our Barrier Reef island', *The Canberra Times* 11 September 1976, p. 11.
Albiston, Valerie (1977). 'Pioneers of Bingil Bay', *The North Queensland Register* 15 January 1977, p. 20.
Albiston, Valerie (1977). 'Where time stood still', *The Advertiser* 13 July 1977, p. 24.
Albiston, Valerie (1977). 'Where time stood still', *The Sydney Morning Herald* 18 July 1977, p. 15.
Albiston, Valerie (1978). 'Timana's toehold in history', *The Cairns Post Weekend Magazine* 14 January 1978, p. 1.
Albiston, Valerie (1978). 'Timana's toehold in history', *The Canberra Times* 5 August 1978, p. 11.
Albiston, Valerie (1979). 'The Dunk Island story', *The Cairns Post* 11 June 1979, p. 12.
Albiston, Valerie (1984). 'Bingil Bay', *This Australia* vol. 3, Spring 1984, pp. 78–79.
Albiston, Valerie (1988). 'Wartime on a tropical island', *This Australia* vol. 7, Spring 1988, pp. 76–78.
Albiston, Valerie (undated manuscripts, c.1990s). 'Time to tell', or 'Raking through the embers'.
Albiston, Valerie (and Yvonne Cohen) interviews with Penny Olsen: 23 January 2000; 19 February 2000; 18 February 2000; 13 May 2000; 9 April 2000; 9 April 2000; 13 May 2000; 2 May 2004.
'Art exhibitions. Georges' Gallery', *The Age* 13 February 1945, p. 4.
'Art in the Tropics', *The Courier-Mail* 7 September 1940, p. 7.
'Atherton personal', *Cairns Post* 13 February 1941, p. 3.

'Barrier Reef paintings. Noel Wood's exhibits', *The Sydney Morning Herald* 27 October 1943, p. 10.
Bell, George (1945). 'Art from tropics', *The Sun* (Sydney) 3 February 1945, p. 11.
'Colorful paintings of Queensland', News (Adelaide) 26 February 1945, p. 2.
Eagle Mary, and Minchin, Jan (1981). *The George Bell School: Students Friends, Influences*. Melbourne: Deutscher Art Publications.
Forwood, Gillian (2003). *Lina Bryans: Rare Modern 1909–2000*. Melbourne: Miegunyah Press.
Fuller, H. E. (1945). 'Noel Wood's paintings of Queensland', *The Advertiser* 26 February 1945, p. 6.
George, Esmond (1945). 'Oils depict colorful scenes in tropics', *The Mail* 3 March 1945 p. 5.
Herbert, Harold (1942). 'High standard', *The Argus* 18 December 1942, p. 3.
Hudson, Alan (2000). *By the Banyan: Tully Sugar, the First 75 Years*. Brisbane: Christopher Beck Books.
Jones, Dorothy (1961). *Cardwell Shire Story*. Brisbane: The Jacaranda Press.
'Large gifts to New Sydney Fund. £5,000 and £2,000', *The Argus* 11 December 1941, p. 7.
Lyon, Mrs. Morris, Townsville, 6 May 1974, letter to The Editor, *The Sunday Mail* (Qld).
McCulloch, Alan (1945). '*The Argus* 13 February 1945, p. 6.
McK., F. (1944). 'Noel Wood's tropical art', *The Courier-Mail* 20 April 1944, p. 4.
'Original indeed!', *The Argus* 27 November 1941, p. 6.
'Passing by. Artist's isle', *News* (Adelaide) 28 February 1945, p. 2.
Pedley, Helen M. (2010). *Tully Street Names: Signs of History*. Tully: Helen Pedley.
Porter, Hal (1966). *The Paper Chase*. Sydney: Angus & Robertson, p. 71.
Porter, James G. (2000). *A Family of Islands: Dunk and Bedarra Island Group, North Queensland*. Brisbane: Boolarong Press.
'Residents of Upper Beaconsfield', http://www.upperbeac.rocke.id.au
Simmons, Ed and Smith, Norm (1991). *Radar Yarns*. Forster, NSW: Ed Simmons and Norm Smith.
'Spotlight on society', *The Australasian* 15 February 1941, p. 26.
'Spotlight on society. Building home on island', *The Australasian* 26 April 1941, p. 37.
'Spotlight on society. Enrolling for the mobile canteen crew', *The Australasian* 7 March 1942, p. 24.
Street, Elizabeth (1945). 'I hear on my rounds. A moon and a barbeque', *The Argus* 18 December 1945, p. 7.
'The life of Melbourne. Thursday night', *The Argus* 22 December 1944, p. 6.
'The Townsville daily bulletin. Monday, October 27, 1941', *Townsville Daily Bulletin* 27 October 1941, p. 4.
'They also serve W.A.A.F', *Sunday Mail* (Brisbane) 16 May 1943, p. 9.
'Town and country', *Cairns Post* 6 January 1945, p. 4.
'Town and country', *Cairns Post* 23 October 1945, p. 4.
'Tully notes. Tully, May 18', *Cairns Post* 22 May 1943, p. 1.
Turner, Herbert G., Editor, *The Sunday Mail*, Brisbane, 11 May 1974, letter to Valerie Albiston, Templestowe.
Turner, Herbert G., Editor, *The Sunday Mail*, Brisbane, 4 June 1974, letter to Valerie Albiston, Templestowe.
'Vice-Regal', *The Sydney Morning Herald* 30 October 1943, p. 8.

Willis, Julie and Hanna, Bronwyn (2001). *Women Architects in Australia 1900–1950.* Red Hill, ACT: Royal Australian Institute of Architects.
Wilson, Gavin (1998). *Escape Artists: Modernists in the Tropics.* Cairns: Cairns Regional Gallery.
'Women to women (continued). Arts and crafts exhibition a record of achievement', *The Argus* 16 October 1935, p. 16.
'Women's letters', *The Bulletin* vol. 62, no. 3222, 12 November 1941, p. 36.

8. LOVE AND LOSS
Timana and South Yarra (1946–1951)

'A few lines', *The Courier-Mail* 18 May 1946, p. 5.
'A few lines', *The Courier-Mail* 25 May 1946, p. 6.
'Advertising', *Cairns Post* 8 November 1946, p. 9.
'Advertising', *Cairns Post* 15 May 1951, p. 6.
'Airmen's report of Townsville cyclone', *Cairns Post* 4 March 1946, p. 1.
Albiston, Norman A. (1932). 'The importance of habit' Pp. 38-55 in *The Growing Child: A Series of Five Lectures on Child Management.* Melbourne: Melbourne University Press.
Albiston, Valerie (1980). Untitled manuscript relating to Norman Arthur Albiston, 1894–1979. NLA MS 6415.
Albiston, Valerie (undated manuscripts, c. 1990s). 'Time to tell', or 'Raking through the embers'.
Albiston, Valerie (1995). 'Early neighbours on Bedarra Island'. Griffith University, *Queensland Studies Centre Newsletter* 3/95, pp. 3 & 6.
'Art of Ian Fairweather', *The Sydney Morning Herald* 21 September 1949, p. 2.
'Art on an island', *Catholic Weekly* 11 April 1946, p. 9.
'Atherton personal', *Cairns Post* 17 August 1946, p. 6.
'Australasian', *Western Mail* 3 March 1927, p. 25.
Bail, Murray (2009). *Fairweather.* Sydney: Murdoch Books.
Bongiorno, Frank (2012). *The Sex Lives of Australians: A History.* Collingwood: Black Inc.
Blackman, Barbara (1997). *Glass After Glass: Autobiographical Reflections.* Ringwood: Viking.
"'Childish concept' about girl", *The Argus* 21 September 1950, p. 6.
'Conference on myxomatosis in rabbits', *Western Star (Roma)* 23 February 1951, p. 6.
Dawson, Betty (1948). 'This week'. *The Mail* 31 January 1948, p. 18.
'Do you want a tropical isle?', *The Argus* 12 February 1951, p. 1.
'Doctor divorced. Melbourne, Feb. 24', *The West Australian* 1 March 1927, p. 11.
'Doctor divorced. Story of desertion', *The Argus* 25 February 1927, p. 16.
'Dunk Island nine tenders received for purchase', *Cairns Post* 5 October 1951, p. 1.
'Dunk Island —no sale', *The Sydney Morning Herald* 30 April 1951, p. 5.
'Dunk leased', *The Courier-Mail* 29 October 1946, p. 4.
'Eagle, Mary, and Minchin, Jan (1981). *The George Bell School: Students, Friends and Influences.* Melbourne: Deutscher Art Publications.
'Family notices', *The Argus* 4 January 1929, p. 1.

'Family Notices', *The Courier-Mail* 12 October 1945, p. 8.
'Fish. A shark and oysters', *Queensland Times* 16 January 1947, p. 3.
'Flashback to war caused shooting', *The Argus* 12 October 1951, p. 5.
'Flemington girl-murder trial doctors clash over killer's insanity plea', *The Argus* 14 October 1954, p. 6.
Gleeson, James (1978). 'James Gleeson Interviews: Valerie Albiston and Yvonne Cohen, 29 November 1978'; http://nga.gov.au/Research/Gleeson/pdf/Cohen_Albiston.pdf
Graham, Jillian (2000). 'The Indomitable Margaret Sutherland: Marriage, Family and Creativity'. *Context* vol. 18, pp. 5–14
Graham, Jillian (2001). *Composer, Wife and Mother: Margaret Sutherland as Conflicted Subject*. MSc thesis, University of Melbourne.
Graham, Jillian (2023) *Inner Song: A Biography of Margaret Sutherland*. Miegunyah Press, Melbourne.
Helmer, June (1985). *George Bell: The Art of Influence*. Richmond: Greenhouse Publications.
Haultain, Ruby (1939). 'Halcyon days on Dunk Island. Calm shattered by war'. *The Sydney Morning Herald* 4 December 1939, p. 8.
'His mind completely broke — psychiatrist', *The Argus* 24 June 1953, p. 22.
'Home-building enterprise', *The Courier-Mail* 30 March 1951, p. 5.
'In contrast', *Cairns Post* 6 October 1950, p. 5.
'Insanity claim in girl murder charge. Psychiatrists' evidence', *The Argus* 13 October 1954, p. 9.
'Intimate jottings', *The Australian Women's Weekly* 7 February 1948, p. 24.
Kershaw, Alister (1991). *Hey Days: Memories and Glimpses of Melbourne's Bohemia 1937–1947*. North Ryde: Angus and Robertson.
'Law list for to-day', *The Courier-Mail* 11 March 1952, p. 5.
Macarthur, Sally (1994). 'Women composers have got Australia covered'. Pp. 173-184 in *Australia for Women: Travel and Culture*. Susan Hawthorne & Renate Klein (eds). North Melbourne: Spinifex Press.
'Macquarie Galleries Catalogue: Exhibition of Drawings by Ian Fairweather', 21 September to 1 October 1949.
'Man having vivid dream could kill wife', *The Argus* 14 August 1952, p. 3.
'Man obsessed by girl', *Newcastle Morning Herald & Miners' Advocate* 24 June 1953, p. 7.
'Melbourne men for reef trip', *Townsville Daily Bulletin* 6 August 1946, p. 3.
'Monday picture page', *The Courier-Mail* 14 October 1946, p. 5.
'Much variety in art show', *The Argus* 13 February 1951, p. 11.
No title. *Townsville Daily Bulletin* 27 August 1946, p. 2.
'Noel Wood's exhibition', *The Sydney Morning Herald* 2 April 1946, p. 5.
'Northern artist returns from overseas trip to work in Cairns', *Cairns Post* 20 May 1950, p. 1.
'Obituary', *Townsville Daily Bulletin* 31 May 1947, p. 2.
Olsen, Penny , Canberra, email from Ann Grocott, Brisbane, 10 June 2014.
Olsen, Penny, Canberra, interviews with Valerie Albiston and Yvonne Cohen, Kew, 18 and 19 February 2000.

Peers, Juliet (1993). *More Than Just Gumtrees: A Personal, Social and Artistic History of the Melbourne Society of Women Painters and Sculptors*. Melbourne Society of Women Painters and Sculptors, Melbourne.

'Personal', *Townsville Daily Bulletin* 17 September 1946, p. 2.

Porter, James G. (2008). *A Family of Islands: Dunk and Bedarra Island group, North Queensland*. Brisbane: Boolarong Press.

'Problem of the child. Question of punishment. Still needed in some cases', *The Argus* 13 September 1935, p. 10.

Rolley, Jack F. (1989). *Pacific Hitchhike—To Jambolana*. New York: Vantage Press.

'R. Glass exhibition is adventurous', *The Sydney Morning Herald* 16 June 1950, p. 13.

'Ruinous failure. Doctor divorces doctor', *News* (Adelaide) 24 February 1927, home edition, p. 1.

'Seized pictures held not to be obscene', *The West Australian* 20 August 1949, p. 8.

Shore, Arnold (1950). 'City art shows reviewed. Modern works in lead', *The Argus* 12 September 1950, p. 6.

'Social chat', *Morning Bulletin* 18 October 1950, p. 8.

'Social news and gossip', *The Sunday Herald* 21 August 1949, p. 9.

'Society of artists' exhibition', *The Sydney Morning Herald* 20 August 1949, p. 10.

'Southern letter', *Townsville Daily Bulletin* 25 May 1946, p. 3.

'Southerners on reef cruise', *Cairns Post* 20 August 1946, p. 5.

Sutherland, Margaret (undated, unpublished manuscript) '1920 and so on—'. Papers of Margaret Sutherland National Library of Australia MS 2967, Box, 1 Folder 2.

Symons, David (1997). *The Music of Margaret Sutherland*. Sydney: Currency Press.

Tamblyn, M. (1990). *Stang, Eleanor Margrethe (1894–1978)*; adb.anu.edu.au/biography/stang-eleanor-margrethe-8621

'Telegraphic chess', *The Sydney Morning Herald* 4 August 1947, p. 7.

'The chess corner', *The World's News* (Sydney) 30 August 1947, p. 27.

'The life of Melbourne', *The Argus* 11 May 1949, p. 10.

'The life of Melbourne', *The Argus* 9 November 1949, p. 7.

'Town and country', *Cairns Post* 28 January 1947, p. 6.

'Town and country', *Cairns Post* 11 December 1947, p. 6.

'Town lots sell well at Tully', *Townsville Daily Bulletin* 12 February 1947, p. 5.

'Triumph by Ian Fairweather', *The Sydney Morning Herald* 11 October 1950, p. 5.

'Tropical island to highest bidder', *The Mercury* 9 August 1951, p. 5.

'Tropic isles of North Queensland', *Pix* 8 June 1946, pp. 12–13.

'Tully notes', *Cairns Post* 30 May 1946, p. 7.

'Tully personal', *Cairns Post* 2 June 1951, p. 6.

'Two wanderers at rest', *Courier-Mail* 24 June 1953, p. 10.

Wallace, Lennie (2012). *From Nanango to Cooktown: The Queensland Memoirs of a Mining Warden's Daughter, 1930–1955*. Brisbane: Boolarong Press.

Watters-Cowan, Chérie (2006). *Reconstructing the Creative Life of Australian Composer Margaret Sutherland: The Evidence of Primary Source Documents*. PhD Thesis, School of Music and Music Education, University of New South Wales.

'Wed at Cairns', *The Argus* 11 July 1950, p. 9.

'Wedding of Lady Gowrie's godson', *News* (Adelaide) 22 November 1948, p. 3.

'What's an isle without those books?', *The Argus* 10 January 1952, p. 3.

Wilson, Gavin (1998). *Escape Artists: Modernists in the Tropics*. Cairns: Cairns Regional Gallery.
'Witnesses defend drawing', *The Canberra Times* 10 February 1967, p. 4.
'Women's letters', *The Bulletin* vol. 67, no. 3452, 10 April 1946, p. 34.
Wright, Katie (2012). '"Help for wayward children": child guidance in 1930s Australia'. *History of Education Review* vol. 41, no. 1, pp. 4–19

9. PAINTERS IN THE HIDDEN VALLEY
Timana and South Yarra (1951–1959)

Albiston, Valerie c. 1970s?). Unpublished manuscript, 'The hidden Yarra Valley'.
Albiston, Valerie (c. 1970s?). Unpublished manuscript, 'No longer up the bush'.
Albiston, Valerie (c. 1970s?). Unpublished manuscript, 'Templestowe's hidden valley'.
Albiston, Valerie (c. 1960). Unpublished manuscript, 'With a Citroen and a pencil in New Caledonia'.
Albiston, Valerie (1978). 'The hidden valley of Templestowe'. *The Mirror* 7 June 1978, p. 19.
Albiston Valerie (1990). 'A hidden valley in Templestowe' *Tirra Lirra* Spring 1990, pp. 12–13.
Albiston, Valerie (undated manuscript, c. 1990s). 'Time to tell', or 'Raking through the embers'.
Armstrong, Judith (1996). *The Christesen Romance*. Carlton South: Melbourne University Press.
'Artists talk of Balinese life and art', *The West Australian* 29 July 1954, p. 31.
'Australia's first cinemascope picture', *Morning Bulletin* 11 August 1954, p. 6.
'Bach and bananas', *The New Yorker* 26 May 1956, pp. 25–26.
'Cairns Art Society eighth annual exhibition opened last night', *Cairns Post* 27 October 1953, p. 3.
'City with definite culture. Painter's opinion of Cairns. Opening of art exhibition', *Cairns Post* 30 September 1952, p. 3.
'Cohen: plans' in Job Files, Box 10, Bar code M06382, Alistair Knox Papers, 1969-1980, MS13243. State Library of Victoria.
'Colony on tropic isle', *The Courier-Mail* 2 March 1935, p. 14.
'Could have cut wife's throat while dreaming', *Queensland Times (Ipswich)* 14 August 1952, daily edition, p. 3.
'Diary dates', *The Argus* 5 March 1953, p 8.
Eagle, Mary, and Minchin, Jan (1981). *The George Bell School: Students, Friends and Influences*. Melbourne: Deutscher Art Publications.
'Family notices', *The Argus* 11 July 1956, p. 12.
Finlay, Keith (1953). 'Woman's Parade', *The Argus* 19 March 1953, p. 10.
Frame, Tom (2005). *The Life and Death of Harold Holt*. Crows Nest: Allen and Unwin.
Furby, Paula (1999). 'Australian Women Artists and the CAS 1938–1959', Flinders University PhD, 1999, p. 91.
Gleeson, James (1978). 'James Gleeson Interviews: Valerie Albiston and Yvonne Cohen, 29 November 1978'; http://nga.gov.au/Research/Gleeson/pdf/Cohen_Albiston.pdf

'Gossip', *Townsville Daily Bulletin* 7 July 1954, p. 8.
Hanley, Frank, Timana Island, letter to Valerie Albiston, Templestowe, 28 December 1956.
'Hazardous trip to hospital', *Queensland Times* (Ipswich) 28 January 1954, p. 3.
Hicks, Gilbert, Timana Island, letter to Valerie Albiston and Yvonne Cohen, Templestowe, 12 May 1957.
Holt, Zara (1968). *My Life and Harry: An Autobiography*. Melbourne: The Herald.
'Hugo Brassey buys another island', *Sunday Mail* (Brisbane) 20 October 1935, p. 5.
Hutton, Drew and Connors, Libby (1999). *A History of the Australian Environment Movement*. Cambridge: Cambridge University Press.
'Island holiday', *The Central Queensland Herald* 11 August 1955, p. 27.
'Island home for new colony', *The Courier-Mail* 6 July 1935, p. 13.
Kerr, Joan (Ed.) (1995). *Heritage: The National Women's Art Book*. Roseville East, NSW: Art and Australia.
Knox, Alistair (1975). *Living in the Environment* . Canterbury, Victoria: Mullaya Publications.
Knox, Alistair [1912–1986] (undated) Chapter 34 in *A Middle Class Man: An Autobiography;* http://alistairknox.org/book/one?sort_order=34&bkid=1
Langer, Gertrude (1953). 'Three artists combine', *The Courier-Mail* 29 September 1953, p. 2.
'"Long John" is something new in Australian films. Hope high for the future of an industry', *The Courier-Mail* 7 July 1954, p. 2.
'Lost his nerve in accident', *The Argus* 12 July 1939, p. 3.
'Melbourne wedding', *News* (Adelaide) 3 March 1953, p. 14.
Mellish, Raoul (1953). 'Tropic isle spirit', *Sunday Mail* (Brisbane*)* 4 October 1953, p. 20.
'Minister says: Migrant aid still scarce for sugar', *Townsville Daily Bulletin* 24 August 1951, p. 1.
Newsome, Mary, interview with Yvonne Cohen, 26 April 1988. Victoria College, Prahran Campus, Victoria.
'Northlander Dicko had only 16/8 when he invaded Tully in 1927', *Townsville Daily Bulletin* 21 June 1954, p. 2.
'Olsen, Penny, interviews with Valerie Albiston and Yvonne Cohen, Kew, 18 February 2000 and 19 February 2000.
Outstanding art exhibition by Cairns society. Officials pleased with display', *Cairns Post* 2 October 1951, p. 5.
'Painted on the Bali Bali beach', *The Sydney Morning Herald* 8 July 1954, p. 11.
'Penrith Branch Pensioners' Assoc.', *Nepean Times* 7 March 1957, p. 1.
Peterson, Richard, and Kuzyk, Bohdan (2014). 'Alistair Knox (1912–1986)'. *RMIT Design Archives Journal* vol. 4, no. 1. 2014, pp. 4–23; mams.rmit.edu.au/p5pu19pzpvfxz.pdf
Porter, James G. (2008). *A Family of Islands: Dunk and Bedarra Island Group, North Queensland*. Brisbane: Boolarong Press.
Rodda, Ballard and Vroland, Solicitors, Melbourne, letter to Yvonne Cohen, Templestowe, 6 December 1956.
'Seized pictures held to be not obscene', *The West Australian* 20 August 1949, p. 8.
'Shell jewels island hobby', *The Argus* 15 September 1954, p. 8.

Shore, Arnold (1954). '£100 prize inspired contrasts in art', *The Argus* 21 September 1954, p. 8.
'Social news and gossip', *The Sydney Morning Herald* 1 July 1954, p. 5.
Sparrow, Jeffrey William (2007). *Engineering Your Own Soul: Theory and Practice in Communist Biography and Autobiography & Communism: A Love Story.* PhD thesis, School of Creative Media Portfolio of Design and Social Context, RMIT University; http://researchbank.rmit.edu.au/eserv/rmit:9551/Sparrow.pdf&sa=U&ei=jGNNU-iZL4OY2QXmg4HQAg&ved=0CD4QFjAH&usg=AFQjCNHf1pUPcuzcEE-qqzG7gsV9jVf_Qw
'Stolen paintings', *Women's Art Register Bulletin* 1990, vol 2., no. 2, p. 18.
'Talkabout', *The Argus* 15 July 1954, p. 10.
'The island bug–and bugs', *Pacific Islands Monthly* vol. 29, no. 9, 1 April 1959 pp. 135–139.
'The Victorian Artist's Society Sixty-third Annual Report 1958'. East Melbourne; VAS.
Thomas, Laurie (1958). 'Strange genius evident', *The Sun* 19 November 1958, p. 40.
'To let and wanted', *Cairns Post* 15 May 1951, p. 5.
'Tully farmers would welcome rain for cane', *Townsville Daily Bulletin* 2 July 1952, p. 5.
'Tully news', *Townsville Daily Bulletin* 11 June 1952, p. 7.
'Tully notes: C.P.S. collections', *Cairns Post* 11 April 1953, p. 3.
Wallace-Crabbe, Chris (1959). 'Art: safety in numbers', *The Observer* 12 December 1959, vol. 2, no. 25, p. 23.
'Worth reporting', *The Australian Women's Weekly* 17 April 1948, p. 18.
Wright, Judith (1977). *The Coral Battleground.* West Melbourne: Nelson.

10. TAPESTRIES IN THE TROPICS: BRUCE AND DEANNA Timana (1965–1969)

'Advertising'. *The Argus* 14 April 1956, p. 44.
Adams, Bruce (1967). 'Island with only one problem'. *The Australian* 11 May 1967, p. 9.
Albiston, Valerie (late 1960s). Unpublished manuscript, 'Island tapestry center'.
'Australian Amateur Championships', *Western Mail* December 1949, p. 43.
'Australian wrestler saves girl. Vancouver, July 27', *The Advertiser* 28 July 1954, p. 12.
'Australia's placings athletes', *The Sydney Morning Herald* 8 February 1950, p. 9.
Balfe, Harold (1954). 'Arthur in top form', *The Argus* 17 May 1954, p. 17.
Balfe, Harold (1955). 'The bigger they are…', *The Argus* 26 November 1955, p. 48.
Curnow, Hugh 'Islands in the sun', *The Bulletin* 1 August 1964, pp. 32-35.
Dunstan, Keith 'A place in the sun', *The Sun* 13 September 1966, p. 10.
Hawley, Janet (1969) 'Couple revive an ancient art on a swinging desert island', *The Australian* 28 November 1969, p. 3.
'If you've ever dreamed of a paradise island…', *The Sunday Express London* 8 March 1970, p. 7.
Johnstone, George (1967). 'Australia: the lucky country', *Vogue* 15 October 1967, pp. 86–89 and 141.
Kendall, Elizabeth (1967). 'Beauty bulletin' and 'Entertaining', *Vogue* 15 October 1967, pp. 32 and 52.

'Live on an island', *Cairns Post* Thursday 29 May 1952, p. 6.
Martyn, Barbara (1967). 'Museum will record island's history'. *The Australian Women's Weekly* 26 July 1967, p. 59.
McCulloch, Alan (1984). *Australian Encyclopedia of Art Vol. 1 A–K*. Hawthorn: Hutchinson.
Porter, James G. (2000). *A Family of Islands: Dunk and Bedarra Island Group, North Queensland*. Brisbane: Boolarong Press.
'Spotlight on sport. Boy of 7 who wrestled champion', *The Daily News* 13 September 1944, final edition, p. 11.
'Sydney is our city', *Sydney Morning Herald* 14 October 1971, p. 12.
'Wrestlers in frock shop', *Advocate* Monday 17 May 1948, p. 5.

11. TROUBLE ON TIMANA: DEANNA AND BERT
Timana (1970–2006)

Albiston, Valerie (1978). 'Tapestry studio on a Barrier Reef island', *Artlook* vol. 5 no. 1, December 1978, p. 31.
"Art', *The Bulletin*, vol. 96, no. 4900, 6 April 1974, p. 48.
Bock, Anna (1983). 'Deanna Conti's woven paintings', *Fibre Forum* (Qld) vol. 2, issue 1, February 1983.
Bottrell, Fay (1972). *The Artist Craftsman in Australia: Aspects of Sensibility*. Crows Nest: Jack Pollard.
Carnemolla, John (1976). 'Art from a sheep's back!', *Australasian Post* 22 January 1976, pp. 10–11.
Cooke, Glenn R. (2008, updated 2011). Noel Wood. http://www.daao.org.au/bio/noel-wood/biography/
'Conti exhibition', *The Age* 27 October 1975, p. 10.
'Deanna Conti', *Bonythperson Gallery Gazette* March 1974, p. 6.
Fessier, Michael (1983). 'On the Road to Mehetia. Part 2', *International Islands Magazine* vol. 3, no. 5, November/December 1983, pp. 31 and 39.
Franks, Sandra (1973). 'Tropic isle is studio for a weaver', *Woman's Day* 26 November 1973, pp. 39–40.
Giffney, Brendan (1998). 'Wrestler in tapestry', *The Australian* 6 April 1998, p. 17.
Gray, Jill (1974). 'Melburnians holidaying in the north', *The Age* 28 June 1974, p. 14.
Heenan, David (1994). 'Other islands in the Family Group', *Australia's Great Barrier Reef: Dunk Island and Beaver Cay*. Red Hill, Qld: Glenmede, p. 9.
Kirkland, David (1987). *The Sydney Morning Herald* 27 June 1987, pp. 9–10.
Lucas, Alan (2010). 'Age of Consent'. *Afloat Magazine*; http://www.afloat.com.au/afloat°©-magazine/2010/october°©-2010/Age_of_Consent#.UoA9aOBC8UU
'Mary Wilson to go solo soon', *The Canberra Times* 21 June 1978, p. 23.
McCristal, Vic (1972). 'People of the sun'. *Walkabout* October 1971, pp 22–26.
McCulloch, Alan (1970). 'Letter from Australia', *Art International*, vol. 4, no. 4, April 1970, pp. 52–59.
Newman, Kate (1979). 'To weave a dream', *The Herald* (Melbourne) 8 January 1979, pp. 17–18.

Olsen, John (1998). 'Convivial creator on a tropical loom', *The Australian* 6 April 1998, p. 17.
Pugh, Judith (2008). *Unstill Life: Art, Politics and Living with Clifton Pugh*. Crows Nest: Allen & Unwin.
Ryan, Ruth (1983). 'Perfect fantasy is one that's yours', *The Bulletin* 6 November 1983, p. 19.
Ryan, Ruth (1984). 'Private islands becoming hot property', *Toledo Blade* 29 January 1984, p. 26; Private Islands Becoming Hot Property; news.google.com/newspapers?nid=1350&dat=19840129&id
Script from the tourist ferry *Lawrence Kavanagh*, Mission Beach, c. 1990s.
Silver, Anneke (2013). 'Remembering Timana', Pp. 43–47 in Searle, R., *To The Islands*. Townsville: Perc Tucker Gallery.
Smee, Bruce. 'Letter to Viewpoint', *Walkabout* January 1973, p. 58.
'Sydney is our city', *Sydney Morning Herald* 14 October 1971, p. 12.
'The battle that can be lost', *The Canberra* Saturday 20 November 1971, p. 15.
'They dropped out to follow their dream: A life of contentment on an island paradise', *Woman's Day* 29 August, 1977, p. 5.
Velik, Gloria (1971). 'Pure wool and hot pink art', *The Australian* 2 October 1971, p. 15.
'Weaver of dreams', *Papua New-Guinea Post Courier* 9 November 1979, p. 34
Willey, Keith, (1972). 'The scent of silence', *Walkabout* October 1971, pp 16–19.

12. CHANGES: WRITING STORIES AND COLLECTING STONES
Templetowe (1960s–1970s)

'Access Press: A Brief History'; http://accesspress.com.au/about-access-press
Albiston, Valerie (1974). 'Where shadows linger', *The Sunday Mail Color Magazine* 10 March 1974, p. 13.
Albiston, Valerie (1975). 'Cooktown: ghost town on the way back', *Parade* April 1975, No. 293, pp. 18–19.
Albiston, Valerie (1976). 'Faded footprints', *Parade* June 1976, no. 307, pp. 18–19.
Albiston, Valerie (1976). 'War years on our Barrier Reef island', *The Canberra Times* 11 September 1976, p. 11.
Albiston, Valerie (1977). 'Pioneers of Bingil Bay', *The North Queensland Register* 15 January 1977, p. 20.
Albiston, Valerie (1977). 'Where tides have turned', *The Messenger* May 1977, pp. 38–42.
Albiston, Valerie (1977). 'Where time stood still', *The Advertiser* 13 July 1977, p. 24.
Albiston, Valerie (1977). 'Where time stood still', *The Sydney Morning Herald* 18 July 1977, p. 15.
Albiston, Valerie (1977). 'Old timers of the north', *Parade* September 1977, pp. 44-45.
Albiston, Valerie (1978). 'Timana's toehold in history', *The Cairns Post Weekend Magazine* 14 January 1978, p. 1.
Albiston, Valerie (1978). 'Timana's toehold in history', *The Canberra Times* 5 August 1978, p. 11.
Albiston, Valerie (1979). 'The Dunk Island story', *The Cairns Post* 11 June 1979, p. 12.
Albiston, Valerie (1978). 'The hidden valley of Templestowe', *The Mirror* 7 June 1978, p. 19.

Albiston, Valerie (1979). 'A town with three lives', *Parade* June 1979, No, 343, pp. 56–58.
Albiston, Valerie (1980). Untitled manuscript relating to Norman Arthur Albiston, 1894–1979. NLA MS 6415.
Albiston, Valerie (1990). 'A hidden valley in Templestowe', *Tirra Lirra* Spring 1990, pp. 12–13.
'An excellent art show', *The Sun* 14 August 1963.
'Cardwell Shire Council. August meeting. Tully. August 19'., *The Northern Herald* 29 August 1936, p. 35.
Eagle, Mary, and Minchin, Jan (1981). *The George Bell School: Students, Friends and Influences*. Melbourne: Deutscher Art Publications.
Furby, Paula (1999). *Australian Women Artists and the CAS 1938–1959*. Flinders University PhD, 1999, p. 91.
Garlick, Margaret (1965). 'Art notes', *The Age* 19 August 1965, p. 5.
Heathcote, Christopher (1995). *A Quiet Revolution: The Rise of Australian Art 1946-1948*. Melbourne: The Text Publishing Company.
Jones, Dorothy (1973). *Hurricane Lamps and Blue Umbrellas*. Cairns: G.K. Bolton.
'Live on an island', *Cairns Post* Thursday 29 May 1952, p. 6.
Lucas, Alan (2010). 'Age of Consent', *Afloat Magazine*; http://www.afloat.com.au/afloat°©-magazine/2010/october°©-2010/Age_of_Consent#.UoA9aOBC8UU
Mackness, Constance (1983). *Clump Point and District: An Historical Record*. Cairns: G.K. Bolton.
McCulloch, Alan (1960). 'Art. MCA show is attractive', *The Argus?* 23 November 1960.
McCulloch, Alan (1962). 'Art. Worth of the rebel show', *The Argus?* 15 August 1962.
'N.Q. Naturalists Club. Annual reports', *Cairns Post* 15 September 1944, p. 1.
'N.Q. Naturalists lecture on snakes', *Cairns Post* 16 January 1945, p. 4.
Ogburn, John (1965). 'Art. It is all so quiet', *The Sun* 3 March 1965, p. 52.
P.M. (1961). 'Excitement, vigour in art exhibit', *Canberra Times* 11 January 1961, p. 2.
'Sanctuary declared', *The Courier-Mail* 28 October 1933, p. 23.
Script from the tourist ferry *Lawrence Kavanagh*, Mission Beach, c. 1990s.
Shore, Arnold (1962). 'Art notes. Lahiff's show an outstanding event', *The Age* 14 August 1962.
Shore, Arnold (1960). 'Art shows. Design dominates exhibits', *The Age* 22 November 1960, p. 2.
'The battle that can be lost', *The Canberra* Saturday 20 November 1971, p. 15.
Thomas, Daniel (1965). 'Lady painters from down south', *Sunday Telegraph* 7 March 1965, p. 91.
'Witnesses defend drawing', *The Canberra Times* 10 February 1967, p. 4.
Wittam, Dick (Richard E.) (2000). *William Frater: A Life with Colour*. Melbourne: Miegunyah.
W.T. (1965). 'Art reviews' (no further details)

13. FROM TEMPLESTOWE TO KEW
Templestowe and Kew (1980–1990)

Albiston, Valerie (1983). 'The Cage', *Peninsula Writing* Winter 1983, pp. 37–41.
Albiston, Valerie (1987). 'Emily's cake', *This Australia* vol. 6, no. 3, pp. 43–45.

Albiston, Valerie (1979). 'Emma and Sam: A true-life story of the goldfields', *Australian Family Circle* 7 September 1979, p. 177.
Albiston, Valerie (1978). 'Tapestry studio on a Barrier Reef island', *Artlook* vol. 5 no. 1, December 1978, p. 31.
Albiston, Valerie (1979). 'A woman of talent', *Artlook* April 1979, p. 25.
Albiston, Valerie (1979). 'Connoisseur of costume', *Artlook* May 1979, p. 23.
Albiston, Valerie (1979). 'Australian landscape—their challenge', *Artlook* vol. 5, no. 7, July 1979, p. 13.
Albiston, Valerie (1979). 'Gold and silver is their medium', *Artlook* September 1979, p. 33.
Albiston, Valerie (1979). 'An artist inspired by Aboriginal myths and legends', *Artlook* November 1979, p. 21.
Albiston, Valerie (1982). 'A place of art and beauty', *Geelong Advertiser* 22 April 1982, p. 19.
Albiston, Valerie (1983). 'Heide–the garden gallery', *Transair* June 1983, p. 28.
Albiston, Valerie (1984). 'A woman's life on the diggings', *The Weekly Times* 4 July 1984, p. 71.
Albiston, Valerie (1985). 'Charming Melbourne gallery', *Panorama* December 1985, No. 42, p. 2.
Albiston, Valerie (1990). 'A hidden valley in Templestowe', *Tirra Lirra* Spring 1990, pp. 12–13.
Albiston, Valerie (1982). 'Tribute to a teacher', *Artlook* vol. 8, nos. 1–2, January-February 1982, p. 19.
Albiston, Valerie (1982). 'A place of art and beauty', *Geelong Advertiser* 22 April 1982, p. 19.
Albiston, Valerie (1983). 'The wide, brown land', *Geelong Advertiser: Lifestyle* 17 February 1983, p. ?
Albiston, Valerie (1983). 'Heide – The garden gallery', *Transair* June 1983, p. 28.
Albiston, Valerie (1984). 'Cigar box treasures', *Standard Post* 4 July 1984, p. 48.
Albiston, Valerie (1984). 'Bingil Bay', *This Australia* vol. 3, no. 4, pp. 78–79.
Albiston, Valerie (1986). 'The Pink Hotel', *This Australia* vol. 5, no. 4, pp. 32–35.
Albiston, Valerie (1987).'Our "Top End"...A vast red land', *The Weekly Times* 11 February 1987, p. 40.
Albiston, Valerie (n.d.). Unpublished? manuscript, 'A town with three lives'.
'A Special Correspondent' (1940). 'Art in The Tropics', *The Courier-Mail* 7 September 1940, p. 7.
Australian Broadcasting Commission (1987). *The Island and the Painter*. ABC TV film. Producer Rob Stewart. Australian Broadcasting Commission.
Cohen, Yvonne (1985). Unpublished manuscript, 'Hospital'.
Costa-Roque, Sylvia da (1985). 'Artist to quit Crusoe existence', *Sunday Mail Color* 17 November 1985, p. 6.
Costa-Roque, Sylvia da (1985). 'Island of dreams: The elegant life of Bedarra's latter-day Robinson Crusoe', *Sunday Mail Color* 8 December 1985, pp. 8–10.
Downes, Jim (1988). 'No Place For a Hermit', Pp. 105–111 in *A Big Country: Stories of Australia and Its People from the ABC TV Series*. Sydney: Angus and Robertson.
Duyker, Edward (Ed.) (1995). *A Woman on the Goldfields: Recollections of Emily Skinner, 1854–1878*. Carlton: Melbourne University Press.

Eagle, Mary, and Minchin, Jan (1981). *The George Bell School: Students, Friends and Influences.* Melbourne: Deutscher Art Publications.
Fitzgerald, Michael (1990). For Australia's city-bred modernists, the tropical north offered both an escape and a homecoming', *Time* 8 February 1999, p. 59.
Mackie, Elizabeth (1981). *The Artists of Kew.* Kew, Victoria: E. Mackie.
'Stolen paintings', *Women's Art Register Bulletin* 1990, vol. 2, no. 2, p. 18.
Searle, Ross (1991). *Artist in the Tropics: Two Hundred years of Art in North Queensland.* Perc Tucker Regional Gallery, Townsville.

14. LAST YEARS
Kew, 2000–2008 (1990–2008)

Albiston, Valerie (undated manuscripts, c. 1990s). 'Time to tell', or 'Raking through the embers'.
Anon. Transcript of interview with Valerie Albiston in Von Cohen's studio, 30 April 2009, possibly by a representative of Heide Museum of Modern Art.
Antonysen, Laeta (1999). 'Sisters' dreams on show', *Progress Press* 29 November 1999, p. 25.
'Australian Artists of Influence', Gecko Studio Gallery, May 2012: http://www.geckostudiogallery.com.au/whats-on/australian-artists-of-influence-exhibition/
Bail, Murray (1981). *Ian Fairweather.* Sydney: Bay Books.
Bail, Murray (2009). *Fairweather.* Sydney: Murdoch Books.
Chipperfield, Mark (2004). 'Australia: Drunken drongos and suntanned soap stars', *The Telegraph Travel Collection* 27 March 2004; http://www.telegraph.co.uk/travel/730023/Australia-Drunken-drongos-and-suntanned-soap-stars.html
Cosic, Miriam (1998). 'Gone troppo', *The Weekend Australian* 23–24 May 1998, pp. 16–18.
Cuthbertson, Natalia (c. 1994). 'Trip into the unknown', *Leader Community News.*
Cuthbertson, Natalia (c. 1996). 'Sisters in fine style', *Leader Community News.*
'First for sister', *Progress Press* 14 May 2001, p. 37.
Heide Museum of Modern Art 2004 Annual Report: http://www.heide.com.au/assets/files/Annual-Report/HeideAR2004.pdf
'Inspiration for Australia', *Torres News* 28 August 1998, p. 36.
Marr, David (1999). 'Northern exposure', *Good Weekend* 23 January 1999, pp. 26–28.
Rothwell, Nicolas (2014). 'Beachcombers escape to paradise'. *The Australian* 17 February 2014, Arts p.13; http://www.theaustralian.com.au/arts/beachcombers-escape-to-paradise/story-e6frg8n6-1226828644133
Searle, Ross (Curator) (2013). *To the Islands: Exploring Works Created by Artists on Dunk, Bedarra and Timana Islands between the 1930s and 1990s.* Townsville: Perc Tucker Gallery.
'Sisters-in-art on show', *Manningham Leader* 2 May 2001, p. 7.
Smith, Sue (1998). 'Cairns exhibition a kind of postcard from the past', *The Courier-Mail* 7 January 1998, p. ?
St John Moore, Felicity (1992). *Classical Modernism: The George Bell Circle.* Melbourne: National Gallery of Victoria.

Stocky, Anita and Stocky, Cathie (2000). 'In the vernacular', *Antiques and Art in Victoria* December 1999 to April 2000, p. 30.
Stocky, Anita and Stocky, Cathie (2002). 'Highlights: The exhibition', *Antiques and Art in Victoria* April to August 2002, p. 34.
Stocky, Catherine (2001). 'Artist profile: Yvonne Frenkel Cohen. Timana Island and beyond', *Antiques and Art in Victoria* April to August 2001, p. 59.
Stocky, Catherine (2001). 'Valerie Albiston – South of Capricornia', *Antiques and Art in Victoria* August to December 2001, p. 65.
Stocky, Catherine (2013). 'The Cohen sisters: painters of the tropics', Pp. 24–31 in Searle, R., *To The Islands*. Townsville: Perc Tucker Gallery.
Wilson, Gavin (1998). *Escape Artists: Modernists in the Tropics*. Cairns: Cairns Regional Gallery.

15. FINDING FAIRWEATHER
2008–2014

Akerman, Pia, and Boland, Michaela (2014). 'Charges over 'faked' Brett Whiteleys', *The Australian* 28 August 2014; http://www.theaustralian.com.au/arts/visual-arts/charges-over-faked-brett-whiteleys/story-fn9d3avm-1227039241897
'Art of Ian Fairweather', *The Sydney Morning Herald* 21 September 1949, p. 2.
Bail, Murray (1981). *Ian Fairweather*. Sydney: Bay Books.
Bail, Murray (2009). *Fairweather*. Sydney: Murdoch Books.
Box, Dan (2014). 'Court challenge to Christie's over "fake" Albert Tucker', *The Australian* 22 July 2014; http://www.theaustralian.com.au/arts/visual-arts/court-challenge-to-christies-over-fake-albert-tucker/story-fn9d3avm-1226996618858
Cascone, Sarah (2014). 'Court Case Claims Australian Art Market Is 30 Percent Forgeries', *Artnet* 22 July 2014; http://news.artnet.com/market/court-case-claims-australian-art-market-is-30-percent-forgeries-64879
Coslovich, Gabriella 92021). 'Guilty verdict in Melbourne fake art scam', *Australian Financial Review* 30 April 2021; https://www.afr.com/life-and-luxury/arts-and-culture/guilty-verdict-in-melbourne-fake-art-scam-20210430-p57nrm
Davies, Anne (2014). 'Art forgery case pits Louise McBride versus the art establishment', *Sydney Morning Herald Good Weekend* 25 October 2014; http://www.smh.com.au/good-weekend/art-forgery-case-pits-louise-mcbride-versus-the-art-establishment-20141024-113tv6.html
Davies, Anne (2014). 'Barrister Louise McBride wins case against Christie's auction house over fake Albert Tucker painting', *Sydney Morning Herald* 4 December 2014; http://www.smh.com.au/nsw/barrister-louise-mcbride-wins-case-against-christies-auction-house-over-fake-albert-tucker-painting-20141204-11zy98.html
Gleeson, James (1978). 'James Gleeson Interviews: Valerie Albiston and Yvonne Cohen, 29 November 1978'; http://nga.gov.au/Research/Gleeson/pdf/Cohen_Albiston.pdf
Mackenzie-Murray, Martin (2014). 'Whiteley or wrongly: alleged con man opens up on art fraud charges', *The Saturday Paper* 6 September 2014; https://www.thesaturdaypaper.com.au/news/law-crime/2014/09/06/whiteley-or-wrongly-alleged-con-man-opens-art-fraud-charges/1409925600#.VOKXZinpgUU

'Macquarie Galleries Catalogue: Exhibition of Drawings by Ian Fairweather', 21 September to 1 October 1949.
McBride, Louise (2014). 'Louise McBride and her fake Albert Tucker painting', *Sydney Morning Herald* 8 December 2014; http://www.smh.com.au/comment/louise-mcbride-and-her-fake-albert-tucker-painting-20141207-121yto.html
O'Malley, Nick (2016).'Convicted of Australia's largest art fraud, Peter Gant prepares for jail', *The Sydney Morning Herald* 2 September 2016; https://www.smh.com.au/entertainment/art-and-design/convicted-of-australias-largest-art-fraud-peter-gant-prepares-for-jail-20160902-gr7axb.html
'Stolen art', *Women's Art Register Bulletin* 1990, vol. 2, no. 2, p. 18.
Wilson, Ashleigh (2016). 'Market hunger for Whiteley's ferocious output inspired daring fraud', *The Weekend Australian* 14–15 May 2016, p. 21.

16. RAKING THROUGH THE EMBERS

Albiston, Valerie (undated manuscripts, c. 1990s). 'Time to tell', or 'Raking through the embers'.
Australian National Gallery Review 1978/79. Canberra: Australian National Gallery.
Chipperfield, Mark (2004). 'Australia: Drunken drongos and suntanned soap stars', *The Telegraph Travel Collection* 27 March 2004; http://www.telegraph.co.uk/travel/730023/Australia-Drunken-drongos-and-suntanned-soap-stars.html
Eagle, Mary, and Minchin, Jan (1981). *The George Bell School: Students Friends, Influences*. Melbourne: Deutscher Art Publications.
Frankel-Cohen, Valerie (1936). 'In a medieval village', *The Herald* (Melbourne) 15 February 1936, p. 33.
Heathcore, Christopher (1995). *A Quiet Revolution: The Rise of Australian Art 1946-1948* Melbourne: The Text Publishing Company.
'Plane fares increased', *The Courier-Mail* 16 April 1940, p. 5.
'Tasmanian Museum and Art Gallery Annual Report 1978–79', Hobart: TMAG.
'The air services', *Townsville Daily Bulletin* 23 July 1938, p. 6.
'The life of Melbourne. Thursday night', *The Argus* 22 December 1944, p. 6.
'What is used to cost'; http://guides.slv.vic.gov.au/content.php?pid=14258&sid=95522
Wilson, Gavin (1998). *Escape Artists: Modernists in the Tropics*. Cairns: Cairns Regional Gallery.

Index

Acknowledgements

This biography is based on Val's writings and secondary sources such as newspapers and archival material. Sadly, whilst there were other first-hand stories to be told, I missed the opportunity to talk to their keepers. I tried, unsuccessfully, to contact Noel Wood in 2000 and he died the following year. Indeed, by the time I decided to fully pursue this biography most of Val and Von's contemporaries were failing or no longer alive.

The sisters didn't date their artwork and made estimates later in life when it was given to galleries, hence the dates are uncertain. Many of the galleries were generous with images of these works. Unfortunately, page limitations meant that not all could be included.

I am grateful to the following people for their help in ways small and large: Murray Bail, Jenny Bars, Barbara Blackman, Jane Bunny, Paulette Clouseau, Deanna Conti, Ben Cox, Jordan Crane, John Cruthers, Eril, Lesley and Chris Deighton, Jill Drews, William and Nancy Ferguson, Gillian Forwood, Sue Gould, Ken Gray, Ann Grocott, Judy Gunning, Robyn Hovey, Jill Holst, Lesley Howard, Helen James, Kelly Jaunzems, Chloe Jones, Peter Kellett, Jade Lalor, Nancy Lowe, Tessa McIntosh, Cosima McPhee, Jan Minchin, Neil Morse, Antoinette Niven, Kate and Charles Nodrum , Katarina Paseta, Juliette Peers, James Porter, Mark Rippon , Raymond Robilliard, Narelle Russo, Ross Searle, Effie Skoufa-Klesnik, Sheryn Smith, Gail Stiffe, Cathie Stocky, Virginia Thompson, Jan Tracy, Monica Trang, Emily Wakeling, Sigrid Warne, and Serena Wong. Special thanks to my brother Peter Woollard and sister-in-law, Artemis Georgiades and, not least, to David, Sophie and Ellen at Melbourne Books. This book was compiled over two decades, and I am two decades older (!); my apologies if I have forgotten anyone.

The Author

Penny Olsen is an Australian ornithologist and author. Cousin to the late Cohen sisters, she has access to unique material and insights on their lives. She has written more than thirty books on natural history subjects, and two major biographies.